Norwegian American Women

HAPPY 19th to
My strong, beautiful &
intelligent wife.
I LOVE YOU!
xoxo

POTS.

2014 A.D.

NORWEGIAN AMERICAN WOMEN

Migration, Communities, and Identities

Edited by
BETTY A. BERGLAND *and*
LORI ANN LAHLUM

MINNESOTA HISTORICAL SOCIETY PRESS

Publication of this book has been made possible through a generous gift from the Ken and Nina Rothchild Fund for Business and Women's History.

www.mhspress.org

The Minnesota Historical Society Press is a member of the Association of American University Presses.

Manufactured in the United States of America.

10 9 8 7 6 5 4 3 2

∞ The paper used in this publication meets the minimum requirements of the American National Standard for Information Sciences—Permanence for Printed Library Materials, ANSI Z39.48–1984.

International Standard Book Number
ISBN: 978-0-87351-820-8 (paper)
ISBN: 978-0-87351-833-8 (e-book)

Library of Congress Cataloging-in-Publication Data

Norwegian American women : migration, communities, and identities / edited by Betty A. Bergland and Lori Ann Lahlum.
    p.   cm.
    Includes bibliographical references and index.
    ISBN 978-0-87351-820-8 (pbk. : alk. paper) — ISBN 978-0-87351-833-8 (e-book)
    1. Norwegian American women—History. 2. Norwegian American women—Social conditions. 3. Norwegian American women—Economic conditions. 4. Norwegian Americans in literature. 5. Women immigrants—United States—History. 6. Women immigrants—United States—Social conditions. 7. Women immigrants—United States—Economic conditions. 8. Women immigrants in literature. 9. United States—Emigration and immigration—History. I. Bergland, Betty A., 1943– II. Lahlum, Lori Ann, 1962–
E184.S2N852   2011
973'.043982—dc22

2010052796

*In memory of Dorothy Burton Skårdal (1922–2010)—
teacher, scholar, mentor, friend*

Contents

Foreword

Norwegian American women forged their lives and their communities at the historical intersections of gender, ethnicity, immigration, time, and place. Not until the 1970s did historians begin to probe what connected these factors, and scant attention has been paid to how they functioned in Norwegian American history. This volume breaks new ground in analyzing the significance of gender for Norwegian American history and Norwegian American women's significance for histories of ethnicity, immigration, and the regions of the American West that drew large numbers of Norwegian immigrants.

In 1976 Sheryll Patterson-Black published her pathbreaking article, "Women Homesteaders on the Great Plains Frontier," in which she identified and challenged the stereotype of the reluctant female pioneer, a stereotype that she associated with a fictional Norwegian American woman. Beret Holm, the leading female character in Ole Rølvaag's novel *Giants in the Earth,* was, according to Patterson-Black, the "best, or worst, example" of this unfortunate stereotype: sometimes "silently courageous" sometimes "utterly despondent and desperate," and always reluctant to join the movement to the American frontier. Rather than embrace the West of pioneer imagination, Beret moaned, "How will human beings be able to endure this place? . . . Why, there isn't even a thing that one can hide behind!"[1]

Rølvaag's fictional Beret represented the reluctant pioneer not only in Norwegian American history but in American history as a whole. The reluctant pioneer became conflated with the stereotypical immigrant pioneer mother: backward, unassimilated, unable to learn English, unable to adjust to her new land. In fact, most of the women depicted in western histories before the development of feminist scholarship were allegedly dragged west against their wills, almost overcome by the harsh living conditions they endured, virtually incapable of independent action. Stock images of western women left them no positive roles, no space to function as historical actors. If they, like western heroes, were adventurous, independent, successful, entrepreneurial, or sexual, they became, by definition, bad women. If they were reluctant, dispirited, worn out, or unhappy with the hardships of settling a new land, they were, by definition, bad pioneers and bad Americans.

Most women have been largely invisible in histories of "battles, dates, and presidents" that privileged the public arenas of state power and influence. The frontier framework of U.S. history shaped a narrative that moved inexorably westward from one frontier to the next but which left each location after initial settlement and the process of claiming the land was achieved. The frontier narrative stopped the action before women cooperated to establish all the institutions so essential to community formation. It raised to mythic proportions the solitary figure of the male frontiersman and portrayed women, homes, families, and communities as encumbrances on his independent spirit. Women played essential roles in settling, accommodating, and community building. But much of their labor was erased because it occurred "after the West was won."[2]

The frontier framework, when coupled with ethnic histories that focused on Americanization, wrote a linear history of immigrants that moved only in one direction—from the Old World to the New, from east to west, from ethnic backwardness to American assimilation. In this framework, immigrants were judged by how well they "Americanized"—how well they learned English, adopted American beliefs, and abandoned backward peasant ways. Immigrant wives and mothers fared poorly in this paradigm. Their husbands and children learned English and interacted with people of different ethnicities as they attended school, engaged in wage work, or conducted business in town. Immigrant women who remained at home learned the new language more slowly and were perceived as backward for preserving ethnic foods and customs.

Norwegian American Women shreds such one-dimensional stereotypes of Norwegian American women and of immigrant women and western women more generally. This volume complicates the historical portrayal of Norwegian American women by revealing them as they were: actors who made history as they built homes, hospitals, religious institutions, and movements for social change. It writes new voices and experiences into Norwegian American history particularly and into ethnic history as a whole. It adds texture and detail to women's history as it grapples with the complex ways that race, ethnicity, class, and region complicate historical understandings of gender. Most importantly, the authors document the histories of Norwegian American women themselves and illuminate the social and historical factors that operated in their lived experiences.

As this volume amply demonstrates, Norwegian American women have negotiated options affected simultaneously by multiple social and historical circumstances, particularly gender and ethnicity, as well as class, marital status, religion, and all the other factors that have differentiated human experiences and options. Their actions and their choices would not have been the same had they been men, had they or their ancestors been born anywhere but Norway, or had they immigrated to another country or another region that offered different social and economic limits and opportunities.

The contributions of this collection go far beyond correcting the distortions and omissions of older histories. This is cutting-edge scholarship, theoretically informed and richly contextualized. The contributors break new ground in probing how Norwegian American women forged their own complex identities and in tracing the enduring links of kinship, community, and identity that were at once personal, local, regional, national, and transnational. Their work places gender at the center of ethnic experience and grounds that analysis in transnational contexts that influenced who immigrated, where they came from, the expectations and skills they brought with them, and the ties they constructed between their old communities and the new ones they established in North America.

New historical assessments become possible from the perspectives of the women in these pages. Collectivity and interdependence become positive values, not threats to rugged individualism. Norwegian religious institutions and foods become not downward drags on assimilation but the positive building blocks of Norwegian American communities. The women who preserved them become not backward peasants but the architects of adaptive communities. Most crucially, family and friends left behind in Norway emerge not as more primitive encumbrances but as enduring and sustaining presences in the lives of Norwegian Americans. The Norwegian feminist movement, we learn, nourished Norwegian American women who organized to empower themselves. Norwegian American women, like other women, performed what the anthropologist Micaela di Leonardo called "kin work"—they wrote the letters and sent the cards and gifts that maintained trans-Atlantic family ties and linked Norwegian women and their Norwegian American sisters. No history of Norwegian Americans can be complete or accurate without taking into account the gendered dimensions of those historical ties or the enduring transnational connections women maintained.[3]

Much more fully dimensional and multifaceted histories of Norwegian American women emerge from these pages to challenge the one-dimensional stereotypes of reluctant pioneers with which historians began some four decades ago. They allow us to challenge the narrow frameworks that judged so harshly the reluctant women Beret Holm came to represent. The fictional Beret, like many real pioneers, was pregnant and isolated and had left her family and all that she knew. In such circumstances, we might admire a woman who embraced the hardships of making a new home in a strange country. But we might also understand the women who had second thoughts. It is only against the imperatives of the masculine frontier narrative that we judge Beret and her sisters as lacking.

In *Norwegian American Women*, Betty Bergland and Lori Ann Lahlum have produced a rich and informative collection that documents an enormous variety of Norwegian American women's histories. They have analyzed these histories using the critical tools of gender and migration histories; located them in the historiographic contexts of Norwegian American history; placed them in the complex contexts of Norway and America, of gender, class, and region; and pointed the way to new directions for further research. The editors' and authors' scholarly labors have generated a significant resource for interpreting our collective heritage. The breadth of vision and careful contextualization that inform these pages help place Norwegian American women at the centers of their own lives and invite them to speak back to the misconceptions that have been written into history. Like the historical legacies of Norwegian American women recorded in these pages, this collective work of scholarship is itself no small achievement.

Elizabeth Jameson
Department of History,
University of Calgary

Notes

1. Sheryll Patterson-Black, "Women Homesteaders on the Great Plains Frontier," *Frontiers: A Journal of Women Studies* 1.2 (Spring 1976): 67–88. Ole E. Rølvaag, *Giants in the Earth*, trans. Lincoln Colcord and the author (New York: Harper and Brothers, 1927), 28–29.

2. Frederick Jackson Turner, "The Significance of the Frontier in American History," *Annual Report of the American Historical Association for the Year 1893* (Washington, DC: Government Printing Office, 1894). This point on the frontier narrative was made by William Cronon, Howard R. Lamar, Katherine G. Morrissey, and Jay Gitlin, "Women and the West: Rethinking the Western History Survey Course," *Western Historical Quarterly* 17.3 (July 1986): 269–90.

3. Micaela di Leonardo, *The Varieties of Ethnic Experience: Kinship, Class, and Gender among California Italian-Americans* (Ithaca, NY: Cornell University Press, 1984), 194–218, and "The Female World of Cards and Holidays: Women, Families, and the Work of Kinship," *Signs* 12.3 (Spring 1987): 440–53.

Norwegian American Women

Introduction

In 1925, Norwegian activist women dedicated a new edition of *Norske Kvinder, 1814–1914 (Norwegian Women: 1814–1914)* to their *norske søstre i Amerika* (Norwegian sisters in America): "This work is dedicated to the Norwegian American women for the Centennial Celebration in the year 1925." The first edition, published in 1914 on the occasion of the hundred-year anniversary of the Norwegian constitution, focused on the collective achievements of women in Norway from 1814 to 1914. In the 1925 edition, Fredrikke Marie Qvam discusses why the Norwegian women decided to publish a sequel. Representing the Norwegian National Women's Rights Association, Qvam explained that her countrywomen initially believed their sisters in America lacked interest in the women's struggle in Norway—until they received the symbolic gift of a peace and freedom clock, sent to Norwegian women for their centennial on behalf of Norwegian American women. Thus, the Norwegian women decided to extend their history up to 1925 and dedicate the new edition to the Norwegian American women to mark *their* hundred years in the United States. Qvam wrote, "the gift must be yours, dear sisters, to enjoy, and promote our intellectual connection—even though an ocean lies between us." Following her dedication, Qvam concluded, "We thank you for your gift and hope that bonds between us may never break."[1]

Across the Atlantic, Norwegian American women conceived a similar book. In 1925 Alma A. Guttersen, who emigrated from Norway in 1866 as an infant and eventually settled in St. Paul, proposed the publication of a work on a hundred years of Norwegian American women in the United States. The Norse American Centennial Daughters embraced the project and voted to support it; published in 1926, the result was titled *Souvenir, Norse-American Women, 1825–1925: A Symposium of Prose and Poetry, Newspaper Articles and Biographies, Contributed by One Hundred Prominent Women*, demonstrating the influence and inspiration of Norwegian Women. Comparable in vision and format to the Norwegian work, *Souvenir* covered one hundred years of Norwegian women in America—including biographies, essays, photographs, and newspaper articles—as the subtitle suggests, and marked the women's conditions and collective achievements. These two publications devoted to Norwegian and Norwegian American women suggest both the continuity and discontinuity of their lives. In addition, the two works, published in 1925 and 1926 in Oslo and Minneapolis, respectively, reveal that Norwegian American women maintained contact with their homeland not only as family members but also as active participants in a transatlantic women's movement. While the centennial occasions that generated these publications signify different moments (a constitution and a migration), the works share the larger context of women's struggles on both sides of the Atlantic.[2]

The Norwegian American women living in North America in 1925—both the subject of and the audience for *Souvenir*—represent first-, second-, and third-generation immigrants, wives and mothers, single and professional women, homesteaders, teachers, nurses, seamstresses, domestic servants, laborers, farmers, missionaries, club women, and activists engaged in social welfare, peace and justice, and women's rights through national and international associations. The re-release of *Norwegian Women* in 1925, its dedication, Qvam's transmission letter, and its influence on the 1926 American work all signify an alliance of Norwegian and Norwegian American women who were internationally engaged, active agents in their communities, an alliance more complex than is generally understood by both descendants and historians. Such an image stands in stark contrast to the prevailing view of Norwegian immigrant and Norwegian American women. This book begins to explore the complexity and diversity of that history by foregrounding the gendered dimensions of migration.

Despite this complexity and diversity, for general readers and scholars a more singular image is posited by the most well-known Norwegian American woman: Beret Holm, a fictional character in the celebrated novel *Giants in the Earth* by Ole E. Rølvaag. Beret represents a gendered perspective on migration from Norway to the South Dakota frontier where the characters homesteaded; however, that image has come to dominate thinking about Norwegian immigrant women. In this imaginative and compelling portrait, Rølvaag's Beret conveys grief on leaving her parents and native land, desperation at the expansive and treeless landscape of the prairie, and anxiety about her family's place in this isolated and desolate land. She is contrasted with her energetic, practical, and future-oriented husband Per Hansa, who leads a small band of immigrants into a new life in the West. In this fictional work, Rølvaag captures the complexity, daring, and vision leading the emigrants in that westward migration, while he also evokes the sacrifices of settlement on the frontier. For most readers, Beret signifies the cost of migration, following her husband into alien and hostile territory, finding regret, guilt, and a deep sense of loss. Furthermore, she has signified the Norwegian immigrant woman as a frontier wife and mother, an image often reinforced by primary source materials centered on the frontier. This prevailing vision of the Norwegian immigrant woman as pioneer, rural wife, and mother struggling on the frontier, often reluctantly, remains incomplete and inadequate: the urban working women, along with their daughters and granddaughters, go unrepresented and unimagined. This book attempts to imagine, document, and interpret these historically neglected women by examining their lives in the context of gendered communities, both American and Norwegian American.[3]

Norwegian women migrating to the United States did so along with millions of other women from Europe, Asia, and Latin America in the nineteenth and early twentieth centuries. In general, as Ingrid Semmingsen and Odd S. Lovoll have demonstrated, women represented 41 percent of all Norwegian immigrants in the nineteenth and twentieth centuries, which totaled just under one million. Also, women were more likely than men to settle permanently. The first Norwegian immigrants, mostly religious dissenters, arrived in the United States in 1825; they were followed in the 1830s, 1840s, and 1850s by farm families responding to population growth and diminished possibilities in Norway in the first half of the nineteenth century. Pioneering Norwegian scholar of migration Semmingsen refers to these early groups as a "preparatory stage in Norwegian migration." Many significant frontier women who documented their experiences were counted among emigrants from this period, including Elisabeth Koren and Elise Wærenskjold. However, a truly mass migration from Norway began after the Civil War and continued until World War I. Eighty percent of all Norwegian emigrants left in this fifty-year period, and, Semmingsen reports, nearly three-quarters of the immigrants came from rural districts. At the same time, women constituted a higher percentage of the urban emigrants. These figures illuminate dramatic population growth in nineteenth-century Norway, a growth that pushed young, single girls into small towns or cities in search of employment; many of these women subsequently journeyed to urban areas in the United States in search of better wages, working conditions, and opportunities. Thus, while Norwegian emigrant women were part of the rural, mostly family migration of the mid-nineteenth century, they also represented a higher percentage of the urban and industrial migration of young and single emigrants at the turn of the twentieth century.[4]

Norwegian immigrants tended to settle in the Upper Midwest, mostly in six states: Illinois, Wisconsin, Iowa, Minnesota, and North and South Dakota. The early settlers sought land and the preservation of a rural way of life, as scholars such as Semmingsen, Lovoll, and Jon Gjerde have argued. Furthermore, Theodore C. Blegen and Lovoll have demonstrated that the Norwegians were the most rural of all emigrant groups, even into the twentieth century. Because successful farming—and the rural way of life—required women's contributions, the rural migration was predominantly a family affair. The urban migration, dominated by the young, the single, and a high percentage of women, centered in the towns and cities of the Upper Midwest, especially the larger urban centers of Chicago, Minneapolis, and St. Paul. In the cities, immigrant women from Norway (and some linked to secondary migrations from midwestern farming areas) sought jobs as domestic workers, where they were in demand because of their experience. Later, immigrants and secondary migrations from earlier colonies moved toward the Pacific Northwest, attracted by fishing, shipbuilding, lumbering, and employment prospects in Seattle and Portland. The highest concentration of Norwegians in the country was (and remains) in Minnesota, no doubt because of the mixed opportunities in both rural and urban areas:

in farming, industry, manufacturing, mining, logging, and fishing and through diverse educational possibilities. For immigrant women, domestic jobs, as well as the needle trades and health-care positions, offered decent wages, economic survival, and better possibilities for the future. By the second generation, many of the American-born children of immigrants had received postsecondary education and secured professional positions, especially in health and education. The prevailing vision of the pioneer wife or frontier mother does not permit those diverse and complex narratives to be told. The lives, experiences, impacts, and legacies of these women remain rich, important, and unexplored.[5]

Contexts of American History

The experiences of the Norwegian immigrant and Norwegian American women explored in this volume must be situated in the context of both American history and Norwegian American history, especially mass migration, westward expansion, industrialization, and urbanization. The mass migration that characterized the nineteenth and early twentieth centuries represented one of the largest mobilizations of people in human history. Europeans, especially in this period, migrated to the United States by the tens of millions, pushed by a growing population and emerging industrialization that left few economic opportunities for the young and the next generation. Simultaneously, they were pulled by land, emerging industrial jobs, and opportunities in the United States. During the early and mid-nineteenth century, much of the migration was rural, but by the late nineteenth century it became mostly industrial and urban. Norwegians migrated as a part of both waves; thus, Norwegian immigrant women were among the homesteaders on public land as well as the laborers in the cities. The year 1882 marked the peak of Norwegian emigration, coinciding with the emerging industrial migration. As industrialization and urbanization fueled immigration, these major shifts altered cities, the labor force, social relations, and the cultural environments of America as reformers and radicals at the turn of the twentieth century sought structural changes to improve living and working conditions, especially among immigrants and the working poor. Norwegian immigrant women contributed to these efforts—in both their Norwegian and American communities.

The experiences of Norwegian immigrant and Norwegian American women also need to be placed in the context of the international women's movement and shifting women's roles both in Norway and the United States at the turn of the twentieth century. Though the first women's rights conference in the United States occurred in Seneca Falls, New York, in 1848, only in 1920 did American women gain full suffrage, while Norwegian women received this guarantee seven years earlier, in 1913. The mobilization for women's rights and emancipation in this country grew out of the abolition movement, part of a larger reform movement in the nineteenth century. As women sought to free their brothers and sisters in bondage, they gained the skills and networks to launch their own struggle. Norwegian women and their emigrant sisters also participated in this movement. Moreover, as post–Civil War industrialization and urbanization altered labor patterns and urban developments, women were in the forefront of the reform movements in American cities and Norwegian immigrant women became part of these efforts. These contexts and their gendered implications have been ignored, however, in Norwegian American history and, generally, in immigration history.

Contexts of Migration History

The larger, systematic study of American immigration/migration now includes several generations and deep roots in the Upper Midwest; nevertheless, gendered perspectives have emerged slowly. Migration historian and scholar Donna Gabaccia has examined in numerous publications the gendered dimensions of immigration history. In one article she identifies the origins of migration studies by professional historians working with Blegen at the University of Minnesota—and refers to the subsequent generations of scholars as the Minnesota School. Her analysis provides a useful framework for understanding migration studies and its consideration of gender. Recognizing three generations and nine decades of scholars at the University of Minnesota, she argues that research has changed in this time but some features remain constant: historians have been at the center of the Minnesota School, they have emphasized the value of archives and the roles of the public intellectual, and, Gabaccia argues, each generation has interpreted U.S. immigration within a framework that is international in context, collaborative, and interdisciplinary and that, at its heart, focuses on "the everyday lives, experiences, and subjectivities of immigrants and refugees." The work of the Minnesota School provides a foundation for this volume: building on these pioneering scholars' contributions, it is grounded in history and archival research and it is international, interdisciplinary, and collaborative.[6]

The first generation of the Minnesota School, led by Blegen and George Stephenson, focused on Norwegian and Swedish immigrants. These two University of Minnesota historians were part of a group of scholars in the Mississippi valley influenced by mass migration into the Upper Midwest and by Frederick Jackson Turner's interpretation of the frontier as a central force in shaping the nation. These "ethnic Turnerians," as Gjerde termed them, embraced Turner's frontier thesis and examined the lives and experiences of millions of immigrants as they developed settlements in the Upper Midwest in the late nineteenth and early twentieth centuries. While documenting this history and building archival resources, they also wrote what Blegen called a "grassroots history," a history of ordinary people, a "history from the bottom up."[7]

The second generation of the Minnesota School emerged in the 1960s with the Iron Range Project, an effort to collect and document the lives of diverse immigrant groups in this northern region of Minnesota. These groups arrived as part of a primarily industrial, proletarian, and urban migration at the turn of the century that came mostly from Eastern and Southern Europe. The generation of immigration scholars who studied these migrants belonged to a broader effort by the so-called new social historians to examine groups rendered invisible in more traditional political and military history—groups such as women, laborers, immigrants, and the oppressed. These migration historians (themselves often second-generation immigrants) emphasized the urban and labor migrations, drew on new quantitative methods, emphasized class, and influenced a whole generation of scholars. With a few exceptions, they tended to neglect gendered dimensions of migration, except those who focused specifically on women's history. A third generation of immigration scholars (at Minnesota and nationally) have emphasized the post-1965 migrations from Asia and Latin America, giving special attention to issues of racial hierarchies, citizenship, nationalism, and related legal concerns.[8]

In this long tradition of migration history, studies of Norwegians were early and ongoing but otherwise steeped in historical traditions and cultural ideologies of the first half of the twentieth century. One might argue, as scholar Kathleen Conzen has, that the Norwegian American historiography has been a "victim of its own success." The institutional leadership—in churches, schools and colleges, newspapers, labor, social, and cultural organizations, and historical societies—long remained male dominated, and patriarchal ideologies about appropriate positions for men and women informed historical writings, research topics, and the historical documents studied. Much of this immigration and ethnic history rested on institutional history: the organizations that immigrant groups developed to help sustain communities provided the archival resources for writing that history, and these very institutions were steeped in patriarchal assumptions. Thus, when historians sought to examine those Norwegian American institutions, the history reflected patriarchal structures, assumptions, and records. Furthermore, when the second generation of social historians began to consider the more urban and industrial labor force, divisions in the "new" social history meant historians of women and historians of migration tended to move in parallel tracks, and the insights from one subfield often did not affect the other: migration historians focused on nationality or ethnic groups, while women's historians focused on gender. Then, as feminist scholars used gender as an analytical tool, many migration scholars had already begun focusing on the new migrations from Asia and Latin America, emphasizing racial constructions and barriers that had affected these groups, and often neglecting scholarship on women and gender.[9]

While some scholars combined women's and migration history in the last two decades, the incorporation of multiple analytical tools by historians in examining migration—such as gender, national origin, class, and religion—has not developed widely throughout the field. In her article "Immigrant Women, Nowhere at Home," Gabaccia writes, "Female immigrants are exceedingly marginal figures" in most of the studies of the 1970s and 1980s. She suggests that women were not "deliberately or accidentally ignored," but she emphasizes methodological and theoretical explanations of why this pattern emerged. A summary of her explanations is useful not only for understanding the general exclusion of gender but also why Norwegian American historiography tended to exclude women and gendered perspectives.[10]

First, Gabaccia argues, immigration and women's studies pursued different topics—the migration historians emphasized community studies (often dominated by men), while scholars of women's studies, in its early stages, focused on notable women, foregrounding differences with men. Second, the academic disciplines did not always share analytical categories. Historians and sociologists both employ categories of race, ethnicity, class, culture, nationality, and religion, but they may overlook gender; thus, those scholars engaged in research on women may be shaped more by their disciplines than by shared categories. Consequently, migration historians may focus on nationality and class, neglecting gender, while scholars of women's studies trained in sociology, for example, may be more focused on race or class, giving little attention to nationality. A third factor dividing immigration and women's history, Gabaccia suggests, involves the diverging approaches to the family taken by migration historians and feminist theorists: migration historians used family studies as a central category because families often migrated together and depended on those networks for survival, yet feminist theorists often studied families as patriarchal institutions repressing women. Furthermore, families were often viewed differently: migration historians saw an extended family, whereas social scientists might focus on the nuclear family. In addition, conceptions of the self in relation to the family often differed between historians and feminists: historians emphasized empirical data and evidence, while feminist scholars emphasized the social and historical constructions surrounding gender, race, and ethnic identities. Finally, different methodologies in the fields of women's studies and the social sciences have often created tensions and divergence. Gabaccia explains that the difference between the interpretive and theoretical approaches used in the humanities and social sciences has made appreciation of alternative modes difficult: the social sciences tend to focus on structures, theories, and measurements, while the humanities tend to foreground experience, the empirical record, and interpretation.

Gabaccia concludes, "Ironically, the very proliferation of specialties that allowed ethnic and women's studies to develop as multidisciplinary fields has also helped institutionalize the conflicting categories, methods, and modes of analysis that contribute to the marginality of scholarship on immigrant women."[11]

Despite these theoretical and methodological challenges, much work on women, gender, and migration—that also incorporates issues of race, class, and religion—has been published since Gabaccia's article first appeared. On the other hand, Norwegian American scholarship on migration—once viewed as a pioneer in the field—has lagged behind in its treatment of women and gender.[12]

Contexts of Norwegian American Studies

In the field of Norwegian American studies, women's and gender history has been largely neglected. At the same time, it must be said that a number of important primary sources have been translated and published in English. Blegen, a pioneer historian of the Midwest and immigration, recognized the importance of Norwegian American women's history in 1930, leading him to collect, translate, and publish primary source materials on women. Indeed, women's historians steeped in gendered perspectives, rather than scholars of Norwegian American migration and communities, have been more likely to use these primary sources in ways that help to explain gender in American society. Until now, however, the only monograph that addresses Norwegian immigrant women and gender from a feminist perspective is L. DeAne Lagerquist's *In America the Men Milk the Cows: Factors of Gender, Ethnicity, and Religion in the Americanization of Norwegian-American Women*. Published in 1991, Lagerquist's groundbreaking and important work challenges church histories that ignore women and uses the "triple lens" of feminist history, ethnic history, and religious history to analyze the lives of Norwegian American women. Gender is central to her analytical framework as she examines the close relationships between ethnicity and religion. Lagerquist's work, drawing richly on primary source materials and employing analytical rigor, has forced scholars to recognize the ways in which women shaped the church and gender shaped women's lives. Moreover, she broadly addresses some of the ways in which living in the United States challenged and changed Norwegian gender roles.[13]

Though not with the singular focus, other scholars of Norwegian American history have examined women's lives in broader community studies. For example, in the 1990s Gjerde and Jane Marie Pederson looked at women's agricultural roles in the Upper Midwest, although they came to different conclusions about the extent to which Norwegian American women continued to participate in agriculture. More recently, Lovoll has richly described life in Norwegian American small towns, exploring the experiences of the men, women, and children who inhabited them in his work *Norwegians on the Prairie.* Likewise, Kathleen Stokker's *Rituals and Remedies* places women healers and midwives at the forefront of her study on folk medicine in Norway and in Norwegian American communities. While these recent developments are encouraging, a need persists for scholarship that more deeply and systematically explores women and gender in Norwegian American communities.[14]

The Present Volume

This volume shares many dimensions with earlier traditions in immigration studies; it also builds on and breaks from them. The shared traditions mean, first, the work is transnational—not only does the collection include two Norwegian scholars and scholarly developments and begin its gendered perspectives in Norway, but the chapters continue to utilize archives and scholarly thinking from both sides of the Atlantic. Second, the work is interdisciplinary, drawing on the fields of history, sociology, geography, American studies, and Scandinavian studies as well as cultural and feminist studies. Third, the work depends heavily on the archival resources collected and preserved, especially by the first generation of immigration historians, and now located at the Minnesota Historical Society and the Norwegian-American Historical Association, in addition to the public records and archival sources found throughout the country in local, state, and national repositories and in church and private collections. At the same time, it also builds on past scholarship, using many of the historical documents the first generation of scholars produced—the letters and diaries collected, translated, and published. Blegen and his contemporaries did not render women wholly invisible; while they did not use gender as an analytical tool, they made many of the women accessible so that today's researchers might more fully explore those gendered categories. On the other hand, this volume breaks from the past, making gendered categories central to its analysis of Norwegian migration.

The chapters in this volume represent a variety of disciplines. By its very nature, Norwegian American studies is an interdisciplinary field, and these new studies display its breadth. As such, the authors have adopted a variety of approaches to their topics. Collectively, the chapters challenge us to understand how Norwegian American women's lives and experiences differed from men's. Furthermore, they demonstrate how using the lens of gender illuminates those differences and their meanings while also shedding light on Norwegian American communities.[15]

Before introducing the scope and content of this volume, a special note on its perspective—gender—is critical. Joan Wallach Scott's book *Gender and the Politics of History,* first published in 1988, lays out theoretical frameworks for analyzing how gender shapes both history and historical writing. The work, now a classic for historians of women, feminist theorists, and scholars examining gender in history and society, remains the best starting point for thinking about gender historically and analytically. The term *gender* (in its recent usage) appeared among American feminists, Scott argues, and denoted a rejection of the biological determinism implicit in the use of *sex* or *sex difference*. The term *gender* also implied the relational aspect of society—that is, the social relations between the sexes sometimes absent in women's history and women's studies— and offered an analytical framework for understanding men and women in relation to each other. Often linked categorically with class and race, *gender* also suggests the inequalities of power and that these inequalities must be examined along, at least, three axes: race, class, and gender. For Scott, the analytical possibility of gender is embedded in her definition of the term. She writes, "The core of the definition rests on an integral connection between two propositions: gender is a constitutive element of social relationships based on perceived differences between the sexes, and gender is a primary way of signifying relationships of power." What this means, essentially, is that social, cultural, and historical elements (ideas, images, symbols, normative concepts, institutions, and ideologies) all shape our perceptions surrounding women and men. Historically, these elements have privileged men over women and affected relations of power—in every dimension of thought and behavior from individuals and families to states. Thus, employing this fundamental category of gender as an analytical tool, historically, we can more fully understand the complexities of human relations, including those surrounding immigration and ethnicity.[16]

Part I of the collection focuses on the world the emigrants left and the migration itself, emphasizing the gendered dimensions of those conditions generally neglected by historians. Thus, Elisabeth Lønnå's chapter on women in nineteenth- and early twentieth-century Norway opens the volume. Addressing the transformations in Norway in the period of migration and foregrounding the status of women and the struggle for gender equity, she tracks the ideological, political, and legal attitudes toward women that shaped their lives and their possibilities and made migration a rational alternative. Lønnå's work provides the foundation for understanding emigration in a gendered context. Eminent scholar of Norwegian American history Odd S. Lovoll looks at female and male immigrants to assess the ways in which gendered opportunities influenced the process of migration. Lovoll compares and contrasts the ways in which women decided to emigrate and the importance of female networks along the way. In Norway, young single women often migrated to cities and urban centers, especially after the 1880s, and in some periods women immigrants outnumbered men.

Part II focuses on the American experiences of immigrants, emphasizing Norwegian Americans in both American and ethnic communities and foregrounding the gendered dimensions of these communities. First, Lori Ann Lahlum uses gender to understand women's labor and community building, both formal and informal, in rural areas. While women's work typically fell within the realm of domestic labor, farm women also played important agricultural roles. Lahlum shows that traditional agricultural gender roles became more flexible in the United States but did not disappear quickly. Then, David C. Mauk examines the migration of Norwegian women to American cities, emphasizing Minneapolis/St. Paul but also referring to Chicago, Brooklyn, and Seattle. Many of these migrants were single women, having earlier left farms in Norway for urban centers before migrating to the United States or having come directly to the new-world cities. Their work and life experiences clearly challenge prevailing views about Norwegian immigrant women as primarily rural and part of a family migration.

The central role of women in the development of Norwegian American communities is examined in two studies that focus on critical contributions of women's work: textile production and health reforms. Laurann Gilbertson's study of Norwegian immigrant and Norwegian American women demonstrates how women's textile production in the United States continued to be critical in sustaining families in the new world and in enhancing their economic survival. Ann M. Legreid's chapter considers how immigrant women adapted to new roles and opportunities in the health professions, founding hospitals and health programs and working toward creating healthy communities beyond Norwegian American circles. Karen V. Hansen's study of Spirit Lake Reservation addresses the complex process of land dispossession at intersections of race, ethnicity, and gender and opens up the racial hierarchies that benefited Norwegians, including women. Hansen's study, focused on a specific historical and geographic moment, examines how Norwegians, especially women, played critical roles in homesteading reservation land on the North Dakota plains, simultaneously comparing Norwegian American and Dakota women's relationships to the land.

Part III focuses on the expressive voices of Norwegian American women, examining the often overlooked fiction and nonfiction that immigrant women produced and which provided interpretations of their experiences and the self-constructions of their lives. Ingrid K. Urberg focuses on four novelists writing fiction for Norwegian American audiences, publications often disregarded in discussions of Norwegian literature. Urberg demonstrates that these writers produced characters reflecting their own desires for education, learning, experience, and opportunity—possibilities often associated with America, the "promised land," and with immigrant fiction. Betty A. Bergland's analysis focuses on nonfiction writings of Norwegian immigrant women, specifically their life writings— letters, diaries, memoirs, and reminiscences—in the absence of full-blown autobiographies by this first generation. Bergland argues that the prevailing pattern within these women's life writings is the fragmented but collective sense of self—a pattern consistent with the writings of other women—signifying the importance of using gender as an analytical framework for examining immigrant, life writing sources.

What these chapters reveal collectively is that by focusing on women's sources and activities, as well as employing gender as an analytical framework, we see a more complete, balanced portrayal of immigrant lives and communities. In a patriarchal world, where women were silenced in the church, kept from voting in the political arena, excluded from decision making and certain life courses, paid less than men, and constructed as the "second sex," their experiences were different from those of men. Of course, these women were not simply passive victims who embraced a subordinated position; rather, we see through an analysis of their lives and the recorded history their agency and autonomy, creativity and endurance, inventiveness and adaptability—despite the constraints. Furthermore, they contributed to Norwegian American communities in vital ways. By recognizing that gender is a socially constructed category and a meaningful analytical tool, we can reimagine this immigrant generation and the ethnic generations that followed in a fuller, more complex and interesting way while moving toward a more complete and truthful history.

Notes

1. Dedication in 1925 edition of *Norske Kvinder: En Oversigt over deres og Livsvilkaar i hundredeaaret, 1814–1914* (*Norwegian Women: A Survey of Their Living Conditions Over One Hundred Years, 1814–1914*), eds. Marie Høgh and Fredrikke Mørck (Kristiania: Berg and Høgh's Forlag, 1924). The dedication reads: "*Dette Verk tilegnes De Norsk-Amerikanske Kvinder ved Hundredaarsjubilæet Aar 1925.*" Translations are the author's.

The one-page note (signed F. M. Qvam and dated 17 May 1925, without label or salutation) follows the dedication, precedes the title page, and is located opposite a photograph of Queen Maud of Norway. Fredrikke Marie Qvam was involved in the Norwegian National Women's Rights Association (*Landskvindestemmeretsforening*) from its beginning in 1885 and was also involved in the Norwegian Women's Sanitation Association (*Norske Kvinders Sanitetsforening*). See Elisabeth Lønnå, *Stolthet og Kvinnekamp: Norsk Kvinnesaksforenings Historie fra 1913* (*Pride and Women's Struggles: Norwegian Feminist History from 1913*) (Oslo: Gyldendal Norsk Forlag, 1996), 17.

2. Mrs. Alma A. Guttersen and Mrs. Regina Hilleboe Christensen, eds., *Souvenir "Norse-American Women," 1825–1925: A Symposium of Prose and Poetry, Newspaper Articles and Biographies, Contributed by One Hundred Prominent Women* (St. Paul, MN: The Lutheran Free Church Publishing Co., 1926). The volume is available online through "Women and Social Movements in the United States," edited by Thomas Dublin, Kathryn Kish Sklar, and Alexander Street Press, LLC: http://asp6new.alexanderstreet. com/wam2/wam2.object.details.aspx?dorpid=1000402456, accessed 29 Oct. 2010.

Although some scholars have written about the centennial celebration of 1925 marking Norwegian migration to the United States, the women's involvement and the gendered dimensions of the celebration remain unexplored. See, for example, April R. Schultz, *Ethnicity on Parade: Inventing the Norwegian American Through Celebration* (Amherst: University of Massachusetts Press, 1994), which does not address women or gendered dimensions. See also Schultz, "How Did Women Shape the Presentation of Norwegian American Ethnicity at the 1925 Norse-American Centennial?" (2009), in eds. Dublin, Sklar, and Press, "Women and Social Movements in the United States": http://asp6new. alexanderstreet.com/wam2/wam2.object.details.aspx?dorpID=1001234510

3. O. E. Rølvaag, *Giants in the Earth,* trans. Lincoln Colcord and the author (New York: Harper and Brothers, 1927), is the first English publication of the two-part novel originally published in Norwegian: *I de Dage: Fortælling om Norske Nykommere I Amerika* (*In Those Days: A Story of Norwegian Immigrants in America*) (Kristiania: H. Aschehoug og Co., 1924) and *I de Dage: Riket Grundlaegges (In Those Days: The Founding of the Kingdom)* (Kristiania: H. Aschehoug og Co., 1925). Rølvaag based the story (in part) on the Berdahl family experiences in South Dakota. The Berdahl Papers are located at the Center for Western Studies at Augustana College, Sioux Falls, SD.

This image of Beret is linked essentially to *Giants in the Earth.* In the two often over-looked sequels, Rølvaag focused on the second generation and widow Beret becomes a strong force in her family and the community: O. E. Rølvaag, *Peder Victorious: A Tale of the Pioneers Twenty Years Later,* trans. Nora O. Solum and the author (New York: Harper and Brothers, 1929), and O. E. Rølvaag, *Their Father's God,* trans. Trygve M. Ager (New York: Harper and Brothers, 1931).

4. Ingrid Semmingsen, "Norwegian Emigration in the Nineteenth Century," *Scandinavian Economic History Review* 8.2 (based on paper read at the Eleventh International Congress of Historical Sciences), 152, 156, 157; and Odd S. Lovoll, *The Promise of America: A History of the Norwegian American People* (Minneapolis: University of Minnesota Press in cooperation with the Norwegian-American Historical Association [hereafter, NAHA], 1984), 23, 28. Lovoll reports that the total number of immigrants from 1846 to 1930 was 851,842, while approximately 677,000 (or 80 percent) migrated from 1865 to 1915. See also Odd S. Lovoll, "Norwegian Immigration and Women" in this volume.

5. Lovoll, *Promise of America,*153; see also his *Norwegians on the Prairie: Ethnicity and the Development of the Country Town* (St. Paul: Minnesota Historical Society Press [hereafter, MHS Press], published in cooperation with NAHA, 2006).

6. Donna Gabaccia, "Reviving a Tradition: The 'Minnesota School' of Immigration Studies," *The Immigration and Ethnic History Newsletter* 39.2 (Nov. 2007): 1, 8.

7. See Jon Gjerde, "New Growth on Old Vines—The State of the Field: The Social History of Immigration to and Ethnicity in the United States," *Journal of American Ethnic History* 18.4 (Summer 1999): 40–65. The early literature of migration historians remains vast; however, Gjerde's article offers a meaningful overview. Theodore C. Blegen, *Grassroots History* (Minneapolis: University of Minnesota Press, 1947).

8. University of Minnesota professors Hyman Berman, Clarke Chambers, and Timothy Smith led the project. Their efforts to collect the records of multiple groups on the Iron Range (newspapers, publications, oral histories, correspondence, church and labor records) became the origins of the Immigration History Research Center. Founded in 1965 and located on the campus of the University of Minnesota, the IHRC

represents one of the largest and most important collections documenting immigration globally. In 1967 Rudolph J. Vecoli came to Minnesota to lead and direct the efforts of the IHRC, where he remained until his retirement in 2005.

From migration historians, see, for example, *A Century of European Migrations, 1830–1930*, ed. Rudolph J. Vecoli and Suzanne M. Sinke (Urbana and Chicago: University of Illinois Press, 1991), as symptomatic of this pattern. The *Journal of American Ethnic History* (published by the Immigration History Society, later the Immigration and Ethnic History Society) began publishing in 1980; however, perusal of its contents for more than a quarter of a century reveals limited attention to women and gender until recently, although many of its contributors write on women and gendered patterns of migration.

Finally, as representative of the "third" generation's work, see Erika Lee, *At America's Gates: Chinese Immigration During the Exclusion Era, 1882–1943* (Chapel Hill: University of North Carolina Press, 2003); Vicki Ruiz and Virginia Sanchez Korrol, eds., *Latina Legacies: Identity, Biography, Communities* (New York: Oxford University Press, 2005). Much of this generation's work is informed by thinking on the constructions of "race" and whiteness, and many of these studies return to earlier European immigrants. See, for example, David R. Roediger, *The Wages of Whiteness: Race and the Making of the American Working Class* (New York and London: Verso, 1991); Matthew Frye Jacobson, *Whiteness of a Different Color: European Immigrants and the Alchemy of Race* (Cambridge and London: Harvard University Press, 1998); Thomas Guglielmo, *White on Arrival: Italians, Race, Color, and Power in Chicago, 1890–1945* (Oxford and New York: Oxford University Press, 2003). See also work of Betty Bergland influenced by these directions: "Norwegian Immigrants and 'Indianerne' in the Landtaking, 1838–1862," *Norwegian-American Studies* 35 (Northfield, MN: NAHA, 2000), 319–50; "Norwegian Immigrants, Wisconsin Tribes and the Bethany Indian Mission in Wittenberg, Wisconsin, 1883–1955," in *Norwegian American Essays, 2004*, ed. Orm Øverland (Oslo, Norway: Norwegian-American Historical Association–Norway, 2005), 67–102; and "Settler Colonists, 'Christian Citizenship,' and the Women's Missionary Federation at the Bethany Indian Mission in Wittenberg, Wisconsin, 1884–1934," in *Competing Kingdoms: Women, Mission, Nation and the Protestant Empire*, eds. Kathryn K. Sklar, Barbara Reeves-Ellington, and Connie Shemo (Durham, NC: Duke University Press, 2010).

9. Kathleen Conzen, "Commentary," in *Scandinavians and Other Immigrants in Urban America: The Proceedings of a Research Conference, October 26–27, 1984*, ed. Odd S. Lovoll (Northfield, MN: St. Olaf College Press, 1985), 196.

In the Norwegian contexts, these institutions would include the Lutheran Church (all synods); ethnic newspapers and publications; the Sons of Norway, a fraternal organization; Lutheran Brotherhood (later called Thrivent Financial for Lutherans), an insurance company; the *Torske Klubbe*, a social club begun by businessmen and reserved for male members only, even today; the *Bygdelags*, regional ethnic societies; and higher education (St. Olaf College was coeducational from its start in 1874, but Luther College excluded women until well into the twentieth century).

10. For some of the work on immigrant women from Europe from the last decades, see, for example, Donna Gabaccia, *From the Other Side: Women, Gender and Immigrant Life in the U.S. 1820–1990* (Bloomington and Indianapolis: Indiana University Press, 1994);

Donna R. Gabaccia and Franca Iacovetta, eds., *Women, Gender and Transnational Lives: Italian Workers of the World* (Toronto and Buffalo: University of Toronto Press, 2002); Hasia R. Diner, *Erin's Daughters in America: Irish Immigrant Women in the Nineteenth Century* (Baltimore and London: Johns Hopkins University Press, 1983); Carl Ross and K. Marianne Wargelin Brown, eds., *Women Who Dared: The History of Finnish American Women* (St. Paul: Immigration History Research Center, University of Minnesota, 1986); Linda Schelbitzki Pickle, *Contented Among Strangers: Rural German-Speaking Women and Their Families in the Nineteenth-Century Midwest* (Urbana and Chicago: University of Illinois Press, 1996); Christiane Hartzig, ed., *Peasant Maids, City Women: From the European Countryside to Urban America* (Ithaca, NY: Cornell University Press, 1997); Suzanne M. Sinke, *Dutch Immigrant Women in the United States, 1880–1920* (Urbana and Chicago: University of Illinois Press, 2002); and Joy K. Lintelman, *"I Go To America": Swedish American Women and the Life of Mina Anderson* (St. Paul: MHS Press, 2009). See also Donna Gabaccia, "Immigrant Women: Nowhere at Home?" *Journal of American Ethnic History* 10.4 (Summer 1991): 61–87.

11. Gabaccia writes, "The category Euro-American or European American, which is increasingly used in ethnic studies and in women's studies to describe white immigrants[,] is almost never used by immigration historians," in "Immigrant Women," 66; see also p74. Early and important work that reflects this pattern includes Virginia Yans-McLaughlin, *Family and Community: Italian Immigrants in Buffalo 1880–1930* (Urbana and Chicago: University of Illinois Press, 1982). The important Norwegian example is Jon Gjerde, *From Peasants to Farmers: The Migration from Balestrand Norway to the Upper Middle West* (Cambridge, London, and New York: Cambridge University Press, 1985).

12. For more recent work on women, immigration, and gendered perspectives, see, for example, Lintelman, *"I Go to America."* See also the works of Florence Mae Waldron and Jennifer Guglielmo.

13. Examples of primary sources include Theodore C. Blegen, ed. and trans., *Land of Their Choice: The Immigrants Write Home* (Minneapolis: University of Minnesota Press, 1955); Pauline Farseth and Theodore C. Blegen, trans. and eds., *Frontier Mother: The Letters of Gro Svendsen* (New York: Arno Press, 1979); *The Diary of Elizabeth Koren, 1853–1855,* trans. and ed. David T. Nelson (Northfield, MN: NAHA, 1955); Solveig Zempel, ed. and trans., *In Their Own Words: Letters from Norwegian Immigrants* (Minneapolis: University of Minnesota Press in cooperation with NAHA, 1991); *The Strange American Way: Letters of Caja Munch from Wiota, Wisconsin, 1855–1859,* trans. Helen Munch and Peter A. Munch (Carbondale and Edwardsville: Southern Illinois University Press, 1970); Janet E. Rasmussen, *New Land, New Lives: Scandinavian Immigrants to the Pacific Northwest* (Northfield, MN: NAHA, and Seattle and London: University of Washington Press, 1993); Elise Wærenskjold, *The Lady with the Pen: Elise Wærenskjold in Texas,* ed. C. A. Clausen (Northfield, MN: NAHA, 1961); Theresse Nelson Lundby, Kristie Nelson-Neuhaus, and Ann Nordland Wallace, *Live Well: The Letters of Sigrid Gjeldaker Lillehaugen* (Minneapolis, MN: Western Home Books, 2004). Theodore C. Blegen, ed. and trans., "Immigrant Women and the American Frontier: Three Early 'America Letters,'" *Studies and Records* 5 (Northfield, MN: NAHA, 1930), 14. For women's historians using these sources, see, for example, Ruth Schwartz Cowan, *More Work for Mother: The Ironies of*

Household Technology from the Open Hearth to the Microwave (New York: Basic Books, Inc., 1983), 30–31; Barbara Handy-Marchello, *Women of the Northern Plains: Gender and Settlement on the Homestead Frontier, 1870–1930* (St. Paul: MHS Press, 2005); Joan M. Jensen, *Calling This Place Home: Women on the Wisconsin Frontier, 1850–1925* (St. Paul: MHS Press, 2006); H. Elaine Lindgren, *Land in Her Own Name: Women as Homesteaders in North Dakota* (Fargo: North Dakota Institute for Regional Studies, 1991); Glenda Riley, *Frontierswomen: The Iowa Experience* (Ames: Iowa State University Press, 1981); Glenda Riley, *The Female Frontier: A Comparative View of Women on the Prairie and Plains* (Lawrence: University of Kansas Press, 1988).

L. DeAne Lagerquist, *In America the Men Milk the Cows: Factors of Gender, Ethnicity, and Religion in the Americanization of Norwegian-American Women*, Chicago Studies in the History of American Religion, eds. Jerald C. Brauer and Martin E. Marty (Brooklyn, NY: Carlson Publishing Inc., 1991), 2–5.

14. Gjerde, *From Peasants to Farmers*, 168–201; Jon Gjerde, *The Minds of the West: Ethnocultural Evolution in the Rural Middle West, 1830–1917* (Chapel Hill and London: University of North Carolina Press, 1997), 135–58; Jane Marie Pederson, *Between Memory and Reality: Family and Community in Rural Wisconsin, 1870–1970* (Madison: University of Wisconsin Press, 1992), 165–71. Lovoll, *Norwegians on the Prairie.* Kathleen Stokker, *Remedies and Rituals: Folk Medicine in Norway and the New Land* (St. Paul: MHS Press, 2007).

15. Some topics may be visibly absent for readers. Religion, for example, appears in most of these essays as a factor in women's lives and in shaping gendered positions, but not as a separate essay. The treatment of the topic in Lagerquist's excellent work, *In America the Men Milk the Cows,* provides an explanation.

16. Joan Wallach Scott, *Gender and the Politics of History,* Gender and Culture Series, eds. Carolyn G. Heilbrun and Nancy K. Miller (New York: Columbia University Press, 1988), especially 28–50, quotation p42. It might be emphasized here that while some students confuse the terms *sex* and *gender,* most scholars distinguish between *sex* (referring to biological difference) and *gender* (referring to socially constructed concepts based on perceived differences).

Acknowledgments

This volume on Norwegian American women's history grew out of discussions we had in Norway during the summer of 2003. Questions about women and gender in Norwegian American communities emerged from conversations at the Norwegian-American Historical Association–Norway Seminar in Bergen and continued throughout June and July as we both studied Norwegian at the International Summer School at the University of Oslo. Our discussions focused on the lack of scholarly work on women and gender in Norwegian America, and these conversations became the starting point for the present volume. This lively exchange, begun in Norway and ongoing for more than seven years, has been enriching and fruitful. In many ways, *Norwegian American Women: Migration, Communities, and Identities* marks the start of a dialogue that will continue for many years to come.

At its core, the essays in this volume illuminate the history of Norwegian American women through the lens of gender. We knew from the beginning that our approach would have to be interdisciplinary because Norwegian American studies has been enriched by the work of scholars from many different fields. We are fortunate to have found scholars who believed the topic as important as we did and were willing to work through multiple versions of their chapters over the past five years. This volume would not exist without our contributors: they bring a richness to this history that would be difficult for one scholar to deliver.

As with a work such as this, we owe a debt of gratitude to many people. Shannon M. Pennefeather, our editor at Minnesota Historical Society Press, wisely guided us through the publication process, cheerfully responded to our many queries, and exhibited the utmost patience as this project took longer to complete than either one of us anticipated. She helped shape this volume in many ways. Likewise, two anonymous readers offered valuable criticisms that informed the final manuscript. Odd S. Lovoll not only wrote a chapter for the book; he has been an enthusiastic supporter of the project from the beginning and fielded questions throughout the process. Donna Gabaccia and the late Jon J. Gjerde offered advice and read our proposal as we sought a publisher. In Oslo, Dina Tolfsby culled the Norwegian-American collection at the Norwegian National Library to create a bibliography for this volume. Elizabeth Jameson generously agreed to write the foreword to the book. The late Dorothy Burton Skårdal, a pioneering scholar in the field, was one of our champions, offering words of encouragement and a cup of tea when we met her in Oslo. Orm Øverland has also supported this project over the years.

The assistance of archivists in the United States and Norway facilitated work on *Norwegian American Women.* Staff at many archives and museums made our work much easier, especially those at the National Archives in Oslo (Riksarkivet), Norwegian Emigration Museum (Norsk Utvandrermuseum), State Regional Archive (Statsarkivet) in Trondheim, Minnesota Historical Society, Wisconsin Historical Society, Latah County (Idaho) Historical Society, and Barnes County (North Dakota) Historical Society. Of special note, our heartfelt thanks are extended to Jeff Sauve, archivist for the Norwegian-American Historical Association (NAHA). Jeff not only saw to it that our research trips to the NAHA archives went smoothly, he always asked about the project, pointed us toward collections with which we were unfamiliar, offered suggestions for research, and provided working space as we finalized the essays. To Jeff: *Mange tusen takk!* Other archivists, librarians, and researchers deserve special mention: Debbie Miller and Linda McShannock at the Minnesota Historical Society; Dee Anna Grimsrud at the Wisconsin Historical Society; Kathryn Otto at the University of Wisconsin–River Falls Area Research Center; Michele McKnelly at the UWRF Chalmer Davee Library; and Joann Dougherty of the Jackson County (Wisconsin) Historical Society.

Colleagues, friends, and family offered advice, encouragement, and support through the book's many stages. We would like to mention a few of these people by name: Mark Anderson, Chris Corley, Kevin Fernlund, Dee Garceau, Cynthia S. Hanson, Kent Hanson, Torild Homstad, Renee Laegreid, Audrey Lahlum, Howard Lahlum, Kirsten Lahlum, Michael Lansing, Joy Lintelman, Roseann Lloyd, Mary Murphy, Leah Rogne, Sally Rubenstein, Joseph M. Shaw, W. R. Swagerty, Claudia Tomany, the late Rudolph J. Vecoli, Florence Mae Waldron, Marianne Wargelin, Monika Zagar, and Solveig Zempel. Colleagues in our respective departments and universities—the University of Wisconsin–River Falls and Minnesota State University, Mankato—also deserve our thanks. Additionally, the College of Social and Behavioral Sciences at Minnesota State Mankato funded a much-needed one-semester course reduction for work on this project. Susan M. Voelker (University of Wisconsin–River Falls) and Amy Kopachek (Minnesota State University, Mankato) provided crucial administrative support, and Dan Semi and Joshua See (UWRF) offered invaluable technical support.

Our collaboration on this project has been extremely rewarding and intellectually invigorating. Although both of us do research on Norwegian immigrants and their descendants, we approach our work quite differently: Bergland from the perspective of immigration, women's, and cultural history and Lahlum from American western women's and gender history. These different frameworks have resulted in a richer volume as we learned from each other over the years.

Betty A. Bergland   *Lori Ann Lahlum*
St. Paul, Minnesota   *Mankato, Minnesota*

PART I

❖

Gendered Contexts: Norway and Migration

Norway underwent rapid change in the period of migration. As in other European countries in the nineteenth century, this change included population growth and the migration of thousands of peasants from the countryside to cities in search of jobs. In Norway, that meant especially Oslo and Bergen but included smaller towns as well. While Norway remained primarily an agrarian nation at the turn of the twentieth century, this growth also spurred migration to the United States, where land and then an industrial economy stimulated the waves of migration. From 1820 to 1914, thirty million Europeans emigrated to the United States. In the midst of these sweeping changes, the place of women also changed. Social disruptions emerged as young, rural women left farm communities for work in towns and cities, often eventually migrating to the United States, and mostly urban women demanded equity, education, and rights. Both men and women emigrated, and most were young, driven primarily by economic motives in pursuit of a better future. Women, however, came from different contexts and shifting expectations about their place in society. Chapter 1 illuminates that world.

The inaugural chapter in this volume, by Norwegian feminist scholar Elisabeth Lønnå, examines those shifting social, economic, political, and legal conditions for women in Norway in the nineteenth and twentieth centuries. It tracks the various campaigns of equity and justice for women: legal rights, including inheritance and equity in marriage; educational rights to higher education; economic justice, especially evident in the Maid Servants' Association (Den kvindelige tjenerstands forening); and political equality, concluding with women's suffrage in 1907. By tracing the positions of women and the struggles for change, Lønnå guides the reader through the gendered dimensions of Norwegian society, emphasizing the changing conditions in the transitional period when emigration occurred. Thus, she helps readers understand the gendered realities in Norway and the circumstances that compelled women to leave. In Chapter 2, eminent scholar of Norwegian migration and Norwegian American ethnicity Odd S. Lovoll situates these migrating women in the larger pattern of Norwegian emigration. Drawing on earlier research and national statistics and offering comparative perspectives on men and women, Lovoll corrects a belief that Norwegian migration was largely a male phenomenon. He also shows that although many Norwegian immigrant women became pioneer wives or domestics in urban settings, their lives, labors, and pursuits in America were far more diverse. Furthermore, he demonstrates that women immigrants were much more likely than their male counterparts to come from urban areas and remain as permanent residents in the United States. The gendered dimensions of life in Norway and the gendered migration patterns to America provide a crucial framework for understanding Norwegian immigrants in the United States.

Gender in Norway in the Period of Mass Emigration

Elisabeth Lønnå

This chapter outlines the changes in the status of women in Norway from about 1865, when the American Civil War ended and mass emigration set in, until the end of the 1930s, when emigration had diminished to a trickle. Also, it examines the gender roles of everyday life, showing how these changed as Norway transformed into an industrial society. Clearly, the legal status, education, and work opportunities for women improved during these years. Whether traditional gender roles also improved is less clear.

Centennial Celebration of 1914

The spring and summer of 1914 was a time of great jubilation in Norway. A hundred years earlier, a national assembly, hastily called together at Eidsvoll north of Kristiania (now Oslo), had passed a new constitution. In a union with Denmark for more than four centuries, autocratic kings had governed Norway from Copenhagen since 1660. But in 1807, Denmark allied itself with Napoleon, who lost to the great powers at the Battle of Nations at Leipzig in 1813. Sweden, among the victors at Leipzig, could now force the Danish king to relinquish Norway to the Swedish king. In a period of international confusion during the early part of 1814, Norwegians tried to establish an independent, constitutional monarchy under the Danish Crown Prince Christian Fredrik. The attempt failed, but the new constitution, signed at Eidsvoll on May 17, 1814, survived in a revised edition. Remarkably democratic for its time, the constitution reflected ideals from the Enlightenment and both the American and French revolutions. Furthermore, it provided the tools to build an independent government even within the union with Sweden that followed later that year. When the union between the two countries was peacefully dissolved in 1905, the 1814 constitution remained the basis of government. No wonder a celebration emerged in 1914.

The country marked the centennial of the constitution with a major, national exhibition at Frogner Park in Kristiania. Here Norwegian industries exhibited their products to an enthusiastic public. A wealth of organizations, along with state and regional governments, presented their achievements in many areas, emphasizing science and the arts. Organizers took care to show the national scope of the celebration; thus, all parts of the country were represented. Traditional rural living styles had a place, as well as the newer and rapidly growing industrial society. Farmers, workers, and the upper and middle classes were all invited. Women also took part, a group that had just recently been accepted as full-fledged citizens into the Norwegian state through the granting of female suffrage in 1913. The Norwegian Women's Public Health Association (Norske Kvinners Sanitetsforening) had its own pavilion. The Housewives' Beneficial Association (Hjemmenes Vel) built an information office for visitors to the exhibition and the School of Women's Industries (Den kvinnelige industriskole) paraded its products in the Industrial Hall.[1]

Still, women played a decidedly minor role in the centennial celebration. At a meeting of the Norwegian Council of Women that summer, women's rights pioneer and council leader Gina Krog summed up the centennial in a speech. She said she was proud that women took part in the celebrations, but she was far from satisfied with the space they received. Furthermore, the organizing committee had not invited women to the opening festivities in Kristiania. During the commemorative service in the Nidaros Cathedral, the only women present were the queen and her ladies-in-waiting. Official speakers did not mention women and historians and authors overlooked their history during the last century. Krog felt this was unfair. She thought the victories women had gained in their struggle for emancipation had changed history.[2]

Presenting Themselves with Pride

By taking matters into their own hands, women had still been able to present themselves in a positive way. In September 1914, Marie Høgh and Fredrikke Mørck, both well-known campaigners for women's rights, published the two-volume work *Norwegian Women: 1814–1914,* a collection of articles about women, both current and historical. One full article focused on the theme "Women in the Home," emphasizing the importance of housewives' work, not only for the family but also for Norway as a nation. A long series of occupations outside of the home were also presented, giving a vivid impression of the range of careers women had entered into during the previous few decades. A host of authors described their fields of work. Among them were gardeners, bookbinders, engineers, nurses, office workers, singers and musicians, midwives, doctors, and teachers. Thus, the publication introduced a variety of careers or occupations (forty-four) pursued by women. The authors showed pride in women's jobs and achievements. Many gave detailed pictures of pay and working conditions. Some were quite satisfied, like the printer Alma Andresen, who wrote: "We female printers have reason to be pleased with our working conditions. The work suits

Scene from the Centennial Exhibition at Frogner Park in Oslo, 1914, in celebration of the 1814 constitution

us well, the pay is increasing, and working hours are getting shorter." Others were more critical and well aware that they were paid too little when compared to men with the same qualifications. At the same time, they were optimistic about future improvements. A telegraph pioneer since 1866, Augusta Schjødt wrote: "When the day finally comes that women in the Telegraph Service are allowed to compete with men for the different positions and only qualifications count when employees are hired, then—and only then—will justice be done to women. May this day not be too far in the future!"[3]

One piece of writing stands out—an article about maidservants. In contrast to the other contributions, the editors point out that this one had been "sent in." That must have signaled to the readers that the article was not asked for and that the editors did not wish to take responsibility for it. Reading it one understands why. The author, Petra Ystenæs, did not join the chorus of praise for Norwegian democracy. She found that the nation's much-celebrated human rights did not include the human rights of maidservants. Those who worked on farms were sometimes not valued higher than the animals, she said. In the cities, they could meet with a contempt that ignited fury and indignation, while organizers faced ridicule and resistance. Ystenæs knew what she writing about. She was the leader of the Maid Servants' Association (Den kvindelige tjenerstands forening) in Kristiania.[4]

The articles in *Norwegian Women* tell us about new opportunities that gave women more freedom to choose their lives. But they also tell us about class differences and a group of women who felt they did not stand to gain through the reforms in political and civil rights. In general, though, it is easy to agree that, in spite of class differences and unfair conditions for large groups, women did have a great deal to celebrate in 1914. Their legal status had improved immensely during the previous two generations. Their opportunities in schools, higher education, and the labor market had also been extended until women were almost on equal footing with men, at least formally. Most spectacularly, women in Norway had achieved universal suffrage only one year before; Norway was the second nation in Europe to provide universal suffrage (after Finland).

Norwegian Citizenship and Gender

The constitution of 1814 established the *Storting* (national assembly). The right to vote for representatives to the Storting was given to citizens over twenty-five years old with stipulated property or position. The premise behind the gender-neutral formulation "citizen" was that the citizen was always a man. This was confirmed in an 1818 ruling by the Storting. Almost one hundred years later, in 1913, a change in Article 50 of the constitution gave women the right to vote and at the same time explicitly defined their citizenship, thereby including them in the nation-state: "Qualified to vote are Norwegian citizens, men and women, who are 25 years of age, who have been living in the country for five years and are now living there."[5]

Just a few days after this great victory in the Storting, a Norwegian delegation arrived at the congress of the International Women's Suffrage Alliance in Budapest. Here Krog greeted the delegates and gave them the news from Norway. The struggle for suffrage had started long ago, she said, "And how far away was the goal, and how steep the road, and what difficulties towered over us. And now! Faith has moved mountains." The feminist magazine *Nylænde* reported, "Her speech was received with wild jubilation." Both for women themselves and for the Norwegian Storting and government, women's suffrage was now a matter of national prestige, something that could add to the image of the recently independent state. That was not the way it had started out. Looking back on the history of women's suffrage shows a remarkable change of heart both in the population and in the Storting.[6]

The organized struggle for suffrage had been ongoing since 1885, when the Women's Suffrage Association (Kvindestemmeretsforeningen) was founded in Kristiania by a small group of middle-class women. A group from *Venstre* (the

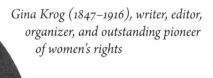

Gina Krog (1847–1916), writer, editor, organizer, and outstanding pioneer of women's rights

liberal party), working in close cooperation with the suffragists, introduced a suffrage proposal in 1886. Four years later, this was debated in the Storting. This group from Venstre viewed suffrage as a human right that had to be given to women if they were to gain equality with men and become true citizens of Norway. They argued that including women as voters would be useful to society at large as well as to women, who would be better able to develop their abilities and fulfill their responsibilities. The main advocate of the proposal and representative from Venstre, Viggo Ullmann, summed up the debate: "any Person claiming some Culture will fully admit that Woman has exactly the same Right to be a Human Being and to obtain Enlightenment (*Oplysning*) as we Men have. This is nothing but a Step on the Way, and therefore it will come in Time."[7]

The proposal was turned down by two-thirds of the members of the Storting. They believed that men and women were created differently, either by God or by nature, and that this was reflected in the different tasks that the sexes were given in human society. They did not approve of women taking part in public life, which was a masculine domain. Instead, women were to fulfill their duties within the private sphere of the home. The harshest contributions to the debate came from Bishop Heuch, a leading conservative member of the Storting. With references to the Holy Scripture, he claimed that letting women vote would be against the "Order of Creation" and therefore dissolve families, destroy morality, and destabilize society. What's more, it would turn women into neuters: "She cannot do the Work of a Man, and she will not do the Work of a Woman. Then what will she become? She will become a deformed Monster, she will become a Neuter, as anyone who has Eyes to see with will see."[8]

The Norwegian state church was (and is) Lutheran and was at this time overwhelmingly pietistic and conservative. Within the church, it was common to think of women's subordination as part of God's plan. However, there were also leading Christians in the Storting who argued in favor of the amendment. The divide in this debate followed party lines rather than religious belief. The main reaction to Heuch's speech seemed to be that he went too far and only managed to create more support for women's rights. Krog printed the whole debate in *Nylænde*, as it had been recorded by stenographers in the Storting, so that people could easily read and judge for themselves.[9]

New proposals for national or local voting rights (national for the Storting, local for the county councils) were considered in the Storting every year, but for a long time nothing happened to bring the cause forward. Strain and political disagreement split the women's movement. A new organization was started, the National Women's Suffrage Association (Landskvindestemmeretsforeningen), and, under the leadership of Fredrikke Marie Qvam, soon grew large and efficient. The new organization continued the struggle for suffrage on an equal footing with men, while the older Women's Suffrage Association now promoted carefully limited rights that would give at least some women the right to vote.

Meanwhile, men's voting rights were gradually extended and in 1898 all men twenty-five and older achieved the right to vote in national elections. The political situation was suddenly changed. Now it was in the interest of *Høyre* (the conservative party) to give upper- and middle-class women the right to vote, in order to balance or outweigh the radical votes of working-class men. In 1901, a proposal for limited suffrage for women in county elections was debated in the Storting. The law was passed in June that year. All women who had an income of their own or who had husbands who fulfilled the conditions for voting were allowed to vote. This meant that about two hundred thousand women, or 42 percent of women over twenty-five years of age, were given local suffrage. In this way, upper- and middle-class women received the right to vote while working-class women did not.[10]

Many privileged women lost interest in working for suffrage when they could vote themselves. However, both suffrage organizations kept up the effort. The final goal was universal suffrage in national elections. For working-class women, now organized in the Norwegian Labor Party's Women's Union (Arbeiderpartiets Kvinneforbund), the 1901 law was proof of the unfair rulings of classed society. To these women, universal suffrage became all the more important.[11]

In order to reach this goal, the constitution would have to be amended—an uphill battle. What finally turned the situation in favor of women was their initiative in the struggle to end the union with Sweden. A conflict with Sweden over the degree of Norwegian independence had been building since the middle of the 1880s. Then in June 1905, Norway unilaterally declared the union to be dissolved. The Swedish government demanded that Norway hold a plebiscite on independence. This was done in August 1905, but women were not included among "the people" who were asked to vote. Women then organized a nationwide petition in support of independence. In a very short time almost three hundred thousand signatures were collected, together with the names of six hundred women's organizations. The relationship between the two countries that summer and early autumn was tense, but the union was peacefully dissolved after negotiations. The women's petition was well received by the Norwegian political elite, and suffragists exploited the campaign to serve their goal—the suffrage amendment. The petition campaign, they claimed, proved that women were patriotic and worthy citizens of Norway. Furthermore, it proved that voting was not only of interest to a small elite. On the contrary, the large majority of women were eager and ready to take part in the affairs of the nation. Even without the right to vote, women had shown they could act politically in a way that served the nation and the state.[12]

In June 1907, women's suffrage in national elections was again debated in the Storting. Opinion had now swung in favor of women. Only one member of the Storting resorted to the kind of harsh arguments promoted in 1890. Liberal representative Johan Castberg commented on this: "In my eyes it is a gratifying testimony of how far we have gotten in culture and common sense in this field that the only thorough defense for continuing the exclusion of women that has been offered here has drowned in laughter." Approximately three hundred thousand upper- and middle-class women were now given the right to vote and the right to be elected. The majority in the Storting thought that it would be best to extend the right to vote gradually; it was understood that this was just a first step and full voting rights would follow in time. This was the breakthrough for the principle of the vote for women. When universal suffrage finally was adopted in 1913, the decision in the Storting was unanimous.[13]

Gendered Legal Status

For women celebrating the centennial in 1914, the right to vote and to be elected was a sign that they were finally taken seriously as members of the nation-state. But other rights had been achieved during the previous fifty years that were just as important and without which gaining suffrage would have been impossible. Together, these newly gained rights gave women a stronger legal status and more economic independence. Some of these legal changes were controversial and difficult to pass, but they were secured in part by the strong standing of women in Norwegian agrarian society, where women's work was considered as important as men's. Farmers and their representatives acknowledged this, which also made other reforms easier to carry through, among them the ones that opened up the educational system to girls and young women.

The 1814 constitution did not mention gender except to secure male succession to the throne. No new statutes of law were passed at that time, so laws dating back to the Danish King Christian V in 1687 persisted far into the nineteenth and even twentieth century. Sons inherited twice as much as daughters. Whereas young men reached the age of legal consent when they turned twenty-five, and could freely dispose of their income and property, women remained dependent—first on their fathers, then on their husbands if they got married. Like children, criminals, and the insane, women never reached the age of legal consent. Only widows could achieve legal authority, and then with the proviso that they had to take on a male legal advisor.[14]

Step by step, the laws were changed. In 1854, women obtained equal rights to inheritance. Although the senior civil servants constituting the governing elite in Norway at the time opposed the reform, farmers supported the new law. Their arguments were based on the economic value of women's work. Then, in 1863, a new law stipulated that unmarried women reached the age of legal consent at twenty-five. They now had a legal status equal to their brothers. Not very controversial, the decision made it easier for unmarried women to make a living on their own, so that they did not turn into burdens to their families. At the same time, the new law did not interfere with the institution of marriage and what lawmakers saw as the husband's natural right of decision making within marriage. The next step—letting married women reach the age of legal consent—met with a good deal of resistance.[15]

Again the farmers took the initiative for change. In their view, women were often more responsible about family finances than men. To give women a chance to gain more control over family economy, Søren Jaabæk, member of the Storting, introduced a bill in 1871 to make it illegal for a husband to sign away more than half of his property without his wife's consent. The intent was to stop careless men from mortgaging and losing the property on which their families depended. It would also extend the rights of women within marriage; this, Jaabæk believed, would be right on principle: "Many a Woman has full Legal Authority before Marriage and after it has been dissolved. During the Marriage she is totally without Rights in many Things; this is believed not to be right." Jaabæk was the leader of the influential Farmers' Friends' Associations (Bondevennforeninger). Of the 118 associations, 110 discussed and voted in support of the bill, reflecting the farmers' belief in women's ability to make decisions that would benefit their families. The bill was not passed, however. The Justice Committee of the Storting argued, "The Opportunity to dispose of and mortgage one's Property without Hindrance is among the fundamental Conditions of a healthy Order of Society, and a Proposal such as this would damage this Right." Dressed in gender-neutral language, this meant that men would keep the power to make financial decisions concerning a marriage and a family. In the debates of the following years, this argument would remain the position of conservatives.[16]

In 1888, a new law passed in the Storting regulating the legal status of property

within marriage. Leading up to it was a heated debate both about the institution of marriage and about women's position in marriage and in general. Radical
members of Venstre and leading intellectuals and writers like Henrik Ibsen and
Bjørnstjerne Bjørnson, together with the newly organized women's rights movement, argued for separate property rights as the legal basis for marriage. This, they
said, would emancipate the woman and lift her status as a human and as a citizen.
Conservatives, on the other hand, thought only joint property was in keeping with
the unity of the family and the Christian idea of marriage. Farmers were for practical marriage reforms, but they also found joint property to be the natural order
of things. The unity of the family as the main building block of society was more
important than individual rights for women. The law that was passed kept joint
property as the legal foundation of marriage, and, with some limitations, the husband kept the right to administer the property alone. At the same time, the law
opened the possibility of establishing separate property rights within a marriage
settlement. It also gave the woman certain economic rights, the most important
being the right to keep the money she herself had earned. In a paragraph in the
same law, married women finally achieved legal authority. Married women had
now reached the age of legal consent, but the contents of their rights were still
restricted, since husbands had the right to manage their joint property.[17]

The next major change in the status of marriage took place in 1927, when
another new law was passed in the Storting. This one resulted from legal cooperation between the Nordic countries and the women's movement as an active
interest group. Typical for its time, the 1927 law aimed at securing the rights of
housewives. Both husband and wife were allowed to dispose of any financial
resources brought into the marriage, and in case of divorce, the property was
equally shared. Spouses were responsible for providing for one another, but the
law specified that a housewife filled her part of this obligation by her work in
the home. At the time, the law was seen as recognition of the contribution of
the housewife and as a long step in the direction of equality. Clearly, the law
supported traditional gender roles, since the assumption was that the husband
was the breadwinner who provided for his wife. The intention of the law was to
place the wife on an equal footing with her husband economically. In practice,
she usually disposed of no more of the family income than the husband gave her,
and the law provided only weak protection for her economic independence.[18]

The Right to an Education and Public Offices

Changes that could threaten the family structure and the established order of
society met with powerful opposition from the ruling elite of senior civil servants (embedsmenn). This was the case for both the radical proposal of separate
ownership within marriage before the law of 1888 and for women's demand for

the right to vote and to be elected to political bodies. In many other cases, however, the ruling elite took the initiative for reforms. Among these were practical measures that made it possible for unmarried women and widows to provide for themselves. There was no organized agitation behind such reforms and almost no opposition to them. They were mostly meant for women from the upper and middle classes and were often initiated and helped along by fathers giving support to their daughters. For instance, this was the case when young girls were allowed to take entrance exams, first at the junior high school and then at the high school level.[19]

Girls and boys without the resources to go to private schools went together to elementary school (*folkeskole*) for seven years. But only boys could go to a middle school (*middelskole*) or to a high school (*gymnas*). Private schools for girls—with a simpler curriculum—became an alternative for those who could afford it. In 1876, girls were officially allowed to take the final exams for middle school, which gradually opened classrooms to girls. This became a popular education for middle-class girls in cities and towns and was an important reform because it provided a large number of young women with an opportunity to seek employment in businesses and offices.

High schools were still closed to girls. The final exam in these schools, the *examen artium,* was also the entrance exam for university studies. Having no access to the examen artium automatically stopped women from studying at the universities. In 1880, an audacious young girl from Eidsvoll, Cecilie Thoresen (later Cecilie Thoresen Krog), decided to take the examen artium and go to the university. Mobilizing first the help of her father and then of women's rights advocate and liberal member of the Storting Hagbard Berner, she worked for a law that would give her the right to carry out her plans. The law was passed in 1882, and Thoresen took the examen artium. The women's movement celebrated. Though Thoresen gave up her study of the sciences after she married, she is still remembered as a pioneer for women's rights.

Clearly, the examen artium was key to university studies, and therefore also to the subsequent exams for becoming a civil servant. A woman civil servant was still quite unthinkable to most people and especially to most civil servants themselves. But once the right to the entrance exam was won, the university was also opened to women. In 1884, women were allowed to study and take the final examination in all faculties of the university. For most young women, studying at the university to become a doctor, lawyer, or college professor would be an unrealistic dream; most planned instead to become a teacher, a secure and accepted job for a woman. For a long time, women had to pay for their own education in private girls' schools, teachers' schools, and governesses' schools. Men could get their schooling for free—for instance at public colleges for teachers. In 1890, these were opened to women, an important step in the direction of equality.

Among the women who now saw the chance to get an education was Helga Eng, a dedicated bookworm who would later become a gifted academic. Born in 1875, the fourth of eight children in a teacher's family in the countryside in Rakkestad, east of Oslo, Eng read an older brother's books and dreamed of studying. Her brother was allowed to attend a private middle school in a nearby town, but the family could not afford to send Eng. But when public teachers' colleges opened to women in 1890, studying became a real option. In 1893, with the economic support of her older brothers, eighteen-year-old Eng enrolled at the public teachers' college in Bærum, outside of Oslo. Many women took this opportunity. When Eng began college, women constituted the majority in her class. Eng took her teacher's exam in 1895. While teaching full time, she continued studying on her own, taking first the middle school exam and then the examen artium as a private candidate, meaning she received no public support. In 1903, she started studying at the University of Oslo, where she specialized in child psychology. Ten years later, she became a doctor of philosophy with a dissertation on that subject. She then faced the question of what she could do with her degree.[20]

In 1904, women joined men in the right to hold positions in civil service. Elise Sem, who had already taken a law degree, opened her own legal practice the very same day permission was granted; by 1912, she qualified as a barrister and was admitted to the bar. That same year, a new law gave women the right of access to most public offices. This meant they could be district medical officers or judges or university professors—if they managed to break through the barriers of prejudice against women. Only three women actually were appointed professors before World War II: Kristine Bonnevie in 1912, Ellen Gleditsch in 1929, and Helga Eng, then sixty-three years old, in 1938. Although the 1912 law opening public offices had little practical impact on the lives of most women, it symbolized the new opportunities opening up for them. It also symbolized the full citizenship women gained with the general right to vote one year later.[21]

Gender in Agrarian Society

During the fifty years between 1864 and 1914, industry, migration, and urbanization turned Norway into a modern country, changing many peoples' lives in a spectacular way. Economic expedience and liberal thinking also gave women basic legal rights and turned them into citizens. But how much had their everyday responsibilities and work changed during the same period? The following sections examine gender in midcentury agrarian society and changes created by the process of modernizing.

In preindustrial Norway, the household was the main production unit. A household consisted of a husband and wife and their children, often together with parents and other relatives. With the exception of cotters or renters *(hus-menn)*, almost all households had at least one servant to assist with the household economy. Servants were young and unmarried people who lodged with a family for the period of their service. To produce enough to make a living for the household, a family had to utilize all possible natural resources, not just those used when farming; therefore, they might be involved in fishing, manufacturing, shipping, or mining, according to the season of the year or job opportunities available. This kind of mixed economy has been called "multiple occupations" *(mangesysleri)*. To make a living this way, work had to be divided between men and women; everyone knew which tasks were theirs. Children were brought up to do either the man's or the woman's work. On larger farms, there was a clearer division of work than on smaller ones; here, men did more of the heavy farm work that on small farms women did themselves.[22]

Northern Norway provides an example of the gendered division of labor in Norwegian coastal regions. The men went to sea to fish for long periods of time year-round. Lofoten fishing, spring fishing in Finnmark, and other seasonal fishing brought cash income to the household—part of the household economy that also brought prestige. The wife of the house cared for the family, did the indoor housework, and farmed the land that provided daily sustenance. Women also took care of the livestock, planted potatoes, shared in seasonal work—like haymaking and spring work—and even sowed the crops, work considered prestigious men's labor in other parts of the country.[23]

Women farmed all along the Norwegian coast. In other parts of the country, too, farming families depended on an able and hard-working wife. The man usually took part in seasonal farm work but also engaged in work outside the farm. When necessary, a woman could step in and do a man's work, but a man had to be careful not to do a woman's work, considered degrading and embarrassing. Worst of all were milking or barnyard activities. In some parts of the country, however, there are examples of men taking over women's work if it meant their wives could earn cash income. There are also plenty of examples of women taking part in cash-earning activities like fishing. In household economies such as these, there was no difference between provider and the provided for; however, the man was the formal head of the family. He was the one who usually signed contracts and was registered as owner when buying and selling. Ideology and tradition placed women in a subordinate position.[24]

The role of women in the household economy was not understood by historians for a long time because men were more visible in the sources. In upper-class homes and on large farms, women administered the housework, but they also shared in the practical work whenever needed. In mercantile households, the wife had extensive responsibilities, including buying the necessary stocks and paying the servants, and there seemed to be no ideological resistance to her

Potato planting at Helgøya in Ringsaker, 1920

taking part in the business itself. Since married women did not achieve the age of legal consent until 1888, they did not have the right to sign contracts on their own. Historian Hilde Sandvik has pointed out that, given the laws regulating family economies, one might believe that women could not be economically active. Looking closer into local, primary sources, however, she has found that married women were often buying, selling, and taking on debts. The law was simply not used against them. It would not have been practical to stop women from being able to provide for themselves and their families.[25]

In the work-intensive economy of traditional society, servants were an essential part of the system. Most young people were servants for a portion of their lives, even the ones from well-situated farming families. The usual age to go into service was about fifteen for girls and about seventeen for boys. The young people did some housework but mainly worked with whatever was needed for the household production, whether fishing, farming, crafts, or trade. Living in the homes of their employers, they learned the skills necessary to make a living and build their own households when they were old enough to marry and start a family. In the last couple of decades of the nineteenth century, the traditional ways of living were changing fast. Young people were flocking to towns and cities, seeking other types of work, or they followed the great waves of emigrants to countries overseas.[26]

Out to Work

Men could always choose within a much larger range of occupations than women. This was the case for the middle class as well as for the working class, but slowly new opportunities opened up. In 1857, the Telegraph Administration started a special course for women aimed at securing well-qualified employees at a reduced wage. From the beginning of the 1860s, women were being hired as teachers in primary schools. This practice was then legalized and by 1869 they had achieved the right to work in both rural and city schools. From the middle of the nineteenth century, social and economic changes emerged, both in the rural districts and in cities and towns, and farming became more efficient and production grew. In addition, fishing, shipping, and logging flourished, furnishing the farming population with work and income. The first wave of industrialization set in, mostly within textile, metal manufacturing, and mechanical workshops. A money-based, more differentiated economy emerged and increased in strength throughout the following decades. The development went on in spurts with occasional economic turndowns. By the time of the centennial celebration in 1914, Norway had turned into a country with substantial industrial production, a modern market economy, and a new, more urban culture. However, the majority of the population still lived in the countryside, where traditional farming with traditional gender-shared work persisted.

In the years between 1815 and 1875 the population grew significantly—from just under one million to almost two million. Until the middle of the nineteenth century, this increased population sought work in the agricultural economy. As the modernizing process went on, there were more jobs and greater opportunities for making a living; many people left rural communities for the town, for the city, or for America. Mass emigration to the United States and Canada occurred in the 1830s and 1840s and accelerated with the end of the Civil War. During the first decades, emigrants left as families, but after the 1880s individual emigration dominated. Young men and women, mostly young men, left for America on their own. In the course of traveling to the United States, women often moved to Bergen, Trondhjem (now Trondheim), or Kristiania, where they sought work in factories, schools, offices, and shops or as servants. The surplus of young women in Kristiania was so large that it became known as "the young girls' city."[27]

Middle- and upper-class women used the opportunities that were offered through education and the opening up of new occupations like telegraph, telephone, and office work as well as in teaching and nursing. Working-class women coming from the countryside went into service or utilized one of the other emerging alternatives, such as crafts, trade, and small-scale production. Women were also an important part of the workforce of the first textile factories in the 1840s, providing indispensable cheap labor. From the 1870s on, they entered into

Shopping in Røkkes Kolonial, a grocery store in Trondheim, 1927

most manufacturing branches. As a whole, though, the labor market was very clearly segmented between the sexes, with women in the textile and clothing industries and men in other manufacturing branches. In some sectors, however, men and women were more equally treated, for instance in teaching and print-ing. After the turn of the century, the service sector became more important than manufacturing for women, and in 1900 women made up 40 percent of all office employees. In 1920, women made up a fifth of the industrial workforce.[28]

Women from all classes had at least two things in common: they did not get the better-paid jobs within their fields of employment, and they were almost always paid less than men doing the same jobs. In manufacturing, men earned twice as much as women. In sectors with a more equal number of men and women, the difference tended to be somewhat smaller. A "lady telegrapher's" pay was regulated to 75 percent of a man's in 1860. Beginner's pay for a female teacher in Kristiania at the turn of the twentieth century was 64 percent of a man's. The rationale was that women, after all, could both cook and sew and care for their own needs, unlike men, and above all they were not supporting a family.[29]

With few exceptions, the new, middle-class jobs were taken by young, unmarried women and many middle-class women never married. This was partly an effect of the surplus of women, making it difficult to find a husband, but it was probably also caused by a more critical view of marriage. Young, educated women wanted more independence and they expected a marriage built on equality and a sharing of burdens. They were trying out new roles and entering new and daring fields of activity—skiing, biking, even traveling alone. These women saw themselves—and were seen—as an alternative type of woman: the "new women" of the new century. They banded together in a wide range of women's organizations, which had roots in women's trade unions, feminist associations, discussion or reading clubs, Christian associations, and charities that had emerged in the middle of the 1880s. Here they found personal challenges and an opportunity to share experiences.[30]

Supporting the new women was a group of liberal, educated, middle-class men—sometimes called "new men." However, the new women were badgered by political attacks and personal harassment from men who were afraid that the old gender order was dissolving and that family life would disappear with it. From about 1900, conflicts over gender relationships persisted, particularly within the upper and middle classes. The "new women" had challenged bourgeois, masculine authority by going out to work, taking part in public life, and demanding rights that had previously been exclusive to men.[31]

Housewives and Servants

Many men worried that women were leaving their homes, neglecting their female duties, and competing in the job market. Actually, they had no great reason to worry. The relative number of women in paid employment did not grow. In relation to all women over fifteen, it was between 31 and 32 percent from 1875 to 1900. In 1910 it grew to 33 percent. But in 1920 it sank to 31.5 percent, and after that the number lowered steadily until about 1970. Most women still worked in private homes, as farmers' wives, housewives, aunts, daughters, or servants. Married women did not go out to work unless the husband for some reason could not provide for the family. They stayed in the home, taking care of the children, the house, and the husband. Working-class women who had to or wanted to earn some money took jobs that were secondary to the work in their own homes—for example, sewing, taking lodgers, or washing for others.[32]

In the countryside, household production and the traditional way of sharing the work along gender lines remained commonplace far into the twentieth century. Housework here was still old-fashioned and heavy. Electricity, running water, and different kinds of machinery became widespread only after World War II. However, new conditions were making headway, mixing with the old. Looking at the countryside in the first half of the 1900s, scholars Anna Avdem and Kari Melby find "a broadly quilted pattern, where old and new are set one against the other in a many-colored pattern, both geographically and socially."[33]

By the turn of the century in the cities, the family had become a consumer unit. The economic importance of household production had more or less disappeared, including the preparing and storing of food supplies. Housewives bought what they needed in shops and markets. At the same time, the fertility rate was falling and there were fewer children to take care of in each family. That did not mean, however, that there was not plenty of work to do in the homes. New ideals for good housekeeping and good childcare set standards that women wanted to meet even though it meant a lot of work. The housewife was to be a professional, the expert in her own home, well informed about matters like cleanliness, hygiene, nutrition, and the bringing up of children. The ideal of the good housewife established itself in the middle class during the last two decades of the nineteenth century, but it was a role model that spread to all classes of society and to all parts of the country.

Although the housewife was considered the expert on domestic affairs, the actual work was done by the maid—at least, this was the ideal in middle-class families. Servants in the cities no longer labored for the economic base of the household; instead, they spent their time doing housework. Earlier, servants and housewives had done much the same work: servants were part of the household and often came from families similar to the ones they served. Now there was a clear and sharply defined difference between mistress and servants. Because boys had more jobs to choose among than girls, it was easier for them to find work that would pay better and allow more freedom. In the first half of the nineteenth century, there were about half as many boys as girls in service, and in the second half of the century, the role of servant became more and more women's work. By 1900, there were already four maidservants for each manservant.[34]

Girls coming from the countryside found it strange that the wife of the house did not take part in the practical work, as the wives in the countryside still did. They also reacted to the way they were treated—they were placed in tiny rooms beside or even in the kitchen, they were expected not to be seen, and they worked long hours with very little private life. *Guide for Maid Servants and Young Housewives,* published in 1912, instructs maidservants to stay in their place: "Do not meddle in the conversations of the family; do not try to entertain guests with talk . . . Do not slam the doors, talk softly, do not sing. In pure rashness girls sometimes start humming and singing, but that is both thoughtless and tactless." Being a maid meant working hard for very little money from six in the morning to nine or ten in the evening, seven days a week. Some got off work every second Sunday before or after noon, and later on Wednesday evenings, too. But, legally, servants had few rights. The laws that regulated their work and their relationship to their employers in many cases dated back to 1754. Up to 1891, employers even had the legal right to punish their servants bodily. While this law was originally gender neutral, by the time it was revoked, it concerned almost only women.[35]

Naturally, many servants wanted to leave this work, and as opportunities opened, they acted. While almost half of all nineteen-year-old girls were in service in 1865, only one-third were in service in 1900. However, this remained the most important job for women up to World War II. Girls kept coming from the countryside to be servants. They were paid much worse than women working in factories, but since they were used to getting their pay in kind, any pay in cash was tempting. Pioneer of women's history Mimi Sverdrup Lunden wrote about servants in times she herself had lived through: "The cash pay could help them to reach their real, great goal. They could save up the money for the fairy-tale country of America."[36]

Though living standards rose and most people's lives became easier during the years from 1865 to 1914, the difference in gender roles did not change much to the advantage of women. Instead of the shared farm work done by both men and women of earlier times, in which many women contributed to the livelihood of the households, married women, at least in the cities, had become housewives in their own homes and were economically dependent on their husbands. If they went out to work, they meant their income to be supplemental, not an equal contribution. The ideal was to stay home and take care of husband and children. It is important to emphasize that working women (mostly unmarried) were systematically paid less than men and kept out of leading positions within their field of work. It is also worth noting that the great majority were kept in totally subordinate positions as servants, a type of work most men were able to avoid.

Post-Centennial Changes: The Long Road from Suffrage to Representation

When Fredrikke Mørck and Marie Høgh published *Norwegian Women,* pride in women's achievement was great and so was optimism about the future. Women had the right not just to vote but to be elected to the county councils and the Storting. However, the struggle to make use of the right to be represented in politics turned out to be at least as tough a process as the fight for voting rights had been. "The right to vote is the duty to vote," said Fredrikke Marie Qvam, who traveled throughout the country canvassing for women voting. But it took a long time before women participated in elections to the same degree as men. Particularly in the countryside, mobilizing women was difficult. In 1930, the percentage of women voting in the cities had reached the level of men, but in the rural districts there were differences at least until 1961. Being properly represented in elected bodies was an even longer process. It has been said that when the men in the Storting consented to give women the right to vote, no one really imagined they would use it to put their sisters into the national assembly. In 1911 and 1912, Anna Rogstad took a seat in the Storting as a substitute, but it was not until 1921 that the first woman, Karen Platou from Høyre, was elected directly to the Storting.[37]

Election to county and city councils was easier, but gaining representation there also took a long time. Before World War II, women never made up more than 2 percent of the county councils in rural districts. In the cities as a whole, representation actually sank from 8 percent during the elections in 1910 and 1916 to a dismal 5 and 6 percent during the 1920s and 1930s. Not until 1937 did it rise again—to 9 percent. There were some exceptions. In a few cities, like Oslo, Bergen, Trondheim, and Drammen, women were elected in numbers that made it possible for them to make genuine political contributions. In the small town of Fredrikstad, for example, where women for a time made up 20 percent of the representatives, they fought visibly and often unconventionally for social causes like school meals and the regulating of rents, sometimes crossing party lines to achieve their goals.[38]

Faced with a bleak picture, the few activists for women's representation were driven almost to desperation. The feminist magazine *Nylænde* kept publishing articles on international developments in every edition, and organized feminists continued to take part in international and Nordic feminist congresses. It was hard to accept the fact that countries achieving female suffrage long after Norway were more successful in electing women to public office. Campaigns for nominating and electing women were held at every election, local or national. Nothing seemed to help.

Political scientist Anne Hilde Nagel has compared the largely male labor movement with the women's movement and shown how women had a much harder time achieving political representation. For instance, while women organized politically years before workers, all men got the right to vote fifteen years before all women. The first representative of the Norwegian Labor Party (Det Norske Arbeiderparti, now Arbeiderpartiet) was elected to the Storting in 1903—the first woman in 1921. In 1928, the Labor Party formed its first cabinet. Women were not represented in any cabinet until 1945, when the Communist Party's Kirsten Hansteen was appointed. Nagel commented on her findings: "The wealthy obtained rights before the poor. But *all* women had to wait for *all* men. In this sense, women were placed lower in the social hierarchy than all men. Gender was the hardest of all criteria when it came to political power."[39]

Post-Centennial Changes: Through War and Recessions

All levels of education and almost all positions in working life had been opened up to women by the 1914 centennial. Many now thought the "doors were open"—it was just a matter of walking through them. This positive attitude was helped along by the fact that the period between 1905 and 1914 was a time when the

Norwegian economy was booming and expectations for the future were generally high. It would soon be clear that it was not to be so easy. Getting the attractive jobs and the pay one deserved might be possible when the economy was good and labor was needed. But the country soon ran into rough waters, both politically and economically.

On August 4, 1914, World War I broke out and belief in progress was replaced by uncertainty and fear. Norway was politically neutral throughout the war and, on a whole, the economy prospered. The export industries and shipping, especially, earned great profits. For most people, though, the war meant rationing, inflation, and a serious and long-lasting shortage of food and everyday commodities. Middle-class housewives tried to make ends meet and find ways to make simple or insufficient supplies into nourishing meals for their families. Their organizations held courses on cooking with untraditional but available raw materials and spread information on what women could do to help the country through the hard times. Working-class housewives protested against inflation and demanded state control of the production and sale of food. In the summer of 1917, there were large demonstrations all over the country.[40]

Due to the war boom, the labor market was extremely tight and women in recently opened occupations found themselves in a new and much stronger position in relation to their employers. It was easy to get a job and easier to get a better position. A direct effect of this situation was that the number of domestic servants declined. "Maid servants in cities and the country-side immediately deserted!" wrote Mimi Sverdrup Lunden. Since servants were in demand, they could ask for better conditions, and many of them actually secured more spare time, better pay, and somewhat better rooms in which to live. Women's trade unions in the telegraph, telephone, and postal administrations put forward aggressive demands for higher wages and to their surprise won on all points. These were "years, when money was available," as a government employee put it. Other groups, like teachers and midwives, also had breakthroughs for their demands. In 1920, a great victory was seemingly won when the state eliminated a special wage scale for women and officially adopted equal pay.[41]

Shortly afterward a serious recession set in, resulting in unemployment and dire economic need. Equal pay turned out to be an illusion: regulations for a special women's wage scale disappeared, but wage differences continued. During the war, a system of family supplements for male breadwinners had been introduced, in reality a way to pay men more than women. This was extended in 1927. In addition, women got less work or other types of work than men. They were not allowed to gain professional qualifications and subsequently did not move up the job ladder. The postwar economic slump was only the start of a series of economic crises. Recessions followed in the middle of the 1920s and the beginning of the 1930s.[42]

Women at work in Bergens Bliktrykkeri A/S (a sheet metal factory), 1930

Among the victims of the recessions was women's free right to work. In 1925, the Norwegian Federation of Trade Unions (Arbeidernes Faglige Lands-organisasjon, now LO), at that time an organization with about one hundred thousand members, passed a resolution against "both man and wife" working. While given a gender-neutral formulation, this was directed against married women. The goal was to protect family households by directing work to male breadwinners. The Labor Party soon adopted the same policy and regulations regarding the employment of married women. These became a part of the party's economic program. As an effective remedy against unemployment, the policy was doomed to be unsuccessful. Many married women had extra jobs or part-time jobs supplementing their husbands' income, but only a few were employed in the type of work that a man could or would want to do. In 1930, only 6.5 percent of women working in jobs that men might want were married. The social economist, working at the statistical office of the Norwegian Federation of Trade Unions, and leading Labor Party member Johanne Reutz calculated at the time that getting rid of all married women who could be fired would free only two to three thousand positions for men—not much compared to the 101,568 registered unemployed men at that time.[43]

The campaign against married women was quite intensive and soon acquired an ideological edge condemning women who did anything other than taking care of their homes. Prejudice against working women flowed freely in the press. One example is the following quotation from a letter to the editor in *Dagbladet* in July 1928: "I think all women hope to be married and have a house, a home and a husband. We see that even as a child a woman has instincts that point her in this direction. They play with their dolls and take care of their kitchens. They like to play with water and to decorate their dolls' houses. Few have ever seen them wanting to play at working in an office or driving a garbage truck." From about 1932, the policy against married women doing paid work met with growing opposition both from established women's organizations like the Norwegian Association for Women's Rights (Norsk Kvinnesaksforening) and from newly founded working-women's organizations like the Norwegian branch of Open Door International. Women in the Communist Party also protested. They were against giving married women the blame for a crisis created by capitalism. The campaign was withdrawn in 1936, when a feminist faction inside the Labor Party, led by Johanne Reutz, mobilized a majority for a resolution against it at the Labor Party's Women's Conference.[44]

It is difficult to evaluate the exact effects the campaign against the so-called "double work" had on women's right to work. Direct unemployment hit men harder than women. But many women were pushed out of work and into unpaid housework. The number of domestic servants, which had gone down during World War I, rose again. Economists Ola H. Grytten and Camilla Brautaset find that, when adding regular to hidden unemployment, total unemployment was higher for women. Particularly married women, who were forced out of employment, were "the losers in the Norwegian interwar market."[45]

Parallel to the trials and tribulations of the interwar years, the housewife ideology strengthened its hold. The good housewife, who took care of her family and was provided for by her husband, had long been an ideal for many women. Now it seemed to turn into a moral obligation to all women. It was based on the thought, believed to be scientifically proven, that women had natural, biologically based abilities for caretaking, and a healthy woman would use her inborn abilities for care both in the home and in society in general. A significant number of women's organizations, with the large and influential Norwegian Housewife Union (Norges Husmorforbund) at the forefront, focused on improving the quality of Norwegian homes and celebrating the good housewife. Working-class women, organized through the Labor Party's Women's Secretariat, also engaged in the housewife cause, and the women of the Norwegian Communist Party organized in housewives' associations (Husmorlag). Women's organizations fighting for equal rights, which had been prominent up to 1914, either disappeared or barely survived. For the most part, only women's trade unions kept up that kind of effort.[46]

During the last half of the 1930s, the limitations on women's options, both socially and economically, sparked a new, feminist drive. A young generation of women demanded equality, independence, and the right to work. Most prominent among the rebels was Margarete Bonnevie. In her book *Marriage and Work (Ekteskap og arbeide)* she enunciated a thought that some young, urban women saw as new and exciting: that they not only could, but ought to have a good marriage and an interesting job at the same time. Bonnevie and her fellow partisans constituted an articulate opposition to the ideology of the housewife, but they remained a small group. The large majority of both men and women subscribed to what Swedish historian Yvonne Hirdman has coined "the housewife contract," the accepted norm for gender behavior and the basis for the gender system in the Nordic countries during these years. The "housewife contract" dominated until the middle of the 1960s, when women started leaving their homes for education and jobs. It was a cornerstone in the policy of the Labor Party, which held political power in Norway from 1935 to the German occupation in 1940 and then again through the entire postwar period up to 1965.[47]

By the end of the 1930s, women had almost the same rights as men and in theory the opportunity to lead independent lives as individuals. But in reality their opportunities to create their own lives according to their own plans were severely limited. Barriers existed both in the social and political guidelines of the time, in women's own acceptance of the housewife ideal and in purely practical circumstances like the workload demanded by good housekeeping and an almost total lack of kindergartens. "The individual rights of women were sacrificed to so-called 'common interests,'" Kari Melby writes in an article exploring what she calls "The Epoch of the Housewife." Although this was an age of modernization, with the flags of liberalism often waved high, both traditional and more recent communal values, like the ones represented in the labor movement, were strong societal forces. Comparing Norwegian and Swedish history, historian Francis Sejersted writes that Norway stuck to a stronger family ideology than Sweden, despite being among the first to give women the right to vote. This stance meant a sharply differentiated set of social roles based on gender. Values were built on collective qualities. The idea of individual rights conflicted with the concept of the family as the basic social unit.[48]

Summing Up: A Promise to Be Fulfilled

When Norwegian women celebrated the constitutional centennial in 1914, they also commemorated women's achievements during the nineteenth century. They had every right to be proud of the goals they had reached. From about 1850 on, the legal, economic, and educational status of women had been brought to an almost equal level to those of men. The high points of this history were many,

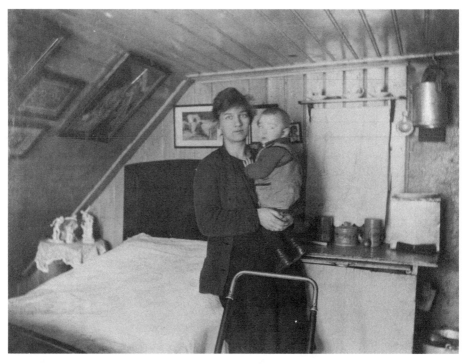

Mother and child in a flat at Rodeløkka in Oslo, about 1930

crowned by the right to enter public offices and become civil servants in 1912 and by getting universal suffrage and full-fledged citizenship one year later. Through the whole period, there had been opposition to the changes, particularly those that let women into politics and the public forum. But there had also been support. Farmers had shown their appreciation of the fundamental role women played in the farming community by giving them economic rights. Well-to-do and influential men had supported their daughters in their struggles for a fuller life. Although pleased with this progress, the women's movement was not satisfied with the place they were assigned both at the celebrations and in society in general. However, they thought this would sort itself out in due time, now that the basic premises had been laid.

They turned out to be wrong. The next twenty-five years would prove that making use of these formal rights would be a long and hard haul. The right to vote did not mean the same as representation in elected bodies. In fact, only eight women were elected to the Storting in all the years from the time women achieved suffrage until World War II. During this same period, 1,024 men were elected. No woman was appointed to the cabinet during these years. The strong economic growth characterizing the years between Norwegian independence in

1905 and the centennial in 1914 was soon replaced by years of war and economic crises. Though some groups of women prospered because of better-paid work during World War I and higher living standards during the interwar years, there was constant pressure to pay women less than men and to keep them out of leading positions and attractive work. After 1925 there was even a campaign to stop married women from going out to work at all.[49]

Women in the premodern, agrarian society played a fundamental role both socially and economically. Life was hard for most people and the choices any individual could make were limited. The goal was to make as decent a living as possible from the resources provided by nature. Then a modernized society opened a wide range of jobs and lifestyles. However, the ideal now prescribed that a woman ought to be a housewife supported by her husband. Collectively, housewives from the turn of the nineteenth century until 1965 played an important role in raising Norwegian models of hygiene, nutrition, and the general standard of living. Individually, many women built good homes for their families, made their hard-working husbands happy, and gave their children a good upbringing. But they paid for it with a lack of personal freedom—almost none had anywhere near the choices in life that men had. In his 1950 book, *Citizenship and Social Class*, T. H. Marshall offered a classical definition of citizenship: "Citizenship is a status bestowed on those who are full members of a community. All who are full members are equal with respect to the rights and duties with which the status is endowed." By the end of the 1930s, women could still not be called full members of the community. The citizenship that had been celebrated in 1914 was a promise that remained to be fulfilled.[50]

Notes

1. Knut Kjelstadli, "Et splittet samfunn: 1905–35," *Aschehougs Norgeshistorie* 10 (Oslo: Aschehoug, 1994), 12. Fredrikke Mørck and Marie Høgh, *Norske Kvinder: En kort oversigt over deres stilling og livsvilkaar i tiaaret 1914–1924* (Oslo: Berg and Høgh, 1924), 3:77, 127, 147.

2. The Norwegian Council of Women was the Norwegian section of the International Council of Women (ICW) and an umbrella organization for middle-class women's organizations. *Nylænde* (15 July 1914), 214–15. *Nylænde (Newly Cleared Ground)*, the magazine of the women's rights movement, was edited by Gina Krog from the start in 1887 and then by Fredrikke Mørck from her death in 1916 until publication ceased in 1928.

3. Fredrikke Mørck and Marie Høgh, *Norske Kvinder: En oversigt over deres stilling og livsvilkaar i hundredeaaret 1814–1914*, Vols. 1 and 2 (Kristiania: Berg and Høgh, 1914), 1:253, 290.

4. Mørck and Høgh, *Norske Kvinder*, 1:429–35. Attempts at organizing maidservants were made in 1886, 1890, 1897, and then again around 1910. Petra Ystenæs was the first leader of the Kristiania branch of the Maid Servants' Association (Den kvindelige

tjenerstands forening), founded in 1910. Sølvi Sogner og Kari Telste, *Ut og søkje teneste. Historia om tenestejentene* (Oslo: Det Norske Samlaget, 2005), 82, 86.

5. Eva Kolstad, *Utsnitt av lovforslag, komitéinnstillinger og debatter i Stortinget om Stemmerett for kvinner 17. mai 1814—11. juni 1913* (Oslo: Fredrik Arnesen Bok-og akcidenstrykkeri, 1963), 6, 119.

6. *Nylænde* (1913), 242.

7. The year before, in 1884, Gina Krog and Hagbard Berner had started the first interest organization for women, the Norwegian Association for Women's Rights (Norsk Kvinnesaksforening). Many of the members thought working for suffrage was too radical. Krog and others then started *Kvindestemmeretsforeningen* (Women's Suffrage Association), which had suffrage as its only goal. Kolstad, *Utsnitt av lovforslag*, 25.

8. Kolstad, *Utsnitt av lovforslag*, 32.

9. Anne Gamme, "'Mandsstemmer har vi saa evigt nok av fra før.': Perspektiver på stemmerettsdebatt for kvinner i Norge 1898–1913" (PhD diss., University of Oslo, 2001), 25.

10. Aslaug Moksnes, *Likestilling eller særstilling?: Norsk Kvinnesaksforening 1884–1913* (Oslo: Gyldendal, 1984), 234.

11. The Norwegian Labor Party's Women's Union (Arbeiderpartiets Kvindeforbund) was founded in 1901. In 1923 it was dissolved and replaced by the Norwegian Labor Party's Women's Secretariat (Arbeiderpartiets kvinnesekretariat). This was not a separate organization but a committee that fell directly under the Labor Party's Executive Committee.

12. Moksnes, *Likestilling eller særstilling?*, 243–46. The 1905 petition was organized by women from the National Women's Suffrage Association and the Norwegian Association for Women's Rights under their leaders, Fredrikke Marie Qvam and Randi Blehr.

13. Kolstad, *Utsnitt av lovforslag*, 103.

14. Hilde Sandvik, "Det økonomiske fellesskapet," in *I gode og vonde dagar. Familieliv i Noreg frå reformasjonen til vår tid*, ed. Sølvi Sogner (Oslo: Samlaget, 2003), 72–118, 204.

15. Sandvik, "Det økonomiske fellesskapet," 99.

16. Stortingsforhandlinger 1871, Indst. og Besl. O., 75.4. Stortingsforhandlinger 1871, Indstilling fra Justiskomiteen, 2:207. Sandvik, "Det økonomiske fellesskapet," 100.

17. Anna Caspari Agerholt, *Den norske kvinnebevegelsens historie* (1937; reprint: Oslo: Gyldendal, 1973), 131, 132. The most important limitation to the husband's rights was that he had to have his wife's permission if he wanted to sell more than one-tenth of their joint property.

18. Sandvik, "Det økonomiske fellesskapet," 107. Elisabeth Lønnå, *Stolthet og kvinnekamp: Norsk Kvinnesaksforenings historie fra 1913* (Oslo: Gyldendal, 1996), 39. Kari Melby, "Del IV. Husmorens epoke. 1900–1950," in *Med kjønnsperspektiv på norsk historie: Fra vikingtid til 2000-årsskiftet*, eds. Ida Blom and Sølvi Sogner (Oslo: Cappelen Akademisk Forlag, 1999), 263.

19. Gro Hagemann, "Del III. De stummes leir? 1800–1900," in *Med kjønnsperspektiv på norsk historie*, eds. Blom and Sogner, 192.

20. Elisabeth Lønnå, *Helga Eng: Psykolog og pedagog i barnets århundre* (Oslo: Fagbokforlaget, 2002), 27–36. The college was situated in Bærum but was called Asker seminar.

21. Women were still excluded from cabinet posts, clerical posts in the Norwegian Church, diplomatic and consular posts, and military offices. Agerholt, *Den norske kvinnebevegelsens historie*, 238.

22. Sølve Sogner, ed., *I gode og vonde dagar. Familieliv i Noreg frå reformasjonen til vår tid* (Oslo: Samlaget, 2003), 13. Sandvik, "Det økonomiske fellesskapet," 78. Ingeborg Fløystad, "Kjønn og språk i gards-og slektshistorie," in *Kvinnekår i det gamle samfunn ca. 1500–1850*, eds. Anna Tranberg and Harald Winge (Oslo: Norsk lokalhistorisk institutt, 2003), 48.

23. Håvard Dahl Bratrein, "Det tradisjonelle kjønnsrollemønster i Nord-Norge," in *Drivandes kvinnfolk. Om kvinner, lønn og arbeid*, eds. Bratrein, et al. (Tromsø: Universitetsforlaget, 1976), 21–39.

24. Fløystad, "Kjønn og språk i gards-og slektshistorie," 50; Brit Berggren, "Kystens kvinner—kystens bønder," in *Brytningsår—blomstringstid. Vol 5, Norges kulturhistorie*, ed. Ingrid Semmingsen (Oslo: Ashcehoug, 1980), 92.

25. Anna Tranberg, "Kjønn og språk i gards- og slektshistorie," in *Kvinnekår i det gamle samfunn*, eds. Tranberg and Winge, 39. Hagemann, "Del III. De stummes leir? 1800–1900," in *Med kjønnsperspektiv på norsk historie*, eds. Blom and Sogner, 157–158. Sandvik "Det økonomiske fellesskapet," 95–96.

26. Sogner and Telste, *Ut og søkje teneste*, 34.

27. Sogner and Telste, *Ut og søkje teneste*, 49.

28. Rolf Danielsen, Ståle Dyrvik, Tore Grønlie, Knut Helle, and Edgar Hovland, eds., *Grunntrekk i norsk historie fra vikingtid til våre dager* (Oslo: Universitetsforlaget, 1991), 241.

29. Ola Honningdal Grytten and Camilla Brautaset, "Family Households and Unemployment in Norway during Years of Crisis: New Estimates 1926–1939," *History of the Family: An International Quarterly* 5.1 (2003): 30. Kommunikasjons-og Teletilsattes Landsforbund, *Med KTTL gjennom 75 år: Et streiftog gjennom landsforbundets arbeid 1914–1989* (Oslo: KTTL, 1989), 7. Lønnå, *Helga Eng*, 47.

30. Ida Blom, "'Nye kvinner'? 'Nye menn'? Refleksjoner over endrete forståelser av kjønn, c.1870–c.1940," in *Erobring og overskridelse: De nye kvinnene inntar verden 1870–1940*, eds. Tone Hellesund and Inger Marie Okkenhaug (Oslo: Unipub, 2003), 259.

31. Hellesund and Okkenhaug, *Erobring og overskridelse*, 5. Blom, "'Nye kvinner'? 'Nye menn'?," 263.

32. Blom and Sogner, *Med kjønnsperspektiv på norsk historie*, 345, see Table 1. Anna Avdem and Kari Melby, *Oppe først og sist i seng. Husarbeid i Norge fra 1850 til i dag* (Oslo: Universitetsforlaget, 1985), 89.

33. Avdem and Melby, *Oppe først og sist i seng*, 123.

34. Sogner and Telste, *Ut og søkje teneste*, 7, 75.

35. Beate Muri, *Kristiania for 100 år siden* (Oslo: Schibsted, 2005), 49, 50. Sogner and Telste, *Ut og søkje teneste*, 68.

36. Melby, "Del IV. Husmorens epoke. 1900–1950," 281. Mimi Sverdrup Lunden, *De frigjorte hender. Et bidrag til forståelse av kvinners arbeid i Norge etter 1814* (Oslo: Tanum, 1944), 160.

37. Lønnå, *Stolthet og kvinnekamp,* 51. Stein Rokkan, *Stat, nasjon, klasse. Essays i politisk sosiologi,* ed. Bernt Hagtvet (Oslo: Universitetsforlaget, 1987), 133. Ingunn Norderval Means, *Kvinner i norsk politikk* (Oslo: Cappelen, 1973), 25.

38. Means, *Kvinner i norsk politikk,* 123, see Table 25. Elisabeth Lønnå, "Da Fredrikstad var på kvinnetoppen," in *Mindrealv. Årbok X. Fredrikstad Museum* (Fredrikstad: Fredrikstad museum, 2003), 213–22.

39. Women's right to take part in the government's cabinet was not included in the new voting rights in 1913 but provided by constitutional change in 1922. Anne Hilde Nagel, "The Development of Citizenship in Norway: Marshall Remodelled," in *Women's Politics and Women in Politics: In Honour of Ida Blom,* eds. Sølvi Sogner and Gro Hagemann (Bergen: Cappelen Akademisk Forlag, 2000), 209.

40. Lønnå, *Stolthet og kvinnekamp,* 45.

41. Lunden, *De frigjorte hender,* 76. Mørck and Høgh, *Norske Kvinder,* 88. Lønnå, *Stolthet og kvinnekamp,* 29.

42. Melby, "Del IV. Husmorens epoke. 1900–1950," 265, 278.

43. *LO* is short for *Landsorganisasjonen i Norge* (the National Trade Union Organization of Norway). Elisabeth Lønnå, "LO, DNA og striden om gifte kvinner i arbeidslivet," *Kvinner selv . . . Sju bidrag til norsk kvinnehistorie,* eds. Ida Blom and Gro Hagemann (Oslo: Aschehoug, 1997), 156.

44. *Dagbladet,* 16 July 1928. Lønnå, *Stolthet og kvinnekamp,* 34.

45. Grytten and Brautaset, "Family Households and Unemployment in Norway," 46.

46. Lønnå, *Stolthet og kvinnekamp,* 76–86.

47. Lønnå, *Stolthet og kvinnekamp,* 85, 92–93, 110. Margarete Bonnevie, *Ekteskap og arbeide* (Oslo: Some, 1932). In 1936, Margarete Bonnevie took over leadership of the Norwegian Association for Women's Rights (Norsk Kvinnesaksforening). Yvonne Hirdman, "Genusanalys av välfärdsstaten: utmaning av dokotomierna," in *kvinnehistorie til kjønnshistorie? Rapport III* (Oslo: Det 22. nordiske historikermøte [The 22nd Nordic Historians' Meeting], 1994). Elisabeth Lønnå, "En feministisk opposisjon til Arbeiderpartiet," in *Arbeiderhistorie. Årbok for arbeiderbevegelsens Arkiv og Bibliotek,* (Oslo: Arbeiderbevegelsens Arkiv og Bibliotek, 2000), 117–35.

48. Melby, "Del IV. Husmorens epoke. 1900–1950," 264. Francis Sejersted, *Sosialdemokratiets tidsalder: Norge og Sverige i det 20. århundre* (Oslo: Pax, 2005), 102–5.

49. Blom and Sogner, *Med kjønnsperspektiv på norsk historie,* 349, see Table 5.

50. T. H. Marshall, "Citizenship and Social Class," in *Citizenship and Social Class,* eds. T. H. Marshall and T. Bottomore (1950; reprint, London: Pluto Press, 1992), 18.

CHAPTER 2

Norwegian Immigration and Women

Odd S. Lovoll

The History of Norwegian Women Emigrants

Norwegian women participated in overseas migrations in large numbers; they fell into assorted social roles, including farming, domestic service, urban work, and in professional pursuits. Many single women as well as women in nuclear families left their homeland to settle elsewhere. A study of their history can benefit from a large body of scholarly accounts, including essays by Ingrid Semmingsen, a pioneer in Norwegian emigration history, as well as from an analysis of national statistics. Though much remains to be learned, the lives of immigrant women can in fact no longer be considered unexplored territory. This chapter intends to draw on earlier research, examine the statistical evidence, offer a comparative perspective of similarities and differences between male and female migratory experiences, correct the general belief that Norwegian emigration was largely a male phenomenon, and temper widely held preconceptions of Norwegian women immigrants as either sturdy pioneer wives on the American frontier or domestics in small towns and metropolitan areas. Women were highly visible in these roles, but these were not their only realities, even though domestic work became the most apparent occupation for young single women.

When we consider the process that made women decide to move to distant lands, the relatively large number of them, and the opportunities that existed in their foreign destinations, we see that the picture of women immigrants becomes much more complex. Beyond the heroic frontier mother and wife and the urban maid, a great variety of circumstances influenced the individual immigrant's actions.[1]

Women's Share of the Overseas Movement

Looking at the period 1866 to 1940, as published by the Norwegian Bureau of the Census, women accounted for 41 percent of the total overseas movement (465,312 men and 320,442 women for a total of 785,754). They moved overwhelmingly to the United States—in the nineteenth century almost exclusively so. The sex ratio varied greatly, with male numerical superiority in periods of increased migration and women augmenting their share of the total

TABLE 2-1
Number of Males and Females Among the Emigrants, 1866–1960

			Number							
	Whole country		Rural districts		Towns		Males per 1000 females			
							AMONG THE EMIGRANTS FROM			IN THE
							WHOLE	RURAL		TOTAL
YEAR	MALES	FEMALES	MALES	FEMALES	MALES	FEMALES	COUNTRY	DISTRICTS	TOWNS	POPULATION
1866–70	41,969	32,379	—	—	—	—	1,296	—	—	961
1871–75	24,546	20,596	—	—	—	—	1,192	—	—	956
1876–80	23,785	16,459	18,693	12,642	5,092	3,817	1,445	1,479	1,334	955
1881–85	59,122	46,582	43,330	31,957	15,792	14,625	1,269	1,356	1,080	944
1886–90	47,417	33,567	32,730	20,456	14,687	13,111	1,413	1,600	1,120	935
1891–95	35,370	25,647	26,347	16,109	9,023	9,538	1,379	1,636	946	932
1896–1900	20,643	13,194	15,889	8,774	4,754	4,420	1,565	1,811	1,079	938
1901–5	65,599	37,596	45,618	23,840	19,981	13,756	1,745	1,914	1,453	935
1906–10	54,403	33,260	38,660	19,767	15,743	13,493	1,636	1,956	1,167	930
1911–15	25,716	18,836	18,900	11,208	6,816	7,628	1,365	1,686	894	932
1916–20	8,393	8,576	4,681	4,202	3,712	4,374	979	1,114	849	943
1921–25	29,608	15,263	20,484	7,915	9,124	7,348	1,940	2,588	1,242	950
1926–30	26,420	15,321	19,669	8,684	6,751	6,637	1,724	2,265	1,017	949
1931–35	1,087	1,465	635	771	452	694	742	824	651	956
1936–40	1,234	1,700	763	987	471	713	726	773	661	964
1941–45	—	—	—	—	—	—	—	—	—	—
1946–50	4,526	5,286	2,402	2,371	2,124	2,915	856	1,013	729	979
1951–55	7,085	6,644	4,061	2,962	3,024	3,682	1,066	1,371	821	988
1956–60	5,620	5,743	3,401	2,755	2,219	2,988	979	1,234	743	992

Source: "Marriages, Births and Migrations in Norway, 1856–1960," *Samfunnsøkonomiske Studier* Nr. 13 (Central Bureau of Statistics of Norway, Oslo, 1965), Table 92, 166.

when migration declined. Women outnumbered men between 1916 and 1920 as well as during the Great Depression of the 1930s when opportunities for employment declined or vanished. The disparity, though both sexes responded to shifting economic circumstances, likely reflected women's gendered motives relating to family issues as well as the reality that the demand for women's work held more steady during changing economic times. Julie E. Backer's analysis of Norwegian statistical evidence regarding motives for emigrating should be noted. "Economic considerations seemingly dominated men's decisions," she writes, "[and] emigration for men consequently was greatly affected by economic conditions on both sides of the Atlantic." The same circumstances influenced women, but not to the same extent: "For women it just as frequently became a question of emigrating in order to unite with the family—a fiancé or husband—who had left beforehand." One may add emigrated siblings, aunts, uncles, and more distant kin to the list of family members ready to welcome and assist new arrivals.

TABLE 2.2
Male and Female Emigrants by Age, Relative Figures, 1866–1960

	Males Age						Females Age					
YEAR	0–14	15–29	30–44	45–59	60–	TOTAL	0–14	15–29	30–44	45–59	60–	TOTAL
1866–70	29.6	39.6	21.6	7.5	1.7	100.0	34.5	34.5	19.9	8.5	2.6	100.0
1871–75	27.2	46.2	18.0	6.9	1.7	100.0	29.6	43.4	16.4	8.4	2.2	100.0
1876–80	19.5	55.9	17.1	5.6	1.9	100.0	26.9	46.4	16.4	7.7	2.6	100.0
1881–85	23.5	52.9	16.5	5.5	1.6	100.0	27.5	47.0	16.1	6.9	2.5	100.0
1886–90	16.1	61.7	16.1	4.6	1.5	100.0	21.3	55.5	15.0	5.9	2.3	100.0
1891–95	14.1	64.8	15.1	4.5	1.5	100.0	17.9	59.9	14.0	5.9	2.3	100.0
1896–1900	10.0	71.8	13.2	3.7	1.3	100.0	14.8	63.9	13.9	5.1	2.3	100.0
1901–5	11.4	71.5	13.2	3.2	0.7	100.0	18.4	62.0	13.6	4.6	1.4	100.0
1906–10	9.1	74.8	12.6	3.0	0.5	100.0	14.6	66.6	13.7	3.9	1.2	100.0
1911–15	8.5	78.0	10.1	2.6	0.8	100.0	11.0	69.8	14.0	3.8	1.4	100.0
1916–20	14.0	59.2	19.2	5.9	1.7	100.0	13.4	55.2	21.9	6.2	3.3	100.0
1921–25	6.9	64.1	22.5	5.7	0.8	100.0	13.5	57.5	22.4	4.2	2.4	100.0
1926–30	9.8	65.8	18.8	4.8	0.8	100.0	15.7	54.8	23.0	4.8	1.7	100.0
1931–35	18.1	37.2	28.9	11.9	3.9	100.0	15.7	38.4	32.1	9.1	4.7	100.0
1936–40	17.0	40.7	25.6	11.9	4.8	100.0	12.9	34.8	35.9	11.7	4.7	100.0
1941–45	—	—	—	—	—	—	—	—	—	—	—	—
1946–50	19.9	37.5	29.2	11.0	2.4	100.0	14.9	35.0	31.6	14.5	4.0	100.0
1951–55	15.5	39.6	34.1	9.3	1.5	100.0	15.2	41.5	27.8	12.8	2.7	100.0
1956–60	16.0	42.8	30.1	9.2	1.9	100.0	15.2	47.3	21.9	12.4	3.2	100.0

Source: "Marriages, Births and Migrations in Norway, 1856–1960," *Samfunnsøkonomiske Studier* Nr. 13 (Central Bureau of Statistics of Norway, Oslo, 1965), Table 93, 167.

Another striking characteristic was the fact that women were more likely than men to settle permanently in the new land, even though women—in the youth labor movement that developed in the postbellum decades—also had a temporary residence in the United States in mind at the outset. They intended to return to Norway after accumulating resources abroad; in many cases, of course, men returned to meet obligations on family homesteads, so their sojourn in America might be considered a means to pay off debt on the home place. As the Norwegian Bureau of Statistics reports, figures on returned overseas immigrants are incomplete. However, they suggest that of the 19,323 repatriated Norwegian Americans listed in the 1910 census, 5,012 were women and 14,311 were men; 85 percent of the men returned to rural communities while 72 percent of women came back to a home in the country. Most of the returning Norwegian Americans, women and men, moved back only a few years after their emigration from Norway. An improved position in gender relationships and new social networks might, at least in part, have influenced women's decision to settle permanently rather than returning to Norway, as well as marriage and American-born children—perhaps the most significant reasons to stay.[2]

Most women, like men, were not married, and immigration might represent a liberating aspect of their lives. As Joy K. Lintelman relates about Hulda Neslund, who came to Chicago at age sixteen in 1915 as "single, Swedish, and female," she adjusted well to her job as a domestic servant. "I was on my own and loved it," Lintelman quotes Neslund as writing. Lintelman challenges the negative image depicted by Theodore Dreiser of his fictional character Sister Carrie as being typical, maintaining that Neslund's real life experience, her "choice to emigrate, her positive employment experiences, and her enjoyment of her life as a single worker in Chicago," was a more familiar and better documented story.

In letters home, women frequently stressed that they received higher wages for less work than they had in domestic service in Norway and, because of high demand for their work, that there were ready opportunities to find new or different employment. The situation created a sense of greater independence. Housework was decidedly preferred by Norwegian and other Scandinavian women over factory work. In her study of Swedish maids, Stina L. Hirsch quoted a Swedish maid who explained that when it became necessary for her to support herself, the question was: "'What can I do?' The answer was plain—housework. I like it best, was used to it at home, and it seems more natural-like." For single women it also provided a place to live.

An immigrant to Council Bluffs, Iowa, from Valdres, Norway, in 1885 wrote home the following, illustrating the point:

> There are six adults in the family, and I have worked here a long time and get 3 dollars a week. They pay every month and I then get 12 dollars. Every Monday I get up at four o'clock and do laundry, and the other days I am up at five thirty. Tuesday I do the ironing in addition to making food, and the other days there is baking and clearing and decorating, because over here you must know everything has to be clean and organized. They are very kind to me and tell me that I am doing my work well, and they give me many things. I also have many free times, three hours nearly all afternoons, and then I can dress nicely and go out on the town and visit the many other Norwegian maids here.

The distinction between the early family character of the overseas exodus, during the founding phase of the overseas movement between 1825 and the 1860s, and the later emerging youth labor migration of unmarried women and men has been too firmly drawn. People continued to move within circles of kin and family. Even women seeking independence through emigration relied on family networks. Friends of the family assisted Neslund with financial help.[3]

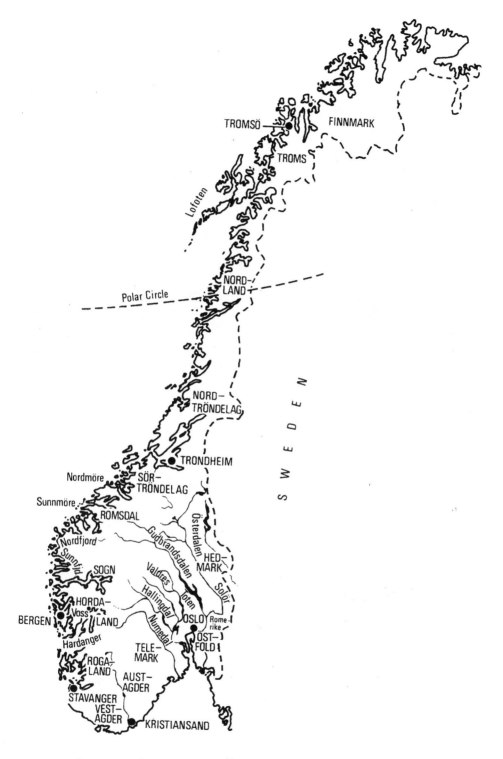

Map of Norway indicating regions of heavy emigration

The journey to America begins

Women on the Farming Frontier

Women participated fully in the conquest of western lands; in most cases as a pioneer's wife and frontier mother, but they also settled on individual claims. The most memorable portrait of a pioneer woman is likely the one drawn of Gro Svendsen, who in 1862 left Hallingdal, Norway, together with her husband Ole to settle in western Iowa. Her firsthand story is recorded in letters written back home in the 1860s and 1870s. Her family in Norway was of the rural aristocracy, with long traditions in landholding and leadership in the local community. Svendsen's move to near-empty territories near Estherville, Iowa, in the interior of America, at the young age of twenty-one, was a hardship and great change. "Through her eyes," to cite the translators of her letters, "we see and feel the experience of an immigrant crossing the Atlantic, 'endlessly vast wearisome, and lonesome,' of the trek in land to the American Midwest, the founding of a frontier home, the rearing of a large family." "It's a fine piece of land," Svendsen wrote in July 1863 about their claim, which they called Skrattegaard after Ole's birthplace in Norway. Like other pioneer women, whether they lived in a sod hut or a log cabin, Svendsen toiled hard in miserable and primitive conditions. Schooling her children at home, she was greatly concerned about their education; her own reading was limited to her periods of confinement. Along with adversity and trial there was progress. In a letter to her parents dated May 30, 1877, she wrote: "We are now well housed, both man and beast. This means a great deal to a pioneer because during the first years he is deprived of many comforts previously enjoyed." The next year Svendsen died in childbirth, giving birth to her tenth child. Both emotionally and physically, pioneer life exacted the greatest toll on women.

A number of examples of how family networks functioned in the western movement may be cited. Anna Koppergard, her sister Vighild, and a cousin, Martha Kjerre, departed from a port in Norway in 1907 and came to an uncle, Nils Koppergard, in Grafton, North Dakota, on June 10 of that year. He had persuaded them to come from Norway to homestead in North Dakota. "I was kind of anxious to see how it was here," Anna said later. She was single and twenty-seven years old when she arrived; after working in the area for two years, she filed on her own land in 1909. During the winters she "worked out," received help from her uncle to break the sod and "some other field operations," but did, as she relates, "drive 4 horses on the binder and I have milked my share of cows. I found it restful and enjoyed doing it." It was by no means uncommon for single women to homestead. Anna married, as did Kirsten Alida Knudsen, who represented the "lone adventurer." She came to North Dakota from Oslo, alone

Carrie Einarson on her homestead, Inland, South Dakota, in 1911. Women as well as men homesteaded alone.

without speaking English, planning to make a fortune and return to Norway. She filed on land in Mountrail County, North Dakota, in 1912, quite a challenge for a young woman from a well-to-do urban family at twenty-seven years old. Instead of returning, she married and remained; as the story goes, Knudsen was a talented singer and violinist with a brief experience as a chorus girl at the National Theater in Oslo (Kristiania) and introduced "the arts . . . into the fabric of everyday pioneer life." These women, like Svendsen, became pioneer wives and mothers but arrived at that stage of their lives by initially settling as single women on land of their own.[4]

The Pioneer Pastor's Wife

Diaries, letters, and other documents delineate the experience of women who accompanied their theologically trained husbands to a Lutheran pastoral call on the American frontier. Especially in the early years of the Norwegian exodus, these women frequently belonged to the "people of condition" (de kondisjonerte), i.e., the cultured upper classes; their encounter with primitive pioneer conditions was consequently a harsh new reality. "I learned to know Norwegian peasants whom I earlier knew so little," the young Else Elisabeth Hysing Koren wrote in her diary. In December 1853, she had arrived at Washington Prairie, southeast of the little town of Decorah, Iowa, with her husband, Pastor Ulrik Vilhelm Koren, who was destined to become a major leader in the Norwegian immigrant Lutheran church.

Koren's diary gives a vivid impression of the crude conditions she and her husband shared with the settlers and is an honest and unromanticized depiction of pioneer life; her aristocratic attitude is occasionally apparent in the narrative. They had only temporary lodging until the parsonage on Washington Prairie stood ready in March 1854; the parsonage became a social and cultural center open to everyone.

Koren had much in common with Caja Munch in Wiota, Wisconsin, whom she had known from childhood. Munch moved to Wisconsin from Norway in 1855 together with her pastor husband, Johan Storm Munch. Like Koren's diary, Munch's preserved correspondence, mainly to her parents in Norway, depicts how she and her husband, while trying to preserve the traditions of accustomed lifestyle, adjusted to the reality of a new land with its egalitarian ideals and abandoned many of the comforts accorded by their station in Norway. Other women also wrote. Linka Keyser Preus, married to Herman Amberg Preus, who served for forty years as pastor at Spring Prairie, Wisconsin, and was one of the major fathers of church establishment, kept a diary from 1845 to 1864. Preus's diary relates her early years there, where a log cabin served as a frontier parsonage, "close to the other cabins in the woods." The congregational affiliation of the three women was with the liturgical high church direction in Norwegian American Lutheranism, the Norwegian Evangelical Lutheran Church of America, generally known as the Norwegian Synod, formed in late 1853. Norwegian Lutheranism in America manifested itself also in competing low-church, pietistic communions, which were embraced by many Norwegian immigrants who praised the greater freedom and equality of America and rejected the ministerial authority and ecclesiastical order of the Norwegian Synod.

The Norwegian Synod was organized by ordained, university-trained pastors, men like Preus, who became its long-term president in 1862. These men were induced to serve the religious and cultural needs of Norwegian settlements in America's Upper Midwest. As members of a professional elite, they and their wives socialized with members of their own class; their lineage and social status set them apart from the vast majority of Norwegian immigrants who hailed from the peasant class. The experience of the cultured wives of pastors from the Norwegian social elite, better educated than most women of that age, made them social role models and their homes cultural centers. Their experience and influence, lasting far beyond their preserved handwritten records, constitute an important chapter in the history of women's overseas migration.[5]

Characteristics of the Migrant Population

It is important to recognize the emotional and social dimensions of immigration. However, current scholarship focuses more on women's resourcefulness in using their old-world traditions to adapt successfully to life in America. Ethnic life is not viewed as an aberration, as Maxine Seller has it, "but as an enduring and valuable, though constantly evolving, feature of the American social landscape." In this context, personal characteristics and social status were significant constituents in the process of adaptation. Consequently, it is essential to know something about the marital status, age, and occupations of Norwegian immigrant women.[6]

The highest immigration intensity in the period 1866 to 1940, for both men and women, was for those age twenty to twenty-four, followed by the age groups fifteen to nineteen and twenty-five to twenty-nine. There were variations throughout the era of mass emigration, which lasted until about 1915, with an especially high immigration intensity among men fifteen to nineteen during the early years of the twentieth century. There were relatively fewer women in this same age group—women typically left for America a few years older. During the years 1891 to 1910, 79 percent of male immigrants fifteen or older were single, while 74 percent of women fifteen or older were single. It was indeed, for both sexes, a movement of unattached people in their most mobile years. These characteristics of a youth labor migration lasted until 1930.

The labor migration often evolved into a family migration by stages. A male-dominated movement during periods of high migration—1866–73, 1880–93, 1900–1915, 1920–29—influenced female family members to follow. However, the discrepancy was not great. Female emigration rose and fell at the same tempo as the male exodus—for instance, 43 percent of the 186,688 people who left Norway in the 1880s were women. The most revealing statistics come during the years affected by World War I. During 1916 to 1920, 51 percent of all emigrants were women; in the following decade, only 35 percent were women, as the final large movement from Norway assumed a strong male composition. Changes in emigration from Norway, neutral during World War I, related to both the dangers associated with the Atlantic crossing and the shortage of appealing employment opportunities. There was a tendency, though not consistently as dramatic as the one cited, for women to join established relatives and neighbors in America during periods of declining immigration. In general, a decline in immigration was largely caused by depression or economic stagnation and the lowered needs of the American labor market; in times of economic growth and prosperity, the need for foreign workers conversely increased, and the movement across the Atlantic swelled.[7]

Marriage Migration

"Marriage migration" was a common occurrence—women joining a fiancé in America. A romantic and illustrative tale may be told of Birgitte Evensen from Arendal, Norway. An intelligent, well-educated, and cultured young woman, she on February 3, 1881, wrote to her former teacher in Norway, Ole Nilsen, then a horse-and-buggy pastor in northern Iowa, asking advice about finding "a teacher's position" in America. Evensen was obviously better equipped to confront a new life in America than most women immigrants. Her initially formal approach to Pastor Nilsen, as evidenced in the more than fifty letters preserved, gradually changed in the correspondence in both directions to become a courtship across the Atlantic. In his letter dated February 25, 1882, Nilsen found the courage to ask, "Will you in God's name be my own dear wife?" Her acceptance of his proposal moved her to America, where the twenty-one-year-old married Nilsen on November 30 of the same year and assumed a pastor's wife role among emigrated compatriots.[8]

Married women regularly emigrated with children to join their husbands in the new land. Examples of women making the journey alone accompanied by children abound. An investigation of family emigration from the city of Bergen in the 1880s by Semmingsen—during the high tide of emigration—show that half of the family units leaving from there consisted of mothers who traveled without their husbands, at times together with a number of children and on

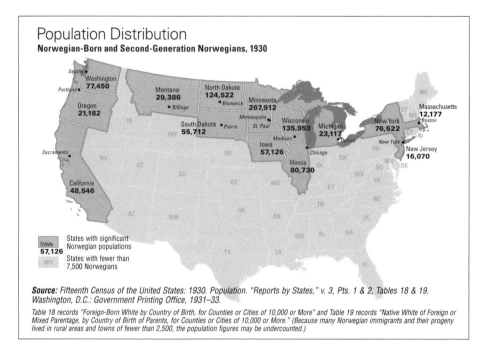

Population Distribution
Norwegian-Born and Second-Generation Norwegians, 1930

Seattle •
Washington
Portland • **77,450**
Oregon **21,182**
Montana **29,386** • Billings
North Dakota **124,522** • Bismarck
Minnesota **267,912**
Minneapolis •
South Dakota **55,712** • Pierre
St. Paul •
Wisconsin **135,953**
Michigan **23,117** • Detroit
Massachusetts **12,177** • Boston
New York **76,522**
New York •
New Jersey **16,070**
Sacramento •
California **48,546**
Madison •
Iowa **57,126**
Chicago •
Illinois **80,730**

Iowa **57,126** — States with significant Norwegian populations
WY — States with fewer than 7,500 Norwegians

Source: *Fifteenth Census of the United States: 1930. Population. "Reports by States," v. 3, Pts. 1 & 2, Tables 18 & 19. Washington, D.C.: Government Printing Office, 1931–33.*

Table 18 records "Foreign-Born White by Country of Birth, for Counties or Cities of 10,000 or More" and Table 19 records "Native White of Foreign or Mixed Parentage, by Country of Birth of Parents, for Counties or Cities of 10,000 or More." (Because many Norwegian immigrants and their progeny lived in rural areas and towns of fewer than 2,500, the population figures may be undercounted.)

prepaid tickets from America. Examining the passenger lists, Semmingsen finds young, unmarried women traveling with a child, "probably . . . to escape from social disgrace," fathers who take with them one or more of the older children "in the hope that they will assist him in establishing himself while the mother stays at home for some time with the younger ones." Semmingsen found only one really big family among the emigrants, "a master joiner 42 years old and his wife of 44 who have 7 children aged from 3 up to 17." This couple was older than most—emigrants in general were younger at the time of departure and thus couples did not have large families.[9]

Husbands and fathers frequently crossed the Atlantic in advance of their families. One may relate how Kristian Eriksen Skotheim from the community of Fræna on Norway's northwest coast immigrated to Seattle, Washington, a few years before the rest of the family "in order to arrange for" their arrival, making a living as a salmon fisherman in Alaska. In May 1913, his wife Inga Johanna and their two children, Marit (Molli), born 1909, and Sivert Olaus, born 1910, made the strenuous journey by boat and railroad to the Pacific Northwest. The loss of her husband at sea in 1921 left Inga to care for the two children, partly dependent on the contribution Sivert could make to the family's economy delivering newspapers.[10]

There were also "mail-order brides," women who arranged marriage to an earlier immigrant, generally from the same home community, before their departure. In a recent master's thesis, Helge Aamodt describes several such instances, including how Marit Helgesdatter Volden, born in 1887, moved in 1904 from Tylldalen in the Østerdalen valley to the Rush River settlement in Wisconsin to marry Jul Lund, the son of Jon and Oline Lund, earlier immigrants from Tylldalen. A shortage of Norwegian women, especially in new regions of settlement, encouraged emigrated Norwegian men to seek a wife from the homeland. As evidenced in preserved correspondence and oral accounts, letters proposing marriage were sent to women the emigrants might or might not know, the latter not infrequently indirectly through an intermediary. In 1868, John Halvorsen, an immigrant from Valdres, sent the following request to Ole O. Ødegaard in Norway from his home in Madison, Wisconsin: "I am sending you my portrait so that if one of your hired girls would like to get married I am available, and she can see how I look." Other men might prefer to return to Norway to seek a wife. Dag Rorgemoen tells about Rikard Eivindsson Espelid who emigrated from Eidsborg in Telemark in 1869 at twenty years old together with four other bachelors. He returned around 1880 and, as the story goes, had "one of the best feasts ever held in Eidsborg." When he left for America again, he was joined by Anne Trondsdotter Hjuringstøyllidi, a cotter's daughter who had been only twelve years old when Rikard emigrated the first time.[11]

Motives in the Overseas Migration

Women, like men, responded to economic opportunities abroad. As the Norwegian Bureau of the Census concludes, "From the earliest beginnings the main reason for emigration from Norway seems to have been young people's desire to improve their economic circumstances." Nineteenth-century Norway, the bureau explains, was not considered well developed economically, and opportunities for advancement or a living wage were grossly inferior to those in the United States.[12]

However, a purely economic explanation of the overseas exodus from Norway is much too limited. Even though Norwegian immigrants were not religious or political refugees but basically economic immigrants, numerous personal motives other than finances influenced their decisions to seek their fortunes in a different part of the world; wanderlust and a desire for adventure might become deciding motives, as well as class prejudice, and even a wish to escape social denunciation for pregnancy outside marriage or other acts found censurable by the community at large. Certain patterns in the movement of people from one continent to another clearly emerged, but all emigrants—women and men—had their own story on how they came to the decision to leave Norway. The human factor may easily disappear in a macro view of this historical phenomenon and in its statistical dimensions. The resolve to emigrate represented for the individual a personal choice. Concentrating on qualitative causalities—rather than simply on economic, demographic, and social circumstances—gives a more positive view of Norway and its dramatic loss of citizens through emigration. It was not a case of people fleeing famine or persecution but rather individuals seeking a better life elsewhere. The image of America as the land of freedom and opportunity was effective throughout the era of emigration; information about conditions and shifting opportunities was obtainable on a regular basis by the time of the American Civil War.

"America letters," correspondence from emigrated kin and neighbors, were for a long time the most common and reliable source of news about the new land; these, as well as the response from Norway, offer insight into how the resolution to seek America was made. Even women could serve as scouts for an entire family intending to emigrate. For example, Augusta Charlotte Laumann, daughter of a glassblower, only eighteen years old and the oldest of nine children, went to America to explore possibilities after the glass factory at Jevne south of Fåberg where her father was employed closed its doors in 1836. Laumann was the first emigrant from her area of Norway. She settled in New York, and to quote her, "after a period of 'a lot of longing and worries' she obtained a job in a store run by another Norwegian." Her success made her encourage the rest of her family to join her, which they did in 1839, later moving to the Sugar Creek settlement in Iowa. Laumann's advance scouting, more commonly a male activity, was a rare incident in the early history of Norwegian emigration.[13]

Scandinavian Female Networks

One may identify functioning female networks in Norwegian emigration, as well as among other Scandinavians. Lintelman relates how Eva Nydahl Wallström decided to emigrate after a visit by two of her aunts, both employed as domestics for rich families in Chicago, who informed relatives of how easy the work was and their high salaries. As a young girl in Småland, Sweden, Wallström experienced hard work with little pay and few prospects to get ahead. Opportunity in America was an appealing alternative. Norwegian examples are many. In 1882, Anne Marie Bøe from Nord Aurdal in Valdres, then living in Dunlop, Iowa, encouraged Anne and Amalie Waagaard to join her because "I am much better off here as a servant and get better wages than they earn in Norway as a housekeeper."

In general, judging by letters from immigrant women back home to Norway, they saw better working conditions than they had had before emigrating. While men frequently mentioned harder work than they were accustomed to, this sentiment is much more rare in letters written by immigrant women. Their salaries were also held to be good even though they earned less than the men. Ingeborg A. Bergene wrote home to Sør Aurdal from Rochester, Minnesota, in 1881 to let her family know that "here the work is different than in Norway.

There is much to be done also here, but the work is much easier for the girls since they here do not have to go out and take care of the cattle. And here we don't stand outside to wash clothes. We are inside in the kitchen. But then we don't beat the clothes either as we did in Norway, instead we have a kind of board we rub *(raabber)* them on or press them on. We think it is hard here in winter to stand outside as long as it takes to hang the clothes on the line."

The experience of Magnhild Torsvik Johnsen, who immigrated to Brooklyn in 1929 at the age of twenty, illustrates the idea of each immigrant having a personal story. She relates: "I decided I was going to go to America. There was one reason. It seems kind of silly to me now, but it was a reason. I wanted to go to Stabekk *husmorskole* [home economics

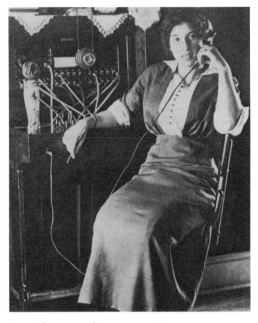

Jessie (Josephine) Jepson, working as a telephone operator in Washington Island, Wisconsin, 1906. Telephone and telegraph companies provided new employment opportunities for women.

school] . . . But to get in there, I had to have one year as a houseworker in one place continuously. And I couldn't see doing housework in Norway; you were not anything if you were working for wages. So I decided I was going to go to America and get a year in there." She had an uncle in Brooklyn who could help her find a position.[14]

The Domestic Calling

America might have represented the "Promised Land for Swedish Maids," as Ulf Beijbom writes, and he could well have included "Norwegian maids." Regardless of employment before leaving for America, young single women's first job in America was most likely to be as a domestic in a family, a boardinghouse, or restaurant. Scandinavian women were also greatly preferred as domestics, as conveyed by a 1910 report of the Immigration Commission, ranked second only to American women in popularity. "The number of maids in this city," Alfred Söderström writes about Minneapolis in 1899, "is quite large . . . but no one can say with certainty how many or where they come from." He estimates that there were about four thousand, and that two thousand were either Swedish or Norwegian, concluding that "The Scandinavian maids are universally sought in this city. They work as we know diligently from morning until evening." Earlier in Chicago, Norwegian women became domestic servants on a full-time or part-time basis. By 1850, about one-fifth of all Norwegian women in Chicago were employed as maids. It was an occupational pattern that persisted throughout the century and beyond. The 1870 census shows that domestic service represented an attractive employment possibility for many young, single women. They could, as announced in the local Norwegian-language newspaper *Skandinaven* in 1871, "get good positions with American families, hotels, and shops by applying to their compatriot Mrs. Johnson at 234 East Oak Street." The demand was thus sufficient to let other women operate a small employment service. In 1880, about three-quarters of Norwegian-born women working outside the home were servants, housekeepers, or launderesses.[15]

The overwhelming majority of Norwegian domestics, as was the case for Swedish domestics, found employment in cities, though there were exceptions. One may, as an example of the latter, cite from Solveig Zempel's insightful anthology of America letters and learn about Berta Serina Kingestad, who in 1886 at age twenty-three emigrated from Finnøy, near Stavanger, to Illinois, where she joined her brothers. In her preserved correspondence she tells about her daily life as a hired woman on farms in the Fox River Valley, an immigrant community in Illinois where many from her part of Norway had settled. In a letter back home dated February 27, 1889, she assures her family that in spite of difficulty, "I have basically never regretted the step I took," that is, emigrating. Her ticket came from an uncle in America.[16]

Women faced more economic barriers than men in financing a ticket to cross the Atlantic and after arriving at their destination in America. Young men had more resources and were better paid. Young women's wages as maids in a city or servant girls in the country were hardly sufficient to cover the cost of emigrating. One may conclude that most single women without means received assistance from relatives and friends established in the United States and either traveled on prepaid tickets or were sent money orders for the fare. Another alternative might have been to borrow money from people in the Norwegian home community before emigrating and repay them from America.

Internal and External Migrations

In considering gendered migrations, it is important to note the difference between rural and urban emigration after the 1880s. The percentage of women emigrating from the countryside declined steadily while the percentage of women emigrating from urban centers increased. Between 1906 and 1910, only one-third of those going overseas from rural areas were women, whereas women made up 46 percent of the emigrants from urban areas.

Migrations within Norway itself and the demographic changes that were occurring explain why during the entire period from 1866 to 1940 women immigrants were more urban than men—37.5 percent as compared to 28.2 percent. Many of the young women departing from a Norwegian city were sojourners, having moved to town from the countryside to seek employment. Julie E. Backer, in her discussion of statistics on emigration, therefore cautions that many of the urban emigrants were in reality more rural than urban. Young people of both sexes sought employment in town, though women clearly did so in greater numbers. There was in fact a surplus of women in the cities, or as a Norwegian parliamentary report of 1921 states, "the abnormal surplus of women" in the nation's population. The greater loss of young men than young women through emigration did indeed create a sex-ratio imbalance. It became for many a worrisome demographic development. It led to more and more women working outside the home, at times competing with men for the same job. Woman's place was, after all, in the mind of most people still in the home as housewife or maid. Internal and external migrations naturally caused a deficit of young people of both sexes in the countryside. After 1880, an increasing number of women emigrated from Norway's cities. The emigration from rural communities in the meantime became all the more dominated by young unmarried men while single young women constituted an ever-larger percentage of urban emigration. In 1907, this category represented 75 percent of all female emigrants from Oslo; that year over half of all emigrants from the capital were women. Apparently, as Semmingsen points out, the biggest and most rapidly growing cities had the largest surplus of women in their populations.[17]

Along with young Norwegian women born in town, young rural women who had worked in town for a while were encouraged to emigrate by the better prospects overseas or chose to join relatives there. As recorded in the police emigrant lists, the most common occupation listed for young women who departed from Oslo in the 1880s is maid (pige). Records for the city of Bergen give better information; in the 1880s there are a few seamstresses (sypiger) and factory workers (fabrikpiger), two teachers, and one telegrapher (telegrafdame). The largest group after 1900 is still maids, but there are also young women registered as nurses, saleswomen, and office girls. Occupations for women emigrants were more systematically collected after 1903. Until 1930—counting all women, married and single—housewives and other domestic workers represented the majority; thereafter followed the occupational group "manufacture and handicraft" and then "shop and office clerks."

After 1905, emigrants were canvassed about their reason for leaving. About one-third of all women reported that they were emigrating to relatives. The remainder, as many as two-thirds, said they wished to make more money, sought larger earnings, or were leaving because they had no income. The majority settled in such large metropolitan centers as New York, Boston, Chicago, Minneapolis, and Seattle. Earlier Norwegian residents and in several of these cities even large Norwegian immigrant colonies created a welcoming environment beyond one's place of employment. Like those who preferred an agricultural setting, single Norwegian women who sought work in a big city most often found a Norwegian American spouse. Women's organizations united and gave comfort. The First Scandinavian Women's Burial Society of Chicago (Den første skandinaviske kvindelige Begravelses-Forening), organized in 1879, appealed strongly to the many single women in the city working in domestic service. It consisted mainly of Norwegian women and gave mutual aid and loans and guaranteed a respectable burial. The society's members encouraged emigration through contacts with young women back home and provided assistance to new arrivals seeking employment.[18]

New Opportunities in America

Chicago offered opportunities not available for women in the homeland. The Norwegian pioneer feminist Aasta Hansteen sought refuge in America from 1880 to 1889; for two of these years she made Chicago her home and noted the greater freedom for women there. There were several Scandinavian schools of midwifery, a specialty women also could enter into in Norway, as well as nursing, but the founding in 1870 of the Woman's Medical School in Chicago opened medical training for women, an opportunity totally absent in Norway. It became an opportunity for the few rather than the many; most women were not in a position to take advantage of the education such institutions offered. However, a number of Norwegian women immigrants enrolled. Helga Ruud came to Chicago from Kongsberg in 1878 when she was eighteen years old. As a governess, she saved money to finance her education and entered medical school in 1882, graduating in 1889. Other Norwegian women followed in her path, coming directly from Norway, like Ingeborg Rasmussen, born in Bergen in 1855; in 1887, at age thirty-two, she abandoned a career as an actress at the Christiania Theater and came to Chicago, where she bravely enrolled in the medical college. She became a prominent member of the Scandinavian medical community. These successful female physicians served as role models, encouraging women to seek medical careers and thus meet the needs of hospitals and other care facilities that were being founded, to serve the Norwegian American community not only as physicians but also as nurses, deaconesses, and matrons at various institutions. Women could play an ever-expanding vocational role.[19]

Many institutions evolved from the social service role of Norwegian immigrant churches. In 1883, Sister Elizabeth Fedde of the Deaconess Home in Oslo came to Brooklyn as the first Norwegian deaconess in America. She started a Lutheran deaconess home and hospital there. Women in Chicago, Minneapolis, and elsewhere embraced the deaconess movement and established homes and hospitals. Education gave access to American society, and the skills gained secured rapid social advancement. With the exception of all theological seminaries, which only accepted male students, most colleges and schools founded by Norwegian immigrants were coeducational. As an example, young Norwegian women

Dr. Ingeborg Rasmussen (1855–1938) graduated from the Woman's Medical School in Chicago in 1892. Her career gave evidence of the expanding vocational role women could play.

The appointment of Agnes Mathilde Wergeland (1857–1914; shown here in 1913) to a professorship in history at the state university in Laramie, Wyoming, from 1902 until 1914 exemplifies the greater opportunity for women in America than in her native Norway.

immigrants enrolled at St. Olaf College in Northfield, Minnesota, founded in 1874, or at Lutheran Ladies Seminary in Red Wing, Minnesota, opened in 1894, or they attended other immigrant colleges or state-run institutions of higher learning. Other women, like Agnes Mathilde Wergeland, sought positions denied women in Norway. Wergeland earned a doctoral degree in 1890 at the University of Zurich, Switzerland—the first Norwegian woman to carry the title doctor of philosophy. In 1902 she received an appointment as professor of history at the University of Wyoming in Laramie. In a letter she assured her friend Aasta Hansteen that she would help make the small "place of employment" as good as any of the older institutions that could boast of "years, standing, and dignity." As their range of educational and business opportunities broadened, women arriving in America from Norway built successful careers in many professions and occupations.

After 1930, the emigration from Norway changed character as the Great Depression caused the youth labor migration to end. It again became a movement dominated by family units; family members continued to reunite in America. About one-third of all male emigrants in the 1930s were married. For women the percentage was even higher; in fact, as many as 43 percent of all women who moved overseas in the 1930s were married.[20]

The Exodus in the Post–World War II Decades

The eruption of World War II in September 1939 and the German occupation of Norway from April 9, 1940, to May 8, 1945, created a long break in the overseas movement to the United States. During the economic severity of the Great Depression, six times as many Norwegians returned to Norway as those who joined the Norwegian community in America. As Carl Søyland discovered, strong tensions existed between Norwegians and those returning "because of the bad times in America . . . since the job market in Norway was not too good either." Norwegian immigration never became large after the war, although in the first years of peace delayed reunions hastened departures from Norway. Men, husbands and fathers, sailors in the large Norwegian merchant fleet, employees in Norway's whaling operations in the South Atlantic, and others caught outside the country when Germany invaded Norway, made their way to the United States in substantial numbers. These men, together with earlier immigrants, to a great extent reunited with their families in America rather than return to a postwar homeland. Emigration resumed in 1946. During the first five years, 54 percent of arrivals were women; the number of children below the age of fifteen increased, as it had done from the 1930s. It was clearly a continuation of the prewar family migratory pattern. As the author writes elsewhere, "The great number of Norwegians who had blood ties in America made a certain flow of people overseas inevitable once normal conditions had been reestablished." More than half of all Norwegian immigrants until 1960 were women; the near sex-ratio balance is a marked difference in the later exodus. Those age fifteen to twenty-nine still dominated, but the thirty and above group was much larger than in the pre-1930 movement.[21]

The total number of immigrants during 1946 to 1960 was 34,904. The relatively small overseas movement reached its absolute maximum for any one year during this span in 1952 with the emigration of 2,958 Norwegians. The Immigration and Nationality Act of 1965 became effective July 1, 1968, repealing the national-origins quota system; it established a general quota for the Western Hemisphere and one for the rest of the world and thus placed all nations on an equal footing; it consequently affected the size of Norwegian immigration to the United States, albeit it had been rapidly declining since the early 1960s. The greatest reduction came in 1969, when there was a drop from 1,574 immigrant visas issued the year before to as few as 434. In the following years, fewer than three hundred visas on the average were issued annually. American sources indicate that between 1946 and 1978 fewer than fifty thousand Norwegian citizens moved to the United States. The era of emigration had clearly faded and by the end of the last century belonged to history.

Analyses of the postwar immigration have focused major attention on the movement of skills and technological knowledge; individuals in this category continue to seek employment for longer or shorter periods of time or to settle permanently, benefiting from the higher wages offered by American companies. And then there are the many young Norwegians who enter on student visas and remain after completing their education. However, the majority of immigrants have, in a broad sense, belonged to the laboring class, though almost no one associated with farming. The occupational picture, for women as well as men, is more varied than in the prewar immigration and shows a larger percentage of individuals with specific skills.[22]

Concluding Observations

Norwegian overseas migration has exhibited increased mobility and greater repatriation than during the mass migration of an earlier age. The rate of remigration compared to emigration has in fact increased more following World War II than during any earlier period. In 1971 and 1972, remigration surpassed emigration. Even so, throughout the era of emigration, Norwegian society has experienced a substantial loss of citizens. Indeed, it was a folk movement that had far-reaching effects on the life of the Norwegian people and greatly influenced national identity.

Norway's sons and, as this study shows, also its daughters left the homeland in large numbers. Between 1866 and 1940, women made up 41 percent of the total overseas movement. In periods of low emigration, their numbers surpassed those of their male counterparts. Regardless of marital status, emigrants moved within family networks. However, the labor movement from the late 1800s until the 1930s was dominated by young, single people. Women, like men, responded to economic opportunities abroad, though opportunities and occupations varied between the sexes. Women chose domestic and social services as major occupations, though they also engaged in farming, took part in founding institutions, and entered professions that at the time were closed to women in Norway. A sense of greater freedom in gender relationships, new social networks, and marriage might to a large degree explain why women were more likely than men to settle permanently in the new land. They displayed great resourcefulness in using their old-world traditions in their adaptation to the realities of life in America. Their circumstances and experiences deserve our attention.

Notes

1. Ingrid Semmingsen, "Kvinner i norsk utvandringshistorie," *Migranten/The Migrant* 1.1 (1988): 7–23; Ingrid Semmingsen, "Noen brevglimt av kvinners liv i Amerika," *By og bygd* 30 (1984): 208–14. See also Donna Gabaccia, "Immigrant Women: Nowhere at Home?" *Journal of American Ethnic History* 10.4 (Summer 1991): 61–87.

2. Julie E. Backer, ed., *Ekteskap, fødsler og vandringer i Norge 1856–1960* (Oslo: Statistisk sentralbyrå, 1965), 166–68, 182–85, quotation p166; Christiane Harzig and Dirk Hoerder, "European Immigrant Women in Chicago at the Turn of the Century: A Comparative Approach," in *Swedes in America: New Perspectives,* ed. Ulf Beijbom (Växjö, Sweden: The Swedish Emigrant Institute, 1993), 91–92.

3. Joy K. Lintelman, " 'On My Own': Single, Swedish, and Female in Turn-of-the-century Chicago," in *Swedish-American Life in Chicago: Cultural and Urban Aspects of an Immigrant People, 1850–1930,* eds. Philip J. Anderson and Dag Blanck (Chicago: University of Illinois Press, 1992), 89; Stina L. Hirsch, "The Swedish Maid: 1900–1915" (master's thesis, De Paul University, 1985), 34; Reidar Bakken, *Lad ingen sladrelystne læse mine brever . . . Nordmenn blir amrikanarar. Brev hjemsendt frå norske emigrantar frå 1844–1930* (Fagernes: Valdres Forlag, 1995), 163; Dag Rorgemoen, *Dei mange val—Utvandringa til Ameika frå Lårdal og Rauland prestegjeld 1837–1899* (Eidsborg: Vest-Telemark Museum, 200), 155–60, quotation p155–56.

4. H. Elaine Lindgren, *Land in Her Own Name: Women as Homesteaders in North Dakota* (Fargo: North Dakota Institute for Regional Studies, 1991), 9, 29, 31, 36, 41, 106, 113, 166, 174, 185, 187, 209, 217, 256; Odd S. Lovoll, *The Promise of America: A History of the Norwegian-American People,* rev. ed. (Minneapolis: University of Minnesota Press, 1999), 139–41; Pauline Farseth and Theodore C. Blegen, trans. and eds., *Frontier Mother: The Letters of Gro Svendsen* (Northfield, MN: Norwegian-American Historical Association [hereafter, NAHA], 1950), front flap, v–xv, 6–8, 41–43, 135–41.

5. David T. Nelson, trans. and ed., *The Diary of Elisabeth Koren, 1853–1855* (Northfield,

MN: NAHA, 1955); Helene Munch and Peter A. Munch, *The Strange American Way: Letters of Caja Munch from Wiota, Wisconsin, 1855–1859* (Carbondale: Southern Illinois Press, 1970); Diderikke Margrethe Brandt Preus and Johan Carl Keyser Preus, *Linka's Diary: On Land and Sea, 1845–1864* (Minneapolis, MN: Augsburg Publishing House, 1952).

6. Maxine Schwartz Seller, *Immigrant Women* (Philadelphia, PA: Temple University Press, 1981), 9.

7. Backer, *Ekteskap, fødsler og vandringer i Norge*, 166–68, 172–73, 177.

8. Frida R. Nilsen, trans. and ed., *Letters of Longing* (Minneapolis, MN: Augsburg Publishing House, 1970), v–vi, 1, 25; Odd S. Lovoll, "Nytt fra løftets land. Det private brev og emigrasjon," in *Amerikabrev. Sogndalseminaret 2000*, ed. Oddvar Natvik (Sogndal: Sogndal kommune, 2001), 5.

9. Semmingsen, "Kvinner i norsk utvandringshistorie," 8–9; Ingrid Semmingsen, "Family Emigration from Bergen, 1874–92," in *Americana Norvegica*, ed. Harald S. Naess, et al. (Oslo: Universitetsforlaget, 1971), 3:42.

10. Niels Juel Drejer, *Gammalt frå Fræna* (Elnesvågen: Fræna sogelag, Hustad sogelag, Fræna bygdeboknemnd, 2000), 276–77.

11. Helge Aamodt, "'Kjæm'n frå Tynset, trivs'n øver alt.' En studie av norske immigrantkolonier i Amerika med vekt på immigrantene fra Østerdalen" (master's thesis, University of Oslo, 2005), 112–13; Bakken, *Lad ingen sladrelystne læse mine brever . . . Nordmenn blir amrikanarar*, 74.

12. Backer, *Ekteskap, fødsler og vandringer i Norge*, 177.

13. Anja Høglien, "The American Option in 19th Century Fåberg and Lillehammer: The Development of a Culture of Emigration" (master's thesis, University of Oslo, 2003), 33–34; Inger Elisabeth Fryjordet and Ola Matti Mathisen, "Glassblåserfamilen fra Vingrom den første som dro," in *Fåberg og Lillehammer. Utvandringen* (Lillehammer: Fåberg historielag, 1986), 46–50.

14. Lintelman, "'On My Own,'" 90; Bakken, *Lad ingen sladrelystne læse mine brever . . . Nordmenn blir amerikanarar*, 18, 150. Janet E. Rasmussen, *New Land, New Lives: Scandinavian Immigrants to the Pacific Northwest* (Seattle: University of Washington Press, 1993), 78–79. Magnhild Johnson returned to Norway in 1939. She moved to Washington in 1948.

15. Ulf Beijbom, "The Promised Land for Swedish Maids," in *Swedes in America*, 110–11; Alfred Söderström, *Minneapolisminnen. Kulturhistorisk axplockning från qvarnstaden vid Mississippi* (N.p., 1899), 90–91; Odd S. Lovoll, *A Century of Urban Life: The Norwegians in Chicago before 1930* (Northfield, MN: NAHA, 1988), 24–25, 79, 155.

16. Solveig Zempel, trans. and ed., *In Their Own Words: Letters from Norwegian Immigrants* (Minneapolis: University of Minnesota Press, 1991), 24–26, 39.

17. Ingrid Semmingsen, *Norway to America: A History of the Migration*, trans. Einar Haugen (Minneapolis: University of Minnesota Press, 1978), 162–63; Semmingsen, "Noen brevglimt av kvinners liv i Amerika," 218–19; Backer, *Ekteskap, fødsler og vandringer i Norge*, 153–64; Ingrid Semmingsen, "Women in Norwegian Emigration," in *Scandinavians in America: Literary Life*, ed. J. R. Christianson (Decorah, IA: Symra Literary Society, 1985), 78.

18. Semmingsen, "Noen brevglimt av kvinners liv i Amerika," 218–19; Backer, *Ekteskap, fødsler og vandringer i Norge*, 173–75; Lovoll, *A Century of Urban Life*, 137, 207–8, 221–25.

19. Lovoll, *A Century of Urban Life*, 212; Lovoll, *The Promise of America*, 265–67.

20. Ingrid Semmingsen, "A Pioneer: Agnes Mathilde Wergeland, 1857–1914," in *Makers of an American Immigrant Legacy: Essays in Honor of Kenneth O. Bjork*, ed. Odd S. Lovoll (Northfield, MN: NAHA, 1980), 111–30.

21. Backer, *Ekteskap, fødsler og vandringer i Norge*, 172. Carl Søyland, *Written in the Sand*, trans. Rigmor K. Swensen (Minneapolis, MN: Western Home Books, 2005), 97; Backer, *Ekteskap, fødsler og vandringer i Norge*, 172–73.

22. Odd S. Lovoll, "From Norway to America: A Tradition of Immigration Fades," in *Contemporary American Immigration: Interpretive Essays (European)*, ed. Dennis Laurence Cuddy (Boston: Twayne Publishers, 1982), 86–107, quotations p91, 93.

PART II

Creating Gendered Norwegian American Communities

When immigrants arrived in the United States, they still faced additional journeys to their final destinations. Overland travel varied through the nineteenth and early twentieth centuries, but for most the final destination would be the Upper Midwest. They came by boat (through the Erie Canal and the Great Lakes), by railroads, and by wagon as they followed the westward movement. In the 1830s and 1840s, the destination was Illinois and Wisconsin; in the 1850s and 1860s, it was Iowa and Minnesota; in the 1870s and 1880s, they journeyed to the Dakotas and farther west. The first settlements in the mid-nineteenth century created communities that provided a base from which the next generation, or the next wave, could continue farther west. After the 1880s, especially, many sought the cities, and by the last decades of the nineteenth century, vibrant Norwegian enclaves could be found in Chicago and Minneapolis as well as in smaller towns. At the same time, significant rural communities of Norwegian immigrants continued to thrive, especially in Dane County Wisconsin, northeastern Iowa, southeastern Minnesota, the Red River Valley, and into the western plains. Wherever Norwegian immigrants settled, they created communities that were predominantly or significantly Norwegian but incorporated components of American cultures. Immigrants and their descendants sought to preserve old-world traditions, language, and culture while adapting to or embracing American customs and traditions when practical and reasonable. The chapters in Part II examine the complex nature of Norwegian American communities at the intersection of gender and ethnicity. Specifically, they explore how a gendered analysis can illuminate the complex dynamics of these communities, not only the experiences of women but also of men.

Historian of women and western history Lori Ann Lahlum employs a gendered analysis in examining rural Norwegian American communities and emphasizes work patterns, the Lutheran church, and community events. She concludes that gendered constructions and perspectives clearly shaped the lives of Norwegian American women and men in these rural communities. Lahlum explores the important labor contributions of women in rural regions as well as the shifting gender roles that created tensions. Such tensions were especially manifested in institutions such as the church and in community events as women and men adjusted to life in America. While the migrating Norwegian population was predominantly rural, many immigrants settled in urban areas, especially in the Industrial Era, a period of mass migration from Europe at the turn of the twentieth century. Migration historian David C. Mauk offers a statistical analysis of those immigrant women who sought employment opportunities in American cities, focusing on Minneapolis and St. Paul in Minnesota. These immigrants often came with skills in domestic service in Norwegian cities and small towns and later found a demand for similar work in the metropolitan areas in the Upper Midwest. They labored in Yankee and Norwegian homes but also found work in the needle trades. Mauk also finds that many Norwegian maids, often second-generation immigrants, migrated from the midwestern countryside seeking work. Perhaps most striking is the extent to which the second generation became employed as teachers or in office positions as the percentage of domestics declined. Implicit in Mauk's work is the underlying pattern of Americanization, especially with the second generation, fostered both by American public schools and Norwegian American institutions of higher education.

Textile curator and scholar Laurann Gilbertson examines Norwegian American textile production and how the traditional practices both persisted and changed in the new world. Historically associated with women's work, home textile production served vital economic functions of survival for immigrant families and communities. Yet this labor also existed in a marginalized realm of women's communities, such as the Ladies Aid. Gilbertson effectively demonstrates that the Ladies Aid both fostered the retention of Norwegian textile skills and encouraged the adoption of American textile practices. Thus, textile production becomes an important practice demonstrating women's vital role in providing economic support through individual and shared labor, in linking the home with the community, and in adapting Norwegian traditions to American conditions. By drawing on letters, diaries, personal narratives, and statistical data, geographer Ann M. Legreid explores the critical roles women played in home health care in Norway and their continuation in the United States. Not only within the families but also within the larger Norwegian American communities, women served critical functions in dispensing information and providing health care. They did this as traditional healers as well as professionally trained workers, primarily as nurses, many in the deaconess movement, but also as physicians. Legreid also discusses the tensions between traditional home health-care practices and emerging scientific medicine in the period of migration. Finally, sociologist Karen V. Hansen examines the effects of the 1904 land lottery at Spirit Lake Reservation in North Dakota. Analyzing census records and plat maps, along with interviews and secondary sources, Hansen contrasts Dakota and Norwegian American women's relationships to the land. As a sociologist less inclined to organize analysis around national origin, Hansen's ethnic coding of land ownership centers on broad categories—Dakota, Yankee, German, and Scandinavian (including Norwegian)—and avoids distinctions among first-, second-, and third-generation immigrants. Because of the large percentage of ethnic Norwegians in the state, Hansen draws the inference that the percentage of Norwegian landowners on the reservation is similar to that in the surrounding counties, although immigration historians might analyze the empirical evidence differently. Critical to her study, however, is the competition over land as a consequence of Norwegian (and European) migration, even into the second generation.

CHAPTER 3

Women, Work, and Community in Rural Norwegian America, 1840–1920

Lori Ann Lahlum

On October 12, 1889, a very pregnant Randi Anderson Rued spent a day bak-ing and cleaning house near Curtiss, Wisconsin. That evening, she walked to a neighboring farm to milk the cows for a Swedish immigrant woman who was attending a wedding (even though the neighbor's husband and children were home). When she was done, she returned home. Later that evening, Rued felt "ill" and went into labor. Alone because she had insisted her husband also attend the wedding, Rued walked back to the neighbor's farm around midnight and sent word to her husband that she had gone into labor. Her husband and the Swedish neighbor woman rushed from the wedding to the Rued farmstead. After a prolonged and difficult labor, Rued gave birth to her first child, a son; a local woman helped after the birth. When her husband went to the lumber camps for the winter, he hired a boy to haul water and care for the livestock, relieving Rued of some of the more onerous farm chores. These few months in Randi Anderson Rued's life highlight many aspects of rural Norwegian American women's experiences, including the centrality of female labor, especially on Norwegian American farms; paid and unpaid female labor; gendered expectations regard-ing work; and the importance of family and community events and female labor exchange in rural communities. Because Rued had newly immigrated, which undoubtedly influenced her perspective, she—not the neighbor's husband—was expected to do the chores: milking cows was women's work. Rued's story also recognizes the fluidity with which young, unmarried women moved back and forth between the countryside and the cities and towns in rural America. The young woman who assisted Rued after she gave birth left the Rueds' home, moved into town, and worked in a hotel. Rued's letters, which, unfortunately, end in 1895, tell a vivid story of women in rural communities: their work, their social interactions, and their community lives.[1]

This chapter addresses women and gender in rural Norwegian America, focusing on the Midwest and northern Great Plains but including Texas and the Pacific Northwest. While Norwegian American communities in the Midwest have received greater scholarly treatment, smaller communities in Texas and Idaho reflect some of the same general patterns for women in rural areas. Moreover, conceptualizing rural Norwegian America beyond the spatial orientation of the

Midwest and northern Great Plains helps readers understand the Norwegian American experience. It also examines gendered labor, as Norwegian immigrants in rural communities encountered American ideals on gender and work. For farm women and their daughters, paid and unpaid labor, as well as the production of goods for sale (eggs or knit stockings, for example), remained key components of the household economy. Finally, the chapter looks at the vital roles women played in creating and shaping their communities, through the Lutheran church, as participants in social activities and civic organizations, and through personal interactions with other women.

By looking at gender in rural Norwegian America, a more nuanced understanding of life in these immigrant communities emerges; more than any other immigrant group, Norwegian Americans stayed on the land and in rural areas. These women and men lived in communities that were at the same time Norwegian and American. Moreover, the intersection of Norwegian and American gender expectations affected their lives, which required Norwegian immigrants to negotiate between ideals on their proper roles in the home and community from Norway and their new situations in the United States. For many immigrant women, gender ideals from Norway framed their experiences, especially in their earliest years in America. As an example, the labor of women, and especially farm women, remained crucial. Farm women often continued working in the fields and milking cows, although these roles generally varied more in the United States. Likewise, girls and young women typically worked as domestic servants in rural Norwegian American communities, just as they had in Norway. Finally, women's domestic skills, for example cooking, remained central to community social activities.

While some gender roles for women remained similar to what they had experienced in Norway, others changed. Generally, broader employment opportunities existed for women in the United States, and they became available sooner than in Norway. Public school teaching is one example: some Norwegian American communities made every effort to hire male teachers, yet in most communities women educators became commonplace by the late nineteenth century. Moreover, in the United States, Norwegian American women could teach in the Norwegian parochial schools operated by local Lutheran congregations; this was not possible in Norway during the same time period. Finally, although women's groups existed in the Norwegian Lutheran Church and engaged in mission activities, the Ladies Aid in the United States became much more egalitarian and engendered broader participation than in Norway. In addition, through the Ladies Aid, Norwegian American women quickly assumed an important financial role within the church (unlike in Norway), which affected the power relationship between women and men within the congregation, and they took on public roles when they served dinners and hosted bazaars.

Women and the Establishment of
Norwegian American Communities

The organized migration from Norway to the United States began in 1825. In America, Norwegian immigrants planted settlements and created Norwegian enclaves that became Norwegian American communities. Most of these communities existed in rural areas, and immigrant women and men participated in the process of settling frontier areas. Many Norwegian women who migrated to the frontier and to rural communities encouraged migration to America as they detailed their lives in a new land.[2]

Some women who settled in rural Norwegian American communities actively advocated emigration and settlement in their areas when they wrote letters back to Norway (called "America letters") describing the United States in glowing agricultural terms. For many, agricultural land became an incentive for migration. Three Wisconsin sisters, Ragnil, Sigri, and Gunild Nicolaisdatter Omland, wrote to their brother Tellef in 1850 and painted a picture of Wisconsin with fertile agricultural options exceeding those available in Norway. The sisters claimed that if Tellef immigrated to Wisconsin, within the span of one year he could purchase a farm of better quality than in their home community in Norway. Not only was agriculture more profitable in America than in Norway, asserted the sisters, the Blue Mound area of Wisconsin was "the most healthful place in America," with "pure" and "clean air" and "plenty of water." According to the Omland sisters, the Wisconsin soil possessed a fertility that resulted in larger crop yields than in Norway. They painted this enticing and optimistic picture of Wisconsin to encourage their brother to join the rest of the family in the state. They also, however, issued a word of caution. Should he immigrate to the United States, the sisters warned: "you [Tellef] will not be so foolish as to go to the warm Texas." The sisters continued that the "hot" Texas climate made it possible to fry bacon on the street. Moreover, whereas in Texas one "can get a completely satisfying meal out of a cob of corn . . . we here in Wisconsin would not be satisfied with such hog's feed." The sisters were clearly boosters for their community, and the exaggeration served to mitigate one of the more potentially undesirable qualities of Wisconsin—the cold winter. Though the sisters addressed their comments to their brother, in many cases these letters circulated among family and friends. In this way, the sisters' potential audience extended beyond the immediate family in Norway, and they could encourage other community members to emigrate as well.[3]

Meanwhile, in Texas, Elise Tvede Wærenskjold countered arguments such as those made by the Omland sisters and actively encouraged settlement in the Lone Star State. In an 1851 letter, she pressed the case for Texas settlement. "I believe Texas is the best of the states to migrate to," Wærenskjold claimed, "partly because the climate is milder and more pleasant than in the Northern states and partly because the land is cheaper. Furthermore, without owning land a person can here acquire as many cattle as he pleases, and, finally, a person can sustain himself with so much less effort, since less is required for house-building [*sic*], for getting food for the animals, etc., etc., than in colder climes." On another occasion, she explained "the thermometer goes up to 100°F;" but, as a resident of Texas for more than twenty years, she could confidently pro-claim "only once" had it reached 112°F. Like the Omland sisters, Wærenskjold also countered images of unfavorable weather, presenting Texas as an ideal place for Norwegian immigrants to settle.[4]

The Omland sisters were more typical of Norwegian immigrant women residing in rural areas than Wærenskjold. The daughter of a Danish minister, Wærenskjold grew up near Kristiansand, in southern Norway, and received a good education. She worked publishing temperance pamphlets, and she edited *Norge og Amerika (Norway and America)*, a magazine that provided information on America and fostered emigration, prior to her own departure for Texas in 1847. From Texas, she sent letters to Norway, a number of which appeared in newspapers and magazines. Indeed, Wærenskjold's purpose for writing some of the surviving letters was explicitly to promote settlement in Texas. As such, the letters highlight American agriculture. In the first letter of the collection, written in 1851, Wærenskjold touted Texas to Norwegians. The letter appeared in two Norwegian newspapers, and in it she compared Norway and Texas as a means of encouraging settlement. "In Norway," she wrote, "if a person wants to turn a piece of unbroken land into a field, it will cost him much labor; even the culti-vated soil must be fertilized if the yield is to be satisfactory—and even so the crop is often destroyed by frost. Here [in Texas] a person merely needs to fence and plow the land and it is ready to be sown." Wærenskjold conceded that her statements applied "only of the prairie; the forest land must be cleared of brush and the large trees must be girdled." While writing about Texas, her letter also implies that establishing a farm was much easier in Texas than in a place such as Wisconsin, where trees had to be cleared. This agricultural orientation dominates Wærenskjold's surviving letters because she sought to encourage emigration.[5]

In addition to serving as immigration boosters, Norwegian immigrant women and their daughters played a crucial role in the establishment and development of Norwegian American communities. In America, some of these communi-ties consisted largely of people from one or two areas in Norway, while others included people from many parts of Norway. The greater context, of course, is that these Norwegian American communities occupied a space in the United States. As a result, residents of these communities, to varying degrees, lived in places with people from outside their home area in Norway and non-Norwegians. Even in parts of the United States with large numbers of Norwegian Americans, immigrants noted the varied ethnic makeup of their communities. For example, Karl Rud, an immigrant from eastern South Dakota, reported that "Americans, English, Norwegians, Germans, Indians, Swedes, Danes, African Americans, and French" resided in the area. Likewise, in the area around Odin, Minnesota, Gina Runningen's neighbors came from a variety of locales in Norway ("Lom, Vaage, Sunmøre, Sogn, Telemark, [and] Hedmark") but also included people from Denmark, Sweden, Germany, and Russia. This great ethnic diversity, she conceded, differed from Norway. She also lamented the fact that no one from her home community of Dovre or neighboring Lesja (both in Gudbrandsdal) resided in the area. Randi Rued described in detail her neighbors, her life, and farmers' efforts to remove trees from the forested land of Wisconsin. At one point, Rued encouraged her family in Norway to "follow me home from church services, [and] I will show you the way and name the farms that lie along the way." She did just that, starting with the German farmer Fedler, the Danish farmer Paulsen, and so on. Rued created a stunning image of her ethnically diverse world that, in turn, connected her family in Norway with her new life in America. While Rud, Runningen, and Rued envisioned themselves in ethnically diverse communities, others saw their communities as consisting only of Norwegian Americans. Johanna Weholt, a young Norwegian American woman, and her family arrived near Genesee, Idaho, in 1887. She later recalled, "The people in that country [around Genesee] were all Norwegians. I don't think I saw an Englishman since I was 12 years and those were those two families we had in Dela[v]an [Minnesota]." Of course, many non-Norwegian Americans resided near Genesee, but Weholt did not consider them part of her community. Perhaps Weholt's social and economic activities were largely restricted to interactions with other Norwegian Americans. Her experience alludes to the fact that even in ethnically diverse communities, individuals' lives could have revolved around smaller Norwegian American enclaves. This, in turn, could serve to segregate Norwegian Americans from broader participation in American society and foster a retention of language and customs from Norway.[6]

In more isolated Norwegian American communities, contact with non-Norwegians became more regular and persistent. Elise Wærenskjold's letters consistently demonstrate links between rural Norwegian American communities in Texas and among Norwegian immigrants and their non-Norwegian neighbors. For the Norwegian immigrants who settled near Waco, Texas, she writes, "most of the world's nationalities" could be found nearby, including French, Germans, Jews, African Americans, Italians, Chinese, Spaniards, Russians, English, Irish, Mexicans, Yankees, Norwegians, Swedes, and Danes. While the immigrants could continue to speak Norwegian among themselves, it became imperative for them to learn English, which was not necessarily the case in rural regions more densely populated with Norwegian Americans. Moreover, the community's diversity promoted marriage outside of the ethnic group. One male letter writer commented that "Norwegian girls [were] marrying Italians," and in the Four Mile Prairie settlement in Texas, Wærenskjold's sons married non-Norwegian girls.[7]

Norwegian American Women and the Rural Economy

Work, whether paid or unpaid, comprised a central component of rural Norwegian American women's lives. "Here [in America]," wrote Ane Vatne in 1886, "there is no shame attached to a woman's working." That sentiment would have been familiar in Norway and throughout Norwegian American and American communities. Much of women's work existed within a gendered space, and for Norwegian American farm women the assumption was they would continue to contribute their labor to the farm. For farm women, regardless of ethnic heritage, their days often included gathering eggs, churning butter, working in the garden, milking cows, cooking for threshers, hauling water, and, for some, working in the fields and the barn. Like their American sisters, Norwegian American women cooked, cleaned, reared children, sewed clothing, and knit, all considered to be "women's work." Of course, when necessary, some men became adept at "women's work." In the early 1920s, Sigrid Lillehaugen described her widower brother, Knut Nelson, as "a good house mother" who "[had] to cook, bake, wash, and iron." According to Lillehaugen, her brother "[did] everything real well just like many women."[8]

On Norwegian American farms, women's unpaid and paid labor played an important economic role beyond the initial settlement period. In this way, Norwegian American farm women and their daughters had much in common with farm women from other backgrounds. Married farm women experienced days filled with work, both in their homes and outdoors. In late 1880s Wisconsin, Randi Rued, newly arrived in the United States, explained to her family in Norway that "around here wives do the housekeeping without hired girls," which differed from many Norwegian farms, where farm women often employed servants. Rued kept busy with housework, food preparation, barn chores and milking, care for the chickens, and spinning, sometimes for pay. Wisconsin newlywed Jonelle Johnson Arntson "found herself helping with all the work as did most of the pioneer women of that day," wrote her daughter, "cows and chickens, butter to make, garden to tend, endless tasks of sewing by hand, babies to raise and hundred[s] of household duties." For other farm women, however, their labor shifted away from the barns and fields. Kari Bjøkne's work consisted of "taking care of the house and caring for little Hendry [sic]." The tasks that most occupied her Norwegian friend's day, spinning and livestock chores, were "those that we don't much do here in America," Bjøkne explained. Norwegian immigrant farm women clearly labored in a variety of ways to support the household, and for many women that included work in the barns.[9]

The idea of women as agricultural laborers came with the immigrants from Norway, and, despite challenges, this gender ideology remained strong in the United States. In Norway, women were responsible for all facets of dairying, including milking, cleaning the barns, and doing cattle chores. Both men and women accepted female agricultural labor. In the period of the mass emigration from Norway after 1865, however, American agriculture transitioned toward male labor as farm families increasingly produced for the market. Despite these changes in American agricultural production, Norwegian immigrant women, and in many cases their daughters, continued to provide agricultural labor beyond butter production and poultry care, especially in their earliest years in the United States and west of the Mississippi River. In Wisconsin, even though some Norwegian immigrant men

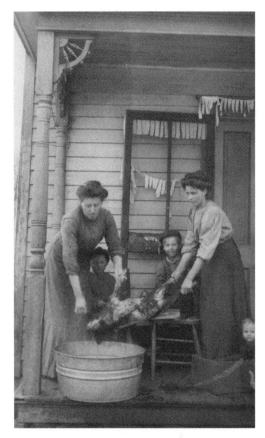

Women butchering a pig near the heavily Norwegian American town of Echo, Minnesota, ca. 1915

took over the barn and milking chores, Norwegian immigrant and Norwegian American women continued to milk cows. One woman who immigrated in 1866 insisted on milking and caring for "her calves," just as twenty years later, Randi Rued milked cows. The movement away from milking was more pronounced in the second generation. While Bell Flamoe Hanson continued her defined role as supervisor of the dairying operation, her daughter Palma, who was born in Idaho, "never learned to milk a cow."[10]

Class certainly influenced the labor patterns of Norwegian American women living in the countryside, and not all rural women were farm women. Elisabeth Koren resided in rural Iowa in the 1850s; her life demonstrates how class affected women's work. The wife of a Norwegian minister and a member of the Norwegian upper class, she lived first in the homes of others and in a small cabin prior to construction of the parsonage. She focused on creating a proper home for her family. At one point before moving into the parsonage, Koren took a stroll around the farm on which she and her husband stayed, knitting as she walked. During the walk, she stopped and "watched Guri [the farm woman] milk and tend her cows." As she reflected on the day, she imagined herself as an elderly woman taking a similar stroll around the parsonage's land, "knitting and looking after her property." Koren's use of "her cows" represents the extent to which women and cattle were linked in Norway. She obviously considered milking the proper work for Norwegian American farm women, but not for her. These classed expectations and what constituted proper work for Koren and for the neighboring women of peasant backgrounds can be found throughout the diary.[11]

Although crop production often took precedence on family farms, rural women's historians have long recognized the importance of the production of butter and the sale of eggs to the family economy in frontier and rural communities. Throughout the United States, Norwegian American women sold butter and eggs. As in American farming communities, the resulting money served as a key source of cash. Additionally, women and men traded these products for store goods, such as sugar, coffee, and cloth.[12]

Women also supported the household economy in other ways. In frontier and early settlement communities, Norwegian American women generated income by doing laundry, baking bread, and sewing for the many unmarried men. Farm women, however, did not limit selling their products to bachelors. In her early years as a young wife, Carrie Lien Sneve worked in domestic positions on the farms where her husband was a laborer. After the family settled permanently at Big Bear Ridge, Idaho, Sneve sewed clothing for others, although, she conceded, the pay was poor. In North Dakota, Anne Bjorlie sewed for herself and for others. Over the course of a year, she saved six dollars by sewing and selling butter, and she used a portion of the money to purchase fabric for a new calico dress.[13]

The purchase of a sewing machine was very important for many Norwegian American women. Indeed, one woman referred to her foster mother's sewing machine as "Mama's choicest possession." In the mid-1880s, one savvy saloon owner in North Dakota recognized this and catered to both men and women. In addition to selling liquor for male customers, he sold sewing machines for female customers. A Wisconsin woman used an inheritance from her parents' deaths in Norway to purchase a sewing machine, while a North Dakota woman hand-stitched and sold quilts to buy one. When Sara Retrum and her husband Ole purchased the family's first sewing machine, women from their Minnesota community dropped in to use it, which may have fostered informal community networks and certainly provided an opportunity for women to work and socialize. Although women typically sewed clothing for the family, in Wisconsin, Amund Flaten, who worked as a tailor prior to immigration, made the family's clothing, while his wife Johanna created the woolen and linen fabrics. Flaten was an exception in this regard, but he demonstrates that families negotiated the division of labor in ways that worked best for them, that labor could be flexible to meet household needs.[14]

Rural women generated income in other ways, too. In addition to sewn goods, women sold items they knit. Sara Retrum used her knitting skills to earn money, selling stockings for "50c per pair" within her Minnesota community. Enterprising Mary Hagan Lee brought stockings she knit into Valley City, North Dakota, and the Parkhouse store sold them. Thus, she sold her knitwear beyond her immediate community. Her products acquired a wider market, which potentially netted Lee more income. In Idaho, one Norwegian American woman traded deer hides for additional income. According to her son, she often invited Native Americans for dinner and personally negotiated the price of the deer hides. In this way, she brought cash into the household. The income Norwegian American farm women generated not only enabled their families to acquire goods in town: in lean years it may have kept the farm in operation. Of course, farm women sewed, knit, baked, and laundered for their own families. When a woman made her family's clothing, for example, those items did not have to be purchased. In this way, Norwegian American women produced products that allowed cash to be spent on other things.[15]

Nicoline Kildahl's experience in rural Minnesota highlights the importance of these female-generated farm revenue streams in the late 1860s and 1870s. Kildahl worked the farm with her sons because her husband taught school. His pay was considered the family's primary source of income. To enhance the family's economic position, the Kildahls sold the farm with plans to move to western Minnesota and acquire another farm. Her husband's subsequent health problems and his inability to teach rendered Kildahl the family's "breadwinner." The family stayed in southeastern Minnesota, and Kildahl made and sold baskets, clothing, and cloth shoes. After crops had been harvested, farmers employed her to glean fields, which provided the family with flour and feed for livestock. One son recalled, however, that the birth of the youngest son "interfered severely" with Kildahl's ability to generate income for the family. For the Kildahls, sewing and basket weaving produced essential income. For other Norwegian American farm families, this income came from the butter women churned, the eggs they gathered, and the stockings they knit. The Kildahls' story may be extreme, but it highlights the importance of income generated from products women produced and points to the importance of women's flexible labor on family farms.[16]

Nicoline Kildahl's experiences on the farm also illuminate an often overlooked component of farm women's labor: women's farm management. Women,

Carrie and Olga Stene, "cookees," inside logging camp cook shack, John Masten Camp, Beltrami County, Minnesota, c. 1917

like Anne Bjorlie in North Dakota and Randi Rued in Wisconsin, managed farms when their husbands secured temporary employment off the farm. Likewise, near Deary, Idaho, Christine Knutson Asplund operated a farm with her husband. When he sought employment away from the farm, she became responsible for most of the farm work, in addition to rearing twelve children. Both Elise Wærenskjold in Texas and Gro Svendsen in Iowa operated their family's farm when their husbands served in the Confederate and Union armies, respectively, during the Civil War. In the case of the Raaen family in northern Dakota Territory, Ragnild Raaen ran the farm, for the most part, because of her husband's struggles with alcoholism. A husband did not have to be physically away from the farm for work to fall on his wife and children.[17]

Other women became permanent farm managers, typically when their husbands died. In Texas, Christine Dahl served as a temporary manager when her husband recruited emigrants in Norway in 1872. During his absence, Dahl corresponded with him about developments on their Texas farm. She informed him that the plowing had been completed, on the price of wheat, that the wheat fields looked good and the corn harvest had been successful, and that all was well on the farm. Not long after her husband returned from Norway, he passed away. As a widow, Dahl managed the farm. In subsequent letters to her family in Norway, she provided extensive detail on farm production. Moreover, her choice of words implies that she made decisions on the farm. For example, in 1875 she wrote, "I have also planted some cotton this year" and one of "my best horses" died. She also "gave" her eldest son some land after he married. Dahl controlled the farm resources, and she further helped her eldest son start farming by giving him mules. After that, she began to write about "we" and "our" farm. O. O. Rossing visited the Dahl family in late 1880, and he obviously respected Dahl's capable management of the farm. Rossing referred to her as "Madame Dahl," and he boasted of her success as a farmer: "She has 30 horses, 80 cows, 12 hogs, and of these 6 fattened hogs."[18]

Despite their important roles on family farms, Norwegian American women are rarely credited in early official pioneer histories except to acknowledge that they married a farmer. Of course, some exceptions exist. Benedick Rekdahl's biographic sketch in the 1903 *Illustrated History of North Idaho*—in which leading citizens of the region are profiled—alludes to Martha Rekdahl's participation on the family's farm. Not surprisingly, few profiles reference women, other than whom they married. Such is the case for Martha. Benedick, an early Latah County settler, was deceased at the time of the book's publication. After listing contributions Benedick made to Latah County, the author wrote of Martha: "the widow has nobly taken up the burdens of life and the added responsibilities and has demonstrated her ability to handle them in a commendable matter." The compilers may have found her management of the farm more acceptable because she was a widow.[19]

Norwegian American women become more visible when their children write about life on the frontier and in early settlement-era communities, in later county or local histories, or in projects designed to recover women's narratives, such as the Pioneer Mothers in North Dakota or the Pioneer Daughters in South Dakota, both carried out by the General Federation of Women's Clubs. In *The Long and Happy Life of Mrs. Peeleyant: An Autobiography,* Elizabeth Ronning Solberg recounts her childhood growing up on a farm in central Minnesota in the early twentieth century. In her account, she described her mother (Johanna Johnson) as the "farm overseer" once her father became ill. While a hired man provided important farm labor, Solberg's mother managed the farm and increasingly worked outside doing chores after her father died, including "cleaning the barn."[20]

Although relatively few Norwegian American farm women managed farms, they routinely employed and supervised hired girls. In Texas, Elise Wærenskjold regularly hired girls to help on the family's farm, doing both agricultural and domestic work. These hired girls were not always Norwegian or Scandinavian. In 1868, Wærenskjold lost a German girl who had worked for her for a number of years. For a few months of the year, when "milking was heaviest," she hired African American women to assist her with her chores. Hired girls were often in short supply in farming communities, in large part because of other job opportunities in towns, cities, and urban areas. Thus, it could be difficult to hire a girl.[21]

Employment opportunities existed for young women on farms and in rural towns and small cities, largely as hired girls or domestics. At some point in their lives, many single, Norwegian American women worked as servants, an extension of a cultural system brought from Norway. The importance of domestic service for Norwegian American girls and young women cannot be overstated. In 1900, 64 percent of first-generation Norwegian American women worked in the domestic services, as did roughly 57 percent of the second generation. These numbers were down from earlier decades when approximately 82 percent of first-generation Norwegian and Swedish women worked as domestics in 1880 and 80 percent in 1890. In a study that looked at women employed as domestics comparatively, only immigrant women from Central Europe worked in domestic services at a higher rate than Scandinavian women in 1900. Although many Norwegian American girls hired out after their confirmation, around age fourteen or fifteen, others needed to help contribute to the family income before that time. These young girls typically babysat or did household chores. Young girls like Hilda Jongren did not show up in the census as servants, which under-represents the extent to which Norwegian American women and girls received compensation for their domestic labor. Jongren, an American-born girl of Norwegian and Swedish parentage, first hired out at age eleven, but in her seventies she "wonder[ed] what an 11 year old could do." She had worked for neighbors, usually caring for children after women gave birth. Most hired girls were older. New Wisconsinite Jannicke Sæhle, formerly of Bergen, worked as a hired girl for a Norwegian immigrant family in the late 1840s. Her compensation reflected a rural orientation. In exchange for her labor, she acquired the right to the proceeds from three acres of land for three years. Winter wheat grew on the acreage, and a successful harvest meant that Sæhle would start fulfilling her American dream of economic success. Her wages appear to be atypical; most hired girls received cash wages, room, and board or cash wages if they lived in the immediate vicinity.[22]

Working as servants on farms or in town became a job option for Norwegian American women and girls, but not all parents wanted their daughters to hire out. For example, the Olesons, who settled in Wisconsin, had been farm owners in Norway. Thorild and Mathis Oleson sold their farm and emigrated in 1866. Life in America challenged them initially. In order to contribute to the household, their oldest daughter (age seventeen) decided to hire out as a servant. The classed expectation of these Norwegian farmers was obvious. A younger daughter indicated "it nearly killed Mother and Father to think of their daughter working as a servant." She was apparently the first in the family to hold such a position, but, in succession, the younger daughters hired out. According to Thurine Oleson, her parents' position was not unusual among more affluent Norwegian Americans. Oleson believed that both affluent Norwegian Americans

Millinery Department, Rossing Department Store, Argyle, Wisconsin, ca. 1907. Helena (Mrs. Lars A.) Rossing (standing), an immigrant from Norway, managed the millinery department, and her daughter, Viola, seated extreme right, worked there.

and Yankees "looked down on the girls who worked out." She also thought this attitude put the daughters of those same affluent Norwegian Americans at a disadvantage because they "kept house in their same old-fashioned ways," whereas the girls who hired out learned more modern, American practices. While some families may have objected to their daughters working as hired girls on farms or in small towns, these same daughters often hired out, as was the case in the Oleson family.[23]

While many Norwegian women worked as domestics for Norwegian American employers, especially in their earliest years in America, others sought to work for old-stock Americans. Some women believed that by working for Americans, they could most effectively learn English and American customs. Others noted that Americans typically paid better wages than Norwegians did, and some asserted that the work responsibilities were less demanding on American farms. In Illinois, Bertina Serina Kingestad initially worked as a domestic for a Norwegian American farmer in 1886, but by 1889 she hired out to an American. Kingestad encouraged her sister to emigrate by focusing on the fact that in America women were responsible for the home and not for the fields and animals. According to Kingestad, "I feel really sorry for [sister Soffia] having to work in that ugly barn . . . in big wooden shoes and shovel manure and go out into the fields . . . and do all kinds of hard work." By this time Kingestad no longer milked the cows nor did much work outside. Her tasks were largely confined to the house, which included collecting eggs, although she continued to feed the livestock.[24]

Farm labor (paid and unpaid) was not the only way women participated in the rural economy. Norwegian American women who migrated to towns and small cities tied to agricultural communities typically found jobs that were in some way connected to the domestic sphere. While on the farm the so-called female and male spheres could become blurred easily; the boundaries were often sharper in cities and towns. Women typically worked as servants/house-keepers, as laundresses, in hotels and boardinghouses, as dressmakers or mil-liners, as small business owners (boardinghouses, restaurants, millineries), and as teachers. These expanded opportunities led some women to encourage young Norwegian girls to migrate to the small rural towns that dotted farming regions. Moreover, these women believed better working conditions existed in cities and towns than on farms and that the pay could be significantly higher in town. One South Dakota woman used both of these arguments in 1892. From Lake Preston, Eline Storaasen asserted that not only was the work "easier and better for a girl" in the United States but that higher wages in town, especially for girls who were "good and fast" workers, made working in town a better option. In a study of three rural, western Minnesota towns with sizeable Norwegian American popu-lations, historian Odd S. Lovoll found that more Norwegian American women resided in towns than on farms, which created a sex-ratio imbalance in the coun-tryside. In North Dakota, Anton Olsen complained about this imbalance. He described a situation in which so "few women" resided in the area that the mar-riage prospects for men were greatly diminished and the women who did live in the community were "stuck-up." Olsen undoubtedly expressed the sentiments of many Norwegian American men when he wrote that the Bottineau area needed more women. This was, of course, a common lament in frontier regions.[25]

In rural towns and small cities, Norwegian American women held a variety of occupations, most frequently as domestics in private homes but also providing domestic labor in restaurants, hotels, and hospitals, among others. For Norwegian immigrant women newly arrived, working in a hotel or boardinghouse enabled them to begin earning an income. "Newcomer" girls often worked in the Palace Hotel in Cooperstown, North Dakota, and most "newcomer" girls to the area came from Norway. Likewise, Johanne Hedemark worked in a "Norwegian" hotel in Lisbon shortly after she arrived in northern Dakota Territory in the 1880s. In South Dakota, both Laura Abrahamson, who emigrated as a young child, and Ingeborg Bergeim, in the United States for nearly four years, worked in Fort Pierre hotels in the late nineteenth century. In Abrahamson's case, she moved back and forth between a job in a hotel and her parents' ranch, where she also labored. After migrating to the United States, Anna Raa and Else Raa worked in an Albert Lea, Minnesota, boardinghouse.[26]

Some Norwegian American women in rural towns and small cities became business owners. The Gilbertson sisters owned and operated a millinery shop in Ellsworth, Minnesota, which they advertised as a "fancy millinery" with "everything up to date." Thus, their fashionable clientele in far southwestern Minnesota could purchase the same hats that their sisters in Minneapolis and St. Paul (the Twin Cities) wore, or they could buy ribbons and notions, which also came from the Cities, for their own designs. The Thompson sisters ran their millinery shop in northwestern Minnesota (Thief River Falls), as did Gustie Johnson and Bell Remmen. Christianna Brandly and Mina Westbye worked as photographers in Hanska, Minnesota, and operated their own studios in the early twentieth century. For some single women, business ownership in rural towns provided them with acceptable career options outside of teaching.[27]

Married women, too, owned businesses. In Idaho, Martin and Gertrude Poyeson owned and operated a boardinghouse, although the census taker listed Martin as the "boarding house keeper." In addition to seven boarders, a Norwegian-born female servant, and Gertrude's mother, all five of the Poyeson children resided at the boardinghouse. The very nature of operating a boardinghouse placed additional responsibilities on women. The women cooked, cleaned, and washed the linens. "Even when a man owned the house or headed the household," asserts historian Wendy Gamber, "the work of boarding fell to women." Ultimately, the success of the boardinghouse hinged on the skill with which the women completed their domestic tasks. Gendered notions of work and proprietorship influenced how census takers recorded occupational status. Thus, Martin Poyeson became the business owner, while Gertrude appears not to be gainfully employed. Yet, the person who truly ensured the boardinghouse functioned was Gertrude Poyeson.[28]

The primary professional occupation open to women between 1840 and 1920 was that of schoolteacher. In the country, in towns, and in small cities, women taught school. Rural schools provided Norwegian American women (especially second and third generation) with the opportunity to start their teaching careers, often in their own or in a neighboring community. In her autobiographical account of growing up in early settlement-era North Dakota, Aagot Raaen described her strong desire to attain an education, the struggles she endured for that education, and her ultimate success as a teacher. Like Raaen, sisters Synneve, Anna, and Bertha Nertrost taught school in North Dakota. Bertha began teaching school at age sixteen, which violated North Dakota law but was a widespread practice in rural areas with a shortage of teachers. A number of the American-born Netteland children from Minnesota went on to become teachers, as did the Lillehaugen daughters in North Dakota and two of the Skatteboe sisters in Moscow, Idaho. Although most Norwegian American women who taught were single, some, like Sophie Noderhus Boe, were married. In North Dakota, Boe often taught terms of school in a Norwegian American community in the early 1890s. Not only was Boe married, she also had a young daughter.[29]

By 1880, the feminization of the teaching profession had occurred. In 1888 when Anne Bjorlie informed her parents that a woman teacher originally from Telemark earned thirty-five dollars per month for teaching school in Nelson County, unsaid was that in most cases women teachers in North Dakota earned less than their male counterparts. For example, in 1890, the average male teacher's salary in North Dakota was $42.33 per month, while women averaged $34.34. Rural teachers earned less than those who taught in city schools, and teachers' salaries also lagged behind other occupational pay. Because of the low pay and short school terms, many rural educators, both female and male, taught in a number of school districts throughout the year. In 1904, Sarah Borreson taught in one North Dakota school, and once that school closed she began a new term in another. Pupils in both of these schools were largely Norwegian American, as was Borreson.[30]

In addition to teaching in American public schools, Norwegian American women and men had an opportunity to teach in church-sponsored parochial schools (Norwegian school)—something that was not possible for women in Norway. In the United States, Norwegian Lutheran congregations frequently established parochial schools because parents wanted their children to receive an education similar to what existed in Norway. This desire to preserve Norwegian language and culture created opportunities for Norwegian American women that would not have been available in Norway. Additionally, through Norwegian parochial schools, women exerted their religious influence on Norwegian American children. In North Dakota, women served on the committees that organized the schools in the first decades of the 1900s and some Ladies Aids funded these schools. Women also became parochial teachers. Perhaps the first was Sigrid Tufte Eielsen, married to Reverend Elling Eielsen of the Haugean Synod, who taught in Chicago in the early 1870s. While women taught in Norwegian parochial schools, in some Norwegian American communities only men served in such capacity. Initially, seminary students and other men conducted the Norwegian parochial schools. By the late nineteenth and early twentieth centuries, however, women parochial teachers had become more

Parochial school with a woman teacher, Bergen, North Dakota, 1910s

common. In Moscow, Idaho, the parochial school met for six weeks during the summer, and for a number of years, Dorthea Dahl, a future noted Norwegian American author, taught her congregation's youth. In the 1910s, Clara and Selma Lillehaugen taught sessions of Norwegian school and English school in North Dakota. In fact, even married women could teach Norwegian school. Though Sigrid Tufte Eielsen was a minister's wife, in the late nineteenth century, farm woman Martha Lima also taught Norwegian parochial school in North Dakota after she married, but before she started having children.[31]

The Lutheran Church, the Ladies Aid, and Community Life

In America, women helped build and shape new Norwegian American communities. These communities assisted immigrant women and men in the transition to life in the United States, although gender proscribed many of the ways in which they could participate. The Norwegian Lutheran Church and the Ladies Aid both functioned as gendered realms—one masculine and one feminine. Ideals on masculine and feminine spaces influenced women's participation in community events and activities. These same ideals, however, also created the opportunity for women to extend their influence to a public space, especially through the Ladies Aid, and shape other social activities in Norwegian American communities.

For many Norwegian American women, the Lutheran church became the center of their community. The purpose of the Lutheran church changed in America as it fulfilled many functions, not just a religious one. The Lutheran church not only played an important role in the everyday lives of Norwegians who immigrated to the United States but, once established in America, the church also acted as preserver of Norwegian culture. Of course, Norwegian immigrants belonged to other denominations, but many retained ties to the Lutheran church. According to scholar Einar Haugen, "To them [Norwegian immigrants,] it [the Norwegian American Lutheran church] was a social as well as a religious center, providing a meeting place where people could discuss crops, politics, and the latest gossip, where they could trade horses and swap stories." He added, "In this country the church socials and the basket suppers, the *lutefisk* dinners and the ladies' aid societies fulfilled the immigrants' need to meet and to mate, to make friends of those who are of their own kind and spoke their own language."[32]

As Norwegian immigrants and Norwegian Americans established settlements, they often organized a Lutheran congregation. For those who sought to retain ties with the Norwegian Lutheran Church, hiring a minister could be problematic. Because the Norwegian settlements in Texas were relatively small and somewhat dispersed, these communities often experienced difficulty securing ministers for their congregations. Elise Wærenskjold referred to this situation as a "serious drawback" and noted "most of the time [the communities] have lacked a Norwegian-Lutheran pastor." Even in areas more densely populated with Norwegian Americans, establishing a congregation and hiring a minister could be challenging. When congregations successfully called a pastor, he might very well serve two, three, or more congregations. For example, in 1883, Realf Ottesen Brandt became the pastor of five congregations in eastern South Dakota. For many Norwegian Americans, ministers provided periodic preaching, which increased the importance of the congregation's members. Laypeople had to take responsibility for many of the spiritual needs of the congregation. Also, in the United States members of the congregation supported the minister and the church financially, whereas in Norway the Lutheran church was the state church. The independence of religious institutions in America greatly facilitated the expansion of female participation within the church.[33]

When Lutheran congregations celebrated the anniversaries of their establishment, they generally wrote accounts that highlighted the roles men played organizing the congregation, because men created and signed the constitutions as well as represented the official congregation. Men, however, were not always the ones responsible for organizing the church. In Hanska, Minnesota, the Zion Lutheran Church congregation formed in 1903, but the Ladies Aid had been established in 1901. Indeed, the purpose for organizing the aid was to raise money "to establish a church in Hanska." The women began serving dinners to the wider community to reach their goal. Members of the aid cooked at home and brought the food to Nundahl's Hall; they also sold items at bazaars. Their hard work paid off. The women helped pay for the building site, and in 1904 construction began on the church. On Christmas Day 1905, parishioners gathered for the first time in the new church for services. The women then managed to pay off the church's debt. Norwegian American women played a central role in the creation of their churches, even if they are not always featured as prominently as the women from Zion. Other churches undoubtedly followed Zion's establishment pattern. In a study of Ladies Aid societies in North Dakota, Erik Luther Williamson found that 15 percent of the Ladies Aid societies predated their congregations. Some of these societies may have been the driving force behind the establishment of a congregation in the same way the women of Zion were.[34]

Once established, internal dissention plagued many congregations. Debates over the church hierarchy, the role of ministers, and the definition of salvation divided Norwegian American communities throughout the United States. L. DeAne Lagerquist perhaps sums it up best: "Norwegian Lutherans' propensity to discuss, disagree, and divide was proverbial." Norwegian Lutheran church schisms occurred regularly, which created Norwegian American communities that could have a number of Lutheran churches belonging to different synods. In most cases when individual congregations split, the resulting churches joined one of the many Norwegian Lutheran synods. In 1881, the Lake Hanska Lutheran Church in Minnesota experienced one of these splits. The congregation disagreed on the location for the new church building, or what one member described as "strictly local matters." In this case, those who left the church organized a new congregation (the Nora Church), and one year later called a Norwegian Unitarian minister, Kristofer Janson, to serve. It appears the congregation's women most strongly supported affiliating with the Unitarian Church. In some ways, Norwegian American women in the congregation had many of the same experiences as their sisters in Lutheran congregations, especially with regard to the Nora Women's Society. One very discernable difference exists, however: from its founding, women in the Nora Church possessed full voting and membership rights. In fact, in the early twentieth century, a woman served as vice foreman of the church council and one man belonged to the Women's Society. The Nora Church was certainly not typical of those established in Norwegian American communities, but it serves as a reminder that communities did exist where women could participate fully within their church.[35]

Gender defined the ways in which women and men participated in Norwegian American Lutheran churches, and it limited opportunities for women to serve in official capacities in most congregations. Congregations typically restricted membership to men. In 1901, the Lake Hanska Lutheran Church boasted a congregation of 577, but a mere 147 could vote because voting rights existed only for adult men. In his study of Ladies Aid societies in North Dakota, Erik Williamson also looked at church constitutions to determine the membership status of women in their congregations. In North Dakota, a few churches had constitutions that did not designate men as voting members, although Williamson asserts that these constitutions "assumed" men would hold the elected positions. Most churches limited voting rights to men, which required male members to change constitutions to allow for female membership and voting rights. It was not until 1895 that the first Lutheran church in North Dakota granted women explicit voting rights, and this congregation was an exception. In some churches, women acquired voting rights rather quickly once the issue was raised. In 1912, the High Prairie Congregation in southeastern North Dakota first discussed granting voting rights to women in the congregation. While the proposal went down to defeat, it again came before the male members of the congregation at the 1915 annual meeting. The following year, church members' sons who had reached the age of twenty-one received "full voting privileges." After seven years of effort, in 1919, the women of the High Prairie Congregation obtained church voting rights with near unanimity. By that time, women in other Protestant dominations typically held voting rights. Generally, Norwegian Lutheran churches in North Dakota granted women the right to vote by the 1940s.[36]

Gender influenced other aspects of church life as well, and women's participation almost exclusively took place within the context of domesticity. Even fund-raising activities represented the public extension of the domestic sphere: sewing, knitting, and serving church dinners. The influence of gender extended beyond participation in church governance and church activities, however. Typically, as families entered the church, they separated based on sex: women and young children on one side, men on the other. In the case of the Lake Hanska Lutheran Church in Minnesota, gender even affected baptism: "All mothers carrying boys were first in line, then came those who carried girls."[37]

Between 1840 and 1920, gender framed Norwegian American women's participation in Norwegian Lutheran churches: though women had no official voice in most of these congregations, they could actively participate in church life and support the church financially through the Ladies Aid. The Ladies Aid afforded women the opportunity to meet socially, to renew their faith, to do good works, and to provide financially for the church. While many stories illustrate the essence of Ladies Aid societies, those of three aids (two in a farming community and the other in a small city) highlight some of their general characteristics. Although the aids discussed are in Idaho, a state not often identified as having a significant Norwegian American population, the patterns shown existed on a widespread basis throughout Norwegian America.

The original Ladies Aid of Genesee Valley (Idaho) Lutheran Church, 1891. Johanna Welholt, far right, middle row; Martha Rekdahl, second from left, front row

In 1884, near Genesee, Idaho, the women of Our Savior's Lutheran Church organized a Ladies Aid despite dogmatic differences that divided the Norwegian American community. Initially, the meetings took place every three weeks from about 10:00 AM until after dinner. While the women studied the word of God, discussed mission activity support, sewed, quilted, and determined the minister's salary, the children played and the men engaged in conversations about farming. When the meeting began, the "first cup of coffee [was] poured" and goodies were served; later, everyone enjoyed a noon meal. Carding wool, with the able assistance of the men, and spinning the wool into yarn also occupied the women at Ladies Aid. In rural communities, it was not uncommon for the Ladies Aid meeting to become a social event for the entire family. At the nearby Lebanon Lutheran Church, organized by members who had earlier split from Our Savior's, women created their Ladies Aid in 1889. Their stated purpose for organizing: "to earn the minister's salary and contribute to mission support."[38]

In Moscow, Idaho, the First Norwegian Evangelical Lutheran Church (also called Our Savior's Lutheran Church) held its organizational meeting in 1901. That same year, "a few women of Norwegian extraction and Lutheran faith" organized the Norwegian Lutheran Church's Ladies Aid. The women organizers held that first meeting at Mrs. John Bue's home and deemed the reason for organizing as "to help establish and maintain Our Savior's Lutheran Church." The women conducted Ladies Aid meetings in Norwegian on Monday afternoons, every other week. The women selected a meeting time that enabled the minister to attend because he came by horse from Genesee. The minister held services on Sunday and then met with the Ladies Aid on Monday. At meetings, the women strengthened their faith with song, prayer, and Bible study. The meetings, however, provided opportunities for women other than spiritual renewal. Conducting the business of the organization took on an added dimension because of the financial contributions the group made to the congregation. Sewing and quilting became mainstays of the meetings. The women sewed and quilted items for missions around the world; for relief work, probably of a more local nature; and for the annual fall bazaar, a fund-raiser.[39]

One of the primary responsibilities of the Ladies Aid involved raising money to support the church. To that end, women commonly held fund-raisers. The first fund-raiser sponsored by the Ladies Aid at the First Norwegian Evangelical Church (Our Savior's Lutheran Church) in Moscow was a *lutefisk* dinner at Mrs. John Bue's home. The women prepared and served a "traditional" Norwegian dinner which included: lutefisk (dried cod reconstituted in a lye mixture), *lefse* (much like a tortilla in appearance, but typically made with potatoes and usually eaten with butter and sugar), potatoes, vegetables, *flatbrød* (flatbread), *primost* (a spreadable, somewhat sweet cheese), blood sausage, *krumkake* (delicate cone-shaped wafers), *fattigmann* (poor man's cookies), and *sandbakkler* (sand tarts), among other tasty items. Though more than sixty people purchased the meal at thirty-five cents per plate, the dinner was so popular that many who arrived could not be served. Because of the initial success, the lutefisk dinner became an annual event.[40]

The financial contributions made by Ladies Aid societies were not trivial. Money raised by the Highland Ladies Aid of Brandt, South Dakota, helped build and furnish the church. Members of the congregation could also borrow money from the aid. In Brookings, South Dakota, the First Lutheran Ladies Aid paid down the church's debt. The High Prairie Ladies Aid in rural North Dakota sewed items for auctions, which provided their only revenue, since apparently no dues were collected and the women did not take an offering for meals served at the aid. They used the income generated by their sewing to fund the parochial school and support mission work. Eventually, the women served a lunch and charged ten cents for it. In time, the parents and later the congregation took care of the parochial school costs, so the women channeled revenue to mission work, especially in Madagascar.[41]

The women of the Rock Valle Lutheran Church in western Minnesota demonstrate the extent to which women played essential roles within their congregations. Between 1888 and 1920, monies generated by the Ladies Aid not only purchased items such as the bell, carpeting, and chairs for the church; they helped a long list of charities that included the local Norwegian parochial school, local people who were in need, orphans' homes, hospitals, missions in Minneapolis, the Bethany Indian Mission, and foreign mission activities. Records, though incomplete, show the women raised more than $8,000 over the thirty-two-year span, and from 1902 to 1912 they donated nearly $2,000 to charities, of more than $2,400 raised. After the creation of a formal budget in 1919, the aid gave "two-thirds of its money annually to the congregation" in support of the church budget. Not only did the women send money to different charitable organizations; they also gave food and clothing to these groups.[42]

While the common perception exists of Ladies Aid groups providing an opportunity for social interaction within the context of religious enrichment, it neglects the important function of the Ladies Aid within the church. Frequently, the Ladies Aid financially supported the church and minister, and through their financial contributions, Norwegian American women exerted influence. The histories of Ladies Aid societies reveal that these women raised considerable amounts of money, often in somewhat difficult economic circumstances, for the benefit of their congregations, charities, and mission work. The Ladies Aid also enabled churchwomen to take on public leadership roles when in all likelihood their congregations prevented them from participating in the governing and decision making of the church.

In addition to their work in the Ladies Aid, Norwegian American women participated in other community activities, and in many ways gender framed the nature of their participation. Indeed, it was often women's domestic skills that made community activities and events possible. When Norwegian Americans gathered socially to celebrate events, especially weddings, women cooked, cleaned, brewed beer, and sewed in preparation for the event. In times like these, the exchange of labor and the sharing of resources became important. Weddings also represent efforts to retain Norwegian cultural traditions as well as the acculturation of Norwegian Americans. Some Norwegian immigrants held to the tradition of hosting large wedding parties like those celebrated by well-to-do farmers in Norway. Other couples opted for small weddings at home with few guests or a ceremony before a justice of the peace.[43]

The large weddings depended on the abilities of women. In 1880, Johanna Wroolie married Chris Weholt in southern Minnesota. As in Norway, the wedding was announced three times in church. Wroolie's mother baked, cooked, and brewed beer, and guests danced "all night." When Ane Vatne married near Cooperstown, North Dakota, in 1889, more than a hundred "Norwegians" attended the celebration. Vatne served veal for dinner and cold cuts for supper. Although the meal consisted of a variety of foods, they were foods unfamiliar to her family in Norway and Vatne did not know how to describe them. She also emphasized that guests feasted on grapes between dinner and supper, again, something not common in rural, Norwegian, peasant communities. A few years later, Vatne's brother, Ole Lima, married. Vatne did the cooking and baking, and the meal consisted largely of American foods. According to Martha Lima (Ole's bride), "To be sure we had neither '*lefse*' nor '*gome*,' but many fine cakes, fruit, and baked spare ribs, and mutton, and many other things." At the time, Martha and Ole lived with the Vatnes, and Vatne also sewed Martha's dress. Christine Dahl estimated that 350 people attended her daughter Martha's 1880 wedding dinner in Texas, many of them staying for festivities in the evening and the following day. In Lac qui Parle County, Minnesota, wedding guests attended a morning ceremony followed by dinner and lunch. Whether a wedding included a dance varied, but when the celebration did so, guests frequently "danced till morning." In some Norwegian American communities, hosts served alcohol to guests, adding to the festivities, and interestingly, in North Dakota this custom continued in some locales even after the state became dry in 1890.[44]

As Todd Nichol explains, these large, community weddings, typical in Norway, were not necessarily continued in America. Consequently, in America the tradition of the large, festive wedding celebration coexisted with much smaller, more intimate events. For example in late 1880s Wisconsin, Barbro Ramseth commented that the "custom" in the United States was not to have a wedding (referring to a public celebration) "unless one absolutely wants to." Ramseth's daughter, Karen, followed this new "custom," and Ramseth seems to make the most of the occasion by remarking that the private marriage "was very ceremonious and quiet and pleasant." North Dakotan Inger Thu Herigstad recalled that weddings became "quiet affairs and not like the weddings of Norway." Herigstad lived in the same community as the Vatnes and Limas; in this one community, both wedding traditions could readily be found.[45]

Weddings were not the only cause for celebration in rural communities. Norwegian Americans near Cooperstown, North Dakota, threw a surprise party for Ane and Andreas Vatne in early 1901. Partygoers presented the couple with a sofa as a gift, in recognition of the Vatnes' tireless devotion to people who were ill or dying. Musicians played and "the entire house rang with music." Near Heimdal, North Dakota, surprise parties were common. In fact, one woman asserted that at some point "every family" should be on the receiving end of a surprise party. Those who attended, as in the case of the party for the Vatnes, brought food and a gift. Sometimes party attendees also danced.[46]

Norwegian Americans also took part in more organized social activities. In 1884, Scandinavians in the Waco, Texas, area celebrated the new year with a masquerade ball. Because it was a leap year, the young women paid for the tickets. Such festivities were not common in all Norwegian American communities

Norwegian community picnic, Wisconsin, ca. 1873

because some Norwegian immigrants objected to such behavior. Dancing was a popular but also a contested activity in Norwegian American communities. Members of the High Prairie Lutheran Church (LaMoure County, North Dakota), for example, opposed drinking, dancing, and gambling. Particularly pious Norwegian Americans objected to dancing, placing it in the same category as drinking excessively. Some ministers used the pulpit to preach against the twin evils of drink and dance. Thurine Oleson recalled that in one Wisconsin community, the church actually split over these issues. Those who objected to the minister's position on drinking and dancing left and formed a new congregation so close that members of the two congregations could "hear each other singing."[47]

The pietism to which some Norwegian Americans adhered precluded drinking, dancing, and playing cards. This pietism celebrated in many Lutheran churches made it easy for Norwegian Americans to embrace the causes of temperance and prohibition. Women and men alike joined such societies, although some groups were all male. In 1850s Texas, Elise Wærenskjold belonged to a temperance society her husband started. The Norwegian American community near Garretson, South Dakota, had an active temperance society in the 1890s in which both men and women held elective office. Although women could not vote in South Dakota in 1896, days before the election one Norwegian American woman extolled the virtues of voting in favor of prohibition candidates to three young men who had just turned twenty-one. She delivered this "advice" at a surprise birthday party for the young men. Another South Dakota woman, Dorthea Dahl, served on the council of Syd Dakotas Afholdsselskab (South Dakota Temperance Society) in 1900. A few North Dakota women demonstrated their opposition to alcohol by attacking two saloons in Hatton in an effort to close them down. Interestingly, this assault occurred just months before the entire state became dry.[48]

The prohibition debate also raised the issues of female suffrage and women's and men's places in American society. The same kinds of chasms that divided American society, generally, on these issues existed in Norwegian America. Near Garretson, South Dakota, a mock legislature composed of men and women voted down female suffrage in early 1897. Thus these young people who largely supported prohibition opposed female suffrage. A 1914 letter from Marie Killy in Minnesota (then past seventy years old) articulates the discussion on female suffrage and prohibition that took place in many Norwegian American communities. According to Killy, "I don't know whether [female suffrage] is good or bad in Dovre [Norway], but the minister says that if women get the right to vote here they will get rid of both the saloons and all the brothels." Indeed, women "would reform all of America." Of course, Killy conceded that women in the United States had not achieved universal suffrage because "men believe that if women get the right to vote, men will have to do women's work and keep house and care for the children." While Killy chuckled at the notion, she also indicated that at her age the issue did not interest her. Killy obviously knew that Norwegian women had secured the franchise in 1913 when she wrote the letter.[49]

Community also existed on a very personal level, and women were typically responsible for remaining connected to family and friends. Visiting was an important component of rural Norwegian American communities, and the letters Norwegian American women wrote back to Norway richly detail visits that took place. Women sometimes sent greetings from visitors to family and friends back in Norway. These visitors were neighbors and family; some made brief visits, while others stayed for months. Shortly after she arrived in Wisconsin in the late 1880s, Randi Rued informed her parents that not only had a number of neighbors visited them; she and her husband had been invited into the homes of their neighbors. At the Oleson home near Winchester, Wisconsin, friends and family stopped by to visit regularly over the years. Thorild Oleson showed guests genuine Norwegian hospitality, which may have included a piece of homemade cheese or a glass of home-brewed beer.[50]

Norwegian American women also engaged in what anthropologist Micaela di Leonardo has referred to as "kin work": maintaining the family connections. America letters often demonstrated the importance of kinship and the maintenance of ties to people from the immigrants' communities in Norway. Women commonly sent greetings from extended family members and other immigrants in their letters. In fact, for children who were born in the United States, women typically noted that the person was the child of someone from the home community in Norway. They also told about people who left the area for opportunities in other communities. To maintain family connections, women hosted family members for holidays and special events. In these ways, Norwegian American women engaged in "kin work."[51]

Conclusion

In 1889, newly arrived Randi Anderson Rued had many hopes and dreams about her life in America. Over the years she had four children, milked cows, cooked and cleaned, attended the Norwegian Lutheran Church, and helped shape the Norwegian American community in Hoard Township. By 1918, the couple owned two hundred acres, which included an eighty-acre woodlot. The farm had been "enlarged and improved" in the years following her husband's immigration, and the couple rebuilt after a devastating tornado in 1905. The Rueds had indeed become successful Norwegian immigrants in America, and Randi played a central role in that process. In this way, she was like so many Norwegian immigrant women.[52]

In Norwegian American communities, gender defined the contexts of women's and men's lives. Rued and other Norwegian American women made important contributions to the household economy, as they had in Norway. Many Norwegian American farm women continued to milk cows and to work outdoors, in addition to myriad chores associated with the house and rearing children. Their work, whether paid or unpaid, typically involved labor that Norwegian American women and men deemed to be women's work. That being said, those traditional, Norwegian agricultural gender roles became less rigid in the United States. Women like Kari Bjøkne stopped working outdoors, and others maintained such labor responsibilities when necessary. To be sure, class also played a role in dictating notions of proper work for women. As Elisabeth Koren demonstrates, although she may have regarded milking cows as being acceptable for women from the Norwegian peasant class, it would not have been suitable work for her. Also as in Norway, female domestic servants worked on farms and in surrounding rural towns. New opportunities existed, too, as

Norwegian American women also filled the ranks of teachers at public schools and Norwegian parochial schools.

In Norwegian American communities women created much of the fabric of social life. The work of women framed wedding celebrations—cooking, cleaning, brewing beer, and sewing. The important "kin work" was also generally considered "women's work," and women maintained familial connections in Norway and in the United States. Women's involvement with the Ladies Aid gave them a say in congregational affairs when many possessed no official voice within the Lutheran church. They used their domestic skills—cooking, sewing, knitting—to raise essential funds for the church. Moreover, they asserted a public presence when they engaged in church fund-raising activities and developed leadership skills. In many ways, it was the women who carried out the actual work of the church.

Notes

1. The author thanks Betty Bergland, Howard Lahlum, Michael Lansing, Leah Rogne, and two anonymous readers for their insightful comments on earlier drafts of this essay.

Randi [Anderson], Curtiss, Wisc., to Dear Parents, 30 Nov. 1889, 1–2, typed manuscript, Oppland folder, Riksarkivet [Norwegian National Archives], Oslo, Norway (hereafter, Riksarkivet). Family members have put translated versions of these letters online. See http://www.cpwhitney.com/RandiRued/, accessed 9 Aug. 2008. I am using my own translations. (All translations in this chapter are mine unless otherwise noted.) The letters are generally signed either Randi Anderson or Mrs. Mattias Anderson; only the last letter (from 1895) is signed Rued. However, the family used *Rued* in the United States. Rued and her husband settled in Clark County, Wisconsin, the cutover region (an area that had originally been logged before it was farmed). Historian Joan Jensen has written elegantly about the area's women and their lives: see *Calling This Place Home: Women on the Wisconsin Frontier, 1850–1920* (St. Paul: Minnesota Historical Society Press [hereafter, MHS Press], 2006).

The woman may have been Matt Rued's sister, and it is unclear whether she received payment for her work. For female labor exchange, see Nancy Grey Osterud, "Gender and the Transition to Capitalism in Rural America," *Agricultural History* 67 (Spring 1993): 23–24; Dorothy Schwieder, "A Tale of Two Grandmothers: Immigration and Family on the Great Plains," *South Dakota History* 31 (Summer 2001): 38–47.

2. The brevity of this essay precludes a discussion on the settlement process and the dispossession of Native American land. For Norwegian American settlement see, among others, Betty A. Bergland, "Norwegian Immigrants and 'Indianerne' in the Landtaking, 1838–1862," in *Norwegian-American Studies,* ed. Odd S. Lovoll (Northfield, MN: Norwegian-American Historical Association [hereafter, NAHA], 2000), 35:319–50; Theodore C. Blegen, *Norwegian Migration to America: The American Transition* (Northfield, MN: NAHA, 1940); Odd S. Lovoll, *The Promise of America: A History of the Norwegian-American People* (Minneapolis: University of Minnesota Press in cooperation with NAHA,

1983); Carlton C. Qualey, *Norwegian Settlement in the United States* (1938; reprint, Arno Press Inc., 1970); Ingrid Semmingsen, *Norway to America: A History of the Migration,* trans. Einar Haugen (Minneapolis: University of Minnesota Press, 1978).

3. Ragnil, Sigri, and Gunild Nicolaisdatter Omland to Tellef Nicolaisen, 18 Nov. 1850, in *Land of Their Choice: The Immigrants Write Home,* ed. Theodore C. Blegen (Minneapolis: University of Minnesota Press, 1955), 267–69. Conevery Bolton Valenčius has discussed the importance of a "healthful place": see *The Health of the Country: How American Settlers Understood Themselves and Their Land* (New York: Basic Books, 2004).

4. Elise Wærenskjold, *The Lady with the Pen: Elise Wærenskjold in Texas,* ed. C. A. Clausen (Northfield, MN: NAHA, 1961), 37: Wærenskjold refers to the widespread practice of running livestock on the open range. Also p89: this letter (believed to have been written in 1869) provides a history of Norwegian settlement in Texas

5. C. A. Clausen, "Introduction," in Wærenskjold, *The Lady with the Pen,* 3–24. Wærenskjold's first husband was the prominent businessman Svend Foyn; they divorced amicably. In Texas, she married Wilhelm Wærenskjold. Elise Wærenskjold to Mr. T. A. Gjestvang, 9 July 1851, Wærenskjold, *The Lady with the Pen,* 28.

6. Karl Rud, Flandreau, SD, to Dear Parents, 12 June 1899, 2, A499, Norwegian Emigration Museum (hereafter, NEM), Ottestad, Norway. Gina Runningen, Odin, Minn., to Marie Thomter, 4 Dec. 1889, 1, A4943, NEM. Four years later, she lived near people "from Lom, Vaage and Sel and Romsdalen . . . and some Americans, Germans, and Swedes." See Gina Runningen, Cedarville, Minn., to Good Marie Tomter, 12 Feb. 1893, 2, typed manuscript, A4944, NEM. Cedarville post office no longer exists; it was not far from Odin. There was a significant Lesja community located around Hanska, Minnesota, not far from where Runningen resided.

Randi [Anderson], Curtiss, Wisc., to Dear Parents and Siblings, 30 May 1889, 1–6, typed manuscript, Oppland folder, Riksarkivet; quotation, p4. In this letter, p4, she compares Wisconsin farmers "plow[ing] between [tree] stubs with Norwegian farmers plow[ing] between stones." Johanna Weholt, "Reminiscences," unpublished manuscript, 17, Day-Northwest Special Collections, University of Idaho, Moscow, ID. Weholt wrote the account in 1938. Eventually she did reside in a non-Norwegian American community.

7. Wærenskjold, *The Lady with the Pen,* 31–34, 72, 129. Johan Moen, Waco, Texas, to unknown, 25 June 1884, 1, typed manuscript, Hedmark File, Riksarkivet.

8. Ane Watne, Watne [near Cooperstown, ND], to Sister Gunnhild, 8 Aug. 1886, 1, P844, NAHA, Northfield, MN. I use the translated version of the Vatne and Lima letters. The name is spelled both *Vatne* and *Watne.* Those who stayed in America typically adopted *Watne,* but Ane and Andreas Vatne returned to Norway in the latter years and used *Vatne.* Sigrid Lillehaugen, *Live Well: The Letters of Sigrid Gjeldaker Lillehaugen,* eds. Theresse Nelson Lundby, Kristie Nelson-Neuhaus, and Ann Nordland Wallace (Minneapolis, MN: Western Home Books, 2004), 122, 116. For a discussion on housework during the period, see Ruth Schwartz Cowan, *More Work for Mother: The Ironies of Household Technology from the Open Hearth to the Microwave* (New York: Basic Books, Inc., 1983); Susan Strasser, *Never Done: A History of American Housework* (New York: Pantheon Books, 1982).

9. Randi [Anderson], 30 May 1889, 1–2. A translation of the Norwegian word *bonde*

to the English farmer is problematic. There was a class status attached to *bonde,* and most peasant women were not married to farmers. For a discussion of *bonde* and farmer, see Lahlum, *Norwegian Women, Landscape, and Agriculture.* Mrs. Nickolais Arntson, 3, Reel 3, Pioneer Mothers Biographies (hereafter, PMB), microfilm, State Historical Society of North Dakota, Bismarck. Kari Bjøkne, no location, to Guro H. Bjøkne, 1, typed manuscript, no date, Oppland folder, Riksarkivet. Kari Bjøkne indicated that she had spun once since she arrived in America. A rich literature on the labor of farm women exists, and I include just a few important works. See, for example, Barbara Handy-Marchello, *Women of the Northern Plains: Gender and Settlement on the Homestead Frontier, 1870–1930* (St. Paul: MHS Press, 2005); Joan Jensen, *Promise to the Land: Essays on Rural Women* (Albuquerque: University of New Mexico Press, 1991); Jane Marie Pederson, *Between Memory and Reality: Family and Community in Rural Wisconsin, 1870–1970* (Madison: University of Wisconsin Press, 1992); Nancy Grey Osterud, *Bonds of Community: The Lives of Farm Women in Nineteenth-Century New York* (Ithaca and London: Cornell University Press, 1991); Glenda Riley, *The Female Frontier: A Comparative View of Women on the Prairie and Plains* (Lawrence: University of Kansas Press, 1988). For immigrant women, see Carol K. Coburn, *Life at Four Corners: Religion, Gender, and Education in a German-Lutheran Community, 1868–1945* (Lawrence: University of Kansas Press, 1992); Jon Gjerde, *From Peasants to Farmers: The Migration from Balestrand, Norway, to the Upper Middle West* (Cambridge, NY: Cambridge University Press, 1985); Jon Gjerde, *The Minds of the West: Ethnocultural Evolution in the Rural Middle West, 1830–1917* (Chapel Hill and London: University of North Carolina Press, 1997); Jensen, *Calling This Place Home,* 90–143; Lori Ann Lahlum, "'Everything Was Changed and Looked Strange': Norwegian Women in South Dakota," *South Dakota History* 35 (Fall 2005): 189–216; Lori Ann Lahlum, *Norwegian Women, Landscape, and Agriculture on the Northern Prairies and Plains, 1850–1920* (Lubbock: Texas Tech University Press, expected 2012); Linda Schelbitzki Pickle, *Contented among Strangers: Rural German-Speaking Women and Their Families in the Nineteenth-Century Midwest* (Urbana and Chicago: University of Illinois Press, 1996).

10. Lahlum, *Norwegian Women, Landscape, and Agriculture,* especially chs. 5 and 6. For the centrality of children's labor on Norwegian American farms, see Gjerde, *From Peasants to Farmers,* 173, 192–98, 210; Gjerde, *The Minds of the West,* 135–58, 171–85, 187–221; Lori Ann Lahlum, "Growing Up in Norwegian-American Communities: A Preliminary Study of Childhood, Adolescence, and Young Adulthood," in *Norwegian-American Essays 2008: "Migration and Memory,"* eds. Øyvind T. Gulliksen and Harry T. Cleven (Oslo: NAHA-Norway, 2008), 110–13.

Pederson, *Between Memory and Reality,* 165–67; Erna Oleson Xan and Thurine Oleson, *Wisconsin My Home* (Madison: University of Wisconsin Press, 1950), 40. Other references to milking exist throughout the remembrance. Erna Xan is the granddaughter of Thorild and Mathis Oleson. She relays the story as told by her mother, Thurine Oleson. Joan Jensen found that immigrant and American-born women in northern Wisconsin milked cows and worked in the fields: see *Calling This Place Home,* 9, 15–16, 21, 26, 90–124. Palma Hanson Hove, interview by Sam Schrager, 13 June 1975, 9–10, typed manuscript, Latah County Museum Oral History Project (hereafter, LCMOHP), Latah County Historical Society, Moscow, ID.

11. *The Diary of Elisabeth Koren, 1853–1855,* trans. and ed. David T. Nelson (Northfield, MN: NAHA, 1955), 261. Class also played a role in Norwegian farm women's labor. Although the wives of well-to-do farmers managed the dairy operation, they generally did not clean the barns or do the milking. Ruth Schwartz Cowan discusses Koren's diary and the "hierarchies" that existed within her world of domestic work. Some work, for example sewing and cooking, had a high status, while laundry and cleaning had a low status. Koren did the high-status chores, but she often hired women or young girls to do the low-status ones. See Cowan, *More Work for Mother,* 30–31.

12. See Handy-Marchello, *Women of the Northern Plains,* 116–41, for a discussion on butter and egg sales in North Dakota. For a discussion on women and the production of butter in Norwegian American communities in North Dakota, South Dakota, Minnesota, and Iowa, see Lahlum, *Norwegian Women, Landscape, and Agriculture,* ch. 6; for South Dakota, see Lahlum, " 'Everything Was Changed and Looked Strange,' " 198–201, 204; for Texas, see Wærenskjold, *The Lady with the Pen,* 72; for Wisconsin, see Xan and Oleson, *My Wisconsin Home,* 72, and Jensen, *Calling This Place Home,* 21. Interestingly, Thurine Oleson described ways in which Norwegian American women tried to sell old butter in the fall by putting newly churned butter on top of butter that stood in jars throughout the summer—butter that was rancid.

13. Nils Jacobsen, 3, Ramsey County, Roll 19, Historical Data Project (HDP), Pioneer Biography Files, 1936–40, microfilm, State Historical Society of North Dakota, Bismarck, ND; Barbara Levorsen, "Early Years in Dakota," *Norwegian-American Studies and Records* 21 (1962): 181; "Story of Pioneer Days—Ida Simpson Kohr," in *Lac qui Parle County Pioneer Stories, 1871–1958,* A Minnesota Statehood Centennial Activity (Lac qui Parle Public Schools, 1958), 11. While Levorsen does not explicitly say that her foster mother received compensation for doing laundry or baking bread for the "bachelor homesteaders," it is reasonable to presume that she did. This account also exists in a full-length memoir: Barbara Levorsen, *The Quiet Conquest: A History of the Lives and Times of the First Settlers of Central North Dakota* (Hawley, MN: The Hawley Herald, 1974).

Gerald Ingle, *Gleanings From Big Bear Ridge* (Moscow, ID: Latah County Historical Society, 1982), 182; Anne Bjorlie, Nelson County, ND, to Hans Jørgensen and Eli Johannesdatter Bjøkne [her parents], Lesja, 19 May 1890, 1, Oppland file, Riksarkivet. Later in the letter Bjorlie mentions selling eggs. It is possible that egg money also made up her savings. For other references to sewing for others, see Anne Bjorlie, Bjorlie [Nelson County, ND], to Dear Parents and siblings, 4 Dec. 1887, 1, Riksarkivet.

14. Levorsen, "Early Years in Dakota," 162; Laurits Larsen Thorstad, Hillsboro, DT, to Johan J. Vangen and Family, 20 June 1884, 2, Oppland folder, Riksarkivet; Randi Anderson, Curtiss [WI], to Dear Brother, 26 Dec. 1895, 2, typed manuscript, Oppland folder, Riksarkivet; Ole Pederson Retrum, "Life of a Pioneer," in *Lac Qui Parle County Pioneer Stories,* 8; "Mrs. Johanna Flaten," 1, Roll 3, PMB.

15. Retrum, "Life of a Pioneer," in *Lac Qui Parle County Pioneer Stories,* 8; Mary Hagan Lee, 2, Barnes County, Roll 1, HDP; Edward Swenson, interview by Sam Schrager, 1 July

1974, 8–10, typed manuscript, LCMOHP; Edward Swenson, interview by Sam Schrager, 2 July 1974, 22–25, typed manuscript, LCMOHP.

16. Harold B. Kildahl, Sr., "Westward We Came: Memoirs of My Youth and Early Manhood as an Immigrant in Minnesota and a Pioneer in Dakota Territory, 1866–1898," rev. and ed. Erling E. Kildahl, typed manuscript, 1991, 22, 29–30, Minnesota Historical Society, St. Paul (hereafter, MHS). The family later operated a boardinghouse in Northfield, Minnesota, before moving to North Dakota and settling near Devils Lake in 1883; see p48, 87. Kildahl also notes that it was his mother who "unrelentingly had sought a farm." Despite all the setbacks, she continued to pursue farm ownership; see p117. A published version of this account now exists: see Harold B. Kildahl, *Westward We Came: A Norwegian Immigrant's Story, 1866–1898,* ed. Erling E. Kildahl (West Lafayette, IN: Purdue University Press, 2008).

17. Anne Bjorlie letter collection; Randi Anderson, 30 Nov. 1889, 1–2; Lahlum, "'Everything Was Changed and Looked Strange,'" 198; Lahlum, *Norwegian Women, Landscape, and Agriculture, passim*; Ann N. Driscoll, *They Came to a Ridge* (Moscow, ID: The News Review Publishing Co., Inc., 1970), 30; Stella E. Johnson, ed. and comp., *History of Troy* (Troy, ID: The editor, 1992), 144–45; Wærenskjold, *The Lady with the Pen;* Pauline Farseth and Theodore C. Blegen, trans. and eds., *Frontier Mother: The Letters of Gro Svendsen* (New York: Arno Press, 1979); Aagot Raaen, *Grass of the Earth: The Story of a Norwegian Immigrant Family in Dakota,* (1950; reprint, St. Paul: MHS Press, 1994), *passim.*

18. Christine Dahl, Bosque, Texas, to Dear Hendrik, 23 July 1872, 1–2, typed manuscript, A5102; Christine Dahl, Dahl [TX], to Dear Loving Husband [Hendrik], 15 Sept. 1872, 1–2, typed manuscript, A5103; Christine [Dahl], Dahl [TX], to Dear Parents and Siblings, 26 Oct. 1875, 2, typed manuscript, A5105; Christine Dahl, Dahl [TX], to Dear Parents and Siblings, 17 Jan. 1876, 2, typed manuscript, A5106, all NEM. See collection of Dahl letters for other references to agriculture. Odd Magnar Syverson writes that Hendrik Dahl went to Norway in 1872 intent upon bringing Norwegian workers to Texas. He arrived back in Texas with seventy-one Norwegians. Dahl also served in the Confederate Army during the Civil War. See Odd Magnar Syverson and Derwood Johnson, *Norge i Texas: Et bidrag til norsk emigrasjonshistorie* (Gjøvik: Gjøvik Bokbinderi A/S, 1982), 115. For references to Dahl's Civil War service, see p104, 267. Dahl letters are located at NEM, Riksarkivet, Statsarkivet i Hamar, and NAHA, and some have been published in Norway. Barbara Levorsen also writes about a widow who managed a family farm in North Dakota after the death of her husband: *The Quiet Conquest,* 89.

O. O. Rossing, Dahl [TX], to Dear Erik and Faster [paternal aunt], 25 Nov. 1880, 1, typed manuscript, Furuset Letters, Hedmark File, Riksarkivet. Another Texas woman, Elise Wærenskjold, also managed the family farm after her husband's murder in 1866: *The Lady With the Pen,* 64–65. For an account on the murder of Wilhelm Wærenskjold, see Charles H. Russell, *Undaunted: A Norwegian Woman in Frontier Texas,* Tarleton State University Southwestern Studies in the Humanities, ed. William T. Pilkington (College Station: Texas A&M University Press, 2006), 122–27. Nils Olav Østrem clarified the translation "fattened hogs" for me.

19. Examples of these official histories are Clement A. Lounsberry, *North Dakota*

History and People: Outlines of American History, 3 vols. (Chicago: The S. J. Clarke Publishing Co., 1917); Doane Robinson, *History of South Dakota Together with Personal Mention of Citizens of South Dakota* ([Logansport, IN?]: B. F. Bowen, 1904), and even county histories such as John W. Mason, *History of Otter Tail County, Minnesota: Its People, Industries, and Institutions: with Biographical Sketches of Representative Citizens and Genealogical Records of Many of the Old Families* (Indianapolis, IN: B. F. Bowen, 1916), and Franklyn Curtiss-Wedge, comp., *History of Clark County Wisconsin* (Chicago and Winona: H. C. Cooper, Jr., and Co., 1918). An exception to this is an early Minnehaha County, South Dakota, history: see Iver I. Oien, H. A. Ustrud, M. G. Opsahl, J. O. Asen, eds., *Pioneer History: Minnehaha County's Norwegian Pioneers, History from the Year 1866 to 1896* (1928; trans. and reprint, Freeman, SD: Pine Hill Press, 1976).

Illustrated History of North Idaho Embracing Nez Perce, Idaho, Latah, Kootenai, and Shoshone Counties, State of Idaho ([S.I.]: Western Historical Publishing Company, 1903); 681–82. The surname is also spelled *Rekdohl.* The *Illustrated History* contains invaluable information relative to where the women were born in Norway, the date of birth, parents' names, date of marriage, date of immigration to the United States, number of children and birth dates, etc.

20. See Elizabeth Ronning Solberg, *The Long and Happy Life of Mrs. Peeleyant: An Autobiography* (N.p.: The author, 1967), 4, 6, 13, 14, P12, NAHA. This commentary is not limited to works by daughters: see, for example, W. M. Oleson, *I Remember 1: Pioneering in Western Dakota* (New York: Vantage Press, 1989).

21. Wærenskjold, *The Lady with the Pen,* 68. By this time, her husband had been killed and the farm rented out. Throughout the Civil War, the aforementioned German girl worked for the Wærenskjolds, as did an African American woman, "a good deal of the time" (p62).

22. Stephen Gross discusses this European model of domestic work as part of a woman's life course: "Domestic Labor as a Life-Course Event: The Effects of Ethnicity in Turn-of-the-Century America," *Social Science History* 15 (Fall 1991): 397–416. For Swedish immigrant women domestics, see Joy Lintelman, *"I Go to America": Swedish American Women and the Life of Mina Anderson* (St. Paul: MHS Press, 2009). For a discussion on Swedish women in rural areas and their work as domestics in Chicago, see Margareta Matovic, "Maids in Motion: Swedish Women is Dalsland," in *Peasant Maids—City Women: From the European Countryside to Urban America,* ed. Christiane Harzig (Ithaca, NY, and London: Cornell University Press, 1997), 99–141; Margareta Matovic, "Embracing a Middle-Class Life: Swedish-American Women in Lake View," in Harzig, *Peasant Maids—City Women,* 261–97.

Olaf Morgan Norlie, *History of the Norwegian People in America* (Minneapolis, MN: Augsburg Publishing House, 1925), 346, 348; Gross, "Domestic Labor as a Life-Course Event," 400–401. Gross's analysis of the census (p409) also found that more than one-half of the Scandinavian domestics worked in rural areas, communities with a population under ten thousand. In 1880 and 1890, the census category was Norway and Sweden, so it is not possible to differentiate between the two using the statistical abstract figures. I also discuss hired girls in Norwegian America more fully in Lahlum, *Norwegian Women, Landscape, and Agriculture.* Hilda Jongren Lahlum, "Memories, Memories,"

5–6, handwritten manuscript, copy in author's possession. Lahlum used the money she earned to buy fabric, which her mother made into a dress. Other women also hired out prior to confirmation. Jannicke Sæhle to [brother] Johannes Sæhle, 28 Sept. 1847, in *Land of Their Choice*, 260–63.

23. Xan and Oleson, *Wisconsin My Home*, 3, 23, 35, 150. Thorild Oleson is described as being from a "well-to-do family," while Mathis came from a "quite wealthy" family: see p3–4. On modern housekeeping, Elisabeth Koren made this same observation: *The Diary of Elisabeth Koren*, 201. Carol Coburn found the same general pattern among Missouri Synod German Lutherans in early twentieth-century Kansas. Young girls from tight-knit German Lutheran communities moved to Kansas City, Missouri, an urban area, or to Paola, Kansas, a neighboring small town, to work as domestics. Such work exposed these young women to American housekeeping practices, and the experience of living away from home made them more independent. Coburn suggests that women who worked as hired girls in Kansas City or Paola became leaders in the Trinity Lutheran Church Ladies Aid. See Carol K. Coburn, "Learning to Serve: Education and Change in the Lives of Rural Domestics in the Twentieth Century," *Journal of Social History* 25 (Autumn 1991): 109–22. Coburn found that in this German Lutheran community around Block, Kansas, the eldest daughter hired out at a much higher rate than the youngest daughter (p112): 74 percent for the oldest; 49 percent for the youngest.

24. Gjerde, *From Peasants to Farmers*, 195–97; Lahlum, "'There Are No Trees Here': Norwegian Women Encounter the Northern Prairies and Plains" (PhD diss., University of Idaho, Moscow, 2003), 226–27; Lahlum, "'Everything Was Changed and Looked Strange,'" 204–6. Bertina Serina Kingestad to Her Sister Anna, 14 Apr. 1889; Kingestad to Her Family, 2 May 1889; Kingestad to Her Family, 27 Feb. 1889, in *In Their Own Words: Letters from Norwegian Immigrants*, ed. and trans. Solveig Zempel (Minneapolis: University of Minnesota Press in cooperation with NAHA, 1991), 40, 42.

25. Eline M. Storaasen, Lake Preston, SD, to Onkel [A. G. Nordhagen], 24 Nov. 1892, 1, A1679, NEM. For separate spheres, see Barbara Welter, "Cult of True Womanhood: 1820–1860," *American Quarterly* 18.1 (Summer 1966): 151–74. Odd S. Lovoll, *Norwegians on the Prairie: Ethnicity and the Development of the Country Town* (St. Paul: MHS Press in cooperation with NAHA, 2006), 152. Anton J. Olsen, Bottineau, ND, 30 March [no year], to Dear friend, 1, typed manuscript, Oppland folder, Riksarkivet.

26. Ruth Lima McMahon, "Introductory Notes" [to Ole and Martha Lima Letters], 1, Folder 3: Ole and Martha Lima Letters, 1893–1902," P844, NAHA; Johanne Hedemark, Englevale [ND], to Sister, Brother and Little Niece Anna, May 1883 [1884 crossed out], 2, Folder 3, Hedemark—Libak Families, letters, P852, NAHA; Philip L. Gerber, ed., "Herding Cows and Waiting Tables: The Diary of Laura Aleta Iversen Abrahamson," *South Dakota History* 20 (Spring 1990): *passim*; Bergeim diaries, spring 1884, *passim*, Ingeborg Olsdatter Bergeim Collection, NAHA; Else [Raa] to Brother Ole, Albert Lea, Minn. 23 Apr. 1893, 3, A013–002, Kåre Hovland Correspondence, Sogn of Fjordane Fylkearkivet, Leikanger, Norway. Bergeim initially worked in hotels in Watertown, Dakota Territory.

27. Mina Gilbertson, Ellsworth, MN, to Petter Olauson, 5 Aug. 1902, 1, A445, NEM; Albert N. Gilbertson, Willmar, MN, to Dear Petter [Olauson], 9 Dec. 1900, 3, A437,

NEM; Albert N. Gilbertson, Willmar, MN, to Dear Petter [Olauson], 21 July 1907, 6, A438, NEM; John H. Ley, *Thief River Falls City Directory, 1909–1910* (St. Cloud, MN: J. H. Ley, 1910), available at the Pennington County Historical Society webpage, http://www. pvillage.org/directorysearch.asp. Before the Gilbertson sisters opened their millinery shop, Mina earned a living sewing in Ellsworth. Sister Maria "learn[ed] millinery" in Sioux Falls, South Dakota. See Trygve O. Gilbertson, Augsburg Seminary, Minneapolis, to Dear Cousin Petter [Olauson], 20 Oct. 1897, 2, A449, NEM. Mina continued operating the shop even after she married. On Brandly and Westbye, see *Hanska: A Century of Tradition, 1901–2001* (Madelia, MN: Preferred Printing Co., 2001), 114, 117.

28. 1900 Idaho Census Roll, Latah County, 219-B; Wendy Gamber, "Tarnished Labor: The Home, the Market, and the Boardinghouse in Antebellum America," *Journal of the Early Republic* 22 (Summer 2002): 179. Gertrude Poyeson is listed as "keeping house."

29. References to teaching school are widespread in letters, reminiscences, memoirs, and community histories. For a brief discussion on teachers in Norwegian American communities, see Lahlum, "Growing Up in Norwegian-American Communities," 118–19; Lovoll, *Norwegians on the Prairie*, 178–79. Raaen, *Grass of the Earth*, 169–238. Raaen taught in rural and city schools. Synneva [*sic*] [Netrost], Manfred, N.Dak., to Onkel John, 6 Sept. 1906, 2, A3295, NEM; Bertha M. Netrost, Manfred, N.Dak., to Onkel John, 3 June 1898, A3297, NEM; Lori Ann Lahlum "'Training the Young Idea How to Shoot': Teaching in Barnes County, the First Thirty Years, 1879–1909" (master's thesis, University of North Dakota, 1992), 15, 80; Anna Netteland, St. Hilaire, MN, to Sister Kristi, 13 Dec. 1919, 1, Riksarkivet; Lillehaugen, *Live Well, passim; Polk's Latah County Directory, 1905* (Seattle: R. L. Polk and Co. Publishers, 1905), 2:62.

30. Anne Bjorli, Bjorli, Nelson, Co., ND, to Parents and siblings, 25 Apr. 1888, 1, Riksarkivet; Lahlum, "'Training the Young Idea How to Shoot,'" 58, 74. Saleswomen and office workers with experience earned nearly twenty to thirty-five dollars more per month than a female teacher. With board, a hired girl earned slightly less than the average female teacher, although in some parts of the state she probably earned more. The situation was similar for male teachers. See p61–62.

31. L. DeAne Lagerquist, *In America Men Milk the Cows: Factors of Gender, Ethnicity, and Religion in the Americanization of Norwegian-American Women* (Brooklyn, NY: Carlson Publishing, Inc., 1991), 52–53. Erik Luther Williamson, "From *Norsk Religionsskole* to Parochial School in Fifty Years: Norwegian Lutheran Congregational Education in North Dakota," in *Norwegian-American Studies,* ed. Odd S. Lovoll (Northfield, MN: NAHA, 1995), 54:304. Fund-raising often became necessary to keep the schools open; see p305. Todd W. Nichol, trans. and ed., "A Haugean Woman in America: The Memoirs of Sigrid Eielsen," *Norwegian-American Studies* 35 (2000): 283; Norlie, *History of the Norwegian People in America,* 216; Xan and Oleson, *My Wisconsin Home,* 89–90; Our Savior's Lutheran Church Register, 37–65, located at Emmanuel Lutheran Church, Moscow, ID; Lillehaugen, *Live Well,* 91, 97; Ole Lima, Cooperstown, to Sister Gunhild, 1 Apr. 1894 [attached to Martha's letter], 1, NAHA. The Norwegian Lutheran parochial school differed from those established by the Missouri Synod German Lutherans, which generally replaced the English (or American) public school. In Norwegian American communities, parochial school typically supplemented the English school

education. For a discussion on Missouri Synod parochial schools, see Coburn, *Life at Four Corners*, 60–80.

32. Carl H. Chrislock, "Introduction: The Historical Context," in *Cultural Pluralism versus Assimilation: The Views of Waldemar Ager*, ed. Odd S. Lovoll (Northfield, MN: NAHA, 1977), 13–14; Lagerquist, *In America the Men Milk the Cows*, 44–52; Lovoll, *The Promise of America*, 62–66. Lagerquist provides an excellent overview of the Norwegian Lutheran Church in America and women's roles within the church. While most Norwegian immigrants did not have official membership in the Lutheran church, membership rates were higher in rural communities: see Lovoll, *Norwegian on the Prairie*, 201. Moreover, those who did not officially join the church (membership generally included financial support of the church which was beyond the means of some poorer immigrants) often participated in the church community. Einar Haugen, "Norway in America: The Hidden Heritage," in *Makers of an American Immigrant Legacy: Essays in Honor of Kenneth O. Bjork*, ed. Odd S. Lovoll (Northfield, MN: NAHA, 1980), 18.

33. Wærenskjold, *The Lady with the Pen*, 88. Mrs. R. O. Brandt, "Social Aspects of Pioneering," *Norwegian-American Studies and Records* 7 (1933): 1.

34. "Zion Lutheran Church, 1903–1978: Seventy-five Years," 7–8, 17, folder 5, box 9d, P537, Minnesota Congregations, NAHA. Episcopalian women in Northfield, Minnesota, first organized the Ladies Social Circle in 1858 and later became the force, both vocally and financially, behind the establishment of All Saints Episcopal Church. See Joan R. Gunderson, "The Local Parish as a Female Institution: The Experience of All Saints Episcopal Church in Frontier Minnesota, *Church History* 55 (Sept. 1986): 307–22. Erik Luther Williamson, "Norwegian-American Lutheran Church Women in North Dakota: The Ladies Aid Societies" (master's thesis, University of North Dakota, 1987), 33. For a discussion on women in the Lutheran Church, see L. DeAne Lagerquist, *From Our Mother's Arms: A History of Women in the American Lutheran Church* (Minneapolis, MN: Augsburg Publishing House, 1987).

35. Lagerquist, *In America the Men Milk the Cows*, 108. For a general overview of the Norwegian Lutheran Church and its internal conflicts, see Lovoll, *The Promise of America*, 98–112. For a case study of antebellum church controversy, see A. Gerald Dyste, "The Twin Churches of Christiania, Minnesota, from 1854 to 1864: A Study of the Causes of Immigrant Church Conflicts," in *Norwegian-American Studies*, ed. Odd S. Lovoll (Northfield, MN: NAHA, 1992), 33:73–98.

"Seventy-fifth Anniversary, 1881–1956, Nora Free Christian Church," 3, Nora Free Church folder, Brown County Historical Society (hereafter, BCHS), New Ulm, MN; "1869—Centennial—1969" [Lake Hanska Lutheran Church], 12, P537, box 9d, folder 5, NAHA; Ella Bjorneberg, "Nora Church 50th Anniversary; Nora Women's Society 40th Anniversary: History of the Nora Women's Scoeity [*sic*] through 1930," in "Nora Women's Society: 100 Years of Service, 1890–1990," 1–2, Hanska, Nora Free Church folder, BCHS; Arlene Schmiesing, "Profile of Early Members: 90th Anniversary Nora Women's Society," in "Nora Women's Society," 1–8; "Nora Free Christian Church, Seventy-fifth Anniversary, 1881–1956," 3–5, 12–13, MHS and BCHS; Ole Jorgensen, "Speech at the Laying of the Cornerstone of the Nora Church Parsonage," 24 June 1906, 1–3, box 3, P809, NAHA; 100th Anniversary of the Nora Free Christian Church, Unitarian-

Universalist, Hanska, Minnesota, 1881–1981 (1981), MHS. Although the impetus for those members leaving the church may have been the location of the soon-to-be built church, the fact that those members then called a Unitarian minister implies that there were also doctrinal issues involved. In fact, the Lake Hanska parish opted to leave the Norwegian Lutheran Synod in a few years. See "1869—Centennial—1969," 12.

36. "1869—Centennial—1969," 13. Williamson, "Norwegian-American Lutheran Church Women in North Dakota," 17–18, 19–22. According to Williamson (20–21), some churches tried to deflate the issue of women voting by providing the Ladies Aid with one vote. Williamson also discusses the issue of women voting in the Lutheran Church briefly in " 'Doing What Had To Be Done': Norwegian Lutheran Ladies Aide Societies of North Dakota," *North Dakota History* 57 (Spring 1990): 10–11. *Hundredth Anniversary, High Prairie Lutheran Congregation of LaMoure County, North Dakota, 1887–1987,* (N.p.: 1987), 10, 13. High Prairie was not a part of Williamson's study.

37. For a description of dividing by sex, see Xan and Oleson, *My Wisconsin Home,* 64, 67; Levorsen, *The Quiet Conquest,* 110; *Lake Hanska Lutheran Church Centennial,* 55.

38. "Genesee Valley Lutheran Church, 1878–1978," 5, 8, newspaper article, no name or date, in "The History of Our Saviour's [sic] Lutheran Church," scrapbook by Our Saviour's [sic] Lutheran Church Ladies Aid, Emmanuel Lutheran Church. One woman recalled leaving around 4:00 PM. Many aids did not contribute to the minister's salary when the subscriptions were successful.

39. Our Savior's Lutheran Church Register, 3, Emmanuel Lutheran Church; Survey of Baptism Records, Records of Ministerial Acts, and the Register for First Lutheran Church, all located at Emmanuel Lutheran Church. *Den Forste [sic] Norske Evangelical Lutherske Mennighed [sic] i Moscow, Idaho* is the Norwegian name for the church. In 1912 when the Ladies Aid created a constitution, the official name became "The Ladies Aid of the Norwegian Lutheran Church, Moscow, Idaho." See "History of Our Saviour's [sic] Lutheran Church," 7. Prior to 1901, a Swedish Lutheran church existed in Moscow, but few Norwegians belonged. "History of Our Saviour's [sic] Lutheran Church, Moscow, Idaho," 1942, 1, 3, typed manuscript, located at Emmanuel Lutheran Church.

40. In the church records, the food names appear in a combination of Norwegian (often spelled incorrectly) and English. "History of Our Saviour's Church [sic] Lutheran Church," 2–3. The church minutes also reflect the financial contributions the Ladies Aid made to the church. See Our Savior's Lutheran Church Register, 51–64. Ladies Aid groups frequently sponsored lutefisk dinners in the Midwest. See *A History of The Nidaros Lutheran Congregation, 1868–1943,* 44, NAHA; "Ladies' Aid Society," *First Lutheran Church, Brookings, South Dakota, Sixtieth Anniversary, 1880–1940* (1940), NAHA; Mrs. Oscar Hellerud, "History of the Valley Grove Ladies Aid," 5, typed manuscript, Congregations Nerstrand, MN, Valley Grove, folder 1, box 13C, P537, NAHA; Handy-Marchello, *Women of the Northern Plains,* 102; Lagerquist, *In American the Men Milk the Cows,* 137–38; Lahlum, " 'Everything Was Changed and Looked Strange,' " 211–13; Lovoll, *Norwegians on the Prairie,* 188; Williamson, "Norwegian-American Lutheran Church Women in North Dakota," 24. The Nidaros Lutheran Church is located in eastern South Dakota.

41. Lahlum, " 'Everything Was Changed and Looked Strange,' " 211–12; "Ladies' Aid

Society," *First Lutheran Church, Brookings; Hundredth Anniversary, High Prairie Lutheran Church,* 24–25. The Ladies Aid members at High Prairie actually paid the salary for a Madagascan who worked with the mission. In 1923, the women began serving a chicken supper to raise funds. Most Ladies Aids charged dues, charged for the meal, or charged for both, with ten cents typical dues for the late nineteenth and early twentieth centuries.

42. Anne H. Odden, ed., "50th Anniversary: Rock Valle Ladies' Aid" (Minneapolis, MN: The Lund Press, Inc., 1938), 21–23, 25–29, 32, 35–36, 41–44. The Rock Valle congregation came into existence when two congregations merged in 1890. Thus, for a time there were two separate aids. Moreover, after the merger, there were three aid divisions within the church. They began meeting as one aid in 1902.

43. Todd Nichol, "Wedding Customs among Norwegian-American Lutherans, ca. 1850–1950," in *Norwegian-American Essays, 2004,* ed. Orm Øverland and Harry T. Cleven (Oslo: NAHA-Norway, 2005), 27–29.

44. Weholt, "Reminiscences of Johanna Weholt," 12; Ane Vatne, Vatne [near Cooperstown, ND], to Oft-remembered Sister, 24 Nov. 1889, 1, NAHA; Martha Lima, Cooperstown, to Malena [Ole's sister], 3 Jan. 1894, 1, NAHA. Ole Lima had returned to Norway after five years in the United States because he promised his father he would take over the farm. While in Norway, he decided to return to the United States. He met Martha and sold the farm to his sister and her husband. See Ole Lima, "Ole Lima Story," 1, NAHA, italics added. *Gome* (also spelled *gomme*) is sweet milk boiled down to a spreadable consistency. It can be used on lefse or bread, for example.

Christine Dahl, Dahl [TX], to Dear Brother Erik, 11 Mar. 1880, 1, typed manuscript, A5110, NEM. For other references to wedding dances, see Randi Anderson, 30 Nov. 1889, 1; Xan and Oleson, *My Wisconsin Home,* 146–49; Nichol, "Wedding Customs among Norwegian-American Lutherans," 30–31; Gilderhus (Mrs. Andrew Gilderhus biography), 7–8 Supplement, 4, Nelson County, HDP; "Mr. And Mrs. Charles Borgendale," in *Lac qui Parle County Pioneer Stories,* 29; Levorsen, *The Quiet Conquest,* 70. Levorsen writes about an 1897 wedding.

45. Barbo Ramseth, Bristow [WI], to Dear Bersven and wife and family, 14 Dec. 1889, in Zempel, *In Their Own Words,* 111. Nichol, "Wedding Customs among Norwegian-American Lutherans," 27–29; Inger Thu Herigstad, 8–Supplement, Griggs County, Roll 11, HDP.

46. Ane Vatne, Vatne [near Cooperstown, ND], to Dearly Beloved, Familiar Sister [Malena], 10 Jan. 1901, 1, NAHA. Levorsen, *The Quiet Conquest,* 90, 96. Many of the biographies for the Historical Data Project contain references to dances, both for weddings and for other special events. It was one of the categories interviewers were encouraged to ask the pioneers about.

47. [Johan Moen], Waco, Texas, to J. Jensen, Hedemark, 19 Feb. 1884, 3, Hedmark File, Riksarkivet. *Hundredth Anniversary, High Prairie Lutheran Congregation,* 8. Xan and Oleson, *My Wisconsin Home,* 74. The two congregations later merged: see p75. Oleson fails to mention that a doctrinal dispute drove the debate over dancing.

48. Wærenskjold, *The Lady with the Pen,* 45, 50; Martha Berdahl, "Extracts from Diary," box 10, folder 2, James Berdahl Papers, 30022, Center for Western Studies, Augustana College, Sioux Falls, SD; Hilde Petra Brungot, "Dorthea Dahl: Norwegian-American

Author of Everyday Experience" (master's thesis, University of Oslo, 1977), 12; Raaen, *Grass of the Earth,* 119–24; Barbara Handy-Marchello, "Land, Liquor, and the Women of Hatton, North Dakota," in *The Centennial Anthology of North Dakota History, Journal of the Northern Plains,* eds. Janet Daley Lysengen and Ann M. Rathke (Bismarck: State Historical Society of North Dakota, 1996), 223–49. The "extracts" is a handwritten reproduction of Berdahl's diary with notations for later additions. It is not known if items have been expunged.

49. Berdahl, "Extracts," 18 Jan. 1897, 26 Feb. 1897; Marie Killi, Sacred Heart, Minn., to [Marie Thomter], 8 Jan. 1914, 3–4, Oppland folder, Riksarkivet. Copies of many of Killi's letters also exist at NEM. The Killi family eventually spelled the name *Killy* in the United States. Andrew Volstead, who introduced the national prohibition amendment, was a Norwegian American from Minnesota.

50. For a discussion on visiting in rural agricultural communities, see Jane Marie Pederson, "The Country Visitor: Patterns of Hospitality in Rural Wisconsin, 1880–1925," *Agricultural History* 58 (July 1984): 347–64. Randi Anderson, 30 May 1889, 3; Xan and Oleson, *My Wisconsin Home,* especially 49–58 and 101–14, although references to visits appear throughout.

51. Micaela di Leonardo, "The Female World of Cards and Holidays: Women, Families, and the Work of Kinship," *Signs* 12 (Spring 1987): 442–43. Also see, for example, the Gilbertson family letters and the letters by Karoline Erickson located at NEM.

52. Rued letters, *passim;* Curtiss-Wedge, *History of Clark County Wisconsin,* 426–27.

CHAPTER 4

Finding Their Way in the City: Norwegian Immigrant Women and Their Daughters in Urban Areas, 1880s–1920s

David C. Mauk

In the late nineteenth century, Albertine Ofstie kept house for her brothers in Minneapolis until she found work at a large steam laundry in the Cedar-Riverside area of the city that was home to a significant Norwegian American community. Later she worked as a live-in domestic in a middle-class, southwest neighborhood until she married. Her younger sister, Anna Marte, who arrived after 1900, had earned a reputation in the family as a "rather wild 'flapper' by the 1920s." When she "settled down" later in that decade, she became a nurse and married a non-Scandinavian stone mason. The sisters' migratory and premarital working lives illustrate the importance of family support networks. The contrasts in their lives also provide examples of the dramatic shifts in education, occupation, and living conditions that took place over forty years among Norwegian immigrant women in urban communities as well as their abilities to adapt to shifting economic, labor, and cultural patterns. This chapter brings together personal narratives found in letters, memoirs, and stories and a statistical analysis of Norwegian and American public sources, chiefly Norway's emigrant protocols and U.S. census data, as a means to illuminate the experiences of the urban Norwegian American women. Together, these sources demonstrate that while the first generation worked primarily as live-in domestic labor, the second generation received better education in American cities and by 1920 increasingly left housework for skilled employment in offices or as professionals in health care. With these changes came more respect and social acceptance, as well as greater integration into the broader American society.[1]

The primary focus here is on the migration patterns of these women to two major centers of migration, New York and the Twin Cities of Minneapolis/ St. Paul, and the working and living conditions they met in those cities. In addition, the chapter incorporates Norwegian American women's work experiences in two other major urban immigrant communities, Chicago and Seattle. The Norwegian enclaves in these four cities represent by far the largest and most influential communities established in the United States. Their size supported

a broad range of religious, social, political, and economic activities and institutions—and with them a greater range of choices for their female residents.
This chapter addresses the period of industrialization and urbanization, thus
the focus is on the working-class majority among these women, most of whom
labored as domestics. To a lesser degree the study makes an attempt to include
the experience and activities of middle-class Norwegian American women.[2]

Indirect Migration: From Rural American Communities to Urban Centers

The paths Norwegian American women took to American urban centers varied,
but they generally fall into two categories—indirect and direct migration. Many
migrated in stages. Thousands first migrated internally inside Norway, especially
from the 1850s onward, as the consolidation of landholdings, the increasing use
of farm machinery, and a growing population displaced rural Norwegians. As
a result, families sought economic alternatives: some left to farm in the Arctic
north; others emigrated to rural America; and still others sought work in Norwegian towns and cities. Generally speaking, women moved from rural districts
to burgeoning coastal, urban centers. While all urban districts grew, the largest—
Oslo, Kristiansand, Stavanger, Bergen, and Trondheim—expanded most and
held the greatest number of opportunities for women. As they moved, migrating
women put domestic skills learned at home or in nearby rural households to use
when they sought available female employment in towns and cities.

Rural-to-rural international migration from the Norwegian countryside to agricultural districts of the American Upper Midwest, followed by subsequent movement to the region's cities for education and work, represented chronologically the
first and, in terms of the size and number of the cohorts of women involved over
many decades, perhaps the most important form of indirect urban migration for
Norwegian American women. Secondary migration came later in these women's
lives (or in their daughters' experience) when they left the farm for opportunities in midwestern urban magnets. Good, cheap farm land constituted the main
attraction for men and women leaving Norway for the United States from 1825
through the 1870s, when Norway was nominally industrialized and its population
mostly employed in agricultural or maritime pursuits. Maintaining traditional
rural Norwegian culture was difficult without land ownership, and good land had
become scarce as the population rapidly grew. America, on the other hand, advertised fine farm land for the taking on the frontier of white settlement for those
willing to work hard. Once Norwegian emigrant scouts, guidebooks, and America
letters pointed the way, emigrants settled in pioneer farm areas of Illinois, Iowa,
Wisconsin, Minnesota, and later in the eastern Dakotas.[3]

This mass migration from rural Norway to rural America later fueled the
secondary migration—the indirect migration—to American cities. The reasons

women migrated to urban areas differed from those of men. Women migrated to the city because their skills (almost entirely domestic) were in decreasing demand on the farm and in increasing demand in the cities. Historians tell us that Norwegian American women left the countryside for several reasons. Women in America did not do as much farm work as in Norway, for example, in caring for cows and other domestic animals, and the growing use of farm machinery in the late nineteenth century reduced the need for manual labor in general. Women's migration to the city often resulted from the farm family's need for additional income—for example, when prices fell for agricultural products, costs for transportation to market grew, or expenses for new machinery demanded capital investment. When young, single women left for the city, fewer family members needed to be supported and the family gained another source of income from the money sent back to the countryside. Once women migrated to urban areas, they less often moved back to the countryside. Many women found better opportunities in cities and had fewer reasons to return to rural life. Unlike women, men were more likely to move back and forth between rural areas and urban centers.[4]

Only a small number of Norwegian immigrants took up long-term residence in America's cities before the 1880s. Earlier, however, the attractions of having some family members, in particular young adult daughters, living in the city for a while or moving in and out became apparent. For instance, in 1840, Andrew Larsen, a Norwegian American father in Chicago, wrote to relatives and friends recommending the advantages of free room, board, and schooling that his two daughters received as maids for men in the city. News of these employment opportunities added to the lure of the city in the farming districts that surrounded it. By the 1850s, the possibilities that housework offered for settling into an urban life became so well known that about one in five Norwegian American women in Chicago had positions as domestic workers. By the 1870s Norwegian American women outnumbered the men in the Chicago census, which, Odd S. Lovoll remarks, "leads one to conclude that employment possibilities, especially in domestic service, represented an attractive alternative" for women compared to living in nearby rural Norwegian American settlements.[5]

A few women emigrants from Norway were drawn to urban life in St. Paul as early as the 1850s. Ingeborg Langeberg migrated first to rural Wisconsin before coming to St. Paul at the start of that decade, when she became a cook for Minnesota's territorial governor, Alexander Ramsey. Around the same time Anne Hovey and Ingeborg Gilberts made the transatlantic voyage and the journey west from New York as domestic servants for a series of Scandinavian immigrant families. When they reached Prairie du Chien, Wisconsin, they converted to Methodism and, after a short time of preaching to rural Norwegian immigrants in nearby Iowa, arrived in St. Paul as Methodist evangelists in 1852.

The Scandinavian congregation their revival helped organize in the city included other young, single, female wage earners. These three women's lives document how opportunities in domestic service encouraged migration for single women at this very early date. Hovey's and Gilberts's experiences demonstrate that domestic employment not only provided economic support for women but also could lead to their contributions in the development of their communities. The Scandinavian Methodist congregational records in St. Paul for the 1850s and 1860s include the names of dozens of single Norwegian immigrant women. City directories for Minneapolis as well as St. Paul between the early 1850s and 1870s, moreover, include many women in domestic service, housekeeper positions, and boardinghouse keeping.[6]

The large majority of Norwegian migrants who became residents of the Twin Cities between 1880 and 1890 relocated to the urban area from surrounding rural areas. Only thirty-seven hundred of the people registered in Norway's emigrant protocols during the 1880s indicated that Minneapolis or St. Paul was their destination, but judging from the U.S. censuses of 1880 and 1890, the Norwegian-born population in the Twin Cities grew by nearly thirteen thousand people in these same years. The large gap between the figures for the decade, combined with the much larger number of emigrants who named rural destinations in the Norwegian records, supports the conclusion that the large majority (around 70 percent) of the Norwegians who came to the Twin Cities in the 1880s were secondary migrants—that is, people who moved into the Cities from the many rural areas where Norwegian emigrants had settled earlier. Family and friends in Norwegian America often assisted international migration and gave their countrymen a first home in rural Norwegian American communities.[7]

When they took up residence in Minneapolis or St. Paul during the 1880s, most Norwegians were thus not newcomers to the United States but Minnesota pioneers. They were very likely people who had come to the region during the 1866–73 wave of Norwegian immigration, perhaps as children. Some were the offspring of emigrants who left Norway even earlier and pioneered in Illinois, Wisconsin, Iowa, or Minnesota between the 1830s and 1860s. Frequently, an aunt, sister, or female cousin moved into town before anyone else in the family. In the same way Norwegian American women contributed to the family economy by taking wage work in Chicago a generation earlier, their more western sisters in later decades increasingly added to family finances by securing employment in Minneapolis/St. Paul in the last decades of the century.

In the Upper Midwest, Norwegian American immigrant women experienced the western movement of settlement and the movement to cities for work as connected processes. For instance, Ione Kadden's grandmother arrived in Springfield, Illinois, early enough to have memories of Abraham Lincoln from her childhood before the family moved farther west to Red Wing, Minnesota. There, she met

Borgina Hylland Johnson worked as an upstairs maid for the James J. Hill family in St. Paul, ca. 1920

and married a young Norwegian American who had moved from the Wisconsin logging camps. Trained as a cobbler in Norway, her husband was offered a job in St. Paul at a shoe factory, and she and the children followed him to the city, where Kadden and the rest of her siblings were born. Mary Jo Thorsheim, a fourth-generation Norwegian American on her mother's side living in Minneapolis in 1998, has a family history that combines these elements, but her story also illustrates how movement in and out of the city followed the family life cycle. Her maternal great-grandmother, who never learned to speak English, emigrated from the Norwegian countryside to a farm in rural Illinois. While she did not re-emigrate from there to Chicago, every summer during the mid-1800s she visited relatives in the city who assisted her with her English. During the rest of the year, she lived in a densely Norwegian rural settlement farther south in Illinois's Fox Valley, where a knowledge of English was unnecessary.[8]

After 1900, women came from the rural areas of the Upper Midwest to the Twin Cities for work and increasingly also for education, which frequently led to employment and personal relationships that kept them there. All socioeconomic classes adjacent to the Twin Cities felt the pull of urban opportunity. For instance, the successful farmland and town developer Albert Soderberg sold his extensive holdings in North Dakota in 1918, and with his wife and three school-age daughters moved to affluent southwestern Minneapolis so that the daughters could attend accredited high schools. Soderberg reasoned that this education would ensure their admission to the nation's best women's colleges. When his savings disappeared in a sudden reversal of fortune, however, his family remained in the city, and the daughters found their educational and occupational futures in local institutions, rather than in the Northeast.[9]

Two to three decades later, Norwegian women also followed this indirect form of urban migration to Seattle. They departed from isolated rural locations in Norway with meager opportunities and searched for "something more." At first traveling in family groups, later they more often traveled alone, perhaps to meet relatives or acquaintances who preceded them. Women kept in touch with friends and family as they migrated, often living and working in rural areas as they moved across North America to the Pacific Coast. Not infrequently, ethnic networks helped maintain connections with other Norwegian Americans and provided them with a community when they made Seattle their home. Developing nearly a generation later than the Twin Cities, rapidly growing Seattle, where Norwegians first settled in the early 1880s, also attracted rural women who moved there in the 1880s and 1890s from the Midwest and adapted to the city's employment and residence patterns when they re-emigrated. By the 1920s, Norwegian American farm women moved in from the settled agricultural counties surrounding the city.[10]

Anne Ormbrekk illustrates the migratory pattern to Seattle through the Midwest. Ormbrekk arrived in small-town Minnesota with her husband Olav and two sons in the 1870s and bore more children there. After only a few years, however, they joined the ongoing westward movement by wagon train and eventually reached the scattered settlement that would become Seattle. In Washington Territory, one of Seattle's founders offered them farmland that was part of rocky Queen Anne's Hill, which later became prime downtown real estate. Rejecting the offer yet becoming urban pioneers themselves, they took better farmland nearby instead and provided dairy products to the growing city until their land was expropriated for expanding highways. In Seattle, the earliest Norwegian female migration resulted from the movement of families rather than single, unattached women. The chief differences between the migration to Seattle and the migration to the Midwest existed in the distance these families traveled across the continent to reach the city.

Another example of Norwegian emigrant women crossing the continent on their own is Sofie Evik, who emigrated from North Trøndelag, leaving just two years before the restrictive national-origins quotas went into effect in 1929. Her path to Seattle and married life there illustrate a number of common elements of rural women's migration to that city. Unattached and not yet twenty years old, she was, in her words, determined "not to stay on the farm and pick rocks," so she immigrated on her own to Canada when an uncle in Minneapolis left unanswered her letter requesting him to sponsor her immigration to the United States. Supporting herself as a domestic and later as a school cook, she worked her way across Canada to the West Coast, all the while keeping in contact with friends from Trøndelag who had settled in Seattle. She visited them on a short-term visa from Canada while a temporary resident in Vancouver, and during her stay met her childhood sweetheart, whom she married in that city a year later. Then, as the wife of a legal resident of the United States, she could settle down permanently with him in Seattle.[11]

Direct Migration: From Urban Norway to Urban America

The second migratory path for Norwegian women to cities in the United States was direct: from a city in the homeland to an American city. This migratory path gained frequency around 1900. By the late nineteenth century, many of the women in this urban-to-urban migration from Norway to the United States had spent most of their lives in urban areas; however, even these women very likely had rural roots. As Norwegian emigration reached its peak in the 1880s, "the intensity of the exodus," as Lovoll notes, was greatest in the country's cities, even though in absolute numbers more people departed from the country's rural districts. Between 1880 and 1895, about a quarter of those leaving Oslo chose Illinois, many of them settling in Chicago. The city appealed strongly to female Norwegian immigrants for several reasons: it was the nation's second-largest employment market, it was close to midwestern Norwegian settlement areas, and it had the largest Scandinavian population of any city in America. Increasingly, the members of this urban-to-urban stream of migrants were single and in their twenties. Most of these immigrants landed in New York and immediately boarded trains bound for the population capital of the Midwest, where the large majority of women among them joined their female Norwegian American relatives from the surrounding rural districts as domestic workers for the city's middle and upper classes. As Lovoll notes in his Chicago study, their increasing youth and single marital status did not mean that family played a much less important role in their migration or employment. Relatives, though perhaps not nuclear families, continued to be traveling companions, and networks of family connections and communications in most cases eased their journey and opened the doors of the employment market in Chicago. In this pattern, men more frequently arrived first, whether as husbands who later sent for family or as brothers, uncles, and male cousins who helped women in the family join them—not infrequently in the expectation of securing help with the housework that they saw as outside a man's province. Growing numbers of women, however, traveled alone (or with female relatives and friends) and were seen off, met, and ushered into work opportunities by other female relatives. This pattern of female-centered migration can be found in other urban areas, for example, in the Twin Cities.[12]

After 1890 the Twin Cities grew to be the undisputed center of Norwegian America and the strongest urban magnet for Norwegian immigrants. People on farms in the whole Upper Midwest looked to Minneapolis/St. Paul for economic opportunity, education, and a broader social life. The special attraction of Minneapolis/St. Paul compared to other urban centers was that the Twin Cities not only contained a large job market and educational institutions but that a larger *portion* of the Cities' population consisted of Scandinavian immigrants and their descendants. Many of these were the descendants of earlier immigrants to the rural Midwest and helped create the indirect migration to the Twin Cities that stimulated the direct migration. Minneapolis and St. Paul also benefitted from their location in the midst of the region with the largest number of heavily Norwegian American rural districts and small towns.

In the 1880s, the period of most rapid growth for the Twin Cities, the overwhelming majority of Norwegian-born newcomers came from the surrounding rural areas rather than directly from Norway. A large minority, however, around three in ten, migrated directly. The thirty-seven hundred people who came directly from the homeland during the 1880s represented the largest group of Norwegian newcomers that the Cities ever received in a ten-year period. In some ways, these immigrants were noticeably different from both the Norwegian Americans already in Minneapolis/St. Paul and those who moved in from the countryside. While the urbanized Norwegian Americans' origins lay in diverse and mostly rural parts of the homeland, 95 percent of the new arrivals directly from Norway in the 1880s came from Oslo (Norway's capital city) and smaller urbanized places in the southeastern region of the country. Conditions in St. Paul and Minneapolis were new to these Norwegian migrants direct from Norway, but many of these people had very likely acquired occupational skills and social attitudes more suitable to their new environment than those of earlier Norwegian immigrants to the Twin Cities.[13]

Many of these direct migrants to the Twin Cities in the 1880s were women. Carl G. O. Hansen, later the long-serving editor of *Minneapolis Tidende,* related a striking example of female migration from Trondheim that combined the paths discussed here. Hansen's mother arrived in Trondheim when she was fourteen and married there. When she became a widow, she showed entrepreneurial skills by building up a knitting business that employed several other young women in the city. In 1881, however, she migrated with her five children to Walnut Grove, Minnesota, near where her parents and most of her siblings lived. After evaluating the opportunities in nearby small towns, Mrs. Hansen decided that those places lacked sufficient opportunities for employment and found work in Minneapolis. Later, she sent for her children. When they arrived, three girls and two boys traveling alone by train, she was at work and they had to find their way to her rooms in the southside immigrant housing block known as "Noah's Ark."[14]

In patterns of direct migration that involved family decision making, men sometimes traveled in advance to find work and shelter, and women and children then followed. Johannes (John) and Peder Larsen came to St. Paul separately, the elder in the late 1870s and the younger in the early 1880s. Experienced shoemakers, they first found work in a small shoe shop and then took wage work in a shoe factory. At that point John sent to Norway for his fiancée, and they married soon after her arrival. In the 1890s and first decades of the twentieth century, the couple ran a grocery store that catered to the Norwegian American community centered in the Mount Airy section of St. Paul, Minnesota's capital city. Family migration decisions may have added security and limited the independence of young, single, and unattached women among the newcomers arriving directly from Norway; however, these same women might exert their independence, as documented by the circumstances of Albertine Ofstie's immigration to Minneapolis in the later 1880s. Ofstie came to America in her early twenties to meet two older brothers who were already established in the Cedar-Riverside area of the city. Her parents supported her move, on the condition that she keep house for her brothers. Initially Ofstie followed the plan, but at the first opportunity she charted her own course: first she took a job in a steam laundry in the area; then she moved to another section of town as a live-in maid; and finally she married a non-Norwegian.[15]

News of economic recession in the United States in the early 1890s, and the resulting economic hardships, sharply reduced immigration in general. The Larsen's grocery store in St. Paul's Mount Airy section had difficulty staying open, and Anna Marte, the younger Ofstie sister, decided to delay her emigration to Minneapolis until the economic situation improved. By 1903 economic recovery produced a renewed large migration from Norway, and the newest arrivals to the Twin Cities were younger and more often single than before. They included nearly equal numbers of both sexes and to an increased degree arrived from Norway's urban areas. The most significant difference in their origins was that they came from urban centers in many parts of the country rather than primarily from the "east country" surrounding Oslo. Albertine Ofstie was followed to the city by four more siblings, the youngest of them Anna Marte, who arrived when she was "hardly 18," just before World War I. The pattern of migration directly from Norway's urban areas to cities in the United States increased in intensity until submarine attacks during the war barred the possibility of safe transatlantic migration.[16]

Norwegian immigrant women also sought opportunities in New York City around the end of the nineteenth century. The prime destination of many shipping lines, the city served as the port of entry for most newcomers and offered the nation's largest job market. New York, renowned internationally as representing the cultural and economic pinnacle of American life, served as a magnet for many immigrants because of the wide range of jobs available (skilled, semi-skilled, and unskilled) and the diversity of commercial, intellectual, and artistic activities. The Norwegian immigrant community in New York, humorously called a suburb of Oslo, was home to people with a plethora of individual pursuits that paralleled the city's broad opportunities and included unusually mobile population elements that frequently "commuted" between Norway and the city. These New York immigrants—primarily fishermen, sailors, and businessmen—also included women who were entrepreneurs, professionals, and cultural figures. In both Norwegian and American terms, the New York "colony" considered itself, and in some respects arguably was, more modern than the Norwegians in other settlement areas. Its population was marked by an exceptionally large number of late emigrants from Norway's southernmost counties. In 1904, two-thirds of those leaving Kristiansand at the country's southern tip, including 768 women, were on their way to Brooklyn or New York, while only 17.6 percent (eighteen women) departing from Bergen and 9 percent (thirteen women) from Trondheim were headed for the two East Coast cities. Well into the 1920s the New York colony thought of itself as in tune with America's most modern city and the latest fashions in Norwegian language, politics, religion, and culture.[17]

In contrast to other urban areas, most of the immigrants to New York City came through direct migration. In the New York metropolitan area, few Norwegian American settlers resided in the city's rural surroundings. In the 1880s only nearby New Jersey towns, such as Hoboken, attracted significant numbers of newcomers from Norway who later moved into the city. New York City's rural Norwegian hinterland was a narrow strip along the adjacent Atlantic and Hudson River coasts, and therefore most of its Norwegian household workers came directly from their country of origin and parts of the city itself instead of remigrating into the city from an American hinterland. Yet, New York's national reputation led to a form of indirect migration of young Norwegian American women, drawn by the hub of business, fashion, and the arts, especially the second generation in the early decades of the twentieth century. Perhaps the best known is the American-born journalist and writer Brenda Ueland.[18]

The experience of Tennie Axelsen exemplifies several trends and attitudes in female migration. She arrived directly from the shipping and fishing center of Risør on Norway's south coast in 1903 and took work as a domestic servant in Brooklyn. After a short while, she seized the entrepreneurial opportunity represented by the intersection of the large New York City market for household help and the wave of emigration from her home region in Norway by opening a Scandinavian *fæstekontor* (an employment office for positions as domestic servants) in Brooklyn. Two years later, however, she closed it after marrying a Norwegian immigrant. The couple lived in Albany, New York, for a few years before returning to New York City and then remigrating to Norway

Suffrage procession, Scandinavian women in national costume with flags, Minneapolis, 1914

with the plan of starting a business there in 1914. Wartime conditions being inhospitable, they returned to New York in 1920. In the middle of Brooklyn's Bay Ridge Norwegian colony, they reopened Axelsen's employment office, this time adjacent to their "well appointed home, where girls just arrived in America are helped and advised in every way until they have got a position." Axelsen's early entrepreneurial ambitions and her husband's cooperative leadership of the women's employment bureau were unusual in the 1920s, but the couple's moves in and out of New York City, as well as to and from Norway, were not. That kind of geographical mobility was typical of the unstable immigrant populations in American cities and characteristic of the transiency and high level of transnational connections in New York's Norwegian community.[19]

The stream of people, male or female, migrating directly from Norwegian cities to Seattle was small until regular railroad and passenger ship service seemed a reasonable project near or after 1900. Most Norwegians landed on the Atlantic coast or traveled down the St. Lawrence to inland Canada or the Midwest and then took transcontinental trains west. As demonstrated earlier, some women in Norwegian and Norwegian American families arrived early in Seattle's history. Male fishermen and loggers from Norway, however, many of them single or living on their own in America, composed the largest part of the Norwegian settlers between the 1880s and 1900. In the new century more men and women who arrived directly from Norway found work in Seattle because its expanding economy created a greater demand for their labor; the Scandinavian American subculture facilitated the transition. By 1910 Swedes, Norwegians, and Danes

accounted for more than 20 percent of Washington's foreign-born population, the state's largest ethnic bloc. They had become even more numerous in
Seattle, where they represented 31.3 percent of the foreign-born population and
Norwegian immigrants predominated. Like Anne Ormbekk, mentioned earlier
in this study, Kristine Hansen's first residence in Seattle was on Queen Anne's
Hill, and like the Ormbrekk family, she and her husband became agricultur-
alists on the edge of the city, supplying Seattle with food products. Hansen,
however, came at a later point—just before World War I—and joined close relatives already well established in the city. Consistent with the main features of
Norwegian women's international migration at that point, she came on her own
by way of one continuous ship and train journey from Norway.[20]

Employment Opportunities for Norwegian American Women

Norwegian women's transfer of working skills from Norway to America's urban
employment market is the most remarkable feature about Norwegian immigrant women's economic choices and activity in these four decades. Whether
they worked without wages at home or became town or city dwellers before
their departure, the overwhelming majority continued in the United States with
familiar domestic work learned at home in Norway. Persuasive evidence of the
transfer becomes evident when women's occupational profiles in the Norwegian
emigration protocols among women bound for selected American cities are
compared with contemporaneous census listings of the work immigrant women
did in these cities.

The overwhelming majority, between two-thirds and four-fifths, of Norwegian
emigrant women engaged in paid work prior to their departure for American cities between 1880 and 1920 earned their living as experienced live-in household
workers. For example, over 99 percent of the women in paid labor who immigrated directly to the Twin Cities from Oslo between 1880 and 1889 worked as
a maid *(pike)* or servant girl *(tjenestepike)*. Over a longer period, from 1886 to
1924 when the records for Oslo, Bergen, Kristiansand, and Trondheim included
specific occupations, the portion in domestic work declined to just under 82
percent (see Tables 4-1 and 4-2). After 1910 a minority of the women arriving had
experience in a wider range of jobs, including "worker" (11 percent), store clerk
(0.1 percent), teacher, tailor, saleslady, office worker, and nurse. However, the
officials who kept the public records in Norway's capital in the first half of the
1880s may have overstated the percentage of women in housework occupations,
too easily assuming what women's work was—that in itself is a most persuasive
indication of gender roles and attitudes in Norway at the time.

The systematic sampling of records from four of Norway's major emigration ports from 1880 to the mid-1920s shows that the most pronounced pattern

TABLE 4-1				
Occupations of Women Leaving Oslo, 1880–89				
Total emigrant women recorded = 1184				
WAGE-EARNING WOMEN (810)			NON-WAGE-EARNING WOMEN (374) (LISTED BY MARITAL/FAMILY STATUS)	
Total recorded	810 (68.4% of 1184)		Total recorded	374 (31.6% of 1184)
Maid/serving girl	807 (99.6% of 810)		Wife	307 (82.1% of 374)
Worker	2 (.2% of 810)		Widow	51 (13.6% of 374)
Shopkeeper	1 (.1% of 810)		Daughter*	13 (3.5% of 374)
			Child	3 (.8% of 374)

*15–21-year-old women listed only as "daughter"

Source: Norwegian Emigrant protocols from Oslo (Kristiania), 1880–89

illustrated above endured for over forty years. An overwhelming four-fifths of Norwegian women leaving continued to report that they were domestic workers, most of them household servants, and the next largest group, over one in ten, worked in the home as family members without wages. In a distant third place, manual workers included both vestiges of the rural past (dairy maid, farmer, fisher) and, after 1890, signs of the future in a larger number of urban "workers," including a handful of women specified as employed in factories. The rural women who moved to Norway's urbanizing coastal areas found a wider range of employment in town in the first two decades of the twentieth century. These jobs give indications of the changing employment opportunities for women that influenced their second-stage migration to cities in the United States. Increasingly women found urban work in Norway in a broader variety of domestic and sewing trades, in health care, and in factories, depending on the opportunities in the region in which they resided. "Maid" disappeared as a generic work title for female emigrants traveling directly to Minneapolis/St. Paul between 1886 and 1924, but very few female emigrants had found work outside a gender-segregated job market before leaving. The first evident development was that emigrating women more often had experience in specific occupations, such as housekeeper, house manager, cook, midwife, and baker, rather than positions in generic household work. Growing numbers worked as weavers, tailors, bookbinders, factory workers, nurses, nurses' assistants, nannies, or teachers. By the 1920s, their occupations included office lady, saleslady, waitress, and dental technician. At the same time, however, by far the most frequent paid work for women remained domestic service, and in a distant second place occupationally, semi-skilled and unskilled labor. The other employment groups with small numbers (see Table 4-2) were typical women's work for the young and single.

TABLE 4-2
Occupations of Women Leaving Norwegian Ports, 1886–1924*

Destination: Minneapolis/St. Paul

TOTAL EMIGRANT WOMEN RECORDED = 1,512; WAGE-EARNING WOMEN = 1,285;
NON-WAGE-EARNING WOMEN (FAMILY RELATION OR STATUS OF "AT HOME") = 227 (15% OF 1512)

OCCUPATIONAL GROUPING AND LARGEST INDIVIDUAL OCCUPATIONS	NUMBER	PERCENT OF 1,285
Total domestic workers	1,052	(81.9%)
Girl (pike)	854	(66.5%)
Servant girl (tjenestepike)	153	(11.9%)
Household worker	16	
Household helper	14	
Nanny	1	
Total blue collar/manual workers (semi- and unskilled)	146	(11.4%)
Worker (unspecified)	135	
Factory worker	5	
Fisher	2	
Baker	1	
Bookbinder	1	
Dairy maid	1	
Farmer	1	
Total clerical/restaurant workers/low white collar	21	(1.6%)
Store assistant	13	
Office clerk	2	
Shopkeeper	2	
Teacher	2	
Waitress	2	
Hostess	1	
Painter (of pictures)	1	
Total needle trades	17	(1.3%)
Seamstress	9	
Tailor	4	
Linen worker	1	
Weaver	3	
Total health workers	15	(1.2%)
Nurse's assistant	10	
Nurse	2	
Midwife	2	
Dental assistant	1	
Total business	4	(0.3%)
Unspecified	2	
Café owner	1	
Clairvoyant	1	
Total no occupation or family status listed (or unclear)	30	(2.3%)
TOTALS	1,285	(100%)

* Recorded every fifth year, i.e., 1886, 1890 . . . 1924

Source: Norwegian Emigrant protocols from Oslo, Kristiansand, Bergen, and Trondheim

Through these positions, women not only received income but gained experience in an urban setting.

New York emigration records reveal the same attitudes toward a woman's place socially and economically in Norway that were found in Minneapolis/St. Paul. Based on emigration records from three Norwegian ports (Kristiansand, Bergen, and Trondheim) to New York in 1904, between 20 percent and 66 percent of the working women had been employed as domestic servants before they left. Furthermore, between 20 and 40 percent emigrating had done unpaid work as homemakers. Around 9 percent had worked as "sewing girls or ladies" and seamstresses. Very small numbers had worked in white-collar office jobs or small businesses before emigrating (see Table 4-3). The most important distinction for female migration to New York was that the majority of women spent their childhood in southern Norway's coastal rural districts. Many followed the paths blazed by seamen, who served as conduits of information, either relaying to family members the attractions of New York or having sojourned there when Norway's commercial sailing fleet experienced a serious economic crisis around 1890.[21]

According to Andres A. Svalestuen, the dominance of men in Norwegian emigration grew especially evident in the late 1880s and reached a peak between 1901 and 1905. The exodus from Oslo to Minneapolis/St. Paul presents a striking exception to this pattern in the later 1880s because women composed the majority of emigrants from Oslo to the Twin Cities in those years. Following 1900, as emigration from Norway was rising to its twentieth-century peak in 1907, women made up varying portions of those departing Norwegian ports

TABLE 4-3
Occupations of Women Leaving Norwegian Ports, 1904

Destination: New York or Brooklyn

PORTS (AND TOTAL FROM EACH):	KRISTIANSAND (768)		BERGEN (43)		TRONDHEIM (61)	
	(NUMBER AND PERCENT OF TOTAL FROM EACH PORT)					
Occupational class						
Professional	2	0.3%	0		0	
White collar/business	8	1.0%	1	2.3%	1	1.6%
Low white collar	27	3.5%	8	18.6 %	3	4.9 %
Skilled worker	69	9.0%	6	14.0%	2	3.3%
Domestic work	378	49.2%	9	20.9%	41	67.2%
Semi-skilled	6	0.8%	0		1	1.6%
Unskilled	5	0.6%	1	2.3%	0	
Misc./wife	273	35.6%	18	41.9%	13	21.3%
TOTALS	768	100.0%	43	100.0%	61	100.0%

Source: Norwegian Emigrant protocol data analysis from David Mauk, *The Colony that Rose from the Sea* (Northfield, MN: Norwegian-American Historical Association, 1997), 227.

for New York City. Everywhere along the Norwegian coast, however, men comprised a large majority of those departing for New York. In 1904, for example, women represented only one in ten emigrants leaving Bergen for New York City and three in ten from Trondheim; four of every ten emigrants from Oslo and Kristiansand for New York were women. Between one-half and two-thirds of these immigrants, however, were city or town dwellers, a range that was higher than average for emigration in general from Norway at that time.[22]

The largest groups of women arriving in the Twin Cities and New York between the 1880s and the 1920s had experience as city dwellers and as domestic workers. They were much in demand as maids, cooks, and housekeepers in American homes or as homemakers in Norwegian American communities. Most of the single women, in their late teens and twenties, planned to work until they had adjusted to American life, established themselves in the Norwegian American community, saved a nest egg (as several termed their savings), and found a suitable husband. Significant numbers intended to take savings back to Norway to help relatives or establish a family there. The large majority felt confident that they mastered skilled housework when they arrived, and many had heard that Norwegian household help was highly regarded and well paid. Frequently this confidence and knowledge of the reception they could expect came from the female friends and relatives who had preceded them to the city and facilitated their chain migration.[23]

Occupations and Working Conditions in the City

The working conditions of Norwegian immigrant women in America's urban centers were in large part determined by their transfer of skills learned in Norway. Until the 1920s, in the United States and in Norway women were generally limited to jobs linked to traditional domestic skills or to semi- or unskilled factory work in, for example, textiles or food processing. All of the big cities with significant Norwegian American enclaves from the 1880s onward possessed an increasing range of factory work for women, from stitching ready-made apparel in New York and the Twin Cities to meat and food processing in Chicago and fish cannery work in Seattle. In each city some Norwegian immigrant women and their daughters found these less traditional kinds of work. The choices of the large majority of the immigrant women, however, showed that they knew their domestic skills were in high demand and that they preferred to take opportunities in that employment market rather than in factory work. Jobs in the needle trades and small dress shops or as self-employed individuals were a distant second-best choice.

In Chicago as early as the two decades before the Civil War, domestic service—usually as a live-in housemaid for families or professional and business men—had become by far the most common employment for Norwegian American women. In the decades just before and after the war, they worked in hotels as well as homes in such large numbers that women topped Norwegian men recorded in federal censuses for those years, notes Lovoll. A Norwegian American business-woman in the city made a living by running an employment agency for fellow immigrants during that period. By the 1880s the preponderance of wage-earning Norwegian American women choosing domestic service was even greater, when fully three of four of them earned a living as servants. Lovoll emphasizes the decided preference of Norwegian and Scandinavian working women generally for housework over factory employment. It seems very likely that this preference is closely related to the women's labor experience in Norway.[24]

By the 1880s in the Chicago community, a much smaller portion of Norwegian American women (13 percent) worked as seamstresses or dressmakers. In 1901 a study claimed that these women often experienced "deplorable working condi-tions" and earned "starvation wages" in sweatshops, even though Scandinavian women received better treatment than the "new" immigrant female workers from southern and eastern Europe doing the same work. A few years earlier, *Skandinaven* found tailoring to be the most common craft among Scandinavians, and Lovoll concludes that a large number of women worked at the trade. The same newspaper report asserted that especially during the winter months, when their husbands were often unemployed, many Norwegian American married women took in sewing at home for pay. As late as 1910, Norwegian American women's occupational profile in Chicago remained largely unchanged, although nursing, customer services in stores, office work, and positions as matrons in charitable institutions had begun to offer broader opportunities.[25]

A study of Norwegian American life in Minneapolis/St. Paul shows the vari-ety of working conditions domestic service could include in the Twin Cities in 1880. As it had been since the 1850s, domestic service remained by far the most important source of wages for unmarried Norwegian American women in the Twin Cities. At that time 32 percent of the Norwegian-born working women in Minneapolis and 68 percent of their immigrant sisters in St. Paul worked as domestic servants. These were high percentages but somewhat lower than those shown by Norwegian American women in Chicago at the same time. The espe-cially low frequency of domestic service in Minneapolis was part of a distinctively diverse employment profile that included over 10 percent in various sewing jobs, 2 percent textile mill workers, and 4 percent doing assorted unskilled clean-ing jobs in businesses and factories. In the small group of second-generation working women in these enclaves, 39 percent in Minneapolis and 56 percent in St. Paul were employed in domestic service, and 22 percent and 28 percent, respectively, worked in sewing trades. Such figures provide no clear signs of occupational change from one generation to another, indicating an enduring interest in domestic service and sewing positions. However, in the early twentieth century this generational shift is more clearly evident. Although the domestic workers ranged in age from eleven to forty-four, most were around twenty—on average younger than both other Norwegian American adults and the general adult population of the Twin Cities. They were also single and living on their own. Only four, all in their twenties, were married, and the large majority lived outside the Norwegian enclaves in the homes of their employers in the more affluent areas. A sizeable minority, on the other hand, worked in the immigrant quarters, living as help in family households or as residents in boardinghouses where they may have been employed. A handful of women described their work more exactly as, for example, "washing and ironing."[26]

The census manuscripts from 1880 reveal a broad spectrum of households employing live-in domestic servants in the Twin Cities that ranged from the mansions of wealthy families to the modest homes of the lower middle class. Not only wealthy business leaders and professionals but also many middle-class proprietors of family stores, agencies, and small businesses relied on live-in help to lighten household tasks before electrical appliances became commonplace. In Minneapolis (called "the Mill City"), the percentage of Norwegian American domestics in the female workforce was less than half that in the state capital; nonetheless, nearly five times the number of women did this kind of work, reflecting the much larger size of the Norwegian American population in the Mill City. In its most elaborate households, for example, the homes of flour mill magnates such as the Pillsburys and Pettits, Norwegian-born and second-generation Norwegian Americans met each other in the workplace and learned to cooperate on polyglot staffs that included Prussian, Swedish, and Irish immigrants and Irish Americans. At the same time they learned the manners and tastes of northern New England, the ancestral home of most of the upper-class and upper-middle-class employers.[27]

In less affluent middle-class homes, Norwegian American domestics learned to interpret a range of cultural differences that was about equally wide, largely because these households usually included boarders. Alice Johnson, for example, twenty-three and Norwegian born, helped grocer Judson Higgins's wife Mary manage a Minneapolis home that included the couple's seven children, only two of whom attended school, and four American store clerks who had moved to the city from three different northeastern states and Wisconsin. Close to the west-side milling district, Julia Hanson served a flour mill worker and his wife from more easterly states as well as their eight boarders. These boarders, who came from Ireland, Germany, Canada, and New England, worked in the mills and as skilled workers in other fields. Norwegian American domestics typically labored in middle-class households, where a single servant performed household duties for a couple and three or more half-grown children.[28]

In St. Paul, Norwegian American household workers experienced as wide a spectrum of situations as they did in Minneapolis, but the circumstances of their employment reflected the capital city's distinctive economy and population. The homes of wholesale merchants, railroad officials, financiers, government officials, and lawyers provided varied positions for Norwegian American domestic workers in St. Paul. Americans from northern New England, however, were again the most influential members in upper-class circles, where some Norwegian immigrants worked, and as in the Mill City, these women served in the homes of middle-class, old-stock Americans from other more easterly states. The different national backgrounds immigrant women encountered in their domestic service occurred not only in upper- and middle-class neighborhoods but also in the city's lower-middle-class and working-class areas. There, first- and second-generation Irish Americans and German Americans more frequently employed Norwegian domestic workers. Anna Tollaas, for instance, worked for an Irish-born policeman in a household that included his wife, two small children, and fourteen mostly Irish and Irish American boarders. Nettie Olsen served in a saloon and boardinghouse run by a couple from Germany that rented rooms exclusively to first- and second-generation German Americans.[29]

The occupational profile of Norwegian American women in the Brooklyn,

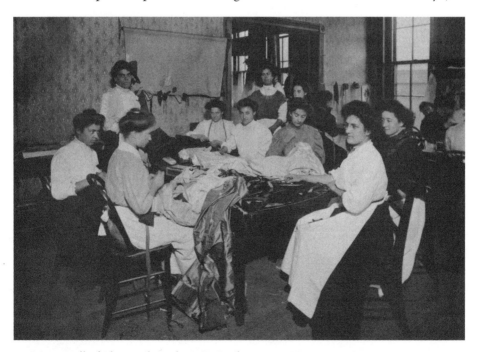

Mary Molloy's dressmaking shop, St. Paul, ca. 1890. Norwegian American women worked in similar shops in the Twin Cities.

TABLE 4-4

Occupations of First- and Second-Generation Norwegian American Women in Brooklyn and Minneapolis/St. Paul, 1892, 1900, 1920

(calculations based on a 10 percent sample of all census districts)

	NEW YORK CENSUS 1892 BROOKLYN		FEDERAL CENSUSES 1900 TWIN CITIES		1920 TWIN CITIES	
Professional	14	(5.2%)	8	(5.4%)	25	(6.9%)
Nurse/deaconess	11	(4.1%)	4	(2.7%)	10	(2.8%)
Teacher	2	(0.8%)	4	(2.7%)	13	(3.6%)
Musician					1	(0.6%)
Psychologist/doctor	1	(0.4%)			1	(0.6%)
Business	11	(4.1%)	3	(2.0%)	6	(1.7%)
Boardinghouse keeper	9	(3.4%)	1	(0.6%)		
Landlady			2	(1.3%)		
Merchant/proprietor	2	(0.8%)			4	(1.1%)
Music school proprietor					1	(0.3%)
Portrait painter					1	(0.3%)
Low-level white collar						
workers (low status and pay)	9	(3.4%)	12	(8.0%)	140	(41.3%)
Bookkeeper					20	(5.5%)
Cashier			2	(1.3%)	5	(1.4%)
Clerk	2	(0.8%)			38	(10.5%)
Saleswoman	3	(1.1%)	7	(4.7%)	17	(4.7%)
Secretary					4	(1.1%)
Stenographer			1	(0.6%)	48	(13.3%)
Telephone/telegraph	1	(0.4%)	1	(0.6%)	7	(1.9%)
Typist	3	(1.1%)	1	(0.6%)	1	(0.3%)
Miscellaneous						
Skilled workers	47	(17.6%)	52	(34.6%)	42	(9.1%)
Dressmaker	17	(6.4%)	21	(14.0%)	9	(2.5%)
Embroiderer			1	(0.6%)		
Fancy sewer (teacher)			1	(0.6%)		
Forelady/supervisor					2	(0.6%)
Glove maker			1	(0.6%)		
Knitter					1	(0.3%)

New York, community in 1892 was strikingly similar to the patterns just discussed for the Twin Cities (see Table 4-4). Two-thirds of wage earners worked in the service sector as domestics and cleaners, almost all of them in private homes. Sewing, which could be done in factories, shops, or at home, comprised the second most-attractive part of the job market for Norwegian women and their daughters. Only two women chose to sew in a factory setting, and altogether less than 2 percent (five women) worked in factories. Office work and

	NEW YORK CENSUS 1892 BROOKLYN		FEDERAL CENSUSES 1900 TWIN CITIES		1920 TWIN CITIES	
Milliner	1	(0.4%)	4	(4.0%)	2	(0.6%)
Seamer/sewer					5	(1.4%)
Seamstress	26	(9.7%)	19	(12.7%)	9	(2.5%)
Shirtmaker			2	(1.3%)		
Tailor			3	(2.0%)	5	(1.4%)
Miscellaneous skilled	3	(1.1%)			9	(2.5%)
Semi-skilled workers	176	(65.9%)	43	(32.0%)	28	(7.8%)
(all Domestic& Service)						
Cook	9	(3.4%)	1	(0.6%)	2	(0.6%)
Hairdresser			1	(0.6%)	1	(0.3%)
Housekeeper	1	(0.4%)	13	(8.7%)	14	(3.9%)
Servant	166	(62.2%)	28	(18.7%)	6	(1.7%)
Waitress/hostess					5	(1.4%)
Unskilled workers	10	(3.7%)	27	(18.0%)	49	(13.6%)
		(½ in housework)		(16.7% in household work)		
Factory sewer	2	(.08%)	1	(0.6%)	5	(1.4%)
Factory worker	3	(1.1%)	1	(0.6%)	13	(3.6%)
Housework			4	(2.7%)	2	(.6%)
Ironer			1	(0.6%)	3	(.8%)
Laundress	2	(.08%)	15	(10.0%)	9	(2.5%)
Washerwoman	2	(.08%)	5	(3.3%)	4	(1.1%)
Miscellaneous						
Unskilled	1	(.04%)			13	(3.6%)
No occupation listed or unclear					71	(19.6%)
TOTALS	267	(99.9 %)	145	(100%)	361	(100%)

Source: Derived from Twin Cities History Project census samples and adjusted work categories from David Mauk, "The Colony that Rose from the Sea: The Norwegians in the Red Hook Section of Brooklyn" (PhD diss., New York University, 1991), Table 6, page 541, for female occupations in Brooklyn 1892.

white-collar service jobs formed a much smaller, third area of employment opportunity. Taking in boarders or running a boardinghouse, however, provided an income to as many women as the whole white-collar sector. At the top of this occupational pyramid were the two women who ran stores, perhaps with their husbands, and the relatively large group of nurses in Brooklyn who worked at the first Norwegian Lutheran Deaconesses' Home and Hospital in America, which Sister Elizabeth Fedde helped establish in 1883.[30]

In 1900, only the married women in Minneapolis/St. Paul whose work was described as "keeps house" comprised a larger occupational group than the women listed as domestic servants. This reflects a very significant change in that a larger portion of the Norwegian female population had left the paid work-force after marrying in those twenty years. Married women with husbands and children now made up the majority of Norwegian-born women in the Twin Cities. Their age, concerns, and priorities had changed. In interviews their children spoke of mothers who were involved in Norwegian clubs, societies, and especially the women's organizations in the churches and Sunday schools. The percentage working as domestic servants, moreover, had dropped drastically to just under 19 percent. If all kinds of cleaning, laundry, and "housekeeping" duties are combined into one occupational group, the women involved make up nearly half (48.7 percent) of the Norwegian American female workforce, but this is a sharp decline from the portion in that kind of work in Brooklyn and Minneapolis in the earlier censuses. Those women, the census data show, were younger and almost all single.

The second-largest category of women workers in the Twin Cities in 1900, skilled occupations in the needle trades, employed a third of Norwegian American women, which was an increase over the earlier Twin Cities and Brooklyn counts. One reason for the change is that increasing numbers of women with experience in these trades emigrated in the 1890s. Another may be that women who came earlier perhaps helped other Norwegians enter this kind of work. The portion of women in professional or white-collar work in Brooklyn in 1892 and the Twin Cities eight years later, on the other hand, had grown only slightly. The women needleworkers and professionals were also, with a few exceptions, unmarried. The younger, unmarried group of women in professional positions, the needle trades, and housekeeping were very likely more recent immigrants. The offspring of Norwegian women who arrived at the end of the 1800s often reported that their mothers or grandmothers did this kind of work until they married. Marriage represented the most important turning point in a woman's life, according to the members of later generations. Despite the continued presence of textile and clothing mills in all three cities, most Norwegian American women, both married and unmarried, continued to avoid factory work.[31]

Within the next twenty years, significant changes again occurred in the work Norwegian American women in the Twin Cities chose, especially among the daughters of Norwegian immigrants. The number of highly educated health professionals and teachers, nearly all of them members of the second generation, more than doubled from 1900 to 1920. The nurses, several of them deaconesses, were American born rather than immigrants from Norway. The phenomenal change, however, appeared in the quintupling of the portion of women working in white-collar jobs, especially as clerks and stenographers. The large majority

Many immigrant women—though only a few of Norwegian descent—worked in the needle trades, such as at Munsingwear undergarment company in Minneapolis

in these positions were second-generation women, reflecting their rapid integration into patterns of women's work among Americans. The active choice of new paths in the job market also seems apparent in the precipitous fall in the percentage of women employed in the needle, domestic, and service trades. Women factory workers increased to a larger number than in 1900 but remained the choice of only a very small percentage of Norwegian American working women, evenly split between the first and second generations. Overall, the 1920 census shows that these women had increasingly moved into new kinds of work, but their concentration in white-collar office work still represented employment in a gendered labor market. Interviews with women in the Twin Cities' Norwegian American communities indicate that most of these women stopped working outside the home when they married.[32]

Women's work among urban Norwegian Americans in Seattle deviated little from the patterns observed in Brooklyn and the Twin Cities. The Norwegian immigrant women interviewed as part of Janet Rasmussen's oral history project with Scandinavian Americans includes several who worked as domestics early in the twentieth century on the West Coast. These women emphasized many of the advantages of domestic service as a way of entering the American labor market that have been outlined here. Rasmussen notes that across the United States in 1900 and 1910, a large majority transferred household skills learned in Scandinavia to demonstrate relevant work experience. She adds that they were unconcerned that some people considered domestic service to be a low-status occupation and that they "displayed a self-determined mobility, moving between households, and between types of service jobs, in search of a better working environment." She also stresses that, as observed in the more easterly cities, live-in domestic service was quite naturally work women did until they married and that many stopped working outside the home entirely at marriage. Significant numbers of married women, she also notes, worked together in small businesses as partners with their husbands.[33]

Norwegian immigrant women in Seattle worked in traditional occupations for women, such as domestic service and the sewing trades, but the labor market on the West Coast, like that across the nation and in Norway, by the teens and 1920s offered a wider range of paying positions that included nursing and office work. Still, well-known paths remained very adaptable for some. Inga Amanda Træland, for instance, followed the migratory path of her older brother and sister to Brooklyn in 1925, where she worked in the homes, as she described them, of "rich people." Later, when her sister moved to the Ballard section of Seattle and asked Inga to join her, she left positions with wealthy New Yorkers for domestic work in affluent homes on Capitol Hill in Seattle.[34]

Life in American Cities: Homes, Family, and Marriage

The experience of Norwegian immigrant women and their daughters in American cities, like their migratory patterns, was in important ways distinctive from men's experiences. To be sure, some features of these women's lives were shared not only by immigrant men and children but also by the general urban working class to which the overwhelming majority of them belonged. Some features that greatly affected Norwegian immigrant women's living conditions will illuminate that difference. In the decades before and after 1900, these laboring classes, whether newcomers or longtime residents, native or foreign born, all lived close to the city center in crowded, commercial-industrial neighborhoods. From the perspective of residents, these districts held advantages and disadvantages. Amidst or adjacent to employers, a location that saved workers transportation costs, these bustling areas usually offered low-cost housing. On the other hand, such neighborhoods were invariably unhealthy because they were noisy, congested, polluted, and commonly the lowest-lying parts of town—canal or riverside districts and dockside flats without adequate sewage or drainage—and so periodically suffered floods and epidemics. Norwegian American women who lived in Red Hook, Brooklyn, and the Cedar-Riverside section of Minneapolis contracted tuberculosis, cholera, and diphtheria under these conditions. They suffered from complications in childbirth and nursed husbands and children as well as lodgers through epidemics that took many lives.[35]

In the 1830s and 1840s, Chicago's first Norwegian community grew up among canal-land squatters on the "Sands," a swampy area near the point where the Chicago River emptied into Lake Michigan and low-cost, unskilled labor was needed. There, sisters, wives, and daughters not only kept house for their immediate family but provided care and hospitality for bachelors or whole families newly arrived from western Norway who commonly lived with the earliest settlers until they could afford their own housing. By the late 1840s such female city pioneers could participate in religious services led by visiting Norwegian clerics who came to Chicago to preach from the rapidly growing number of farming communities Norwegians founded in this period in nearby areas of Illinois, Wisconsin, and Iowa. In New York City Norwegian immigrants first clustered in the dockside districts of lower Manhattan in the 1850s and 1860s and from the 1870s through the 1900s in bay-side neighborhoods of Brooklyn, where pneumonia and malaria, among other illnesses, cost more lives than in other areas of the city due to the dampness of these low-lying districts. Here, too, the family's female members made room for relatives and others, in this case usually from southern Norway or sailors from the country merchant fleet. In Minneapolis/ St. Paul, Norwegian newcomers crowded into working-class immigrant quarters close to factories or the flour and lumber mill districts along the Mississippi River, the least successful among them squatting at river level in Minneapolis on Bohemian Flats or in a ravine in St. Paul called "Swede Hollow." In those areas, too, women created homes for families and new arrivals amidst the worst physical conditions of city life.[36]

Financial necessity forced people with little capital to get a start in the city in precisely such areas. These were the first settlement areas of immigrants where one foreign group succeeded another with the passage of time. For the newly arrived foreigner, such immigrant quarters often provided the guidance and comforts of familiar enclaves, whose institutions eased their adjustment to American city life. As soon as circumstances allowed, most people relocated to more salubrious and attractive parts of town. As long as they remained in the first settlement districts, however, they offered food, shelter, and advice for later arriving relatives and acquaintances who followed chain migration patterns like their own. Of female immigrants, wives and young girls spent the most time in the immigrant quarters of town. Male immigrants' work, as dirty and dangerous as it often was, not infrequently took them to the port, out on the river, lake, or sea, or to construction sites in other parts of the city. Male children had chores, but more often these consisted of outdoor work, and they took paid jobs as news-paper carriers and delivery or errand boys at a young age. Married immigrant women and their underage daughters stayed at home or in the district, where they shopped for supplies and food, cooked, cleaned, and cared for the old, the sick, and the very young under the difficult conditions described above.[37]

Women unemployed outside the home cared for the stream of newcomers who followed the path to urban America. By common custom and economic need, women and girls, in addition, made and mended clothing and preserved foods for the family and its temporary guests (if they were male). Jorunn Wolden, for example, explained that her mother had emigrated from one end of the Odal valley in south-central Norway and her father from the other. While she was growing up, their home in south Minneapolis therefore became the temporary residence of newcomers from both ends of the valley until they got their feet on the ground and could find their own housing in the city. Similar accounts of a family home where women performed extra household work for new arrivals and sojourners appear in interviews and documents of immigrants in Brooklyn and Minneapolis/St. Paul.

Women in these urban enclaves, moreover, frequently added to the house-hold income by taking in laundry, boarders, and lodgers. In Minneapolis/St. Paul during the 1880s and 1890s, the most common small business among first- and second-generation Norwegian Americans was the boardinghouse; the large majority of these were run as family enterprises in which wives and daughters did the cooking and cleaning. Boarding was much more commonplace in American cities between 1880 and 1920 than at any time since, and the Norwegian immi-grants in Minneapolis/St. Paul show no exception to this pattern. A large major-ity of Norwegian American households, regardless of socioeconomic class, included boarders, usually just a few but occasionally a half dozen or more—even though most of these families did not declare taking in boarders as an occupation. A typical Norwegian American home included parents, children, boarders, and not infrequently a young female domestic servant, who may have helped out with the household work or done domestic duties elsewhere. The Norwegian-born boarders in the Twin Cities' homes and lodging houses were so overwhelmingly single and youthful that they gave the immigrant community as a whole a distinctively youthful, single character compared with the rest of the population. Nine of ten of these boarders were single, and their median age was twenty-three.[38]

In 1880 and 1890 the majority of boarders in the Twin Cities were men, seasonal workers who moved into the countryside for the harvest or work in logging camps, then back to the city for jobs in the flour and lumber mills or construction. Even as early as the 1880s, however, young single women consti-tuted a growing part of the boarding population, and from 1900 into the 1920s the balance tipped so that young, single women moving into Minneapolis/St. Paul made up the majority of migrating workers coming to the Twin Cities and taking up residence as boarders. Although this was part of a national trend, Minneapolis/St. Paul represented an extreme example of an urban environment experiencing the arrival of large numbers of unattached women. A 1900 Federal Census Bureau study of working women showed that a greater portion in the Twin Cities found room and board away from their families than was the case in twenty-five other large American cities. In St. Paul just over one-third and in Minneapolis just under one-third of adult working women were living as unattached individuals with room and board arrangements. In contrast, Chicago ranked eighth and New York eleventh among the twenty-seven cities for which the living conditions of the female workforce was studied. The foreign born made up a little over 40 percent of the women boarders in the Twin Cities: German, Swedish, and Norwegian immigrants comprised the three largest groups. In Minneapolis/St. Paul, moreover, over twice as many second-generation immigrant women, the daughters of foreign-born parents, boarded or lodged than was the national average. The unusually high rate of urbanization of young single women from the rural Upper Midwest to the Twin Cities resulted from continuing crises in agriculture and the attractions of Minneapolis/St. Paul.[39]

In Brooklyn's Little Norway around the turn of the twentieth century, wives so frequently ran a boarding business out of their homes or apartments that the community coined the Norwegian American word "table-*bord*" to describe them. The word meant a private family home where people could buy meals. Its mixture of a Norwegian word (*bord*) and the English word for the same object (table) indicated to Norwegian Americans that they could sit at the table for meals at a house with a sign advertising a "Table-bord." Norwegian American women so often shared their homes with single, unrelated men lodging in the upstairs corridor that people in the group called these lodgers "hallboys." Women's nonwage domestic labor coupled with wage work required long hours during and outside of normal working times; however, this was often seen as their natural lot in life. Furthermore, it was best carried out with a cheerful stoicism, according to stories handed down by generations of Norwegian American women in Brooklyn and Minneapolis/St. Paul.

Boarding brought nonfamily into the home, but quite often these people were Norwegians or Norwegian Americans who appeared after work in the evenings. Norwegian American women frequently reported that married women's daytime lives were lived almost exclusively within the domestic round of stay-at-home wives' unpaid household duties and their social contacts with other women in the same situation inside the ethnic community. As a young girl in Sunset Park, Brooklyn, for example, Serene Sortland heard from her mother that gainful employment in service or offices had to stop when a woman married.

That attitude found broad confirmation in a Norwegian American community of the 1920s in which only 18 percent of married Norwegian-born women and their married daughters worked outside the home. Sortland spent her preschool days at home with "mor," where housework and sewing and laundry jobs for neighbors were relieved by visits from stay-at-home Norwegian-born female friends of her mother. Sortland learned her "English" from her mother and these women. Her father, a deep-sea sailor, was seldom at home. After her first day at school, Sortland reported that her teacher was "no good because she [her teacher] can't speak the language [English] right, not like you [her mother] and your friends." Sortland's story, though perhaps exaggerated through family retelling, nonetheless echoes in the memories of many married women and young girls in the Norwegian communities in New York and the Twin Cities. Women and young girls moved in a daytime, weekday world bound by female company and extended largely only by forays to nearby ethnic shops for household goods. It can be argued that the Norwegian culture in the city—and later Norwegian American ethnic identity in urban life—found its strongest bulwark in the private home life maintained by married women.[40]

Carl G. O. Hansen, a member the editorial staff of *Minneapolis Tidende* from 1897 and the paper's editor in chief from 1923, expressed commonplace attitudes of the period concerning the importance of the ethnic households maintained by Norwegian American mothers on the occasion of the 1925 centennial celebrations of Norwegian immigration to the United States. Norwegian American mothers in the Midwest, he wrote,

> provided the most essential foundation for the strong feeling of Norwegian-ness that is often to be found among people who were born and have grown up in America . . . Right up to recent times homes have been Norwegian to the degree that the mother preserved the best of Norwegian tradition. The man in the family associated with all kinds of people in his work or business and in time became more of an American in his behavior, but the wife in all her activity remained Norwegian . . . Not infrequently the man . . . became Norwegian the moment he entered his living room . . . Mother has been the guardian of Norwegian-ness in Norwegian American homes.

Hansen wrote this about the Norwegian American mothers in the Midwest, but the Americanizing effects of the father's dealings with "all kinds of people" became most pronounced in urban settings. An ethnic identity preserved in the home was surely valuable in the city, where wives walked between the home and Norwegian-language stores, churches, and other ethnic institutions in the local neighborhood; the women's preservation of old-world culture in the homes was validated and reinforced in the world around them.[41]

In such strongly ethnic urban enclaves, marrying and making a life within the ethnic group was demonstrably possible, as is documented by the very low intermarriage rates in Chicago and the Twin Cities. Around 1880, if Norwegian American women in Chicago left work for marriage, nine of ten married a man from Norway. The increasingly skewed sex ratio among recent Norwegian immigrants to the city, reports Lovoll, likely contributed to the decline in endogamous marriages to a little over three in four in 1910. In Minneapolis in 1880, around eight of ten Norwegian-born women and their daughters chose Norwegian American men. The rest found spouses outside their national-ity group, most of them among Swedish or Danish American immigrants or Americans of unknown background (see Table 4-5). In neighboring St. Paul, where the Norwegian immigrant community was much smaller, only a little over seven in ten married inside the group, but when they did not their preference for Scandinavian Americans was so strong that the maintenance of Nordic marital ties was equally pronounced in both of the cities. In Minneapolis, endogamous marriages dropped to three in four by 1900, and during the following twenty years the intermarriage rate and choice of other Scandinavians, when it did occur, remained nearly constant. In St. Paul, by contrast, endogamous marriages fell to two-thirds by 1900 and stayed at that level in 1920. In the same years, though Norwegian American women in the capital city found partners whose origins more often lay outside Scandinavia, Swedish Americans remained by far the first choice among non-Norwegians.[42]

The Norwegian women who arrived in the Twin Cities after 1900 contin-ued to be remarkably young. The community's women in their twenties were

TABLE 4-5
Intermarriage in Percentages: Minneapolis/St. Paul, 1880, 1900, and 1920

(first and second generations)

	ENDOGAMOUS	TO SWEDES	TO DANES	TOTAL
1880 (100% sample) Minneapolis	79.5	9.0	2.6	91.1%
1880 (100% sample) St. Paul	72.1	11.9	7.9	91.9%
1900 (20% sample) Minneapolis	74.1	16.1	2.6	92.8%
1900 (20% sample) St. Paul	67.7	12.2	0.1	80.0%
1920 (20% sample) Minneapolis	74.2	15.2	1.8	91.2%
1920 (20% sample) St. Paul	65.3	18.4	0.4	84.1%

Source: 1880, 1900, and 1920 U.S. Census samples for the Twin Cities History Project

almost evenly divided between the first and second generations (18 percent and 12 percent, respectively) at the start of the 1920s. Those arriving as youths between 1913 and the mid-1920s mixed socially with women their own age in both generations and had Norwegian girlfriends from Norway, the Twin Cities, and the region. Perhaps the most dramatic change among young women born in Norway was that only 14 percent of them were single. Nearly seven in ten of the American-born women, on the other hand (one-third of them in their twenties), were unmarried. In general, the majority of marriageable Norwegian American women had shifted from the foreign-born generation to their daughters, the first American-born generation. These daughters, brought up in the Twin Cities in the years since 1900, had reached young adulthood and were dating or thinking about starting families. If they considered dating inside the group, they found many single Norwegian-born men but far fewer unmarried Norwegian-born women. Thus, since the large majority of Norwegian Americans in the Twin Cities still chose to marry inside the ethnic group in 1920, more couples formed between the Norwegian-born men and second-generation Norwegian American women. A study of the marriage patterns among Norwegian Americans in the Twin Cities in the 1920 census confirms the frequency of such unions. The women who, like Hansen's mother, had small children in the 1880s had become the community's grandmothers by the 1920s. Their daughters were far more likely to marry men born in Norway than in the United States or elsewhere.[43]

Conclusion

The earliest movement of Norwegian immigrant women to American cities most often took place via the rural midwestern agricultural districts where the great majority of Norwegians settled in the 1800s. Some of the early female emigrants from Norway, women like Anne Hovey and Ingeborg Gilberts, worked their way to America as servant girls in the mid-1800s and quickly relocated to urban areas. Others came to Chicago and New York between the 1830s and 1880s as unmarried daughters in the families who formed the early communities in those cities. Many in these contingents of women used the transferable household skills they had from Norway to make a living in the city as domestic workers after their arrival. Letters to relatives and friends in the American countryside or in Norway spread the news of their success and the conditions of their work. From the 1880s onward, increasing numbers of Norwegian women migrated to the United States alone or with friends, and growing numbers moved directly from Norwegian cities to American cities. Still, the great majority of first- and second-generation Norwegian American women, especially those migrating in or to the Midwest, repeated the pattern of settling as part of family groups on farms and then moving to urban areas later. It was mostly young, unmarried Norwegian-born women and young, unmarried American-born daughters who moved to big cities like New York, Chicago, the Twin Cities, and Seattle. They worked there for some years, mostly in domestic positions, until they married. The Norwegian women who moved to New York City more often came directly from Norway as single people. They chose New York both because it was a center of later Norwegian immigration and because the number of Norwegian immigrants in the vicinity of the city was relatively small. In the period of this study, Seattle attracted women migrating directly from Norway as well as Norwegian American women relocating from the Midwest; only later did it attract larger numbers from Norwegian American rural districts in its vicinity. After marriage, almost all these Norwegian American women left the paid workforce and instead cared for home, family, boarders, and lodgers without pay.

A significant portion of the Norwegian American population left its first urban settlement areas in the decades after 1900 and spread out in American cities between then and 1930. As that happened, the married woman's "Norwegian home" that Hansen celebrated more often stood alone, and a growing portion of daughters chose not to maintain traditions of their Norwegian heritage to the same degree in their domestic lives. To an important extent many women simply could not follow their mothers' model because they lacked the community support that a close-knit concentrated ethnic quarter had once provided. Another important reason for changes in Norwegian ethnicity in these years was language loss. By the 1920s, many young women of Norwegian descent in American cities had not learned Norwegian or they only remembered fragments of it taught to them at home during their preschool years. By that decade, moreover, not only strong continuities but striking changes had appeared in the occupational profile and working conditions of the largely unmarried Norwegian American women in the cities studied here. Between 1900 and 1920 large numbers of women, though by no means all, continued to bring transferable household skills from a modernizing Norway to urban centers of the United States. For many in the second, American-born generation, however, employment choices related to social patterns and occupational skills learned in urban America rather than to traditional roles for women in Norway. In the public schools they had learned fluent English and the skills to leave the manual labor of cleaning and domestic service behind. Instead, they most often did well enough at school to enter some form of higher education and then take positions as clerks, stenographers, teachers, nurses, and other health professionals. The pronounced agency of the second generation in opting for different occupations while single, however, stands in marked contrast to their continued marriage inside their ethnic group.

Notes

1. Lorraine Ofstie, interview by author, 22 May 2000.

2. For the most part, material from other scholars' work concerning Norwegian American women in Chicago and Seattle are cited in the text and notes. Norwegian immigrant communities appeared in other cities, for example in San Francisco and Philadelphia, that are not discussed here. Other secondary sources about women immigrants and their gendered employment and living conditions have also influenced the interpretation of sources in this essay. Among these are Solvi Sogner and Kari Telste, *Ut og søkje tjeneste—historia om tjenestejentene* (Oslo: Universitetsforlaget: 2005); Christiane Harzig, ed., *Peasant Maids—City Women: From the Countryside to Urban America* (Ithaca, NY: Cornell University Press, 1997); Donna Gabaccia, *From the Other Side: Women, Gender, and Immigrant Life in the U.S., 1820–1990* (Indianapolis: Indiana University Press, 1994); Alice Kessler-Harris, *Out to Work: A History of Wage-Earning Women in the United States* (New York: Oxford University Press, 1982); David M. Katzman, *Seven Days a Week: Women and Domestic Service in Industrializing America* (New York: Oxford University Press, 1978).

3. Odd S. Lovoll, *A Century of Urban Life: The Norwegians in Chicago before 1930* (Northfield, MN: Norwegian-American Historical Association [hereafter, NAHA], 1988), 79; Odd S. Lovoll, *The Promise of America: A History of the Norwegian American People,* rev. ed. (Minneapolis: University of Minnesota Press, 1999), 232, 250–56.

4. L. DeAne Lagerquist, *In America the Men Milk the Cows: Factors of Gender, Ethnicity and Religion in the Americanization of Norwegian American Women,* Chicago Studies in the History of American Religion (Brooklyn, NY: Carlson Publishing, Inc., 1991), 73–74, 94, 102–3; Merle Curti, *The Making of an American Community: A Case Study of Democracy in a Frontier County* (Stanford, CA: Stanford University Press, 1959); Jon Gjerde, *From Peasants to Farmers: The Migration from Balestrand, Norway, to the Upper Midwest* (New York: Cambridge University Press, 1985); Lynn Weiner, "'Our Sisters' Keepers': The Minneapolis Woman's Christian Association and Housing for Working Women," *Minnesota History* 46.5 (Spring 1979): 189–90; Lucile M. Kane and Alan Ominsky, *Twin Cities: A Pictorial History of St. Paul and Minneapolis* (St. Paul: Minnesota Historical Society Press, 1983), 144; Rhoda R. Gilman, *The Story of Minnesota's Past* (St. Paul: Minnesota Historical Society Press, 1989), 171–72; John S. Adams and Barbara J. Van Drasek, *Minneapolis–St. Paul: People, Places and Public Life* (Minneapolis: University of Minnesota Press, 1993), 45–47. Interviews by author with Mary and Alan Austensen (10 Jan. 1999), Carl and Jean Brookins (1 Nov. 1999), Eileen and Luther Forde (12 Aug. 1998), Krista Sande and Gannerud Johnsen (20 Oct. 1998), Helen Pedersen (12 May 2000), Marilyn Sorensen (3 May 1999), Mary Jo Thorsheim (18 Dec. 1998), Joel Torstensen (27 Apr. 1999).

5. Mari Lund Wright, "The Pioneer Community in Chicago before the Great Fire (1836–1871)," (master's thesis, University of Wisconsin, 1958), 50. Lovoll, *A Century of Urban Life,* 24–25, 79.

6. Carl G. O. Hansen, *My Minneapolis: A Chronicle of What Has Been Learned and Observed about the Norwegians in Minneapolis through One Hundred Years* (Minneapolis,

MN: The author, 1956), 12. Arlow Andersen, *The Salt of the Earth: A History of Norwegian-Danish Methodism in America* (Nashville, TN: Norwegian-Danish Methodist Historical Society, 1962), 39–41, 51–53, 54–55. Letter from Rev. Thomas M. Fullerton to Benjamin F. Hoyt, 22 Mar. 1859, Methodist Episcopal Church—Minnesota Annual Methodist Conference Papers, 1840–1909, box 1, Minnesota Historical Society, St. Paul (hereafter, MHS). A systematic sampling and analysis of the occupations listed for Scandinavian-named residents in city directories for the Twin Cities in the 1850s, 1860s, and 1870s completed for the Twin Cities History Project (hereafter, TCHP) reveals many women in domestic service, housekeeping, and boardinghouse occupations.

7. The U.S. Census of Population totals for St. Paul and Minneapolis in 1880 (p538–41) and 1890 (p670–73) indicate an increase of 12,830 Norwegian-born residents during the decade. In the same ten years, 3,514 Norwegians departing from Oslo (Kristiania) gave their destination as one of the Twin Cities and small numbers of Norwegians leaving the country's other major emigration depots announced the same goal. A total of 3,709 people—equivalent to 29 percent of the 12,830 increase in the Norwegian-born population in the Twin Cities between 1880 and 1890—left Oslo, Kristiansand, Bergen, and Trondheim directly for one of the Twin Cities. Included in that total were very likely Norwegians who named Minneapolis or St. Paul as their destination not because they intended to stay in town but because one of the cities was the place where they left a train for more local means of transportation to a location outside the urban area.

8. Interviews by author, Ione Kadden (17 Nov. 1998) and Mary Jo Ann Thorsheim (28 Oct. 1998).

9. Evelyn and Mary Flaten, interview by author, 17 Dec. 1998.

10. The sources for this and the next paragraphs about female immigration to the West Coast include Kristine Leander, ed., *Family Sagas: Stories of Scandinavian Immigrants* (Seattle, WA: Scandinavian Language Institute, 1997), 128. On the early settlement of Norwegian immigrants in Seattle and the importance of the remigration of Norwegian Americans from the Midwest in the city, see Camilla Rokstad, "Bringing Home to America: The Significance of Holiday Traditions in the Establishment of a Norwegian American Ethnic Identity in Seattle" (master's thesis, Norwegian University of Science and Technology, 2006), 18–20, 23; and Kirsti Alette Blomvik, "Heritage, Sisterhood, and Self-Reliance: The Evolution and Significance of the Daughters of Norway, 1897–1950" (master's thesis, Norwegian University of Science and Technology, 2002), 25–35.

11. Leander, *Family Sagas*, 25–26.

12. Lovoll, *A Century of Urban Life*, 152–53, 155–56.

13. TCHP analysis of emigrants all departing for the Twin Cities from Oslo, 1880–89; see Table 4.1.

14. Hansen, *My Minneapolis*, 48–49.

15. Eunice Baker, interview by author, 12 June 2000.

16. Lorraine Ofstie interview. TCHP demographic findings concerning emigrants leaving for the Twin Cities from the Norwegian emigrant protocols in Trondheim, Bergen, and Oslo for five-year intervals between 1890 and 1924.

17. Lovoll, *The Promise of America*, 267–68; David C. Mauk, *The Colony that Rose*

from the Sea: Norwegian Maritime Migration and Community in Brooklyn, 1850–1910 (Northfield, MN: NAHA and University of Illinois Press, 1997), 3–5, 29–36, 224–26.

18. Brenda Ueland, *Me* (St. Paul, MN: The Schubert Club, 1983), 123–24, 133, 135. U.S. Census, 1900, 1930: see http://mapserver.lib.virginia.edu/, accessed 7 Dec. 2010. Ueland's father was a Norwegian immigrant but her mother was an American.

19. Johannes Wong, ed., *Norske Utvanderer og Forretningsdrivende* (New York: J. Burner and Co., 1914), 92; Molla Bjurstedt's career, p93. Author's translation.

20. "Norwegians in Seattle and King County," in *The Free Online Encyclopedia of Washington State,* www.historylink.org/essays/output.cfm?file_id=3476, accessed 29 Oct. 2010. Kay F. Reinertz in *Passport to Ballard* (Seattle, WA: Ballard News Tribune Co., 1988), 47. Leander, *Family Sagas,* 89.

21. Mauk, *Colony that Rose from the Sea,* 31, 33–35, 37, 39.

22. Andres A. Svalestuen, "Om den regionale spreiing av norsk utvandring før 1865," in *Utvandringa—det store oppbrotet,* ed. Arnfinn Engen (Oslo: Det norske samlaget, 1978), 79. Findings from the TCHP, 100 percent sample of data about female emigrants whose destination was one of the Twin Cities during the 1880s. Mauk, *Colony that Rose from the Sea,* 33–39, 227.

23. Wong, *Norske Utvanderer og Forretningsdrivende,* 84; Mauk, *Colony that Rose from the Sea,* 24–227; interviews by author, Former Domestics 2 and 3 (23 Jan. 1986), Gyda Andersen (9 Nov. 1986), Sigurd and Synnøve Daasvand (2 Feb. 1986), Helen Livingstone (9 Dec. 1985; 18 May 1986), Lina Logan (26 July 1985).

24. For the source of materials in this and the next paragraph, see Lovoll, *A Century of Urban Life,* 24–25, 79, 82, 155–56, 235.

25. Lovoll, *The Promise of America,* 315–16, offers a useful, concise overview of the evolving employment and educational opportunities for Norwegian American women.

26. North American Population Project–Twin Cities, 1880, and statistical analyses by William Block and the author, (NAPP-TC). Interviews by author, Jorunn Wolden (19 Apr. 1999), Gyda Andersen, Sigurd and Synnøve Daasvand, Lina Logan, Mary and Alan Austensen, Helen Pedersen, Ione Kadden, Nina Draxten (8 May 2000), Clarice Johnsen (12 Jan. 1999), Dolores Smaadalen King (25 May 1999), Ardis Munther (26 Oct. 1998), and Lorraine Ofstie. The preliminary version of the NAPP data for 1880 does not include addresses, but city directories and other records reveal the location of residences in the cities. What we learn about domestics and lodgers in one federal census provides a basis for comparison later with similar information from the next. Norwegian American men made up only a very small group among servants in any of the cities in the study.

27. The discussion of ethnic mixing in the households where Norwegian American domestics worked derives from analyses of the household patterns revealed in NAPP-TC 1880 for both cities.

28. The occupational percentages and details in these paragraphs come from the TCHP and its analysis of NAPP-TC data on Norwegian-born and second-generation Norwegian American women in Minneapolis/St. Paul in the 1880 and 1900 censuses.

29. The examples here come from the TCHP sample for 1900.

30. Mauk, *Colony that Rose from the Sea,* 228–29; interviews by author with Former

Domestics 2 and 3, Helen Livingstone, Lina Logan, Birgit Rasmussen (16 Nov. 1986), and Hjordis Mortensen (10 May 1986); "Søster Elisabeths (Elisabeth Fedde's) Optegnelser, XII," *Nordisk Tidende,* May 16 1933, 5.

31. Interviews by author with Jorunn Wolden, Gyda Andersen, Sigurd and Synnøve Daasvand, Lina Logan, Mary and Alan Austensen, Helen Pedersen, Ione Kadden, Nina Draxten, Clarice Johnsen, Dolores Smaadalen King, Ardis Munther, Lorraine Ofstie, Enice Baker, Luther and Eileen Forde, Gracia Grindal (16 Apr. 2000), Krista Sande Ganderud Johnson (13 Jan. 1999).

32. Interviews with Enice Baker, Luther and Eileen Forde, Gracia Grindal, Krista Sande Ganderud Johnson.

33. Mauk, *Colony that Rose from the Sea,* Appendix 2, Table 6, "Female Occupations in 1892," 541. Interviews with Former Domestics 2 and 3, Lina Logan, Hjordis Mortensen, Birgit Rasmussen; Janet E. Rasmussen, *New Land, New Lives: Scandinavian Immigrants to the Pacific Northwest* (Northfield, MN, and Seattle: NAHA and University of Washington Press, 1993), 169–75, quotation, p171.

34. Leander, *Family Sagas,* 115–16.

35. See Ingeborg Sponland, *My Reasonable Service* (Minneapolis, MN: Augsburg Publishing House, 1938), ch. 4, "Pioneering in the Northwest," esp. 40–41, 49–50, 53; and Laura Ringdal Bratager, *Over Hav og Land: Lyngblomstens Historie, Pionerliv i Minneapolis med flere skildringer* (Minneapolis, MN: Lutheran Free Church Publishing Co., 1925), especially 25–32. The letters and diaries of Theodore Kartevold, in the author's possession, tell in detail the tragic story of his beloved first wife, who contracted tuberculosis in Red Hook, Brooklyn.

36. Lovoll, *A Century of Urban Life,* 11–21, 24–25, 28. A distinctive dimension of the development of Norwegian America is that the group's rural society evolved first, before the colony in Chicago crossed a threshold of size that permitted organized group institutions and public activities. Mauk, *Colony that Rose from the Sea,* 60–63, 77, 84–87, 93–95, 228–29; interviews by author with Bertha and Gudrun Kartevold (28 Dec. 1985; Apr.–May 1986), Rolf Broun (15 Nov. 1986), Walter Lee (2 June 1986), Stanley Solaas (27 May 1986); TCHP interviews by author with Eunice Baker, Ione Kadden, Lorraine Ofstie, Carl Chrislock (16 May 1999), Lloyd Hustvedt (19 Nov. 1998).

37. Mauk, *Colony that Rose from the Sea,* 154–78; interviews with Luther and Eileen Forde, Gudrun and Bertha Kartevold, Lorraine Ofstie, Paul and Ruth Qualben (13 May 1986), Tom Svennevik (27 Nov. 1985); Odd S. Lovoll, *A Century of Urban Life,* 68–73, 149, 164–67, 212–21, 225.

38. TCHP interviews by author with Jorunn Wolden, John Akslen (18 Jan. 1999), Sam Bergaas (20 Apr. 1999), Ione Kadden, Hilda Kringstad (26 Mar. 1999), Aase Lervik (3 June 1999), Christian Skjervold (3 Feb. 1999), among others. Interviews by author with Johannes Aardahl (18 Nov. 1986), Hans Beerggren (30 Dec. 1985), Cecilia Tessdal Felt (7 Sept. 1986), Kari Alice Hesthagg (31 May 1986; 17 Nov. 1995), Bjørn and Kitty Jakobsen (24 May 1986; 18 Nov. 1995), and Birgit Rasmussen, among others. See Mauk, *Colony that Rose from the Sea,* 228–29, for a complete list of interviews. Ronald Allen Goeken, "Unmarried Adults and Residential Autonomy: Living Arrangements in the United States, 1880–1990" (PhD diss., University of Minnesota, 1999), 39, 41–45. The

figures on the marital status and median age of Norwegian American boarders were derived by the author from William Block's compilation and analysis of NAPP-TC 1880.

39. U.S. Census, 1900, *Statistics,* Table 20, 29; Table 26, 198–207; Table 28, 218–305; Mildred L. Hartsough, *The Twin Cities as a Metropolitan Market* (Minneapolis: University of Minnesota Press, 1925), 28–64. See also Weiner, " 'Our Sister's Keepers,' " 189–200, for a well-documented overview of single women's living and working conditions and the YWCA's efforts to assist these women in the Twin Cities in the late nineteenth and early twentieth centuries. Joan M. Jensen, "Out of Wisconsin: Country Daughters in the City, 1910–1925," *Minnesota History* 59.2 (Summer 2004): 48–61, offers a useful family study of how young and single second-generation women dealt with the urban conditions they found in the Twin Cities in the first decades of the twentieth century.

40. Serene Sortland, interview by author, 6 Sept. 1985.

41. Carl Gustav Otto Hansen, "Norske Kvinner i Midtvesten," *The Norseman* 31 (1938): 286–90, available in Det løftrike land database, http://www.nb.no/emigrasjon/, accessed 3 March 2001.

42. Lovoll, *A Century of Urban Life,* 231, 235.

43. Analyses of TCHP 10 and 20 percent samples are the basis for this overview of the changing demographic characteristics of Norwegian Americans in the Twin Cities between 1880 and 1920. The following are some representative TCHP interviews during which Norwegian Americans talked about the ethnically mixed crowd they associated with in high school and in leisure-time activities: John Akslen, Jens Anker (29 Feb. 2000), Marilyn Chiat (10 Nov. 1998), John Futcher (10 Feb. 1999), Ione Kadden, Dolores King (26 May 1999), Hilde Kringstad, Lorraine Ofstie, Mary Ann Olsen (11 May 1999), and Marilyn Sorensen (24 Mar. 1999).

Matilda (Telia) Lilleby McReynolds

The life story of Matilda Lilleby McReynolds (Telia to her family) exemplifies migration and work patterns for Norwegian American women in urban areas. Her parents emigrated from Norway in the mid-1850s, married, and settled in Nicollet County, Minnesota, in 1856. In 1862, during the U.S.–Dakota War, the family left their farm and relocated to St. Peter. They later moved westward to Renville County and lived in Sacred Heart. Born in 1870, McReynolds was the seventh of twelve children. Her parents operated a hotel in Emmet Township (Renville County) in 1880. Six people, most of them Norwegian, resided at the hotel. The Lilleby daughters most likely assisted their mother with domestic work.

Like many other young Norwegian American women in rural communities, some of the Lilleby daughters, including Telia, sought employment in the city. Family played a role in Telia Lilleby's migration. In the late 1880s, elder sister Hannah relocated to Minneapolis. By 1894 Telia had moved to the city as well and secured employment as a dressmaker. Five years later she worked for the Misses McGahn and lived in a boarding-house operated by her sister, Anna Mason, on Twelfth Street South in a working-class, ethnically diverse neighborhood.

It appears Telia Lilleby married Lucian Alden McReynolds in 1901 and began using Lilleby McReynolds as her name professionally. After her marriage, she continued working as a dressmaker. The couple lived on Second Avenue, and McReynolds operated her dress business on the second floor of their home. With her husband's unexpected death in 1910, McReynolds became the family's sole breadwinner, which made her sew-ing and business skills all the more important. She sewed dresses for some of the Cities' leading women, including Bessie Pettit Douglas, and had up to fifteen employees. Son Richard helped his mother by riding his bike to Amluxon's fabric store to pick up goods. McReynolds traveled to New York City twice each year to purchase "fabrics for her business."

As a second-generation Norwe-gian American, Telia Lilleby McRey-nolds saw her future not on the farm but in the city. Many of the Cities' dressmakers and seamstresses in the late nineteenth and early twen-tieth centuries were Norwegian Americans, some working in the needle trades temporarily and others

Matilda (Telia) Lilleby McReynolds portrait, ca. 1915

Dress sewn by McReynolds for Bessie Pettit Douglas

Lilleby McReynolds
1617 Second Avenue South
will return from
New York
March sixteenth, nineteen hundred & eight

McReynolds's calling card

becoming career seamstresses and dressmakers. McReynolds, a career dressmaker, used her sewing skills to create a business that catered to fashionable Minneapolis women. Her life and experiences allude to the broad contours of life in the city for Norwegian American women.

Note

This biographical sketch is based on Linda McShannock's research on dressmakers in Minneapolis and St. Paul; McShannock is a collections curator at the Minnesota Historical Society. "Albert K. Lilleby (1888)," in *A History of Yellow Medicine County,* Arthur P. Rose (Marshall, MN: Northern History, 1914), 395; 1870, 1880, and 1900 Roll Censuses, Renville County, MN; 1885, 1895, and 1905 Minnesota State Censuses; *Davison's Minneapolis Directories,* 1888–89, 1889–90, 1894–95, 1900, and 1901 (Minneapolis, MN: Minneapolis Directory Company, 1889–1901); 1900 and 1910 Roll Censuses, Minneapolis, MN; Marion J. McReynolds, telephone interview with Linda McShannock, 1 Feb. 2007; Minnesota Death Certificate, www.ancestry.com. Records provide a number of birth years for McReynolds, although 1870 is the year used most frequently. She also lived at different addresses over the years.

CHAPTER 5

Textile Production in Norwegian America

Laurann Gilbertson

No one artifact at Vesterheim Norwegian-American Museum offers a glimpse into the lives of Norwegian immigrant women in America; in fact, the museum houses hundreds of telling artifacts, such as ten looms, twenty-six pairs of wool carders, more than seventy spinning wheels, and eighty-three weaving shuttles. Vesterheim's collection also includes numerous handwoven and handknit textiles, such as the shawl that Jorund Halvorson of Fertile, Minnesota, wove in the early twentieth century from yarn that she had carded and spun. Halvorson emigrated in 1899 from Østre Slidre, Valdres. There, and throughout rural Norway, women wove cloth and made most of the clothing and textiles for the family and for both male and female servants, if they had any. Women who emigrated expected to continue producing textiles in the United States. Norwegians in America reinforced this expectation with recommendations to bring spinning wheels, looms, and other equipment. As a result, many women emigrated with textile tools and with something even more valuable: textile skills. Once in their new midwestern homes, women again produced clothing, bedding, and other household textiles for their families. Often they continued to spin, weave, and knit for economic and social reasons. From the perspectives of skills and textile processes, we can see that women's productive labor helped ensure the financial stability of their families. By sharing labor and equipment and by organizing with other women, Norwegian immigrants further strengthened families and communities both socially and economically.

Scholars have found that after emigration many Norwegian women and men quickly replaced their rural clothing with American-style fashions. Likewise, instead of the traditional handwoven wool bedding, immigrant women made and used cotton piecework quilts, relatively unknown in rural Norway. Although the textiles themselves often changed dramatically after emigration, the skills used to create textiles did not. Norwegian immigrant women adapted their skills to the new materials and American textile forms.[1]

This chapter focuses on the Norwegian women who settled in rural areas or in small towns in Illinois, Wisconsin, Iowa, Minnesota, South Dakota, and North Dakota and on their skills in preparing raw wool and linen fibers, spinning, knitting, weaving, hand sewing, and doing fancy work. The study is limited to the years between 1836, the start of annual emigration from Norway, and the 1920s,

Shawl woven by Jorund Halvorson from wool she carded and spun, early 1900s, Fertile, Minnesota

when U.S. immigration laws severely restricted the number of Norwegians who came. In addition to the histories of artifacts in museum collections, sources for this study include diaries, letters, and memoirs. Most often the writers were women, either the immigrants themselves or their daughters and granddaughters. Few men recorded information about textiles and textile production in their writings, probably because they were less involved with and less interested in the processes of creating or acquiring clothing and household textiles.[2]

The Migration and Adaptation of a Tradition

The textile tradition in rural Norway at the time of mass emigration was diverse. Women utilized both locally raised and imported materials to create clothing and household textiles with a variety of weaving and decorative techniques. The regional preferences for color and pattern were perhaps most evident in folk dress *(folkedrakt)*, which often varied by valley or church parish. Regionalism was also evident in wool coverlets *(åklær)*. These textiles were both functional and decorative. Women wove them for bed coverings but also used them for christening blankets, funeral palls, and wall hangings in the main room of the house for color on festive occasions. Rural women created few textiles that were purely decorative. They would find the emphasis on creating and using decorative textiles very different in America.[3]

Norwegians who had emigrated earlier strongly recommended in letters to friends and family that women bring spinning wheels to America. The writers also occasionally suggested packing wool carders, looms, sheep shears, and shears for cutting woven cloth. As for clothing, many letter writers recommended bringing fabric rather than finished garments because Americans dressed differently. "American women wear clothes like those worn by the upper class in Norway," Anders Anderssen Qvale informed his sister in Valdres in 1851. Immigrants were, however, to bring coverlets or sheepskins because they had to provide their own bedding on the ships to America. Once in the United States, immigrant women could choose whether they would continue textile production. With money, they could purchase yarn to speed the process of weaving cloth or eliminate the weaving process completely by buying fabric and ready-made bedding and clothing. Even with access to fabric, however, the accounts of women suggest that a good deal of textile production continued in America. The type and amount of production varied, but overwhelmingly they spoke of raising sheep for wool, spinning, weaving, sewing, and knitting.[4]

Norwegian American women were not the only ones to produce textiles at home in the late nineteenth and early twentieth centuries. Even though factory-woven cloth and some ready-made garments were available for sale, immigrants from Scandinavia and Europe and people living in remote or frontier areas throughout the United States tended to rely most heavily on home textile production.[5]

To begin the process of textile production, women acquired and prepared the raw fibers. Animal fibers, most often wool from sheep, were very commonly used. Primary sources tell us that many immigrant families raised sheep on their midwestern farms, especially during their early years in America. Gro Svendsen, an immigrant from Hallingdal, had only one sheep on her farm in Estherville, Iowa, in 1865. "I have sheared the sheep twice this year," she reported. "The wool, which was of excellent quality, weighed all of seven pounds." Sigrid Hippe Rogness considered one sheep to be sufficient for her needs and "always" kept a big white ram for wool for knitting stockings. When the Ole B. Iverson family prepared to leave Decorah, Iowa, for Minnehaha County, South Dakota, in 1868 they took two pigs, four cows, three calves, and twenty sheep. Larger numbers of sheep do not necessarily mean greater textile production. Some of the sheep were intended for food and some for sale. According to Andrew Veblen, on his parents' farm in Manitowoc County, Wisconsin, the family kept one sheep in the yard near the house as a pet. An additional two or three sheep would be similarly cared for as the source of wool for handwork. The Veblens also kept up to one hundred merino crossbreed sheep that provided the family and others with high-quality wool for textile use. Neighbors eagerly bought any surplus wool produced on the farm.[6]

Women also used plant fibers, such as cotton, linen, hemp, and nettle. Cotton had not been grown in Norway, nor was it being grown in the midwestern United States. Immigrant women were not accustomed to working with the raw fibers, so they tended to purchase cotton as yarn, quilt batting, or finished fabric. They used fibers from the stalk of the flax plant to make linen in a multistep process. First, they retted, or rotted, the stalk by long-term soaking or exposure to rain and sun. Next, they removed the woody part of the stalk, to access the fibers inside, by roasting and breaking. Finally, they combed the fibers and could begin spinning. Women used linen fabric for toweling, for sheeting, and for some garments, such as underclothes and shirts. Immigrants in Wisconsin, Minnesota, and North Dakota wrote about growing and using flax for linen textiles. In Norway women occasionally used hemp and nettle fibers, but no written evidence proves that women continued to use hemp and nettle in the United States.[7]

Compared to flax, wool required relatively little processing. The sheep were sheared; the wool fibers washed and then straightened by carding. At this point, the fleece would be ready for quilt batting. Women could also spin the fleece into yarn for weaving or knitting. They could color white yarn with plants or purchased dyes. Some immigrants raised gray or black sheep to provide greater color options.

In rural Norway, women typically cared for the flocks of sheep and sheared them. Once in America, some immigrants observed a different practice: men were responsible for animal husbandry, including milking cows and shearing sheep. However, many immigrant women, like Svendsen and Rogness, followed the traditional division of labor in caring for and shearing the family's sheep. Rogness, who emigrated from Valdres in 1871, knit with the wool from her sheep and gave stockings to her sons for Christmas "every year until her death" in 1942. Scholar Jon Gjerde found that early immigrants in Wisconsin benefited financially from a traditional Norwegian division of labor. To switch to an American work pattern and hire men to care for the livestock, families would have had to deplete their cash savings. When Norwegian immigrant women continued to care for and shear sheep, they helped preserve the family's cash flow.[8]

Tilla Dahl's family did not raise sheep in Lyon County, Minnesota, in the 1870s but received boxes of wool from her grandparents in Wisconsin. "Mother sat up late nights at her spinning wheel or knitting. Of[t] evenings [Dahl's brother] Herman helped to card the wool she spun." Carding, the process of cleaning and straightening wool fibers in preparation for spinning, was a task that could be

Kristi Skjervem Nestegaard spinning and Torine Endresen Skjervem carding wool, 1910s, Rock Dell, Minnesota. Notice Kristi's feet on the treadle that powers the spinning wheel.

done by children or sometimes adult men. The first carding, done with a pair of "cards" with coarse wire teeth, removed plant material and other debris in the wool. During the second carding, fine wire teeth aligned the fibers.[9]

Spinning twisted the wool (or flax) fibers into a firm yarn that women could then use for weaving or knitting. Spinning wheels were as common in the immigrants' luggage as trunks, concluded art historian Tora Bøhn after interviewing immigrant families that had arrived in the mid-nineteenth century. Women brought spinning wheels from Norway to America because they expected to need them in their new homes. In 1851, Marta Monson brought three spinning wheels from Land, Norway: one wheel for herself and one each for her twin daughters, then only three years old. Monson must have expected that both she and her daughters would continue textile production. If an immigrant had not brought a spinning wheel, she might borrow one from a neighbor or ask that one be brought by a later immigrant. She might even try to acquire one in the United States. Because of demand, some Norwegian carpenters continued to make treadle spinning wheels in the Midwest in the nineteenth century. Salve Anderson arrived in Iola, Wisconsin, from Næsverk in 1855. He had a shop on his farm and made wheels for the local spinners, who were also immigrants from Norway. Alfred Andresen & Company in Minneapolis, Minnesota, imported treadle spinning wheels from Norway and sold them by mail order from 1894 to 1922. The Andresen wheels were also available in some midwestern dry goods stores.[10]

Most sources indicate that women used the Norwegian treadle spinning wheels they brought or acquired. Kari Bunde Veblen requested a second wheel from Norway after the first one, brought by a newcomer, "did not prove satisfactory in that it growled slightly in running." In addition to the "noiseless" second Norwegian wheel, Veblen used a great wheel, "an American spinning wheel, of the large wheel variety, which is operated standing up." She used it often because she could spin more quickly than on the smaller Norwegian treadle wheel. The technique used to spin standing up on a great wheel was quite different from the technique used to spin seated at a foot-powered Norwegian wheel, but the immigrant women's skills were adaptable. Helene Maria Synstelien, an immigrant from Nord-Torpa living in Rock County, Wisconsin, also adapted to using an American great wheel in order to spin quickly and with less effort. She wrote to her family in 1867, "on this wheel one can spin from 3 *merker* to 2 *pund* a day so I think that it is much better to spin on a great wheel than on a Norwegian wheel. I can spin the whole week and be no more tired on the last day than the first, but I cannot do that on a Norwegian wheel."[11]

After women completed the spinning, they could begin to weave. To do this, they placed warp threads under tension on a loom and interlaced weft yarns at right angles; for example, they passed weft yarns alternately over and under the warp yarns. Some women used warp and weft materials of the same fiber and weight, while other women preferred the warp to be thinner and of a different material than the weft. Weft might be homespun wool yarn or rags. Depending on the materials and how the loom was set up, the cloth produced could be fine or coarse, simple or complex. While looms were common in homes in rural Norway, they were less available in the United States. A few immigrants brought looms to the Midwest, and some men made looms for their wives. For example, Johan Falde of rural Hudson, South Dakota, made a loom for his wife Ingeborg after they married in 1871. Because looms were less common in the United States, many women borrowed them from friends and neighbors for textile production. In the late nineteenth century, Anne Fedkje Nelson of Windom, Minnesota, wove on "a very large loom which belonged to a neighbor."[12]

With their own or borrowed looms, immigrant women often wove bedding, for example blankets, in the early years. There is no written evidence that women continued to weave Norwegian-style *åklær*, or "coverlets." Helene Synstelien wrote home in 1867 that, while staying with her uncle Hans Tollefsrud in Orfordville, Wisconsin, she had woven two lengths of cloth, presumably of linen or cotton. One was a piece of twill weave for mattress ticking and one was for underclothes. Homewoven wool cloth was often intended for men's trousers and jackets as well as for women's and children's dresses. Sigrid Tufte Eielsen of Muskego, Wisconsin, recorded that in the 1840s, "My mother and I . . . wove woolen material which we used for clothing such as we were accustomed to [in Hallingdal]." Svein Nilsson reported from Jefferson Prairie, Wisconsin, in *Billed-Magazin* in 1869, "Home crafts are not inconsiderable. The women spin and weave; for everyday use, clothes of homespun are usually worn." The Monsons were among the southern Wisconsin families in the 1870s that produced cloth, which they continued to call *verken* (the Norwegian word for wool-and-cotton or wool-and-linen fabric).[13]

Immigrant women could purchase fabric for clothing at stores, but they were concerned about the cost. Store prices for yard goods were high, especially during and shortly after the Civil War. All-wool fabric was particularly expensive, but Svennung Kjærkebøn noted in 1866 that some sturdy wool-and-cotton fabric was available for less money in southwest Wisconsin. At times, cotton fabrics, like muslin and calico, were also expensive, but immigrants writing home generally considered them a good buy. The quality of store-bought fabric was another concern, as Svendsen bemoaned in 1862: "So it is with everything: shoddy and careless workmanship everywhere . . . Norwegian clothes, too, are better and much warmer." Immigrant women and men agreed that the American-made wool fabric and garments available for sale were poor quality. They valued the items they had brought with them from Norway and wrote home asking for more. The perception that handwoven and Norwegian goods were warmer and more durable, along with the high cost of store-bought fabric and clothing, likely contributed to women's decisions to continue weaving wool fabric for dresses and suits.[14]

There was a general trend among immigrant handweavers beginning in about 1890 away from the production of fine fabric for clothing and toward making rag carpets or rugs and coarse blankets. This trend is also evident in collections at Vesterheim Norwegian-American Museum and in observations made by Marion Nelson, an expert on Norwegian American material culture, of numerous looms sold at auction with remains of rug warp. Women may have felt less compelled to weave fabric for clothing when the price and quality of store-bought fabric improved. Even if the cost and quality did not improve significantly, immigrants may have become more resigned to American products and prices. Fashions for women after 1900 increasingly called for fine, lightweight cotton or silk fabrics that even talented weavers would have difficulty producing themselves.[15]

Although rag carpets and rug weaving were less technically difficult, they should not be ignored because the production of rag rugs enhanced the homes of some women and provided income for others. Caja Munch described the rag carpet she and her husband purchased to cover the bedroom floor in their cold Wisconsin parsonage: "It is very nice; we got it from a Norwegian for about 40 cents per yard; underneath we have filled in richly with straw." Rug and carpet weavers often required that clients provide prepared rags. The preparation of rags for weaving involved several steps, sometimes beginning with dyeing the fabric. In October 1858, Caja Munch was planning to get another carpet and this time was intimately involved with the process: "My work these days is to sew rags. A woman is going to weave me a rug, my old chemises were good for nothing else, but as they are white, I want to color them yellow with lye and vitriol." During the next step fabric strips were torn or cut, sewn (stitched end to end into long lengths), and wound into balls to be used as weft. Hilda Thompson Quickstad remembered helping with the process.

> I well recall Mother sitting at her sewing machine sewing many, many scraps of material into long strips. Beside her on the floor we four youngest [children] sat.
> . . . Our job was to roll these strips into balls. We girls tried our best to get fine, round balls, but Swen insisted on making his football shaped. After that process, Mother took the balls to a neighbor woman, Helga Tollefson, who did weaving. She wove these long strips of rugs according to room measurements, which Mother sewed together and used as carpet stretched to cover the parlor floor.[16]

In the nineteenth century, sewing machines were not yet as common in rural Norway as they were in the Midwest. Immigrant women had hand-sewing skills that they adapted for sewing on a machine. Sewing machines could save time and labor, so women quickly made the transition. Clara Jacobson remembered that in Daleyville, Wisconsin, in the 1870s, "The first large sewing machines in the settlement were bought by Mr. Dahle, the merchant, and my father. A machine cost nearly a hundred dollars then. Father was the first to sew on them and he instructed others. Many came to inspect our sewing machine and Mother had to demonstrate how it worked." Owners of the first sewing machines often shared them with friends. Not only was this a gesture of kindness to help ease the burden of textile work, it also provided women with an opportunity to socialize.[17]

As sewing machines became less expensive, they joined the list of items women needed to start their married lives. Helen Olson Halvorsen described setting up a household in rural Leland, Minnesota, after her marriage in 1884: "Halvor bought a table, four chairs, and a rocking chair. I had bedding. I had nothing much from home. They needed what they had. I took comforters that I had pieced and quilted while at Uncle's . . . I had some grey linen that was my mother's. I had a sewing machine. I had put ten dollars into that and mother gave the rest of the money it cost—I think about $30 or $35." Thalette Galby Brandt of Ridgeway, Iowa, received a sewing machine as a gift from her mother when she and Realf Ottesen Brandt married in 1883. The gift was intended to help Thalette with her productive labor, ensuring the success of the new family. Historian Barbara Handy-Marchello notes that laying hens were given as wedding gifts for a similar reason.[18]

Many immigrant women distinguished between plain sewing, "useful sewing that keeps household and person neat and orderly," and fancy work, which was needlework of a primarily or exclusively decorative nature. Fancy work included crochet, tatting, lace techniques, and embroidery. Some rural Norwegian women used these techniques on clothing for festive occasions and textiles for ritual use, such as embroidered linen cloths wrapped around infants at baptism.

Wedding portrait of Thalette Galby Brandt, 1883, by Relf, Decorah, Iowa

Fancy work tended to be associated with higher social and economic classes in both Norway and the United States because it required the purchase of supplies and the leisure time in which to complete it. Despite the cost and time demands, fancy work was extremely popular in America in the late nineteenth and early twentieth centuries. Many immigrant women were interested in doing fancy work because they wanted to be and to look American. For example, American fashion motivated Gertrude Christopher Smith of Decorah, Iowa, to sew crazy quilts, a highly decorative form of quiltmaking. She described crazy quilts in a letter to her sister-in-law in Norway in 1885, and then explained her reason for making one: "There is an interest among the ladies here, for a work called Japanese or crazy work; it consists of pieces of silk, plush, or velvet, satin too, of all colors, sizes and shapes, joined with fancy stitches; plain pieces are often embroidered prettiest so. I haven't found time for this but of course I must do crazy work, since every body else does so."[19]

Not surprisingly, men and women viewed some textile tasks differently. Andrew Veblen thought that knitting "was hardly regarded [as] work but rather as a *pick-up* matter to occupy the fingers when not doing formal *work."* While it is true that Norwegian immigrant women "picked up" their knitting during quiet moments, they also knit while they walked to town and to church and while hunting for eggs. Women viewed knitting as a necessary and important task that needed to be accomplished whether they had a quiet moment or not. When Barbara Levorsen described her mother's role in the household, knitting was included: "She made all the butter, baked all the bread, prepared five meals a day, knitted our stockings, sewed her own and my everyday clothes, and often helped Papa in the field." Dikka and Caia Wulfsberg would have placed knitting in the category of work as well: "Mother was very industrious and very good at various handwork, but it was mostly knitting as there were so many feet to cover. They always had homeknit stockings and sox [*sic*] in those days. When she had knit 22 stockings there was one pair for each." Gertrude Berg was so impressed with the work of her neighbor, Severina Sande, who knit full-length stockings for her ten children, that she remarked that some of these "everyday events" seemed more like "myths." Caroline Mathilde Koren Naeseth elucidated: "Though Mother was helped by a young girl who was staying with us, she has told me that she had to exert herself to keep us all supplied [with stockings]."[20]

Many immigrant women were involved in all steps of textile production, including raising sheep, growing flax, spinning, weaving, knitting, and sewing. They used equipment brought from Norway and, increasingly, American tools and machines they purchased here. Women continued to use some of their Norwegian textile skills almost unchanged, as with knitting. They could knit while doing other tasks, so it was one of the easiest textile activities to do to provide for their families. Other skills, such as sewing, were traditional but adaptable to new American styles and equipment. Many women from rural Norway learned about fancy work and made time for this textile activity, once more common among upper-class urban and wealthy rural women.

Shared Labor and Ladies Aid

Immigrant women shared not only textile equipment, such as looms and sewing machines; they shared productive labor as well. Sharing gave women opportunities to socialize and increase their productivity. When they could create more textiles for their families more quickly, they might have time to make extra items to benefit their local and global communities, often through the work of Norwegian American Lutheran churches.

Immigrant women living in the rural Midwest frequently mentioned in their diaries, letters, and reminiscences that they participated in Ladies Aid, a women's organization at their church. Textile production was an important part of Ladies Aid and was, in fact, the reason some of the first organizations formed. Diderikke Ottesen Brandt began a sewing society with members of her church in Decorah, Iowa, in 1865. She invited some of the women to her home, the parsonage, to knit socks and mend clothing for the students at Luther College. Similarly in 1879, women met in Madison, Wisconsin, to knit and mend for seminary students. A. C. Anderson, the student who suggested creating the group, conducted devotions during the biweekly work meetings.[21]

The format of the Madison group's meetings was typical of Ladies Aid societies throughout the Midwest in the late nineteenth and early twentieth centuries. Though the names of the groups changed over time, from *Syforening* (Sewing Society) to *Kvindeforening* (Women's Society) to Ladies Aid to Mission Society, the goals were the same: to raise money through dues, meals, and the sale of textiles for the benefit of the church and its work in the community, nation, and abroad. Fund-raising was important, but Christian education and fellowship were as well, so devotions or Bible readings were given at Ladies Aid meetings by the pastor, the pastor's wife, or the *klokker* (sexton).[22]

Ladies Aid societies had formed in many established churches by the 1890s. Some aids began as a way to raise money to build churches for existing congregations. The Osterdalen congregation and Ladies Aid of Aure, Minnesota, formed in 1900. They used the local school for services from 1901 until 1914, when their church was completed, with "much credit . . . given to the Ladies Aid." Aid meetings were most often held in members' homes, though in later years groups were more likely to gather in the parsonage or church basement. Scholars, such as DeAne Lagerquist, Erik Luther Williamson, and Lori Ann Lahlum, researched the complex history of the Ladies Aid in Norwegian American Lutheran churches, but they did not describe the textiles or discuss the role of textiles in the success of the churches and communities. Textiles were an important way, and in many congregations the primary way, of raising money for projects that ranged from local parochial schools to regional hospitals to foreign missions.[23]

A common Ladies Aid fund-raiser was the sale or auction of garments and textiles. Aid members sewed aprons, men's shirts and work clothes, and children's dresses as well as pillowcases, piecework quilts, rugs, and pieces of fancy work. A large number of Ladies Aid textiles were sewn by hand or machine from purchased cloth. Members' dues, income from sales, and special donations paid for the cloth. Dues totaling $2.50 were collected at the first meeting of the Mouse River Ladies Aid in Minot, North Dakota, on July 7, 1887. With the dues, Oline Ramstad bought materials and then planned a project for the second meeting. The members began a quilt in a pattern called "Chase the Fox." The men attending a luncheon served in 1890 by the Dovre Ladies Aid near Willmar, Minnesota, gave most of the offering. Society members used the

James River Kvindeforening at the home of Thore and Beathe Gunderson, 1888,
near Menno, South Dakota. Women are spinning, sewing, and knitting.

collected money to purchase materials for their upcoming sewing, quiltmaking,
and knitting projects.[24]

Once they raised the money and purchased supplies, Ladies Aid members
devised systems either to share or to distribute them. The president of the
Arendahl Ladies Aid transported the green chest that held the group's fabric
and sewing projects from meeting to meeting. Because of the distance between
members' homes, the women of Trefoldighed Lutheran Church's Ladies Aid
decided in 1882 that a small group should meet to cut purchased fabric into
pieces for shirts, aprons, girls' dresses, and pillowcases. They tied the pieces into
parcels and, at the next church service, handed out the parcels to members to
sew at home. Although it was unusual for the women to work independently on
projects, they were quite successful. To the garments were added knit stockings
and mittens and crocheted doilies. Two sales held in 1882 raised a total of $83.[25]

Many women, like those at Trefoldighed, preferred to spin and knit rather than
sew. Sigrid Lillehaugen wrote in 1920 that she had knit eight pairs of mittens for
Ladies Aid. "Now these days," she explained, "I have been spinning, and I am making yarn for many others . . . I am about the only one around here who spins and
have [sic] wool, so I have to be ambitious, then." A similarly ambitious family near
Henry, South Dakota, often supplied wool from their sheep for quilt batting. The
quilts were made and sold by the Ladies Aid of Our Savior's Lutheran Church.[26]

"Hole in the Barn Door" quilt, purchased by Mattie Anderson in the 1920s at a Thanksgiving Ladies Aid bazaar at Our Savior's Norwegian Lutheran Church, Henry, South Dakota

The time of year that churches held Ladies Aid sales varied. For some groups it was only at Thanksgiving; for others it was a summer event. Often women held the sales in conjunction with meals and programs promoting mission work. During the 1890s at Trefoldighed Lutheran Church in Battle Lake, Minnesota, "The main event each year was the handiwork sale—always an all-day affair held in some member's grove. Tables and benches were built under the trees. Rev. Normann was always present and conducted a mission service in the forenoon. At noon the women served a bountiful dinner, which was followed by a social hour and then the sale."[27]

Not only were meals and bazaars selling Ladies Aid textiles popular with church and community members; they also became important fund-raisers. For example, one "friendship" quilt made by the women of Valley Grove Lutheran Church in Kloten, North Dakota, brought in $104.30. The Ladies Aid of Highland congregation in Deuel County, South Dakota, raised and contributed seven hundred dollars toward a new church building in 1892. During the 1910s in Madison, Wisconsin, the Bethel Ladies Aid "continuously helped to pay off the church debt" while funding several other large projects. Through their productive labor, Ladies Aid societies raised significant amounts of money—crucial support for the operation of Norwegian American churches in the Midwest.[28]

In addition to fund-raising, Ladies Aid societies touted an educational component. Some congregations offered *Pikeforening* (Girls Aid or Little Helpers) organizations for young women. The aim of the Pikeforening of Perry Lutheran Church near Daleyville, Wisconsin, was typical of these groups: create an interest in missions, provide a good social time, and offer "able instruction in domestic art and in Christian literature and singing." Thalette Galby Brandt described the response to the newly formed Pikeforening at her South Dakota church in 1886:

> So much interest was shown that mothers asked if their daughters might join, even those down to six years of age! I said, "All right; if they can hold a needle, send them along" . . . They were given pieces of unbleached muslin on which simple designs had been drawn with lead pencil, and a needle with common black thread. They were to learn outline work to start with. When they had learned to make even, smooth stitches and to turn the curves neatly they were promoted to stamped linen pieces and colored embroidery silks. The older girls started center pieces.

The handwork made by Brandt's Pikeforening was sold at a bazaar held upstairs in the parsonage. Not only were the girls learning textile techniques, they were involved with fund-raising. Initiated by two teenagers, Julia Boyum and Karina Knutson, who spent recess at school piecing quilt blocks, a Pikeforening formed

Women with their contributions to or successful bidders following a Trinity Ladies Aid sale at Trefoldighet Lutheran Church, Dawson, Minnesota, c. 1890

in 1886 at Arendahl Lutheran Church near Peterson, Minnesota. The girls' handwork sold well at auctions, raising $235, for example, in 1902 for a new organ.[29]

Over time, as churches were built and equipped, Ladies Aids societies and Pikeforenings looked increasingly outward toward foreign missions and other global needs. During World War I, churchwomen contributed funds to the Red Cross, and their projects benefited the war effort. The Trefoldighed Girls Aid, for example, knit socks, scarves, and sweaters for men in training camps and overseas.[30]

The Ladies Aid Society is a dramatic example of how shared textile equipment and productive labor could strengthen immigrant communities socially and financially. Important social bonds formed when women worked together for the benefit of their families or local communities. When the women's textiles were sold, the communities publicly acknowledged that handmade textiles and textile skills had value. Women were crucial to the social and financial success of immigrant communities, and by training young women and girls, they sought to build strong Norwegian American communities into the future.

Continuing Traditional Practices in a Cash Economy

Clearly many Norwegian immigrant women chose to continue to raise sheep, process fibers, card and spin, weave, knit, and sew for their families and communities in the rural Midwest. The dramatic degree to which traditional Norwegian women's productive labor continued after immigration necessitates a thorough examination of possible causes. Interpretation of information in primary sources suggests three broad categories into which most individual situations fell. Personal reasons included continuing textile production at home out of enjoyment, habit, and a belief that store-bought textiles were of poor quality. Limited assimilation was a socio-cultural reason for continuing home textile production. Economic reasons included the challenges of acquiring, saving, and using cash for purchases.

When immigrant writers discussed clothing and textiles, they also often mentioned money. For example, "to get a new outfit was no easy thing; as money was an unknown article in this area in those days," wrote A. J. Risty about Minnehaha County, South Dakota, in the 1870s. Risty trapped muskrats and foxes for skins to trade for cloth. Because cash was often scarce, writers noted precisely how they acquired the money for fabric or clothing. The Losen family caught quail, sold them for twenty-five cents each, and bought dress fabric. Berries were an important source of cash. Cranberries bought goods for Gunhild Jacobson's first American dress after arriving in Muskego, Wisconsin, in 1844. Likewise, Aagot Raaen described the gooseberry season in Traill County, North Dakota, which ran for five weeks starting in early July, as "a time of plenty" because it meant money for clothing for the whole family. Some years, she said, the gooseberries even paid interest on the farm loan.[31]

Once cash was in hand, the next obstacle was getting to a store. Many immigrants lived hours if not days from a town and stores. Commonly the trip to the store for cloth or clothing corresponded with harvest season. Each fall during the 1850s, John Sevalson Losen of Hesper, Iowa, took wheat to a mill on the Mississippi River to be ground into flour. He would return after four or five days with enough flour for the winter as well as brown sugar, green coffee, dried fruit, salt, and calico for summer dresses. Women might go to town by themselves, especially if they were selling butter and eggs, though the trips could still be lengthy. In the 1880s, Gro Viken Mork packed butter in tubs and stored them until fall when she took them thirty-five miles to Grand Forks, North Dakota, to sell. She brought back clothes and other necessities. Barbara Handy-Marchello clarifies that payment for butter and eggs often came as store credit, so the items purchased from the sale of butter and eggs would be groceries or dry goods, such as shoes, clothing, cloth, and sewing supplies.[32]

Somewhat later in the immigration and settlement period, peddlers brought fabric and sewing supplies to rural homes, thereby eliminating the obstacles of distance and transportation. Simple clothing, for example men's work clothes, might also be available. Twice a year during the 1910s, Joe Alick from Sioux Falls visited the Berg farm in southeastern South Dakota selling yard goods, clothes, bedding, and small items like pencils. Written accounts from North and South Dakota described the peddlers most often as Arab or Jewish men, like Alek and Albio Hadjo, Syrian cousins from Crookston, Minnesota, who came to farms near Northwood, North Dakota, after the turn of the twentieth century. Aagot Raaen recalled visits from Syrian and Arab women from Grand Forks and from Ole Knudson, the Norwegian peddler from Telemark, in the 1870s and 1880s.[33]

Continuing to produce textiles enabled some Norwegian immigrant women to participate in the cash economy. In early written accounts, immigrant women most often described creating textiles for their own families. By producing additional items, however, women could sell them to provide an income, which was an especially good option for women who could not work outside the home. Gjertrud Rumohr Haug Hilleboe of Arkdale, Wisconsin, supported her family with knitting and weaving after her husband returned from the Civil War an invalid. She knit stockings, leggings, mittens, scarves, and sweaters to sell to lumberjacks in the area and wove cloth and blankets to sell "wherever she could." H. B. Kildahl's mother wove rag carpets, a common sale item. Shortly after arriving in Red Wing, Minnesota, in 1866, Kildahl's father became ill. He recalled: "The care and provision for the family developed upon mother, who was equal to the occasion. Mother was a very practical and resourceful and energetic woman, and did everything honorable that she could do." Not only did home textile production provide income; it allowed her to care for her children and family in a way that was considered socially acceptable. As Ingeborg Olsdatter Bergeim's diary reveals, textile production could be hard work and, at times, unpleasant when dealing with clients. In May of 1885, she knit five pairs of stockings for Swedish laundry girls in Watertown, South Dakota: "They paid me 1½ d. for the work. I am glad I am through with that work. Found the Sweed [sic] girls very bossy—did not stay long."[34]

Even if they had learned to produce textiles in Norway, not all women chose to continue spinning, weaving, and knitting after they emigrated. Caja Munch purchased stockings for her family because, as she explained to her parents in a letter on March 31, 1857, "I am not too clever at knitting." The decision to continue or discontinue home textile production was often related to exposure to the prevailing American or "Yankee" styles of clothing and textiles. Women living in rural Norway in the mid-nineteenth century had somewhat limited experience with European fashion. They knew that women in Norwegian and American cities dressed differently because they had seen fashionably dressed tourists and photos from the United States. They were probably not familiar with some of the techniques required to sew *motedrakt,* fashionable clothing, nor were they comfortable with the speed at which fashions changed in comparison to their more steady dress. Immigrant women would have to learn about and adopt fashion along with many other aspects of American life.[35]

As textile historians have demonstrated, many immigrant women wanted to look American by wearing fashion and decorating their homes in the American style. But the transition from Norwegian clothing and textiles to American clothing and textiles was delayed when immigrants settled in rural areas or in communities of predominately Norwegian or European immigrants. The experiences of Anna Hedalen Ellestad suggest the difference between urban and rural America. After arriving from Valdres in 1856, Ellestad worked the first winter in the home of former Wisconsin governor Leonard J. Farwell. She had difficulty understanding the language and culture, so she left to work in a Norwegian farm community near Madison before marrying and settling there. Rather than purchasing clothing and bedding, as would have been more the custom in cities like Madison, Ellestad produced homespun and homewoven textiles for her family of thirteen. Because her exposure to an American household had been limited, she may not have absorbed enough information and interest in fashion. She may also have rejected urban styles after she found her time in an American household unpleasantly challenging.[36]

The story of Gro Viken Mork introduces the variable of economics into women's decisions to retain or abandon textile traditions. After arriving in Northwood, Iowa, from Hol, Hallingdal, in 1864, she announced that she wanted to work for the Yankees to learn English and the American way of life and earn money. This accomplished, she married and, in 1874, moved to Steele County, North Dakota. Mork advised a neighbor to keep her cupboard from Norway, flour barrel, spinning wheel, and sacks of wool upstairs and out of sight, so her home would look more American. Mork taught American-style cooking to other pioneer women and was a good dressmaker, one of the first in the community to own a sewing machine. She also "sheared sheep, [and] spun and dyed yarn for necessary knitting and weaving." Her biographer, Aagot Raaen, does not explain this apparent contradiction between new American and old Norwegian customs, but does give a few clues. At the time of Mork's untimely death in 1887, the family had added land to the farm. Both floors of their house were freshly painted and papered. They had a new extension table in the dining room and cane chairs, a sofa, and a reed organ in the living room. It would not have been due to a lack of acculturation that Mork continued textile production; more likely it was due to economics. Cash was needed to pay for land, wallpaper, and furniture. Mork could help her family save money and protect the cash they were accumulating by raising sheep and producing textiles from the wool. Traditional textile production enabled immigrant families to purchase modern, American products.[37]

Economics was one of several factors that motivated Kari Bunde Veblen to continue intensive textile production. Veblen and her husband emigrated from Vang in Valdres in 1847, settling first in Ozaukee County, Wisconsin. Although they had saved money for the trip, they were nearly penniless when they arrived.

They worked hard, bought and cleared land, built a house, and sold the property, repeating this process several times as they moved slowly north toward established settlements of Norwegians in Manitowoc County and finally west into Minnesota. Needing cash to purchase and prepare the land for farming, they buffered the uncertain income from crops on poorly developed land by raising more livestock. They also benefited from labor shared by recent immigrants in exchange for temporary lodging. Another boost to the family's finances was Veblen's textile work. Andrew, her oldest son, wrote with great detail about his mother's production of textiles during their seventeen years in Wisconsin. She processed flax and wool, spun, and wove. She used the handwoven fabric for clothing for her family, the hired men, and less-fortunate neighbors. Andrew explained that the family was isolated, both physically and socially, from the Yankees. Furthermore, the family and neighbors (both Norwegians and non-Norwegian immigrants) respected and appreciated her fine weaving and knitting. These factors, combined with the ongoing need to preserve cash, motivated Veblen to continue to use the textile skills she had developed in Valdres.[38]

As immigrant women decided whether or not to continue producing textiles in America, they considered several, often personal, reasons; but economics was commonly in the forefront of their minds. By continuing home textile production, women like Veblen and Mork could save cash and protect savings. They could buffer the economic hardships of large families, poor crops, and recessions. Women's textile skills helped ensure the survival and then the success of their immigrant families.[39]

Conclusion

Women from rural Norway immigrated to the United States with the skills to prepare fibers, weave fabric, and knit and sew garments. These skills continued to be useful in the American Midwest despite the differences in clothing and household textiles. Women's textile skills contributed to the financial stability and success of families living in small towns and rural areas by helping to accumulate and save cash. Although the income or cash savings from home textile production is not quantifiable, as are butter and egg production, economic benefits encouraged women to continue producing textiles, often from fiber to finished product, long after settling in the Midwest. Additional production meant that items could be used to benefit the community through Ladies Aid sales, local benevolences, and international efforts. Shared equipment and labor, at home or at church, also strengthened the community socially and financially. Textile production must be explored through a gendered perspective, because men were only occasionally involved and not usually interested in the details of creating textiles.[40]

Notes

1. See Carol Colburn, "'Well, I Wondered When I Saw You, What All These New Clothes Meant': Interpreting the Dress of Norwegian American Immigrants," in *Material Culture and People's Art Among the Norwegians in America,* ed. Marion Nelson (Northfield, MN: Norwegian-American Historical Association [hereafter, NAHA], 1994); Aagot Noss, "Tradition and Transition: Norwegian Costume from Norway to the United States, 1840–1880," in *Norwegian Immigrant Clothing and Textiles,* ed. Catherine C. Cole (Edmonton, AB: Prairie Costume Society, 1990). Laurann Gilbertson, "Patterns of the New World: Quiltmaking Among Norwegian Americans," *Uncoverings* 27 (2006): 157–86.

2. Andrew A. Veblen is a notable exception to the lack of male writers about textiles. Because of his interest in preserving and sharing the traditions of Valdres, Norway, and Valdres Americans, he recorded in great detail his immigrant parents' work and leisure activities.

3. Helen Engelstad, *Dobbeltvev i Norge* (Oslo: Gyldendal Norsk Forlag, 1958), 137–38. Engelstad describes secondary functions of doubleweave coverlets, though it is commonly believed that other types of handwoven coverlets were used the same ways (at birth, at death, and for color).

4. Carlton C. Qualey, trans. and ed., "Seven American Letters to Valdres," *Norwegian-American Studies* 22 (1965): 147.

5. Carol Colburn, "Immigrant Handweaving in the Upper Midwest," in *Norwegian Immigrant Clothing and Textiles,* 45; Paul E. Rivard, *A New Order of Things: How the Textile Industry Transformed New England* (Hanover, NH: University Press of New England, 2002), 2–7; Betty J. Mills, *Calico Chronicle: Texas Women and Their Fashions, 1830–1910* (Lubbock: Texas Tech Press, 1985), 19, 43.

6. Pauline Farseth and Theodore C. Blegen, eds. and trans., *Frontier Mother: The Letters of Gro Svendsen* (Northfield, MN: NAHA, 1950), 72. *Moe Parish Pioneers: A History of the Pioneers of the Lands, Romsdal and Trinity Lutheran Churches, rural Hudson, South Dakota* (Hudson, SD: Moe Lutheran Parish, 1982), 44. Iver I. Oien, H. A. Ustrud, M. G. Opsahl, J. O. Asen, eds., *Pioneer History: Minnehaha County's Norwegian Pioneers History from the Year 1866 to 1896,* trans. Emily Brende Sittig and Clara Brende Christenson (Freeman, SD: Pine Hill Press, 1976), 79. Andrew Veblen, "The Veblen Family, Immigrant Pioneers from Valdris" (unpublished, n.d.), 64, 71, Andrew A. Veblen Papers, vol. 43, Minnesota Historical Society, St. Paul, MN.

7. Marta Hoffmann, *Fra fiber til tøy: Tekstilredskaper og bruken av dem i norsk tradisjon* (Oslo: Landbruksforlag A/S, 1991), 16.

8. *Moe Parish Pioneers,* 44. Jon Gjerde, *From Peasants to Farmers: The Migration from Balestrand, Norway, to the Upper Middle West* (Cambridge, NY: Cambridge University Press, 1989), 194.

9. Tilla Regina Dahl Deen, *Chronicles of a Minnesota Pioneer* (Minneapolis, MN: Burgess Publishing Co., 1949), 4.

10. The simplest way to spin fibers is to roll them between the hands or along the thigh. A spindle, a stick with a round weight called a whorl at the end, can speed up the process. The spinner drops the spindle with a twist of the wrist to cause the device to

spin and thereby spin the fibers that are caught by a notch at the end of the stick. The spinning wheel was invented in India, probably during the first century. Indian spinners mounted the spindle horizontally onto a wooden frame. The spinner turned a wheel that turned a belt that then turned the spindle. This general type is known as a great wheel, and the style spread to neighboring countries and into Europe. It is important to note that the spinner turned the wheel by hand and stopped periodically to wind the yarn around the spindle for storage. The next innovation was the addition of a foot pedal, or treadle, so that the spinner could keep the wheel in motion with her foot, leaving her hands to manipulate the fibers. During the sixteenth century, a U-shape flyer was added to treadle wheels to wind and store the finished yarn for continuous spinning. Kax Wilson, *A History of Textiles* (Boulder, CO: Westview Press, 1979), 7–10; Eliza Leadbeater, *Spinning and Spinning Wheels* (Buckinghamshire, UK: Shire Publications Ltd., 1992), 3–7.

Tora Bøhn, "A Quest for Norwegian Folk Art in America," *Norwegian-American Studies and Records* 19 (1956): 129. Elizabeth R. Forell, *The Rossings and Their Store, 1870–1970* (Iowa City, IA: The author, 1970). Malcolm Rosholt, *From the Indian Land: First-hand Account of Central Wisconsin's Pioneer Life* (Iola, WI: Krause, 1985), 159. Victor Hilts and Patricia Hilts, "Spinning Wheels in the Alfred Andresen Catalog," *The Spinning Wheel Sleuth* 53 (2006): 6.

11. Veblen, "The Veblen Family," 59. Helene Maria Synstelien, letter, 15 Jan. 1867, Clara Monson Collection, Norwegian-American Historical Association, Northfield, MN (hereafter, NAHA). Three *merker* equals 24 ounces or 680 grams. Two *pund* equals 34 ounces or 965 grams. According to Marta Hoffmann, *Fra fiber til tøy* (73), spinning wheels with large wheels were known in Norway as *skotrokk*. They were brought from Denmark in the 1740s for use in the prison workhouse in Oslo. They were primarily used for cotton or short-fibered wool to be used as weft yarn.

12. *Moe Parish Pioneers,* 22. Gertrude Berg, "Roots from Norway" (unpublished, 1981), 17–18, Gertrude Berg Collection, Vesterheim Norwegian-American Museum, Decorah, IA (hereafter, Vesterheim).

13. Synstelien letter. Todd W. Nichol, trans. and ed., "A Haugean Woman in America: The Autobiography of Sigrid Eielsen," *Norwegian-American Studies* 35 (2000): 275. C. A. Clausen, ed. and trans., *A Chronicler of Immigrant Life: Svein Nilsson's Articles in Billed-Magazine, 1868–1970* (Northfield, MN: NAHA, 1982), 65. Forell, *The Rossings and Their Store.*

14. John A Houkom, ed., "Pioneer Kjærkebøn Writes from Coon Prairie," *Wisconsin Magazine of History* 27 (1944): 442. Farseth and Blegen, *Frontier Mother,* 29.

15. Marion Nelson, "Folk Arts and Crafts of the Norwegians in America," *Migranten / The Migrant* 1 (1988): 58.

16. Textiles woven from rags were used in Norway beginning in about the mid-nineteenth century. They were used in beds over straw or straw mattresses and then increasingly on the floor of the best room. Rag rugs were most commonly used in the winter, rolled out with space between the lengths to show the wooden floor. They were less often sewn together lengthwise to make "carpeting," as they were in the United States. Rugs were typically made of worn-out clothing, but a registration project in Romerike (eastern Norway) recorded examples made with the addition of burlap

sacks, fishing nets, rabbit fur, and straw. Anne Guri Gunnerød, "Fillerye registrering på Romerike—gamle filleryer, er det noe å bruke ti'a på da?" *Maihaugen Årbok* (1997): 72–81. An English translation by Katherine Larson appears in *Norwegian Textile Letter* 8.2 (2007): 1–8.

The Strange American Way: Letters of Caja Munch from Wiota, Wisconsin, 1855–1859, trans. Helene Munch and Peter A. Munch (Carbondale: Southern Illinois University Press, 1970), 68, 154. As a pastor's wife, Caja Munch would have been part of the immigrant upper class, but she faced many of the same challenges while creating a home in a new country as did other immigrant women. See Gracia Grindal, "The Americanization of the Norwegian Pastors' Wives," *Norwegian-American Studies* 32 (1989): 199–207. Hilda Thompson Quickstad, "Memories of My Childhood" (unpublished, 1982), 5, Hilda Quickstad Collection, NAHA.

17. Domestic sewing machines first became available in the United States in 1859. In 1863 the Singer Company reported sales of twenty thousand home machines. The machines were quite expensive until the 1870s, when patents expired, manufacturing competition increased, and shipping costs decreased, especially for states west of the Mississippi. Manufacturers marketed aggressively to women, offering demonstrations, installment purchase plans, and trade-in allowances. The decrease in cost and increase in marketing efforts meant that more and more women bought sewing machines. Sales of Singer sewing machines, one of the more than fifty American brands available, soared from 170,000 units in 1870 to 500,000 units in 1880 to 1.35 million units in 1903. Anita B. Loscalzo, "The History of the Sewing Machine and Its Use in Quilting in the United States," *Uncoverings* 26 (2005): 175–208; Singer Sewing Co. website, History: http://www.singerco.com/company/history.html, accessed 19 Nov. 2007. Clara Jacobson, "Memories from Perry Parsonage," *Norwegian-American Studies and Records* 14 (1944): 143.

18. Helen Olson Halvorsen and Lorraine Fletcher, "19th Century Midwife: Some Recollections," *Oregon Historical Quarterly* 70.1 (1969): 42–43. Mrs. R. O. Brandt, "Social Aspects of Prairie Pioneering: The Reminiscences of a Pioneer Pastor's Wife," *Norwegian-American Studies and Records* 7 (1933): 3. Barbara Handy-Marchello, *Women of the Northern Plains: Gender and Settlement on the Homestead Frontier, 1870–1930* (St. Paul: Minnesota Historical Society Press, 2005), 124–25.

19. Eva M. Niles, *Fancy Work Recreations: Knitting, Crochet & Home Adornment* (Minneapolis, MN: Buckeye Publishing Co., 1885), 5. Gertrude Smith, letter to Anne Bugge, 20 Jan. 1885, Gertrude Smith Collection, Vesterheim.

20. Veblen, "The Veblen Family," 68. Barbara Levorsen, "Our Bread and Meat," *Norwegian-American Studies* 22 (1965): 196. Dikka Wulfsberg Hove and Caia Wulfsberg Thoen, "Memoirs of Fathers and Mothers Pioneer Life in Freeborn County Minnesota" (unpublished, n.d.), 46, Reference Library, Vesterheim. Berg, "Roots from Norway," 133. Caroline Mathilde Koren Naeseth, "Memories From Little Iowa Parsonage," trans. Henriette C. K. Naeseth, *Norwegian-American Studies and Records* 13 (1944): 69.

21. O. M. Norlie, O. A. Tingelstad, Karl T. Jacobsen, eds., *Luther College Through Sixty Years, 1861–1921* (Minneapolis, MN: Augsburg Publishing House, 1922), 471–72. Bethel Lutheran Church website, "The History of Bethel Lutheran Women," http://www.bethel-madison.org/historyBLC%20Women.htm, accessed 31 May 2006.

22. L. DeAne Lagerquist, *In America Men Milk the Cows: Factors of Gender, Ethnicity, and Religion in the Americanization of Norwegian-American Women* (Brooklyn, NY: Carlson Publishing, Inc., 1991), 54, 148–50, 200.

23. Conrad H. Stai, "A Brief History of Buzzle Osterdalen Church" (unpublished, n.d.), Reference Library, Vesterheim. Lagerquist, *In America Men Milk the Cows;* Erik Luther Williamson, "'Doing What Had To Be Done': Norwegian Lutheran Ladies Aid Societies of North Dakota," *North Dakota History* 57 (Spring 1990): 2–13; and Lori Ann Lahlum, "'Everything Was Changed and Looked Strange': Norwegian Women in South Dakota," *South Dakota History* 35 (2005): 189–216.

24. Martha Reishus, *The Builders: Chapters of History of the Pioneer Lutheran Church at Minot, North Dakota* (N.p., 1933), 73. Borghild T. Estness, *Josie Rykken's Family* (Minneapolis, MN: The author, 1983), 64.

25. Quickstad, "Memories of My Childhood," 14. *100th Anniversary, 1870–1970: Trefoldighed Lutheran Church, Battle Lake, Minnesota* ([Battle Lake, MN: Trefoldighed Lutheran Church], 1970).

26. *Live Well: The Letters of Sigrid Gjeldaker Lillehaugen,* ed. Theresse Nelson Lundby, Kristie Nelson-Neuhaus, and Ann Nordland Wallace (St. Paul, MN: Western Home Books, 2004), 123. Bella Anderson, letter to Vesterheim Norwegian-American Museum, 28 July 1992, Vesterheim.

27. *100th Anniversary.*

28. *Valley Grove Lutheran Church, Kloten, North Dakota, 100th Anniversary* (Finley, ND: Steele County Press, 1982), 15. The money raised by the friendship quilt came from both the sale of raffle tickets and the amount people paid to have their name embroidered on the quilt. Brandt, "Social Aspects of Prairie Pioneering," 17 and n12. Bethel Lutheran Church website.

29. C. O. Ruste, ed., *Sixty Years of Perry Congregation* (Northfield, MN: Mohn, 1915), 125. Brandt, "Social Aspects of Prairie Pioneering," 17. Ernest M. Maland, *Remember the Days of Old: The Centennial Saga of Arendahl Evangelical Lutheran Congregation, 1856–1956* (N.p.: Arendahl Evangelical Lutheran Church Centennial Committee, [1956]), 42–43.

30. *100th Anniversary.*

31. Oien, et al., *Pioneer History,* 96. Hilda Marie Thingwold Burreson, "Memories of Grampa and Grandma Losen" (unpublished, 1946), 2, Reference Library, Vesterheim. Gunhild A. Larsen, "Gunhild Andrine Jakobsdaughter Larsen, Born Nov. 4, 1835" (unpublished, 1923), Gunhild A. Larsen Collection, NAHA. Aagot Raaen, *Grass of the Earth: Immigrant Life in the Dakota Country* (Northfield, MN: NAHA, 1950), 21, 90.

32. Burreson, "Memories of Grampa and Grandma Losen," 1. Aagot Raaen, "Gro Viken Mork" (unidentified newspaper clipping, n.d.), Hildegarde Johnson Collection, Vesterheim. Handy-Marchello, *Women of the Northern Plains,* 120.

33. Berg, "Roots from Norway," 51. Orville Bakken, Palmer J. Sougstad, Louis R. Thompson, and Courtney J. Sather, eds., *Northwood, North Dakota Diamond Jubilee, 1884–1959* (Oklahoma City, OK: Semco Color Press, 1959), 108. For more on the immigration of Arabic speakers to the Midwest and the profession of peddling, see William C. Sherman, Paul L. Whitney, and John Guerro, *Prairie Peddlers: The Syrian-Lebanese in North Dakota* (Bismarck, ND: University of Mary Press, 2002). Raaen, *Grass of the Earth,* 170.

34. Anna Regina Hilleboe Christiansen, "Wife and Mother: Gjertrud Rumohr Haug Hilleboe, 1833–1909," in *Souvenir "Norse-American Women" 1825–1925,* ed. Alma A. Guttersen and Regina Hilleboe Christiansen (St. Paul, MN: Mrs. Gilbert Guttersen, 1926), 36. N. N. Rønning, *Fifty Years in America* (Minneapolis, MN: The Friend Publishing Co., 1938), 132. Ingeborg Olsdatter Oye Bergeim, diary entries 27 April and 10 May 1885, Ingeborg Olsdatter Bergeim Collection, NAHA.

35. *The Strange American Way,* 82.

36. See, for example, Colburn " 'Well, I Wondered When I Saw You,' "; Noss, "Tradition and Transition," and Gilbertson, "Patterns of the New World." Erling Ylvisaker, *Eminent Pioneers: Norwegian-American Pioneer Sketches* (Minneapolis, MN: Augsburg, 1934), 43–46.

37. Raaen, "Gro Viken Mork."

38. Veblen, "The Veblen Family," 5, 13, 21, 50, 59; [Emily Veblen Olsen], "Memoirs of Mrs. Sigurd Olsen (Emily Veblen)" (unpublished, [1940]), [1, 6], Emily Veblen Olsen Collection, NAHA; Ylvisaker, *Eminent Pioneers,* 1, 11; William C. Melton, "Ideal Immigrants: Thomas, Kari, and Haldor Veblen," paper, Vandringer: Norwegians in the American Mosaic 1825–2000, St. Paul, MN, 7 April 2000, manuscript at Minnesota Historical Society, St. Paul, MN.

39. Later generations of Norwegian American women were also involved in benevolent societies and shared labor. This involvement is, however, almost the only thing that directly links them to the skills and efforts of the immigrant women from rural Norway. Second- and third-generation women might have helped as children with some stages of textile production, and they likely learned to knit and sew. But even if they had learned to spin or weave, they rarely continued the practice and concentrated their efforts on sewing garments, making quilts, and doing fancy work. During the twentieth and twenty-first centuries, there have been several revivals of textile handwork for economic and other reasons, such as identity. The American Bicentennial in 1976 inspired many women to take up quiltmaking and explore other Colonial (or pioneer) textile and food customs. A more recent example is the interest in traditional folk art classes at Vesterheim Museum. Many female students perceive weaving as a way to express their Norwegian heritage.

40. For one family's annual expenditures for clothing and help in sewing, see Valborg Adelaide Fynboe and Carl Teslow Fynboe, eds., *An Account of the Life of Anders N. Teslow: A Diary 1828–1908,* trans. Gunnar J. Malmin (Tacoma, WA: Carl T. Teslow, 1976).

Home, Health, and Christian Respectability: Norwegian Immigrant Women in Family and Community Health

Ann M. Legreid

Norwegian American and Norwegian immigrant women played active and vital roles in the health care of their families, and many of them also played roles in advancing American public health and sanitation campaigns in the nineteenth and twentieth centuries. These women administered medicines to their husbands and children, fought infectious diseases, made medical advances as doctors and researchers, and brought American norms of cleanliness and domesticity into their homes and communities.

Most Norwegians came from rural settings and traditional backgrounds and were not well versed in Victorian and Edwardian ideals. In America, it became obvious to them that a decent home, good health, education for their children, and Christian respectability were Victorian ideals to which middle-class Americans aspired. Some women took up the gospel of reform as formal educators, promoting improved school hygiene and scientific farming and housekeeping.

Clergy and clergy wives, schoolteachers, and professionally trained medical personnel were among the leaders in the campaigns for public health improvement. In *Souvenir,* the booklet prepared for the 1925 centennial of the beginning of Norwegian immigration, we see a remarkable record of involvement by Norwegian American women in American reform movements, including the League of Women Voters, the Woman's Christian Temperance Union, the Red Cross, Young Women's Christian Association, parent-teacher associations, and the boards of hospitals and humanitarian groups. Through these involvements, Norwegian American women challenged and redefined gender roles, which paved the way for female participation in a broader public arena.[1]

Norwegian immigrants were also influenced by currents of change flowing within Norway in the provision of medical care, particularly in the last decades of the nineteenth century. Some of those changes emanated from Western Europe, while others came from North America. As in the other Nordic states, in Norway there were longstanding traditions of folk medicine and support for the poor, aged, and sick through home- and community-based care. Wives and mothers were the family's primary health-care givers. Physician districts were organized in Norway as early as the 1830s, and as more doctors trained at university (at the time, only men had access to formal medical training), the practice of medicine began to professionalize. With the onset of professionalization, men assumed a greater role in the overall health maintenance of the Norwegian family, dispensing modern medicines and employing scientific methods of healing. Educational reforms in the late nineteenth century opened doors to women at Norway's teaching seminaries and universities, eventually granting them access to medical education.[2]

Many other currents of reform were emerging at the time, adding momentum to the changes in the Norwegian medical system. For example, the Norwegian Feminist Society was organized in 1884 and the National Women's Suffrage Union in 1898. The consumer cooperative movement flowed to Scandinavia from England, social democratic impulses emanated from Germany, and temperance pleas came largely from the pulpits of Europe. There were also efforts within Norway to develop best practices for such matters as child labor, housing standards, and public sanitation. Norway's mortality rate from leprosy dropped to nearly zero after G. H. Armauer Hansen's discovery of the leprosy bacillus in 1874, only a few years after Louis Pasteur demonstrated the link between disease and bacteria. In sanitation, Norway's reforms bore resemblance to those sweeping across the United States.[3]

This chapter illustrates the pivotal role of Norwegian American women in tending to the health of their families and communities. Women are largely absent from county and local histories published during the immigrant era; thus, their stories and contributions must be gleaned from a mix of family and community resources such as letters, diaries, and newspapers. Similarly, women's roles in hospitals and other health-care facilities are quite obscure, usually lacking the detail afforded their fathers, husbands, brothers, and sons. In his address at the Norwegian American Centennial in Minneapolis in 1925, Carl Kolset noted that "so little has been written about our medical men." Even less has been written about the contributions of women. This chapter draws on such sources (letters, diaries, family histories, newspaper accounts, and public health records, mostly from the Midwest) to paint a broad picture of women's roles in family and public health in Norwegian America.[4]

Norwegian Americans and Public Health

Death and disease were ever-present themes in nineteenth-century America, as evidenced in the diaries, letters, and ledgers of innumerable pioneer families. Pioneer women faced daunting challenges in caring for those afflicted with typhoid, cholera, smallpox, malaria, whooping cough, scarlet fever, and countless other ailments and disabilities. In a report to the Minnesota Board of Health on the condition of Norwegian immigrants, one doctor noted, "The newcomers suffer frequently . . . from protracted diarrheas." He continued, "The diarrheas of small children are far more frequent and severe than in the old country. Especially in the cities is the number of infants carried away by these diseases very great." The doctor identified "chronic gastritis and dyspepsia" as the most common complaint from the Norwegians, a condition he attributed to a "diet more difficult to digest." Norwegians in Minnesota also suffered from infectious diseases like influenza and diphtheria to a greater degree than their friends and family back in Norway.[5]

The Wisconsin State Board of Health, created in 1876, ran a public health campaign that was a microcosm of the national campaign to educate and reform the American public on health and sanitation issues. The board routinely disseminated health information to Wisconsin residents through posters, pamphlets, and newspaper circulars titled, for example, "Diphtheria . . . causes and precautions," and "The proper means of sewage disposal." One La Crosse authority was adamant that circulars from the board be placed in the hands of all families. The Wisconsin Medical Society lobbied the state legislature in the interest of public health; at the same time, it endeavored to "educate the public and the profession regarding the importance of sanitation and preventive medicine."[6]

The medical community faced daunting challenges in educating the public on germ theory and the value of personal and public hygiene. "People perish for lack of knowledge," noted the health officer at Trimbelle, Wisconsin. Bad water and poor drainage were two of the greatest public hazards, routinely giving rise to epidemics of diphtheria and cholera. In the heavily Norwegian Christiania and Coon townships in Vernon County, Wisconsin, a local health officer in 1888 submitted this statement to the Wisconsin State Board of Health regarding the challenges there: "We have done all in our power to enforce isolation and other precautionary measures in both towns and in cases of contagious disease, but have failed in destroying the poison of Diphtheria and Scarlet Fever in many instances by reason of the disease occurring in rotten, tumble-down log houses."[7]

The drive for sanitation reform in the United States emanated, in part, from the horrors of disease witnessed by thousands of soldiers and civilians during the Civil War. Epidemics of diseases like cholera and scarlet fever, too, propelled people into community cleanup campaigns. Public health officials rightly recognized that sanitation was more effective than quarantine.

The American cleanliness campaign grew robustly after the Civil War and reached its pinnacle in the years following World War II. The campaign had two branches, personal hygiene and public sanitation, and Catharine Beecher, sister of the famous abolitionist Harriet Beecher Stowe, was a leader among those who championed the domestic values of efficiency and cleanliness. In 1841, Catharine Beecher published *A Treatise on Domestic Economy for the Use of Young Ladies at*

Home and at School, in which she championed American domestic values and defined a dual role for women in the home and in the larger society. In 1873, the sisters copublished *The New Housekeeper's Manual: The American Woman's Home,* in which they asserted that women should devote more time to assuring neatness, order, comfort, and cleanliness in the home. Catharine Beecher wrote about the "underestimated importance" of women's roles in society.

By the late nineteenth century, Beecher and other reformers had begun to affect middle-class attitudes about public health and personal hygiene, helping the public to see the relationship between filth and disease. Sylvester Graham, best known for the cracker named after him, was an active proponent of good hygiene and argued profusely for proper diet, regular bathing, and well-ventilated, cleanly homes. William Alcott, cousin of the author Louisa May Alcott, published prolifically on the importance of personal hygiene, a vegetarian diet, and regular outdoor exercise.[8]

Norwegians in America created their own flourishing media—newspapers and periodicals that addressed the issues of the day and presented them in a format the immigrants could understand—in their native tongue. *Kvinden og Hjemmet (Woman and Home),* a monthly magazine for Scandinavian women established in Cedar Rapids, Iowa, by two emigrant sisters from Norway, was the only Norwegian American publication established and edited by women for women. Its editor and cofounder, Ida Hansen, wanted to soften the transition of Scandinavian immigrant women to American life by giving them a journal that would help them learn about American ways and at the same time make it possible for them to contribute their heritage to the American experience. With popular columns like "Our Mothers" and "Our Children," it claimed the greatest readership of any Scandinavian periodical in the American Midwest and circulated from 1888 to 1947, an impressive sixty years. In addition to providing information on traditional foods and crafts, the publication offered short stories, poetry, serialized novels, and special interest items, including many on health, and served as an important vehicle for feminist writings on reform. Its progressive, feminist voice exposed immigrant women to American perspectives on social and political matters and acted as a discussion forum for issues of the day, such as suffrage, public health, and child rearing.[9]

On most indicators, Scandinavian immigrants were healthier than members of many other immigrant groups who entered the United States. The Scandinavian countries promoted health services on a mass scale, allowed contraception, and mandated vaccination against smallpox from early in the nineteenth century. These countries' childbirth and child-rearing customs, including breastfeeding and good child nutrition, contributed to some of the lowest infant mortality rates among all immigrant groups in America. According to the 1900 U.S. census,

Scandinavians had the lowest death rates for diseases of the female reproductive organs and had a well-below-average rate of diseases related to pregnancy.[10]

Norwegian immigrants, with their strong traditions of home health care and folk medicines, were generally progressive in addressing health-care issues and sanitation reforms. They involved themselves in public health at many levels as concerned citizens and parishioners, local sanitary officers, educators, midwives, and health-care personnel. In 1925 Olaf M. Norlie noted that Norwegians in America constituted 2 percent of the population and had produced 2 percent of the "medical men, there are 2,900 Norwegian physicians and surgeons in America, also 100 osteopaths, 270 veterinary surgeons, 1,125 dentists, besides 2,982 nurses." The data show that Norwegian Americans were well represented in the American medical community, at least proportionate to their numbers in the general population.[11]

Folk Traditions and Home Health Care

Wives and mothers became the frontline providers of medical care among Norwegian immigrants. They worked from an oral tradition of treatments and cures passed through the generations, combined in practice with advice from a domestic medicine book and probably a sturdy faith in God. Folk healing had been practiced for centuries in Norway, usually by women, who were often viewed as witches. Practices that led to witchcraft charges often employed rituals, spells, and potions linked with superstition. Such rituals involved warding off "evil" and appeasing the *huldrefolk,* troublesome creatures from the forest and a major concern of many folk healers. To prevent a healthy baby from disappearing out of the cradle and into the hands of the huldrefolk, who would replace the baby with one with rickets, mothers were instructed to place three dolls in the cradle, each wearing garments sewn from the baby's clothing. A mother could cure a child's fever with chills if she wrote a special code on nine pieces of bread, feeding the first eight pieces to the child on consecutive days and burning the last. Such ancient rituals were prescribed for broken bones, labor, and afflictions of every kind, including emotional distress. Premodern Scandinavians long believed that disease was caused by demons, and Black Book formulas brought magical relief to those who believed in such powers.[12]

On the other hand, folk healing also meant remedies that rested on rational and scientific grounds, passed down through the oral tradition and brought by immigrants to North America. As noted in Viking-era sagas and in records kept by Christian monks, herbs were an essential element of these remedies, as were everyday ingredients with healing properties. Nineteenth-century Norwegian and immigrant records show that these included camphor, cod liver oil, poultices, potatoes, pork, honey, goose grease, mustard plaster, kerosene, turpentine, lead, and spirits.

Significantly, the folk healers employing these methods most often were women. As medicine became more professionalized, healers often faced challenges from authorities, who questioned their "old wives remedies" (kjerringsråd). Still, many female healers provided scientifically sound advice—for example, Norwegian women advocated for sunshine and cod liver oil as a preventative for rickets long before the disease was fully understood. Folk medicine widely practiced in Norway met resistance in America also; the formal medical community led campaigns for criminal laws and penalties against folk healers. Folk medicine, nonetheless, remained a central part of family health in Norwegian America into the twentieth century, especially in areas underserved by formally trained doctors and nurses.[13]

Norwegian folk traditions and modern, scientific medicine often came together in the home. Fascinated by traditional homemade cures, one Minnesota pioneer recalled her mother rubbing skunk fat, intended for greasing boots, on her four little girls who were very ill and then noted their miraculous recovery. She also recalled another incident:

My brother had cried all night because of a foreign substance in his eye. Flax seed, blowing his nose, pulling the eyelids over each other, mother looking and working with a clean cloth—nothing helped. A neighbor happened in in the midst of our trouble and she had a cure. Shoot a woodpecker and take a pellet out of his gizzard and put it in the eye. Mother thought that finding a woodpecker at this time was rather difficult so she put my brother on a riding pony and sent him in to Brandon to Dr. Meckstroth.

The intersection of folk and modern medicine in this pioneer story is striking. Similarly, Norwegians in America often used modern medical instruments in home medical care. For example, they used forceps to remove teeth and a "cupping" instrument to suck away "bad blood." Anesthesia was not a part of the picture in most home remedies, however, and reminiscences often note excruciating pain.[14]

Norwegians often sent medicines and suggestions for remedies, both folk and modern, to their immigrant relatives. Some even sent smallpox vaccine. (Norwegian law mandated the vaccination for smallpox in 1810.) In a letter dated December 5, 1864, Gro Svendsen acknowledged receipt of the vaccine she had requested: "Thank you, Father, for the vaccine. One bottle was crushed, and the second was damaged, but the third was intact. I haven't used it yet because my little Niels has been ill. He is getting better so I shall soon use it."[15]

Norwegian immigrant Severine Hovelsrud of North Beaver Creek, Wisconsin, kept a diary in which she made note of administering nursing care to family members and others in her immigrant community. The diary provides no detail on her methods or medicines, but from the names it is clear that Hovelsrud provided nursing care to her family and a circle of neighborhood friends, thus only within her own ethnic group. Her patients were almost exclusively born in or descended from the Hardanger region in western Norway; these were the people who shared her dialect and populated the social circles of her valley. She and her husband, the community's parochial school teacher, were obviously community nurturers and leaders and involved themselves in a steady schedule of social and congregational engagements.[16]

Norwegian women were at the interface of Norwegian folk and modern medicines, and as such they sometimes found their work impeded by age-old beliefs and practices. At times the barriers to health care and reform were profoundly challenging. In preindustrial times, a thorough cleaning of house and barn followed slaughtering and brewing, which was done seasonally, right before Christmas. People bathed and washed their clothes infrequently and used soap and water sparingly, except, once again, at Christmastime. Clothing was not washed daily or weekly but in several large washings during the year. Tradition, however, dictated that the Norwegian home and farm, including the barnyard, needed a thorough pre-Christmas scrubbing. Norwegian sociologist Eilert Sundt traced these practices to pre-Christian times in his book *On Cleanliness in Norway* (1869) and associated the thorough cleaning with renewal and protection. In the early folk belief, the wash water was linked to the sign of the cross, fire, and steel—all elements that could protect the people from the mythical huldrefolk.

Such beliefs may have persisted in some regions over the centuries, but by the 1800s ideas about cleanliness began to change. The forces of change ranged from the Enlightenment to industrialization and the exposure to modern practices by sailors and workers who had traveled outside of Scandinavia. Norwegian rural life was rooted in tradition, and these traditions influenced peasant immigrants, but more modern beliefs about health and sickness were beginning to take hold.[17]

By religious conditioning, many Norwegians felt that disease and death were the will of God. One health official noted the fatalism among Norwegians in Colfax, Wisconsin: "And there are many among them who say that when their time comes they must die, and so will not call in a physician, no matter what the trouble may be." Svendsen noted that her own health "is not always the best, but so far God has spared me from any prolonged illness, and so I feel that I cannot complain. Rather I should thank God for his infinite goodness." Her story was not uncommon: she mourned the loss of her "little Sigri" who "has gone to her

Heavenly Father," feared that her next child would not live long, and died herself at age thirty-seven following the birth of her tenth child.[18]

America's modern medical methods were not uniformly accepted by immigrants from Norway. Many feared quack doctors, impure vaccines, and draconian methods like cupping, vomiting, and bloodletting. Some Norwegians feared the night air, believing that diseases were linked to electricity or gases in the air, a common understanding before the gradual acceptance of germ theory. Naturally, they would have felt most comfortable with the time-tested remedies of home. Hospitals at that time were viewed as houses for the sick, where people went to die. Doris Weatherford has noted that Scandinavians viewed their old-world health-care systems as superior to American methods. For example, they "protested the lack of stringent licensing for doctors in America and missed their own government-regulated system." Cooperating with American public health administrators must have been awkward and confusing at times, especially since many viewed sanitation laws with suspicion and as authoritarian and unevenly applied. The language difference, too, deterred some immigrants from seeking treatment by English-speaking doctors or dealing with health officials.[19]

The Church and Health

Ministers and their wives were particularly well situated to administer health care, to introduce new scientific methods, and to preach the gospel of good health and hygiene. They were usually educated and well respected, and they functioned in vast networks both within and beyond the communities they served. Public health officials depended heavily on the clergy in combating disease and, in fact, much of the sanitation reform literature was directed toward clergymen and their wives. "The clergyman," wrote the Reverend John Faville for the Wisconsin Board of Health, "must teach the ethics of sanitation." Moreover, continued Faville, "The clergyman as the expounder of the Christian religion must be a health officer" because "[our] bible is a book of life. It remembers the body. A considerable part of its history is that of sanitary reform. It sends out boards of health in the name of Jehovah." Clergymen were admonished to have "good personal habits of hygiene," to monitor the heating and ventilation in their church buildings, to be a "guardian of health" at public funerals, and to be in "perfect harmony" with the medical community.[20]

Clergymen, along with civic leaders, endorsed these sanitation campaigns. Pastors and deacons mobilized local citizens in support of the work of state and local boards of health. Many pastors doubled as community doctors and pharmacists, lending their stature and guidance, a tradition continued from Norway. Mrs. Assur Groth recalled that Reverend Clausen doubled as a doctor for her community to the extent that he was capable. In the absence of trained physicians, ministers often functioned as doctors, dispensing medicines along with comforting prayers and scriptures. Thalette Galby Brandt, wife of a Norwegian Lutheran minister in South Dakota, noted that her husband had brought smallpox vaccine to the parsonage, and "many people, old and young, came to the parsonage for free vaccination."[21]

Yet it was usually pastors' wives who served as the primary workers in the actual provision of health-care services. Elisabeth Koren's diary from the Iowa frontier, 1853–55, demonstrates that she was knowledgeable about botanical preparations. Because she was a pastor's wife, parishioners came to her with expectations that they would be cured. As the community's untrained pharmacist, she regularly referred to medical books to concoct preparations of powders and other remedies. Ministers' wives, no doubt, played a complementary role by hosting people in their homes for medical and spiritual attention, and in some cases, like Koren, they undoubtedly took the lead. There were vaccines to unpack, children to tend, and mothers to comfort and reassure.[22]

Ministers and their wives could provide some medical assistance and education to parishioners, giving vaccines and sharing the latest missives from the state, but the primary responsibility for health care remained in the home and in the hands of wives and mothers.[23]

Medical Wives

In addition to their role as caregivers in the home, the wives of medical doctors were well positioned to have an impact on community health; in fact, some were nurses, and many dedicated their lives to working in supportive roles alongside their husbands. The life of Kari Larsdatter Rockne Quales is a case in point. Niles Theodore Quales of Kinsarvik, Norway, emigrated to America in 1859, enlisted in the Union army, and served as supervisor of the veterinary hospital in Nashville. He graduated from Rush Medical College in Chicago in 1866, served as city physician in charge of the smallpox hospital from 1868 to 1870, and later was appointed surgeon in chief at the U.S. Marine Hospital in Chicago. Because the hospital had only minimal furnishings, Quales moved in his own furniture and library and took residence there himself. He later married Kari Larsdatter Rockne of Voss, Norway, who may have been quite typical of doctors' wives in that era. She "raised the children, advised and supported her husband, and took an active role in several institutions," serving more than thirty years as a Sunday school teacher.[24]

In the Great Chicago Fire of 1871, the Qualeses, with the help of two Danish nurses, transported all of the patients from the Marine Hospital out of harm's way to the safety of other facilities. Dr. Quales helped to establish the Tabitha Hospital, Lutheran Deaconess Home and Hospital, and the Norwegian Old

People's Home at Norwood, Illinois, where he was the attending physician. He was elected president of the Norwegian Old People's Home Society of Chicago and hosted its monthly meetings in his home, his wife and daughters emerging at the end of each meeting with coffee and cake. The records suggest that together the Qualeses provided caring, dynamic leadership, a leadership that inspired others in the Chicago community to action in the campaign for better health.[25]

Helga Sara Isaksaetre Gundersen is another example of an active spouse. Married to Adolf Gundersen, the founder of the Gundersen Hospital in La Crosse, Wisconsin, Helga was known variously as Mother Gundersen, Madam Gundersen, and Mother Norway, although her preferred title was Mrs. Doctor Gundersen, in the Norwegian style. She was dedicated to the local community, admired and loved by many, and deeply devoted to family. As one historian notes, "Helga Gundersen was the center of authority in the Gundersen home. When she gathered the children for prayers, for lessons, or for meals, they did not argue with her. A teacher before she was married, she had a great love of books and an understanding of how to raise children. Adolf Gundersen usually deferred to her when it came to child rearing and matters of the home." When a cholera epidemic struck many in her community, she acted cautiously: "I give him [son Carl] practically no other food than cooked milk for the time since a bad children's cholera goes around here during the summer months." This statement suggests a central role for Helga in the health care of her family, a telling detail considering that her husband was a distinguished medical doctor.[26]

Helga yearned to return to her native Norway, but Adolf enjoyed the freedom of American medicine and perhaps also his status as the local "premier surgeon." In Norway, doctors were more strictly controlled; certain procedures, such as gynecological examinations, were forbidden, so Adolf could not envision himself in Norway, except as a periodic visitor. Helga relished her journeys home and made every effort to assure that her children "learned and kept the Norwegian language, literature, and music." Helga was upper class and educated, and like her counterparts in Victorian America, she was the purveyor and guardian of culture and domesticity, a moral authority, a nurturer and guide for the Gundersens' many children.[27]

Midwifery

Female hygiene issues and health concerns, particularly pregnancy, were generally not considered appropriate topics for public discussion. Immigrant letters suggest that infants appeared quite abruptly in the family home; they were said to be gifts from God or delivered by an angel. There is scant mention of pregnancy and its various complications. Even when a pregnancy was a particularly difficult one, there were few, if any, references to this condition and, in fact, the mother may have characterized it as simply "feeling tired" or "not feeling well."

Gro Svendsen, emigrant from Hallingdal, Norway, built a life with her husband in a pioneer community near Estherville, Iowa. Her letters home contain frequent and matter-of-fact references to personal and family afflictions such as toothaches and bad coughs. She called her pregnancies "my confinements" and noted inflammation in her breasts and a lack of mother's milk but did not elaborate on what, if any, treatments she tried.[28]

Because sexuality and female body issues were taboo topics, women relied on old family remedies or the help of midwives and wet nurses or, in rarer cases, availed themselves of mail-order booklets and brochures written by doctors. Dr. La Croix's book *Physiological View of Marriage* was advertised widely for American women "who need a confidential medical adviser with regard to any interesting complaints to which their delicate organization render them liable." Some Norwegian immigrant women might have viewed La Croix's English-language guidebook with hesitation and suspicion, however; they were more likely to favor old remedies handed them by folk healers or by their mothers and grandmothers.[29]

Lesley Biggs has studied midwifery practices among Icelandic settlers in Canada and found that these practices varied "over time, according to class, race, ethnicity, region, levels of industrialization, and colonization." She makes the distinction between "neighborhood midwives," those who learned on the job, and "trained midwives," who had taken formal midwifery schooling. She recounts the extraordinary story of an Icelandic-trained midwife, Gudrun Gudmunddottir, who performed a successful Caesarean section on a mother who had just been torn up by the horns of an ox and killed. Physicians in Europe often used midwives to do Caesarean sections on dead or dying women and to remove dead fetuses. European midwives also performed more common procedures such as vaginal examinations and postdelivery treatment of illnesses. In addition, midwives arranged for wet nurses, dealt with foundlings, and examined women suspected of practicing abortion and infanticide. Midwives had highly specialized knowledge and skills and served vital functions in American settlements in the medical treatments of the day, either working alone or assisting doctors and nurses.[30]

Norwegian immigrant women tended to prefer Norwegian midwives to American doctors for deliveries: the midwives were familiar and empathetic, spoke the same language, were very affordable, and could assist in the home following delivery. Severine Hovelsrud of the North Beaver Creek community in Wisconsin was a neighborhood midwife who had learned the art of midwifery on the job. According to one of her descendents, her delivery fee was fifty cents, unless the delivery took two days; then the fee was a dollar. Norwegian immigrant

Ole and Anne-Marie Lindberg, who was a midwife

Anne-Marie Lindberg, who lived in nearby Mill Creek, Wisconsin, was another neighborhood midwife, trained by her mother back in Norway. She delivered hundreds of babies, performing her last delivery at age ninety. Unlike Hovelsrud, however, she left no record of her midwifery apart from the reminiscences of her children and grandchildren.[31]

Midwifery instruction in Norway was well developed and gave the midwife delivery skills similar in caliber to those of physicians. Sonnova Knutson, a formally trained midwife from Norway, delivered many babies and sometimes engaged in practices licensed physicians usually performed, including cupping and bloodletting.[32]

Goro Dahl of Kathryn, North Dakota, a graduate of the Midwife's School in Oslo, brought her midwifery skills to the Dakota frontier. People in the Kathryn community remembered Dahl in a local history:

> Goro Dahl had not intended to practice her profession in this country, but when people heard of her training, they came for her help and although she had to endure many hardships, such as traveling in open rigs, walking in all kinds of weather, becoming lost on the prairie at night with nothing but the stars to guide them and going out in snowstorms in the middle of the night to deliver babies or to help sick people, she would always go. She delivered hundreds of babies as daughter Annie recalls, but never kept any records.
>
> She vaccinated communities for smallpox and on occasion pulled teeth for people when asked to do it . . . Her home was opened to many newcomers from Norway and several times she took in children and kept them when they needed a temporary home.[33]

Some Norwegian American women who provided
health care advertised their services. Mary (Marie)
Skryseth, a Norwegian immigrant midwife living
in Minneapolis, hung a sign on her family's house
on North Aldrich Avenue advertising her services
in the mid-1890s (above). In Fargo, North Dakota,
Sophia Stavnheim (Mrs. Lauritz) regularly placed
an ad in the Norwegian-language newspaper
Dakota in 1896 (at right). Stavnheim, a recently
arrived immigrant from Norway, lived in a
decidedly Norwegian American section of the city.
In the ad, she emphasized that she received her
midwife training in Bergen, a detail that would
have been important within her community.
Among Norwegian Americans, many believed that
medical training in Norway (for midwives and for
doctors) was superior to the training available in
the United States. Stavnheim's ad on January 22,
1896, appeared with those for Norwegian American
doctors and one for a private hospital operated by
Mrs. Hoff.

Norwegian American Women and Modern Medicine

Norwegian American women sought formalized training as doctors and nurses and established themselves in the health professions—not in large numbers, but in numbers sufficient to open new doors for women in professional life and to allow them to lead health reforms. Women were slow to be accepted as medical doctors in America; in fact, the doors to medical education did not fully open to women in America until the first years of the twentieth century. Gender roles were rigidly prescribed, antifeminism was strong, and men controlled the trained medical community.

Elizabeth Blackwell (1821–1910), a champion of women's rights, worked as a governess in physicians' homes and schooled herself in medicine by reading her employers' medical texts. After being shut out of numerous all-male medical schools, she was eventually admitted to New York's Geneva Medical School (now Hobart College) in 1847, paving the way for other women in the medical professions. Welcome opportunities came in 1870 when Swiss universities and the University of Michigan opened their medical classrooms to women. In Sweden, women were permitted to take university admissions exams beginning in 1870, but equal access to all programs was not granted until years later.[34]

In 1904, when the first woman joined the staff of the Gundersen Clinic/Lutheran Hospital in La Crosse, Wisconsin, founder Adolf Gundersen expressed his concern in a letter to his brother, Gunnar: "The new woman doctor, Dr. Hansen, gives a good impression, but it's too bad she's a woman. It's too bad that she wears a skirt." He was concerned that her reputation would suffer by working among mostly men. He noted, "There will certainly naturally soon be talk and gossip about Dr. Christensen and her." Later that year Gundersen wrote that Hansen, then his assistant, planned to leave the practice and return to Norway; he gave no reason for her departure. Gundersen encouraged several of his sons to enter the medical profession, but true to his patriarchal nature, he "squelched any idea of his daughter sharing the family tradition."[35]

"Dr. A [Adolf Gundersen] was 'royalty,'" noted Lenore Hanson Schnabel, a nurse at the Lutheran Hospital Training School for Nurses, class of 1926. Gundersen led an entourage of doctors on morning rounds, while nurses stood at attention in white, starched uniforms. Schnabel described the scene: "Prior to their arrival we, as student nurses, were expected to have every patient and every room looking immaculate. We rushed around carrying breakfast trays, straightening bedding, combing hair, picking up any mess, and lastly, all window shades must be at the same level. This accomplished, we were told to disappear." Such a gendered approach was not unique to Gundersen and the Gundersen Clinic; it was widespread throughout the medical profession.[36]

Though Norwegian American women entered the medical field as physicians in small numbers, their work left a lasting legacy that opened doors for the generations that followed. Medical doctor Susan Ackerman of Vadsø, Norway, settled in Chicago just before World War I. She never married, but she raised several orphans and became "active in work for the poor and sick, especially those of Norwegian descent." In addition to serving on the staff of the Norwegian American Hospital in Chicago for twenty-two years, she was active in the American Medical Association, the Chicago Medical Society, the Medical Women's National Association, and the Chicago Medical Women's Club. King Haakon of Norway awarded her the Royal Gold Medal in 1934 in recognition of her attention to a sick child who arrived in Chicago on the Norwegian training vessel *Sørlandet*.[37]

Ingeborg Rasmussen received her medical degree from Northwestern University and served several hospitals in Chicago, held membership in the Women's Medical Society and Women's Press Association, served as editor of *Skandinaven*, and received the Royal Gold Medal from King Haakon VII for "her services to humanity." Valborg Andersen Sogn, born at Horten, Norway, in 1858, emigrated to America in 1886 and graduated from the Woman's Medical School at Northwestern University in Chicago in 1895. For the next fifteen years, she practiced medicine in Chicago. She was a pioneering instructor of gynecology at Northwestern's Medical School and an instructor of nurses and a practicing gynecologist at Tabitha Hospital. In 1910 she chose to return to Norway, where she became a licensed physician and practiced medicine until her death in 1916.[38]

In 1878 Helga Ruud, born in Kongsberg, Norway, emigrated to Boston at the age of eighteen. For a time she worked as a governess, then wrote a book about the experience and sold it to finance her way through medical school. With her medical degree in hand, she accepted a position at the Dunning Psychiatric Hospital in Chicago and was purportedly the first Norwegian doctor in that city. She was a practitioner at the Norwegian Hospital in Chicago, had a private practice, and taught obstetrics at Northwestern University for thirty-four years. Like most female physicians, Ruud recognized the tremendous need for doctors specializing in women's concerns and focused her practice on the female specialties. She was involved in many medical and cultural organizations, serving as president of the Medical Women's Club and founder of the Federation of Norwegian Women's Societies and the Norwegian Women's Club. She supported the women's suffrage movement and peace movement, prohibition, and the numerous cultural programs sponsored by Norwegians in Chicago, including Nordmanns Forbundet. She was described as a "symbol and ideal to those who have been touched by her."[39]

These examples demonstrate that female physicians became role models and leaders in civic and women's societies, groups that opened the doors to more and more women for participation in the public arena. Furthermore, women's talents were no longer confined to the home as women formed organizations and became active in causes such as suffrage and prohibition. As women learned to work together in their sisterhoods and to lead and exert authority, they created women's spaces in which they could work within a larger world managed and led by men.

Besides doctoring, women pursued other avenues in health care, including the diaconate, secular nursing, child welfare, and the Catholic sisterhood. Religious groups were intimately involved from the beginning in caring for those affected by disease, disability, and difficult life circumstances. The work of the Catholic Church was broad and profound and became a model for other religious groups. Both Catholic and Protestant congregations trained health and charity workers and teachers and engaged in fund-raising through bazaars and church dinners. According to Norlie's 1925 history of Norwegian Americans, Norwegian American Lutherans sponsored twenty-eight hospitals, twenty hospices, twenty homes for the aged, fourteen children's homes, three deaconess homes (including one jointly sponsored with the Methodists), numerous rescue homes for unwed mothers, and a home-finding department for orphaned children.[40]

The Lutheran deaconess movement was a part of the larger Protestant movement to train women for Christian service. To be accepted into the diaconate, women had to be unmarried, have a high school education, and be between the ages of eighteen and thirty-two. These women trained in "motherhouses," usually as nurses, although diaconate education eventually expanded to include home and foreign missions, social services, and forms of health-care administration. Norwegians in America established three motherhouses in Brooklyn, New York (1883, incorporated 1892), Minneapolis (1889), and Chicago (1897), and though they had a modest number of members, the women of the motherhouses were influential beyond their numbers. They served as overseers in hospitals, orphanages, and other care facilities. Not only did women who trained in motherhouses learn the skills of their profession; they also built a sisterhood from which they drew strength and inspiration to function in a sexist society.[41]

Deaconess Elizabeth Fedde stands prominently among those who provided both spiritual and medical care for Norwegians in America. Born on Christmas Day, 1850, near Flekkefjord, Norway, Fedde entered the Lovisenberg deaconess house in Norway and received her training from Mother Katinka Guldberg, who, in turn, had been trained in Germany and was prominent in the Norwegian deaconess community. After working for some time in Troms, she accepted a challenge from her brother in New York to set up a ministry for Norwegian seamen there. Just months after arriving in New York in 1883, Fedde established the Norwegian Relief Society, adjacent to the Norwegian Seamen's Church. At the outset, the relief society was just a three-room boardinghouse. Two years

Elizabeth Fedde (front row, center) and deaconnesses, Norwegian Deaconess Home, Minneapolis

later, she opened a deaconess house to train women to assist her in her "outdoor relief" efforts, which consisted of outpatient services, relief for the poor, and pastoral care. Over time, more and more women became deaconesses, public servants, and social activists.

Fedde's work in New York eventually evolved into an incorporated hospital and motherhouse with fifty beds that was supported by an ambulance service. Her diary is a sketchy but revealing record of her service to Norwegian settlers, noting their hardships and heartaches and chronicling her own disappointments and challenges. Her diary entry of May 10, 1883, testifies to the breadth of her duties: "On board a ship with a sick seaman, and afterwards to four families; hunted for a place for a child, five months, but have not secured anyone who will take it." Three days later, she noted, "Today I placed the little boy and am glad and thank God that a door and heart were opened for him. Then to a woman for whom I care each day with dressings." Her March 19, 1885, entry reads: "Six sick calls. Came home tired, and then saw a poor woman here with a sick child and after talking a long time with her, gave her a ticket for coal." In April of that year, she noted that "Mrs. Juhl died here at 7 AM after a hard night. Then to arrange with undertaker and pastor. Home and washed the body, and am dead tired." The next day she bought "flowers for the casket, and prepared the house"; the day after, she "put Mrs. Juhl in casket; large funeral."

Fedde lived in an age with limited opportunities for women, particularly in the public sphere. Her board of managers added three new female members to "protect and guide" Fedde's efforts. While she was satisfied in her work, Fedde was distressed about the degree of contention between members of her board; the question of a lottery at the bazaar was a particularly troubling issue, and on March 9, 1886, she wrote, "Board meeting; always opposition. God, it is thus in Your Kingdom. The way is hard and narrow." On several other occasions, she noted problems at board meetings, and in one instance, she lost sleep in response to them: "I am tired of many torments and pray for peace."[42]

After moving to Minneapolis, Fedde established the Lutheran Deaconess Home and Hospital of the Lutheran Free Church in 1889. She wrote an important chapter in the history of social services in America by pioneering "outdoor relief" and deaconess education and working in Christian service beyond her immigrant community.

The role of Norwegian-speaking doctors and health-care personnel in the public health campaign cannot be underestimated. Norwegian doctors were respected as leaders and role models; they were effectual as liaisons and educators in making medical improvements acceptable at the grassroots level. Immigrants often resented the intrusion of American-born or Yankee doctors, suspected their motives, and suffered in silence rather than allowing themselves to be treated by them. Likewise, American doctors and health officers were often harsh and condescending regarding Norwegian hygiene and folk medical methods and did not give Norwegian patients requisite attention. The second-class treatment of Norwegian immigrants by American doctors angered Adolf Gundersen, who was determined from the outset to provide quality medical care to his Norwegian compatriots, often free or in exchange for produce from their farms and gardens.[43]

The Cleanup Campaigns

Upper-class Victorian women saw in the public health campaign an opportunity to instill middle-class values in immigrant minds. The campaign for sanitation reform played on the emotions of women, and women with stature in the community, like Helga Gundersen, were well positioned to make a difference. A clean house and a healthy family were sources of female pride and self-esteem.

Milk could carry diseases like typhoid and tuberculosis, so safe milk for children became a moral imperative. Women were important players in boy-cotts, demonstrations, and legal efforts to force improvements in milk produc-tion, ensuring the safety of the public milk supply. Helga Gundersen was widely known and admired by Norwegians in west-central Wisconsin in part because of her work on community health issues. There is no doubt that her support of the local milk safety campaign lent it extra urgency and power.[44]

Government on state, county, and local levels played an important role in promoting public health. In Wisconsin, for example, an 1883 state law required that every town, village, and city in the state organize a board of health. A local board consisted of three members, two appointed by the president of the town or village from the town council, plus a health officer, such as the local physi-cian. The board's mission was broadly defined to include identifying and cor-recting potential health hazards, such as open sewers, bad ventilation, crowded classrooms, and contaminated milk and water. These boards represented the most active grassroots effort to control infectious diseases. In the early years, health officers and board members tended to be American born or old-stock Americans. Almost without exception, these boards were composed of com-munity leaders, primarily men, and men comprised the overwhelming share of health officers. Except for the few with medical degrees, women assumed sup-portive roles as wives and health-care assistants. Over time, more Norwegian Americans, including women, assumed leadership roles as health agents and advocates of reform.

In the early 1890s, a Scandinavian health officer in Barron County, Wisconsin, implored the state to pass laws making vaccination, burial permits, and doctor licensing mandatory. One Mr. Mattson, a local health officer, strictly enforced the regulation that "no dead body shall be taken into a school house for funeral services unless a certificate" was signed by two physicians confirming that the disease leading to the death was noncontagious. The health officer in Trimbelle, Wisconsin, called for pamphlets to educate farm families on the dangers of dung heaps, privies, cesspools, and other unsanitary conditions.[45]

Boards of health worked in concert with boards of education to bring the message of reform to Wisconsin schoolchildren. Publications by the state board included titles such as "School hygiene and what the teacher can do to promote it." Teachers took charge of school hygiene by virtue of their salaried status, often cleaning the facilities themselves or with the help of community mothers. Schoolchildren received special booklets and instructions on hygiene in the hope that they, in turn, would educate their parents and other family members, which could be especially important in immigrant families. Perhaps the most dreaded visitor to the rural school was the county nurse, who often came in search of "a louse in the house," using her fine-toothed comb to search for lice in students' hair. The decrepit condition of schoolhouses was an ongoing area of concern;

many were log cabins with poor lighting and ventilation, filthy hovels resembling "pest houses." Entire families pitched in to clean, renovate, or build new facilities, usually a broad community effort. By century's end, most of the old log schoolhouses had been replaced by more hygienic clapboard structures.[46]

American insurance companies jumped on the cleanliness bandwagon by educating policyholders on matters of public and private hygiene. The fraternal insurance companies, Lutheran Brotherhood and Aid Association for Lutherans, which had a large Norwegian American clientele, used company agents to bring messages of health and hygiene into the homes of Norwegian American women. By the first decades of the twentieth century, along with life insurance policies, the insurance companies began offering health insurance options.

At the same time, cleanliness had become big business. Colgate, Ivory, Lever Brothers, and Fels-Naptha products had entered the homes of Americans across the country. Home economics courses took hold in the schools in the 1930s. During the same decade, cleansing agents like Bon Ami Soap and Dutch Cleanser became popular. Electric washers replaced maids in the 1930s, and by the 1950s, "whiter than white" and "cleaner than clean" were standard American phrases.[47]

Norwegian immigrant women readily adopted Victorian ideals, with the result that school teachers and mothers cleaned, painted, and primped to give churches and schoolrooms a look of culture and domesticity. Woman-to-woman networks whose purpose was to enhance the appearance of schoolrooms with framed pictures, flowers, and handmade curtains and rugs emerged. Lutheran congregations had Ladies Aid societies that worked to raise money for building enhancements. Women made church buildings look more refined and domesticated by adding artistic touches in the form of wall hangings, curtains, carpets, and embroidered altar cloths. From *Kvinden og Hjemmet,* Norwegian immigrant women and their daughters gleaned new ideas for using American textiles and patterns in interior decoration.

In addition to their aesthetic efforts, women's societies raised money for poor relief, hospitals, orphanages, and other charitable causes. Women's organizations within congregations gave women a bridge to the secular world, allowing them to move into activist roles in the public sphere, such as the campaign for public health.

Health and sanitation reforms were inexorably tied to religious doctrine to the extent that cleanliness suggested Christian respectability. "Cleanliness is next to godliness," attributed to John Wesley, the founder of Methodism, became a national mantra. Norwegian Americans worked toward acceptance in their new American home, and some came to see their clothing, housing, diet, and personal hygiene as symbols of status and accomplishment.

Laundry was the most time-consuming of hygiene-related chores. Norwegian American women made soap from lye and ashes, collected rainwater in barrels,

Women washing clothes in Harmony, Minnesota

boiled the water, beat the heavily soiled clothes with pounders, and labored over a washboard, sudsing, rinsing, and wringing the clothes dry. Articles and editorials in *Kvinden og Hjemmet* introduced modern American methods and products to Norwegian Americans and encouraged them to be fastidious, refined Americans.[48]

Women used wallpaper, whitewashing, curtains, and doilies to visually soften the hardness of rural life in Norwegian American communities and to create a sense of Victorian refinement. Goods purchased from catalogs and traveling salesmen helped to bring culture and elegance into even the roughest of cabins and clapboard homes. Scandinavian girls (including Norwegian Americans), valued as domestics in American homes, brought back American Victorian ideals of cleanliness to their immigrant homes. Art, music, etiquette, and hygiene were some of the many expressions of nineteenth-century gentility immigrant communities adopted.

As they added signifiers of civilization, like china and kitchen tools, to their homes, women also adopted values of good hygiene and cleanliness. Cleanliness intertwined with self-esteem and moral respectability. In 1894, the founder of the Lutheran Ladies Seminary in Red Wing, Minnesota, wrote in the institution's first catalog, "The welfare of our homes depends in the highest degree upon what

Issues of Kvinden og Hjemmet (Woman and Home)

These Red Cross workers, many of them Norwegian Americans, fought the 1918 flu epidemic in North Dakota

type of woman is making them. Thrifty, neat, and well-trained homemakers create thrifty and well-ordered households. Intelligent, educated and cultured mothers and wives understand how to make the homes centers of noble interests and elevating influences."[49]

Facing Pandemic

Great strides had been made in the public health and hygiene campaigns that emanated from the nineteenth century. The American public had come to accept germ theory and to take basic precautions against the spread of dangerous contagions. Norwegian Americans filled seats at medical training schools and sought active roles in public health campaigns. Yet nothing could have prepared them for the Spanish influenza pandemic in 1918, which struck with a virulence and ferocity unequaled in modern history, killing more than six hundred thousand Americans and tens of millions worldwide. This pandemic engaged women from all classes and backgrounds in a common battle and brought even greater numbers of female health-care workers into the public sphere.

The household of Norwegian immigrants Albert and Mary Lindberg, in Mill Creek, Jackson County, Wisconsin, was a microcosm of the larger flu experience that ravaged the world. The Lindbergs' home was a veritable boardinghouse for extended family, including uncles and cousins who passed through as they entered jobs and military duty. Mary had lost friends and relatives in the community to the flu, and on December 6, 1918, Mary herself died of flu complications, a quick demise caused by a fierce immunological response. Because of her robust immunity, a veritable explosion of antibody reactions killed her; white blood cells rushed to her lungs, accelerating bronchial pneumonia. Although extremely ill and near death for days, the couple's four children survived and remained in the home with their father. In the years that followed, grandparents, aunts, and neighbors filled in for Mary.[50]

Carl and Alida Johnson of Madison, Wisconsin, responded to the influenza outbreak by converting their home into a convalescent hospital for stricken residents. The *Wisconsin State Journal* reported that "chauffeurs were kept busy all day driving autos back and forth from the grocery stores, bringing milk, cocoa, soups and other supplies for the sick" to the Johnson home. Madison women devoted night and day to the care of young men in the university infirmary.[51]

Gunnar Gundersen, finishing medical school in New York, wrote this account of the siege in the east: "People were dying like flies. They were almost drowning in their own secretions. They carried off 40 dead people one night. They would take these people out on the porches thinking the air from the East River would help . . . That was my initiation into clinical medicine. It was totally and completely discouraging." Alf Gundersen, Gunnar's brother, sailed with soldiers from New York to France; many of his comrades became sick, died, and were buried at sea. "Ship doctors offered little help," Gunnar noted, "only aspirin and advice . . . Two maids in the Gundersen home, sisters from Vernon County, died within minutes of each other." Gunnar continued, "We came home at Christmas not knowing of this. It was a thoroughly depressing picture for a young person getting into clinical medicine. You are all steamed up thinking you could do good and all of a sudden you were faced with complete and total frustration."[52]

Medical practice in 1918 offered no miracle drugs, no respiratory equipment, and no effective remedy for the scourge of influenza. The bulk of the responsibility rested with local people, trained and untrained, paid and volunteer. There was no cure; bed rest was the best prescription, and health-care workers could only hope to limit the spread of this odd contagion. Cities like Chicago imposed quarantines and closed theaters, schools, and all nonessential gathering places, yet people still mingled, sharing germs on the streets, in streetcars and subway corridors, and when registering for the draft in post offices and city halls. Communities mandated the wearing of masks, and some factories staggered work hours; in Philadelphia, authorities suggested kissing through a handkerchief. In many places there were fines for coughing and sneezing without a handkerchief or for shaking hands.[53]

The correlation between pregnancy and flu mortality was staggering; stillbirths were common and expectant mothers died quickly as their lungs filled and outgrew their thoracic cavities. No story could be more poignant than that of little Viola Venden. Born of Norwegian parents in Dane County, Wisconsin, she died of the flu just two hours before her baby brother also died, born prematurely because their mother lay afflicted with influenza. The children were buried together, the baby boy cradled lovingly in his sister's arms.[54]

No disease in modern history had killed so many or swept the globe with such terrifying swiftness. For Americans from Norway, like others, the Spanish flu shattered dreams and lives, orphaned children, and generated a century of research into its many mysteries. Norwegian American women were a part of the army that faced the flu and fought it, some as doctors and health officers but most of them as mothers and sisters offering home care—and, in so doing, demonstrating neighborliness and incredible kindness.

Though the pandemic itself did not last long, the Spanish flu served as a catalyst for increased female activism in American public life. Child welfare workers were swamped as children's parents sickened and died; ordinary citizens were stirred to volunteer to care for these children. Generally, children were not sent directly to orphanages for fear that they would contaminate more children. Instead, they were placed in sick houses or with willing relatives and neighbors.

From the Norwegian Lutheran Orphans Home at Beloit, Iowa, came this report: "We were particularly spared . . . in that we did not have the influenza, although it raged all around." As a result of the epidemic, officials at the orphanage reported a waiting list of children who needed homes. Maryllia Dahl described her experience at the orphanage: "We were taken there after our mother's death during the 1918 flu epidemic. We were five children ages from two to twelve years." The Scandinavian Lutheran synods responded to the epidemic of orphaned children by supporting Lutheran children's homes and supervising the Lutheran Children's Home Finding Society. Gender roles were clearly prescribed in the operation of these homes. The men constituted the boards of directors, handled the finances, and took responsibility for construction and heavy maintenance. Women, on the other hand, constituted the major day-to-day workforce of cooks and nurses, teachers and managers. Regarding child welfare, the events of 1918 lent greater urgency to plans that were already in motion to develop Norwegian Lutheran child placement programs and state funding for social services. In the coming decades, states assumed a much greater role in the care of disadvantaged and orphaned children within their boundaries.[55]

Conclusion

Norwegian immigrants depended to a large degree on the traditional systems of home care and folk medicine, in which wives and mothers provided primary care for ailments ranging from fevers to toothaches to colic. Most immigrants were receptive to preventive and curative medicine; others brought with them to America strong fatalism or antimedicinal views. Folk medicine in the home intersected with modern medicine in beneficial ways, so Norwegians as a whole were a comparatively healthy group. The urgency of sanitation and pandemic, of course, superseded factors such as class and national origin. Norwegians and non-Norwegians, men and women, rich and poor, worked side by side to clean their communities and quarantine disease in the health interests of all.

For women, entering the medical profession was fraught with challenge, particularly as more and more men filled its ranks. Folk medicine and midwifery, largely considered women's work, were stigmatized in ways that persist to the present day. Nonetheless, Norwegian American women became custodians of care at a variety of levels, public as well as private. They sought community involvement at a time when gender lines were firmly drawn. They were active and influential in their congregations, skilled in nurturing, and well positioned to lend their voices to groups organized around issues such as health care and suffrage. The 1918 flu pandemic drove home like never before the urgency of guarding family members' health.[56]

Campaigns for better health and sanitation played on women's emotions. A clean house and a healthy family were sources of female pride and self-esteem. Community involvement built female confidence and solidarity, helping women develop a common sense of accomplishment and identity. Whether mother, maid, or medical practitioner, these women helped to promulgate the gospel of cleanliness and reform, and in the process they found new horizons for themselves and for other women to follow.

Notes

1. Mrs. Alma A. Guttersen and Mrs. Regina Hilleboe Christensen, eds., *Souvenir "Norse-American Women," 1825–1925: A Symposium of Prose and Poetry, Newspaper Articles and Biographies, Contributed by One Hundred Prominent Women* (St. Paul, MN: The Lutheran Free Church Publishing Co., 1926). Joan M. Jensen highlights frontier women in *Calling This Place Home: Women on the Wisconsin Frontier, 1850–1925* (St. Paul: Minnesota Historical Society Press, 2006).

2. Reforms are discussed more fully in T. K. Derry, *A History of Scandinavia* (Minneapolis: University of Minnesota Press, 1979), 263–323.

3. Byron J. Nordstrom, *Scandinavia since 1500* (Minneapolis: University of Minnesota

Press, 2000), 248–53. The contributions of Louis Pasteur and Robert Koch to the germ concept of disease are discussed in Roy Porter's *The Greatest Benefit to Mankind: A Medical History of Humanity* (New York: W. W. Norton and Company, 1997), 431–48.

4. Kolset's address was titled "The Pioneer Physician": Ludwig Hektoen Papers, 9 Sept. 1904–9 June 1940, Norwegian-American Historical Association, Northfield, MN (hereafter, NAHA).

5. Ch. Gronvald, "The Effects of the Immigration on the Norwegian Immigrant," *Sixth Annual Report of the State Board of Health, Minnesota* (Minneapolis, MN: Johnson, Smith and Harrison, 1878), 24–25, available at http://reflections.mndigital.org/. Influenza, chronic rheumatism, and neuralgia are listed as the most frequent diseases in Minnesota among Norwegians. Bronchitis and pneumonia are noted as much higher in Norway than in Minnesota. Gronvald. E. Kraft wrote about the "physical degeneration" of Norwegians in America in "Den norske Races fysiske Degeneration i Nordamerika," which appeared in *Norsk magasin for laegevidenskapen* (1891): 1040–45.

6. *Annual Report of the State Board of Health of Wisconsin, 1877* (Madison, WI: Atwood, Printer and Stereotyper, 1878), 140. Ronald L. Numbers, "Public Protection and Self-Interest: Medical Societies in Wisconsin," in *Wisconsin Medicine: Historical Perspectives,* eds. Ronald L. Numbers and Judith Walzer Leavitt (Madison: University of Wisconsin Press, 1981), 24.

7. *Annual Report of the State Board of Health of Wisconsin, 1880* (Madison, WI: Democrat Printing Company, 1881), 141. *Annual Report of the State Board of Health of Wisconsin, 1888* (Madison, WI: Democrat Printing Company, 1889), 290.

8. Suellen Hoy, *Chasing Dirt: The American Pursuit of Cleanliness* (New York: Oxford University Press, 1995), 18–23, 113–14.

9. Odd S. Lovoll, *The Promise of America: A History of the Norwegian-American People* (Minneapolis: University of Minnesota Press, 1984), 137–38. Aase Elin Langeland has·done a thorough analysis of *Kvinden og Hjemmet;* see "Adjusting to America. A Study in *Kvinden og Hjemmet:* A Monthly Journal for the Scandinavian Women in America, 1888–1947" (master's thesis, University of Bergen, 2001).

10. See "Locality in Relation to Deaths," Section 11, Twelfth U.S. Census (Washington, DC: Government Printing Office, 1900). Scandinavian numbers were high on diarrheal diseases and the infectious diseases of diphtheria, typhoid, and whooping cough.

11. Olaf M. Norlie, *History of the Norwegian People in America* (Minneapolis, MN: Augsburg Press, 1925), 466.

12. Kathleen Stokker, "Narratives of Magic and Healing," *Scandinavian Studies* (Fall 2001): 399–415.

13. Kathleen Stokker, *Remedies and Rituals: Folk Medicine in Norway and the New Land* (St. Paul: Minnesota Historical Society Press, 2007). Stokker has combed through hundreds of original documents to write a detailed history of folk healing; her volume also includes a sampling of recipes for home remedies. Emphasizing the nineteenth century, Stokker foregrounds the transfer of folk healing knowledge in the process of migration and especially the role of women in this process. See, particularly, chs. 1 and 2 on folk healing and female healers, ch. 6 on birthing practices, and ch. 7 on rickets.

14. Mrs. Wilmer Dorothy, "Reminiscence" (1949), and Mrs. Gust Peterson, "Minnesota Territorial Centennial" (1949), *The Farmer* Collection, 1949 to 1958, Minnesota Historical Society, St. Paul, MN (hereafter, MHS).

15. Pauline Farseth and Theodore C. Blegen, eds., *Frontier Mother: The Letters of Gro Svendsen* (New York: Arno Press, 1979), 57.

16. Diary of Severine Hovelsrud, North Beaver Creek, Trempealeau County, WI, 1909–10, in author's collection.

17. Kathleen Stokker, *Keeping Christmas: Yuletide Traditions in Norway and the New Land* (St. Paul: Minnesota Historical Society Press, 2000), 38–40.

18. *Annual Report of the State Board of Health of Wisconsin, 1882* (Madison, WI: Democrat Printing Company, 1883), 201. Farseth and Blegen, *Frontier Mother,* xiii, 121, 130, 134.

19. Doris Weatherford, *Foreign and Female: Immigrant Women in America, 1840–1930* (New York: Facts on File, 1995), 47. William K. Beatty notes the language issue in "Medical Care for Norwegian Immigrants in the Chicago Area," *Proceedings of the Institute of Medicine, Chicago* 36 (1983): 148.

20. John Faville, "The Clergyman as a Health Officer," in *Annual Report of the State Board of Health of Wisconsin, 1891–92* (Madison, WI: Democrat Printing, 1893), 113–19.

21. Mrs. R. O. Brandt, "Social Aspects of Prairie Pioneering," in *Norwegian-American Studies and Records* 7 (Northfield, MN: NAHA, 1933): 6.

22. Elisabeth Koren, *The Diary of Elisabeth Koren, 1853–1855,* trans. and ed. David T. Nelson (Northfield, MN: NAHA, 1955), cited in Weatherford, *Foreign and Female,* 49.

23. Knut Gjerset and Ludvig Hektoen, "Health Conditions and the Practice of Medicine Among the Early Norwegian Settlers, 1825–1865," *Norwegian-American Studies and Records* 1 (Northfield, MN: NAHA, 1926): 11.

24. William K. Beatty, "Niles T. Quales—Physician and Leader in the Norwegian Community in Chicago," *Proceedings of the Institute of Medicine, Chicago,* 41.2 (1988): 54.

25. Beatty, "Niles T. Quales," 54–58.

26. Susan T. Hessel, *Medicine: The Gundersen Experience, 1891–1991* (La Crosse, WI: Gundersen Clinic, 1991), 31, 34.

27. Hessel, *Medicine,* 32.

28. Farseth and Blegen, *Frontier Mother,* 98, 105, 136.

29. Glenda Riley, *Frontierswomen: The Iowa Experience* (Ames: Iowa State University Press, 1981), 82.

30. Lesley Biggs and Stella Stephenson, "In Search of Gudrun Goodman: Reflections on 'Doing History' and Memory," *The Canadian Historical Review* 87.2 (June 2006): 2, 13. For a more full-blown account of midwifery in Canadian settlements, see Lesley Biggs, "Rethinking the History of Midwifery in Canada," in *Reconceiving Midwifery,* eds. Ivy Bourgeault, Cecilia Benoit, and Robbie Davis-Floyd (Montreal: McGill-Queen's University Press, 2004), 17–45. Merry E. Weisner provides a very detailed account of midwifery procedures and regulations in Nuremburg, Germany, in "Early Modern Midwifery: A Case Study," in *Women and Work in Preindustrial Europe,* ed. Barbara A. Hanawalt (Bloomington: Indiana University Press, 1986), 94–113.

31. Hazel Tjerstad-Knutson, "Remembering Beaver Creek" (1985), recorded oral

history in author's private collection. Tjerstad-Knutson is a member of the Hovel-srud family. Lindberg Family History, Jackson County, WI (2002), author's private collection.

32. Weatherford, *Foreign and Female*, 49.

33. Norman C. Saugstad, *Kathryn, North Dakota, 75th Anniversary, 1900–1975: 100th Anniversary of Our Community, 1876–1976* ([Fingal, ND]: The author, 1976).

34. Carol Lopate, *Women in Medicine* (Baltimore, MD: Johns Hopkins Press, 1968), 3, 14; Nordstrom, *Scandinavia since 1500*, 253. See also Mary Roth Walsh, *"Doctors Wanted: No Women Need Apply": Sexual Barriers in the Medical Profession, 1835–1975* (New Haven, CT: Yale University Press, 1977). Barriers to women in nursing are well articulated in Philip A. Kalisch and Beatrice J. Kalisch, *American Nursing. A History*, 4th ed. (Philadelphia, PA: Lippincott, Williams, and Wilkins, 2004).

35. Hessel, *Medicine*, 12.

36. From a letter describing her experiences as a student nurse at the Lutheran Hospital Training School for Nurses, cited in Hessel, *Medicine*, 8.

37. Knut Gjerset, "Medical Doctors," 1–2, Knut Gjerset Papers, box 5, file 7, NAHA.

38. Norlie, *History of the Norwegian People in America*, 468–69. Ludwig Hektoen Papers, 1904–40, 148.

39. Gjerset, "Medical Doctors," 1–2. "Dr. Helga Ruud 90 aar," *Nordmanns-Forbundet*, Feb. 1951, 26.

40. In European Lutheranism a *diaconate* is a non-ordained ministry with responsibility for such pastoral and charitable ministries as, for example, work in nursing, social welfare, education, and parish work. For a history of the Lutheran diaconate, see James Monroe Barnett, *The diaconate—a full and equal order*, 2nd ed. (Philadelphia, PA: Trinity Publishing, 1995). Norlie, *History of the Norwegian People in America*, 426–33.

41. Laurann Gilbertson, "Careers of Service: The Norwegian Lutheran Deaconesses," *Vesterheim* 5.1 (2007): 42–48.

42. Elizabeth Fedde's life story and diary can be found on the website of the Norwegian-American Historical Association, the diary translated and edited by Beulah Folkedahl: http://www.naha.stolaf.edu/pubs/nas/volume20/vol20_9.htm. Fedde's relationship with the board of managers is detailed in David C. Mauk, *The Colony that Rose from the Sea: Norwegian Maritime Migration and Community in Brooklyn, 1850–1910* (Northfield, MN: NAHA, 1997), 113–15.

43. Hessel, *Medicine*, 5–21.

44. See Judith Walzer Leavitt, *The Healthiest City: Milwaukee and the Politics of Health Reform* (Madison: University of Wisconsin Press, 1996).

45. *Annual Report of the State Board of Health of Wisconsin, 1891–1892*, 123. *Annual Report of the State Board of Health of Wisconsin, 1882*, 246. *Annual Report of the State Board of Health of Wisconsin, 1880*, xli.

46. *Annual Report of the State Board of Health of Wisconsin, 1878* (Madison, WI: Atwood, 1879). The upgrading of local schoolhouses because of health concerns was common. Refer, for example, to *Many and Memorable. A History of the 110 Rural Schools of Trempealeau County* (Galesville, WI: Trempealeau County Historical Society, 1988).

47. Hoy, *Chasing Dirt*, 123–49.

48. See Langeland, "Adjusting to America," 1–33.

49. For examples, see Mona Domosh and Joni Seager, *Putting Women in Place: Feminist Geographers Make Sense of the World* (New York: Guilford Press, 2001), 1–20; Elizabeth Hayes Turner, *Women, Culture, and Community: Religion and Reform in Galveston, 1880–1920* (New York: Oxford University Press, 1997). Lutheran Ladies Seminary quote cited in DeAne L. Lagerquist, "As Sister, Wife, and Mother: Education for Young Norwegian-American Lutheran Women," *Norwegian-American Studies* 33 (Northfield, MN: NAHA, 1992), 113.

50. *Melrose Chronicle,* 13 Dec. 1918.

51. *Wisconsin State Journal,* 7 Oct. 1918.

52. Hessel, *Medicine,* 21–22, 45.

53. Alfred W. Crosby, *America's Forgotten Pandemic: The Influenza of 1918* (New York: Cambridge University Press, 1989), 87; Gina Kolata, *Flu: The Story of the Great Influenza Epidemic of 1918 and the Search for the Virus that Caused It* (New York: Touchstone, 1999), 19.

54. *Stoughton Daily Courier-Hub,* 28 Oct. 1918.

55. George Hanusa, ed., *All About Beloit* (Des Moines, IA: Privately published, 1998), 42–43.

56. For a discussion of the role of women in the boycotts, demonstrations, and legal efforts to force improvements in public hygiene, including water and milk quality, see Leavitt, *The Healthiest City.*

CHAPTER 7

Land Taking at Spirit Lake: The Competing and Converging Logics of Norwegian and Dakota Women, 1900–1930

Karen V. Hansen

My Norwegian grandmother, Helene Haugen Kanten, told stories about grow-ing up on an Indian reservation: "[My mother] took land; she took homestead on the Indian Reservation. And that's where they chased the Indians off, you see, and took the land away from them." The idea seemed incongruous: what cir-cumstances would allow a young girl, recently emigrated from Norway with her widowed mother, to live on land belonging by treaty to Native Americans?[1]

When I first had occasion to visit the Spirit Lake Dakota Reservation in North Dakota, I discovered that my great-grandmother was not the only Norwegian to homestead there. Nor was she the only woman. And while Helene Haugen Kanten got it right that the Dakotas were dispossessed of large amounts of land, in fact, most tribal members remained on the reservation. In the early twentieth century, the Dakotas and the Norwegians vied for resources, made competitive bids for land, haggled over the price of rent, shared the burdens of rural life, and lost children to epidemics. With the grave injustice of Indian dispossession as a backdrop, these unlikely neighbors endured fierce winters, cultivated gardens, and rooted their kinship in the land.

When the reservation was established in 1867, a territory covering approxi-mately two hundred forty thousand acres was recognized as Dakota tribal land. The treaty founding the reservation used Devils Lake as its northern border and the Sheyenne River as its southern one. The lake's name had been changed to reflect the white Christian interpretation of its meaning, and the reservation was named accordingly. It included a military reserve, with Fort Totten at its geographic and administrative center.[2]

Starting in 1890, reservation land was allotted to individual Dakota men, women, and children, and the remainder opened to white homesteaders in 1904. Land quickly passed out of the Dakotas' hands. By 1910, only half of privately owned reservation land belonged to individual tribal members. In the decades that followed, white settlers continued to move onto the reservation, Norwegians in even greater numbers. By 1929, the Dakotas' share had diminished to one-quarter. By then, nearly half of the reservation land was owned by first-, second-,

Helene Haugen Kanten, confirmation portrait, ca. 1907

and third-generation Scandinavians, predominantly Norwegians. And, like my great-grandmother, almost a quarter (24 percent) of those Scandinavian landowners was female.[3]

This chapter details the processes by which the Dakotas were allotted land at Spirit Lake and Norwegians, including women, came to homestead the unallotted land. Despite the fact that property holding for one group was predicated on the dispossession of another, both groups were poor. The two dislocated peoples came to the region by profoundly different routes and entered land ownership with sometimes converging and other times clashing cultural logics of land. I argue that land ownership provided both Dakota and Norwegian women a means for their livelihood, a center for their kinship networks and community, long-term insurance to support themselves in widowhood and old age, and a place to live and practice their culture. Remarkably, land offered both Dakota and Norwegian women a base for survival and the prospect of a multigenerational legacy.

The Competing Logics: Territorial Use versus Land Ownership

On the reservation, divergent histories meant that Dakotas and Norwegians both revered land but imagined using it in different ways. Historically the Dakotas had approached land as a gift that yielded the means for living and as a territory that had to be negotiated with competing tribes. Norwegians had the advantage of wanting to own land for themselves and embracing the logic of land accumulation, consonant with U.S. property laws and the dominant American ethos. Even though they came as poor people, they devoted their collective energies to cultivating land and retaining it over generations.

The convergence of immigration, economic opportunity, and federal policy positioned Norwegians to gain from the opening of homestead land at the Spirit Lake Dakota Reservation. The costs to land seekers of the government's offer of land—relocation, back-breaking labor, and participation in usurping Indians' resources—were balanced by the benefits: satisfaction of the unrelenting peasant hunger for land and the promise of a viable economic future for the family. The costs to Dakotas included further erosion of their land base and the social and economic intrusion of white settlers. The tribe was to benefit financially from the payments for the land and, from the perspective of non-Native reformers, an Americanizing influence on the reservation. Ironically, although the U.S. government cast homesteading first- and second-generation immigrants as representatives of American culture who would help assimilate the native people as they lived side by side on the reservation, many spoke little English and most arrived with few resources other than kin and labor power. However, many homesteaders, coming as they did from farms in Norway or other midwestern states, had some knowledge of subsistence agriculture.[4]

The reservation was designated by treaty as the tribal base for the Sissetons, Wahpetons, and Cut-Head (Pabaksa) bands of Dakota. Like the Norwegians, many of the Sisseton-Wahpeton Dakota had traveled far to make a life there. Although the region south of Devils Lake had been a hunting territory for the Yanktonai, or Ihanktonwanna (of which the Cut-Heads were a part), it had not been a place of permanent settlement for the Sisseton and Wahpeton, whose primary territory for generations had been southern and central Minnesota. The U.S.–Dakota War of 1862 sparked violent repression, prompting these Dakotas to venture north and west in search of refuge.[5]

As American Indians, the Dakotas had a unique relationship with the federal government, which regulated land ownership and the prospects of moving on (or not) and influenced how they could use land. Living on a reservation created a sometimes tense, always dependent relationship with the U.S. government that was mediated by the Indian agent and federal employees, which included soldiers until 1890 when Fort Totten was decommissioned and demilitarized.[6]

In 1887, Congress passed the General Land Allotment Act, also known as the Dawes Act, with the stated intent to assimilate American Indians into the agricultural economy by granting privately owned property—allotments—to individuals. The law allotted tribal members parcels of land on reservations that had formerly belonged to a tribe as a whole. Informed by an idealization of the yeoman farmer and a desire to take Indian land, the Dawes Act was based on the presumption that enabling individual Indians to own a plot of 160 acres (instead of sharing vast acreages owned collectively by their nation) would encourage them to develop farms, learn the logic of private property, and assimilate into the agricultural economy and U.S. culture. In addition to attempting to transform the communal character of Native society, the Dawes Act was designed to transfer millions of acres from American Indians to European immigrants and Yankees, who would utilize the land "efficiently" and serve as an example of individual enterprise to the Natives among whom they lived. According to Indian agent F. O. Getchell, by 1902, 1,132 Spirit Lake Dakota had received allotments totaling 131,506 acres.[7]

The Dawes Act mandated that each man and woman who was head of household be allotted 160 acres. Unlike the Homestead Act, married Dakota women were allotted land, but only half the amount allotted to men. Children were each allotted eighty acres. The Dakotas' land allotments were concentrated in three areas on the reservation: St. Michael's Mission, Crow Hill, and Wood Lake, in the northern and western areas, which tended to be hillier and more wooded, more similar to terrain enabling mixed use of the land.[8]

The imposition of the logic of private land ownership and the push to engage exclusively in sedentary agriculture clashed with the Dakotas' historical approach to land. In Minnesota, the Dakotas had treated land as territory they collectively controlled in order to hunt, gather foodstuffs, and cultivate seasonal crops. From their perspective, their band was entitled to use the land and reap its resources. Tribal member Phillip John Young said, "The Indians, they felt that traditionally they shouldn't own land. You *couldn't* own land because it's not yours." Mari Sandoz writes that land "was held for tribal use and for posterity." For the Sioux, "sale of land . . . meant sale of the use." Selling or negotiating that right implied use of the land but not proprietary control. In contrast, white settlers viewed ownership as entitling them to monitor access and make absolute and authoritative decisions. Their beliefs embraced the principle of private property as the foundation of the legal system and the agricultural economy. This clash in logics led to profound misunderstandings and sometimes had disastrous consequences.[9]

In recognition of Indians' unfamiliarity with and opposition to private property ownership, the Dawes Act stipulated that the allotted land be held in trust by the U.S. government for twenty-five years. Thereafter the allottee was to obtain the patent—the legal title—to the land. The trust status of the land was to prevent scheming, land-hungry whites from defrauding Indians and to allow Indians to adjust to a landowning logic and family farming. Indians whose land was held in trust did not enjoy the same privileges and responsibilities as non-Indian landowners. For example, allottees could not take out a mortgage on the property. Nor could they sell the land; first they had to petition for the patent to the land and prove their fitness, or "competence," to act independently. By design, full-blooded tribal members were assumed to be "incompetent," that is, unable to manage their legal affairs. However, they could make a case to the Indian agent that they were "competent" to handle the responsibilities of land ownership and petition to receive the patent. Importantly, because an allottee did not own land outright (it was held in trust) and was not formally a citizen of the United States (but rather a member of a domestic dependent nation), he or she did not pay property taxes on the land. Being declared "competent" enabled a person not just to take the title but to obtain a mortgage. Ironically, competency, and hence outright ownership, could encumber the owner with debt and taxation and consequently was often a fast path to dispossession.[10]

In accordance with the Dawes Act, after a period following allotment, the Spirit Lake Dakota signed an agreement in 1901 conceding one hundred thousand acres to white homesteaders with the promise of receiving fees for the acreage. The U.S. Congress delayed but finally approved the agreement and passed legislation in 1904. To organize the process of land taking, the federal government designed a lottery to select potential homesteaders. The first six hundred names chosen won the right to claim a quarter section of land (160 acres) on the reservation for $4.50 an acre and a pledge to improve the land. The appearance of equal opportunity in the lottery was undermined by the entrance rules that favored adult men, who could enter whether single, married, or widowed, as long as they were twenty-one or older. In keeping with the stipulations of the Homestead Act, married women could *not* enter the lottery; women had to be twenty-one or over and single, widowed, divorced, or head of household.[11]

Women homesteaded for a range of reasons, but all sought the economic foothold that landowning provided. For single immigrant women, whose primary occupation in the United States was domestic service, land taking offered a unique opportunity. Were they to marry, they would no longer be eligible to homestead in their own names. Katherine Harris writes that for young women in northeastern Colorado, "one of the essential attractions of homesteading was the independence that proving up a claim offered. Self-determination was not an option generally available to their sex." Widowed women, regardless of age, shared many of the same obstacles to self-sufficiency, as did married women who had few employment options, particularly while raising children. Homesteading offered a potential investment with prospects for long-term productive labor. Barbara Handy-Marchello reframes our thinking about the legislation, the constraints on women's marital status notwithstanding, by pointing to the opportunities previously unthinkable to women.[12]

On August 9, 1904, it was a single woman, Carrie Fisher of Grafton, North Dakota, who stood first in line at the Grand Forks Land Office when it opened to register people for the land lottery. She was followed by a "long line of women" who wanted a chance to homestead cheap land. These women, and the many who joined them later, understood and valued privately owned land. Their pursuit of private land ownership promised them a major advantage in planning their futures. Over the course of two weeks, 15,076 people entered the lottery, and six hundred names were chosen, many of them female, some Norwegian. Six years later, women constituted 13 percent of the Scandinavian landowners on the reservation. By then, Scandinavians owned virtually half of the new homesteading land. Homesteading resulted in the migration of many white landowners and their families to the reservation and created a local and immediate clash of cultural logics. The new inhabitants brought different languages, religious beliefs, food, and approaches to land.[13]

The settlers and the Indians found a common ground in leasing land. To provide income, Indian land could be leased by non-Indian farmers, an arrangement often encouraged by Indian agents. It had a rationality of its own: renting or leasing land was consistent with Dakotas' sense of territorial use, and it allowed Dakotas to live on a portion of the land but not have to cultivate it themselves. Renters would pay with half the crop in lieu of liquid cash or make an annual payment after harvest. For the most part, the Dakota farmers at Spirit Lake were not producing for a national market; most plots were too small and their farms undercapitalized. Importantly, funds from leasing could be easily divided among multiple owners, which the land could not if it were to support a household.

At the same time, leasing benefited Norwegians who needed to expand their acreage under cultivation in order to succeed under an industrializing system of agriculture. Renting land required less capital than outright purchase, so it created a way for Norwegian farmers to expand their production without investing money (that they might otherwise have to borrow). The Dakotas' willingness to lease land to them on a case-by-case basis enabled them to become commercially viable in an environment that required economies of scale. The process of leasing—sometimes negotiated directly and other times through the Bureau of Indian Affairs—engaged Norwegians and Dakotas directly with each other and allowed them to pursue their sense of the best use of land while they lived as neighbors. In this way, the shared logic of the use of land for a fee enabled Dakotas and Norwegians to find common ground.[14]

Norwegian Demographic Dominance

In 1904, when the Spirit Lake Dakota Reservation was opened to white settlement, Norwegians were the largest ethnic group in the state. Importantly, they were concentrated in the counties surrounding and overlapping with the reservation: Benson, Eddy, and Nelson. They were well positioned to claim land when it became available.

Norwegians had been coming to the United States since the 1820s but began arriving in large numbers after the Civil War. The peak period of Norwegian immigration was from 1876 to 1890, just when Dakota Territory was surveyed and vast tracts of homestead land made available on the Upper Great Plains.

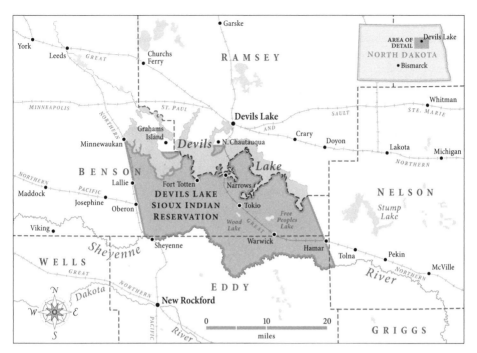

Map showing Devils Lake region

Norwegians were actively recruited by the territorial government through propaganda published in Norwegian and agents sent to Norway.[15]

Many Norwegians came to North America in pursuit of land. Under the strain of Norway's population growth and limited arable land base, Norwegians immigrated to the Midwest in general and North Dakota in particular; many sought land they could own, land that would support them and their children in a way denied them if they remained in Norway as farm laborers or cotters. Some had recently lived in Minnesota, Wisconsin, or Iowa and relocated as communities. Farming allowed them to be their own bosses. John C. Hudson argues that in seeking economic opportunities in North Dakota, people were escaping farm tenancy, which resulted from the lack of available land to buy or homestead in other states. They came to North Dakota to expand their generational prospects, for cheaper and more abundant land that would accommodate their children and extended kin. They sought to stay together in extended family groups and often took land in the vicinity of their kin and former neighbors from Norway in an effort to gain land and economic autonomy while maintaining social ties and culture.[16]

Sigrid Lillehaugen articulated the power of autonomy as a motivation for owning a farm. She lived in southern Walsh County, North Dakota, among her relatives and others from her district in Norway. Her husband, Tosten, claimed a homestead and bought land. In a 1903 letter to her father back in Norway, Sigrid commented on the leverage that land provided: "It is good to have more in the hand or it will be as it has always been to work for others." Many preferred the modicum of autonomy in farming to working in a factory or being a hired farm worker or domestic servant. Owning a farm meant self-employment, although farmers could not control either the weather or the price of grain. Many land-owners had to work for wages as well, but they had taken a key step toward self-sufficiency.[17]

North Dakota was a state of newcomers. In 1910, the vast majority of the state's population (70.6 percent) was of foreign birth or parentage. As Table 7-1 demonstrates, foreign-born whites (27.1 percent) combined with whites of for-eign or mixed (foreign and native-born) parentage (43.5 percent) significantly outnumbered native-born whites, or what I call Yankees (28.2 percent). Native American Indians constituted only 1.1 percent of the whole population and lived primarily on reservations. As mentioned above, many of the Dakotas at Spirit Lake had migrated from southern and central Minnesota.

Of those foreign-born whites, 29.4 percent were born in Norway (see Table 7-2). Another 7.8 percent were born in Sweden and 3.4 percent in Denmark, making 40.6 percent of those born outside the United States Scandinavian. Their presence shaped North Dakota's economy, politics, and culture.[18]

Norwegians predominated in the region surrounding the reservation. To put things in perspective, in 1902, 1,043 Dakotas lived on the reservation. While whites on the reservation were not enumerated, it is possible to generate an estimate of Norwegian concentration using the two counties (Benson and Eddy) in which the reservation falls, in addition to the adjacent county to the east (Nelson). Table 7-3 reveals that for each of the three counties, foreign-born whites and whites with at least one foreign-born parent made up over half of the population in 1910. Of those who were foreign born, Scandinavians constituted the vast majority. In turn, of those Scandinavians, Norwegians accounted for

---

TABLE 7-1
Racial-Ethnic Composition in North Dakota, 1910

RACIAL-ETHNIC GROUP	NUMBER	PERCENTAGE
Whites: born of "native" parents	162,461	28.2
Whites: born of foreign or mixed parents	251,236	43.5
Foreign-born whites	156,158	27.1
Indians	6,486	1.1
Negroes	617	.1
Total	576,958	100

Compiled from U.S. Census, 1910

77.5 percent in Benson County, 64.1 percent in Eddy County, and 88.1 percent in Nelson County. Clearly, Norwegians were the dominant Scandinavian group in a region heavily populated by immigrants. Given the demographic distribution of the area, it is reasonable to assume that Norwegians were the majority of the Scandinavian population living on the reservation as well.[19]

Landowning on the Reservation

The unallotted lands available for homesteading were concentrated on the southern, flatter part of the reservation, which perhaps made it even more attractive to Norwegians interested in farming. The nearby Sheyenne River provided drinking water for people and animals, and the valley offered wood for building and fuel, better hunting, and easier fishing. The Norwegians tended to take land in areas already populated by Norwegians, initially along rivers and creeks. Scandinavian women's land was concentrated on the southern part of the reservation along the Sheyenne River.[20]

Those who moved onto the reservation were not "pioneers" as those a generation before had been. In 1904, the living conditions mixed isolation and a lack

TABLE 7-2

Countries of Origin of Foreign-born Whites, North Dakota, 1910

COUNTRY OF ORIGIN	PERCENT
Norway	29.4
Russia	20.4
Canada	13.5
Germany	10.6
Sweden	7.8
Denmark	3.4
Austria	3.3
England	2
Hungary	1.8
Ireland	1.6
All other countries	6.4
Total	100

Compiled from U.S. Census, 1910

TABLE 7-3

Foreign-born Whites and Scandinavians in Benson, Eddy, and Nelson Counties, North Dakota, 1910

	BENSON COUNTY	EDDY COUNTY	NELSON COUNTY
Total county population	12,681	4,800	10,140
Foreign-born whites	3,042	1,133	2,955
Norway	1,650	430	1,886
Sweden	388	215	190
Denmark	90	26	64
Total Scandinavian as percentage of foreign born	2,128 (70%)	671 (59.2%)	2,140 (72.4%)
Whites born to foreign or mixed parents	3,466	1,456	3,469
Foreign born + those with at least one foreign-born parent	6,508 (51.3%)	2,589 (53.9%)	6,424 (63.4%)

Compiled from U.S. Census, 1910

of electricity, indoor plumbing, and inadequate roads with advanced transportation and unprecedented connections to the world economy. As railroads pene-
trated the area—to Warwick on the reservation, to New Rockford in the south,
and to Devils Lake in the north—small villages had greater access to urban centers and regional grain markets. Unlike farmers of the previous generation, who
broke sod with a walking plow pulled by oxen, many of the homesteaders hired
out the land breaking to a Yankee who owned a big steam engine rig and lived
on the reservation.[21]

Many of the settlers did not stay for long. The hardships were too great and
farming too unpredictable. Prompted by the diminishing supply of affordable
land (North Dakota land values more than tripled between 1900 and 1910) and
searching for a way to make a living in the wheat economy, some continued west
while others ventured north. Sigrid Lillehaugen, who lived in Walsh County
off the reservation, observed in a letter home in 1903, "All the land around here
is taken. Those who want Homestead land have to go to Minot or to Canada."
Land available for purchase had risen in value: "Here the land is up to two, yes,
even $3,000 a quarter. That is a lot of money. The poor can never pay that price
when they buy." Amid these rising prices, we can imagine the clamor for these
vast acres of reservation land, seemingly "unused" to the Norwegian and the
Yankee eye, suitable for farming and available at below-market rates.[22]

And yet, many ethnic Norwegians remained over generations. North Dakota
was a rural state with an agriculturally based economy. The majority of Americans
dwelled in cities as of 1920, but in 1930, 83 percent of North Dakota's population was still rural. Norwegians, more than any other Euro-American group,
including other Scandinavians, tended to stay clustered in rural communities
for generations. With the Norwegians' proclivity for farming and rural living,
Norwegian communities consolidated and endured on the reservation as they
did elsewhere in North Dakota.[23]

By 1929, the staying power of Norwegians became clear as they continued to
accumulate land on the reservation. Scandinavian landowners held an average
of 212.6 acres each (see Table 7-4), reflecting growth and consolidation of farms
since the initial land taking in 1904 (average acreage was 149.5 in 1910). Still, their
acreage was less than half the average farm size in the state as a whole: 500 acres
in 1930. On the reservation, the land had been made available to homesteaders
only in 160-acre parcels, and a person could acquire more land only through
purchase, marriage, or inheritance.[24]

While the Norwegians gained, the Dakotas lost. By 1929, more than a generation after allotment, Dakotas' average landholdings had shrunk to 83.8 acres
each, smaller than the average size in 1910 and even less adequate to sustain a
family through cultivation. While Dakota landowners were more numerous than
Scandinavians, the total acreage owned by Dakotas had declined significantly as

TABLE 7-4
Acreage Owned at Spirit Lake Reservation by Gender and Race-Ethnicity, 1929

	TOTAL ACREAGE OWNED	MEAN ACREAGE (N)	FEMALE (N)	MALE (N)	GENDER UNKNOWN (N)
Indian	49,209	83.8 (587)	83.0 (205)	84.4 (380)	60.0 (2)
Scandinavian	73,331	212.6 (345)	152.7 (83)	237.2 (242)	163.2 (20)
Yankee	30,238	200.3 (151)	127.7 (33)	229.3 (109)	113.9 (9)
German	20,024	241.3 (83)	182.6 (16)	262.2 (64)	106.7 (3)
Canadian and other foreign born	13,119	305.1 (43)	242.0 (5)	313.4 (38)	—
Unidentified Ethnicity	16,746	119.6 (140)	145.8 (48)	111.6 (55)	97.6 (37)
Total	202,667	115.5 (1,349)	150.2 (390)	168.1 (888)	117.5 (71)

well, from 99,038 acres in 1910 to 49,209 acres in 1929. Most Dakotas did not own their land outright at this point; their land continued to be held in trust. When an allottee died, the land was divided among the heirs. If no heirs could be identified, a patent was assigned to the land, and it was put on the market for closed bidding. In this way, many original allotments were sold to whites. While some Indians did attempt to purchase land, they were greatly outnumbered by local farmers, speculators, and land investors with more resources.[25]

Dakota women represented the largest group of female landowners on the reservation. The growing scholarship on the indigenous ownership of land tends to neglect gender, making this analysis of landowning at Spirit Lake all the more striking. As evident in Table 7-4, Dakota women were significant landowners, comprising 35 percent of Dakota landowners in 1929. These rates are astonishingly high in comparison to those of non-Indian women. In her studies of homesteading, which was just one path to land ownership, Elaine Lindgren found that women claimed an average of 10 to 12 percent of homesteads in North Dakota. A 1920 study examined the ownership of farms rented to tenants in the north-central states and found that only 8 percent of the owners of North Dakota farms were women, even though the average was about 16 percent in the region overall. By all of these standards, the proportion of Dakota women owning land was high, as was that of Scandinavian women: 24 percent of Scandinavian landowners were women in 1929.[26]

The comparative amount of land women controlled is equally important in assessing the gendered dimensions of landowning on the reservation. Consistently across the region and across ethnic groups, men owned more land than women. However, Dakota women came close to parity with men; they owned on average 98 percent of the amount of land that men owned (83 acres versus 84.4 acres). This parity may reflect the consequences of receiving allotments and

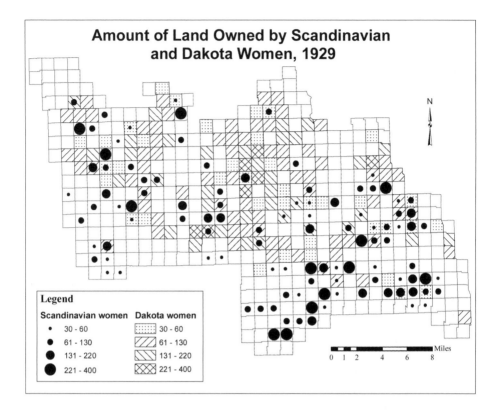

inheriting land in equal numbers. When allottees died, their land was divided equally among their heirs, male and female alike. By 1903, one-third of the original allottees had already died. Over time, the disparity between men and women narrowed, and Dakota women continued to be major landholders in the tribe. As evident in the GIS-generated map of female land ownership in 1929, Dakota women's holdings were largely in the northern, central, and western areas of the reservation.[27]

At the same time, Scandinavian women became a larger proportion of land-owners, yet the inequality of acreage owned increased between men and women. Of the various ethnic groups, Scandinavian women owned approximately 64 percent of the average acreage of Scandinavian men. Still, Scandinavian women owned an average of 152.7 acres, almost double that of Dakota women and men. Canadian and other European and German women owned a considerably higher ratio compared to men (77 percent and 70 percent, respectively). Interestingly, the largest disparity in acreage owned was between the holdings of Yankee women—those identified by Lindgren as the most active home-steaders elsewhere in North Dakota—and those of Yankee men. In 1929, on average, these native-born women owned just 56 percent of the acreage owned by Yankee men.

The Meanings of Land

Land taking was shaped by culture, history, and individual inclination, as well as by law. While Norwegian and Dakota women differed in how they acquired land and in how much land they owned, they shared some perspectives on the meanings and use of land. Both groups faced economic and cultural challenges in the U.S. economy that land ownership helped them meet. Land provided the means to feed the family. It enabled both groups of women to grow vegetable gardens, raise chickens and cows, and engage in other subsistence-oriented work.

For most of the Dakota women, the reservation was not ancestral territory, but two generations after the reservation was established, it had become a tribal base. With that designation came some shelter and food, however limited. Over time it became home, a place where kin lived and visitors gathered. Eunice Davidson relayed her Dakota grandmother's perspective about her land: "She always made that remark that the land was one of the greatest gifts. That's what it was to her, a gift, she said . . . when you give something to an Indian, back then and now, that's really a gift you get, and you really cherish it." Dakota women were determined to maintain a base to practice their culture and raise their children. The land provided a vital foundation on which to build a physical and metaphorical home. Individual holdings were too small to farm profitably, although women were able to plant huge gardens. Nor was most Indian land a fungible asset because of its trust status.[28]

On the reservation, both Dakota and Scandinavian women commonly leased out their land. Some Dakota women also made efforts to accumulate land to generate income for their families. Mary Blackshield was one of the few Dakota women who made a bid to purchase available Indian land in 1913. Approximately ten years later, she rented land to the Knudson family, who lived on the reservation. Bjorne Knudson recollects a time during the 1920s when, as a boy of twelve, he drove a team of horses north of Fort Totten with a rig to plow a field belonging to Blackshield. Because the land was so distant from his home, he stayed at the Blackshield home and took meals there for a week while he plowed.[29]

Norwegian women recognized that land could generate annual income as well, through renting it for cultivation or harvesting the wild hay that grew abundantly on the reservation. For example, my great-grandmother, Berthe Haugen, testified in her final proof of homestead claim that she cultivated oats and flax on sixty-five acres, harvested wild hay, and rented her twenty-one-acre pasture to a neighbor for his cattle. Renting out the land could provide the owner a dividend, paid in either crops or cash. Gust and Annie Berg struggled to remember the name of the woman from whom they rented land after they were married in 1922: "We just had eighty acres. That belonged to somebody, some lady that homesteaded. Her name was . . . what was her first name?" Annie replied, "Albert Olson's . . ." Gust interrupted, "Sister, yeah."[30]

In addition to generating income, owning land gave women the power to say no. When Norwegian immigrant Bertine Sem proved up her claim in Bottineau County in 1904, three neighbors attested to the fact that she had lived on the land and cultivated eighty acres. "Satisfied that she was in fact a *bona fide* farmer, the government granted her a deed to the land." She married Erick Sannes almost immediately thereafter and started a family.[31]

To meet the needs of the family, it eventually became necessary to expand the size of the farm. Most farmers used their land as collateral to buy more land, but Bertine, who had worked so hard to retain the title to her land in her own name, refused to risk mortgaging her farm. She insisted they find another way. Her independent ownership of land entitled her to veto a maneuver that would risk her financial security. Because her name was on the patent, she could say no.[32]

For Norwegians, land was an anchor in the new world, a place to make a living and raise a family. Norwegian women sought economic independence, long-term security, and the ability to make strategic contributions to their current kin and future households. As Lori Ann Lahlum found in her study of farming practices on the Great Plains, Norwegian women took an "agricultural rather than aesthetic" perspective on the land. Lois Olson Jones, of Swedish and Irish ancestry, framed the issues grandly: "We're the people that feed the world. And if you have land, you can have cattle and you can have gardens and whatever."[33]

Elizabeth Hampsten has found that while white women in North Dakota were unlikely to identify emotionally with the land in their diary and memoir writing, they focused on the continuity and livelihood it provided. As one Norwegian woman living near Devils Lake wrote in 1889 to her cousin in Norway, "You say aunt wonders whether I still own land. Well I have it mainly because as long as I keep it we have a home. Mother lives there mostly alone. I am at home in the winter time and gone in the summer." (Her summer job cooking for a "tight American" helped to pay for food and wood to support her mother and herself through the winter.) The letter writer continued, "You know I cannot take care of the land like a man. All I can do is to live there as much as I can and to plow what I can so that no one can take it away from me because I hope in time to sell and maybe get a couple of thousand dollars for it if we get railway over here."[34]

Hopeful speculation aside, the letter writer's land, at the very least, was a home for herself and her mother. She realized that her crops might not yield much, depending on the weather. Land was a place to live, it potentially yielded annual income, and if a person got lucky, he or she could turn a handsome profit from selling it. Though it seldom generated riches, land was a prudent investment that owners assumed would increase in value, regardless of its annual crop yield or improvements.

In addition to providing income, land could enhance women's and men's prospects on the marriage market. Single women with land were surely more attractive to male farmers than women without. Presumably the reverse held true as well. Julius Fjeld, who grew up in Nelson County and later homesteaded in Ward County, married a homesteading woman, Mary Rue. Using his neighbors as an example, Julius explained that "you couldn't take a homestead if you was married, a lady couldn't. But, she had a homestead and he had a homestead. And one of them proved up so that they could marry." Sem left Norway expressly to homestead land in North Dakota. She settled in Bottineau County in 1902 and worked the land to improve it. In two and a half years, she took title to her homestead. A month after filing for her patent, she married.[35]

Land and kinship were deeply intertwined in Norwegian law and culture. According to Mark R. G. Goodale and Per Kåre Sky, "traditionally, farms were thought not to belong to individuals only, but to all related kindred if the farm had been in the possession of a family for a certain period of time." Informed by their history of working the land, Norwegians were aware of the intense labor and commitment required to operate a successful farm. Handy-Marchello articulated the long-term multigenerational approach to land and posterity: "In North Dakota, many women identified their personal or their family's security with ownership of a productive farm. Farm families expected to prosper through generations linked to each other by their work and presence on the land." While she found the land-keeping ethic across groups, it perhaps held true more for immigrant groups that came from agricultural societies. Particularly on homesteads and previously uncultivated land, it was essential to take the long-term view, as it took years to create a farm. Success could only be measured over time as land stayed in family hands and continued to produce. In interviews with contemporary women landowners of all different ethnicities, researchers found that women "kept their land primarily for family reasons. They either lived on the farms or maintained ownership from a distance because of a desire to keep the land in the family."[36]

The endurance of Norwegian communities was linked to the kin-based, labor-intensive (rather than capital- and machinery-intensive) form of agriculture they practiced. Farmers had to muster many hands to help with periods of harvest. Drawing on extended kin was as important as having many children. Having a network of relatives meant that farmers could share not only equipment and labor but also information and support.[37]

Like the Dakotas, the Norwegians sought to live as close to one another as possible. Brothers and sisters homesteaded on adjacent sections of land. Adult children staked out land for their parents, who followed them to the new country. Parents purchased more land when possible to sell to their children later at below-market prices. Clusters of neighbors moved from villages in Norway to townships in the United States. Newcomers sought out people who spoke their language, made their favorite foods, and told jokes they understood. Handy-Marchello argues that Norwegian women fought to keep their land because it anchored them in a familiar culture in a foreign country: "These Norwegian immigrant women understood that losing the farm might mean moving out of the community. If they had to move, they might end up in a Yankee community where they would be outsiders."[38]

This pattern is visible in the clustering of family names on the plat maps. Oral histories attest to the importance of choosing land near relatives. Geographic clusters of kin-owned land facilitated sharing labor and farm equipment, which was too cumbersome to transport on bad roads. Because of the isolation of dispersed households founded through homesteading and allotment, companionship was also a motivating factor. Barbara Levorsen told of the joy people found in speaking with others from the same village or valley in Norway, people who spoke the same dialect and might have news of the folks back home. As Lahlum puts it, the shared language and culture helped to mitigate the extreme "strangeness" of the new land and its economy.[39]

The link between place and kinship shows up in numerous stories of illness and grief. Gravestones rooted losses in a particular place. The Lillehaugens of Walsh County lost five of their eleven children to disease and accidents in the early twentieth century. Yet they remained among their kin and fellow Norwegians. Handy-Marchello astutely articulates the paradox: "The bond between family and farm was both beneficial and tyrannical: land was a powerful benefactor that supported large families over generations, and land was an enemy that drained families of money, health, hope, and sometimes even life." For some families, surviving meant staying where people knew them and could help them. As Norman Forde put it, "I don't think they had any choice . . . they had to live some way."[40]

For the Dakota as a people, the loss of ancestral land frames stories of the past. Grace Lambert, a Dakota elder, reveals the impact of a family tragedy a generation after military defeat.

> My father was farming . . . my parents were on a homestead. So, naturally we were there. And that was really good I thought, because I can always remember seeing scenes like my dad used to plow, plow the field, to put in his grain . . . Then when I became about eight years old I think,

my grandmother got killed by lightning. [She was] my dad's mother . . . And my dad . . . just couldn't stand it, . . . so we left the homestead, and then some white man got it.

"Some white man got it." With this simple statement, Lambert expresses her feeling that her family had been robbed of something rightfully theirs. The passage of Dakota land to whites was repeated over decades. The Dakotas held less land on the reservation as their Euro-American neighbors acquired more. Her statement about the consequences of this incident rings with inevitability, a despairing acceptance that the invisible arm of the market had joined with the heavy hand of the federal government to take Indian land from a Dakota family and transfer it to a white owner. Her reflections on how it *felt* as an eight-year-old obscured the particulars of the land sale. Yet her statement exposes traces of the bitterness that she, an elder of the tribe who was sixty-eight years old at the time of the interview, felt after witnessing the cumulative impact of sixty years of land transfer from Indian to white owners.[41]

The paradox of the land—that it both gave and extracted life—existed in tension with a deep-seated land-keeping ethic. Land gave sustenance, fed people, and provided a safe harbor. It simultaneously demanded bone-wearying work and provoked worry and fear of loss. Land was everything. Lois Olson Jones, of Swedish and Irish ancestry, reflected, "It's instilled on *me* that land, you don't sell land, once you get it. You hang onto land." In a similar vein, Eunice Davidson, of Dakota ancestry, recalls clearly the message of her grandmother:

She said, "Don't ever sell the land." Both my grandmas did. On my mom and my dad's side. They both felt strongly about the land. My grandma, Alvina Alberts, she always said, "Don't sell the land. Whatever you do, don't sell the land." So they both felt very strong about that. And I think it was because they were nomads for, you know, from back to their parents to their grandparents. They always

Two Dakota women on a wagon trail

moved around, but they always had land. They didn't have to fight for it. Then all of a sudden they were fighting the whites for their land.

The grandmothers' advice rang true for the granddaughters of the reservation, be they Scandinavian or Dakota. Both groups of women embraced this ethic, a belief that coalesces the competing logics of land in the next generation. Divergent histories led these peoples to the same place. The Scandinavians were more or less able to act on the grandmothers' wisdom. The Dakotas as a whole were not. In the face of dispossession, this shared insight takes on tragic dimensions.[42]

Farming and the Gendered Division of Labor

Scholars have posed theoretical questions about the relationship between the gendered division of labor, women's economic contribution to households, and their status in society. The question remains: do women's economic resources—in the form of labor, wages, and wealth—translate into more power? While debating definitions, dynamics, and consequences, historical studies of women's work consistently document the extent to which women's labor and wage-earning were essential to the farm economy. To this perplexing conundrum I want to add the matter of land ownership. The value of a woman's labor is critical, but so is the value of her property. Did owning land, working the land as a partner farmer, or building community networks translate into decision-making leverage, bargaining power, old age security, or greater respect for women? What were the consequences, in both the long and short run, of women's economic contributions to their families as landowners, farm workers, and community builders?[43]

Women as Partner Farmers. While decidedly male dominated, the farm economy was also deeply gender integrated. On the Great Plains, women's labor was essential to family success and well-being, whether as gatherers or as farmers. Handy-Marchello frames these gender relations as a "partnership"; "marriage and family stability depended on the economic contributions of both husband and wife." Linking the centrality of women to the type of crop cultivated, Handy-Marchello argues that "the instability of wheat farming made women's productive activities on the farm central to the family's survival and success, not peripheral." Handy-Marchello's conception of women as partner farmers renders their work visible and important in ways that conventional portraits of women as helpmates or housekeepers ignore.[44]

The labor provided by partner farmers placed a premium on marriage. As Carrie Young insightfully observes in her biography of her Norwegian mother, "Homesteading men were desperate for wives." The sex ratio favored women; the surplus of men in the state gave women some leverage in their marital and economic choices. With the labor-intensive demands of rural life, male farmers needed women to make their farms viable.[45]

Without electrification or indoor plumbing, in remote areas where roads were impassable a good part of the year, women in cash-poor households made do through ingenuity and hard work. They hauled water, washed clothes in big tin tubs, warmed the house, and cooked with wood and cow chips. Each task required strenuous physical labor. For example, when Dakota elder Lambert described her life in the 1920s, she spoke of her responsibility for chopping mountains of wood to keep warm in winter. She boasted that chopping wood made her "strong and mighty." Grace Pearson, a second-generation Norwegian who lived just off the reservation, told a similar tale about hauling logs from the Sheyenne River: "When [my husband] was out working in the field, threshing and that, then I'd go down to my sister's, and she'd help me load it. And I'd haul wood home, in that old Model T." Women cooked five meals a day, took care of children, milked cows, churned butter, baked, cleaned, laundered, sewed, and knit. Men's list of chores was equally long. For example, Barbara Levorsen's father dug wells, turned the soil, tilled the fields, tended horses, hauled hay and straw for the animals, cleaned the barn, hauled manure, and made trips to town.[46]

The division of labor on the farm had to be flexible, although adaptations differed between racial-ethnic groups. Every group had a gendered division of labor, and which chores were appropriate for whom varied by culture. As Handy-Marchello says, "To make a northern plains farm produce, families developed an integrated system of productive and reproductive labor that extracted a huge physical and emotional toll from women, men and children. In this system, the assignment of tasks according to gender operated under rules that were both flexible and subtle." Historians of the West have found many more similarities than differences among groups of farming women, regardless of ethnicity, in part because of the work they do. Hampsten finds a common workaday reality for women in North Dakota: "Depending on where he lives, a man can be a cattle raiser, a whaler, or a miner; what women do all day long is much the same from one place to another." Glenda Riley argues that differing resources and econo-mies of the prairies and the plains did not significantly affect women's daily lives. Rural women performed hours of back-breaking labor in the barnyard and in the house, regardless of ethnicity. Even those with sufficient resources to hire help pitched in alongside.[47]

Like the Norwegians, the Dakotas practiced a deeply gendered division of labor. Historically, Dakota women were responsible for cultivating crops. In addi-tion, they dried meat, tanned hides, and foraged for edible food on the prairies. Importantly, they owned household items as well as tipis. On the reservation, Dakota women planted gardens, produced ceremonial objects such as beadwork and quilts, and occasionally snared small game. They had the power to divorce men without stigma, and in the process they retained possession of the household and its goods. Relations between men and women "were complementary and consistent with a wider Dakota ethos which idealized both individual integrity and collective responsibility." According to anthropologist Patricia Albers, "Men did not exert any control over the products of female subsistence and manufacturing activity. Women had the right to determine how the products of their labor would be used." This autonomy contrasts dramatically with the practices of Norwegian households, where women's work contributed fundamentally to the household economy but decisions were made largely by men.[48]

On the reservation, forms of economic subsistence shifted from growing squash and corn and seasonal hunting and fishing to a life based primarily on sedentary farming supplemented by wild game. In this transformation, the responsibility for growing crops was shifted uneasily and incompletely from women to men. The federal government set policies of tool distribution and ran educational programs that privileged men in agriculture and the cash economy and excluded women. Women continued to garden, forage, and manufacture goods for trade or sale at home.

Despite the similarities across groups, Norwegian women did more work in the fields than women of other ethnic groups. Norwegians seemed amenable to interpreting these gendered boundaries flexibly or simply disregarding them. In Norway, through the mid-nineteenth century, women were responsible for the house and barn, often running farms while men worked elsewhere in fishing and forestry. Although some chores shifted in the United States (e.g., men began milking cows), Norwegian women continued to work in the fields, at least seasonally.[49]

The seasonal rhythms of farm labor demanded numerous workers. Barbara Levorsen told many stories about haying and harvest time, which required all available hands, including women and girls: "Papa would guide the horses along, one on either side of the windrows, and the rake would dump constantly, leaving the hay in piles. Mama shaped these piles into haycocks and I trotted along with a big wooden rake, supposedly gathering up all the stray tufts of grass." Levorsen's skepticism about whether her work was actually helpful is countered by other accounts that reveal that children provided substantial help. She recalls her neighbor, Ann, not yet eleven, driving a plow: "I distinctly remember her plowing the big field next to the road, with five horses on the gang plow."[50]

Levorsen's childhood chores included hoeing weeds around newly planted trees and shoveling manure among them. Clearly remembering the weight of the expectations placed on her, she recalls exclaiming, "It was no fun being a Norwegian!" She protested not only the amount of work she had to do on the farm as a child but also her mother's proprietary sense of how things should be done: "The way they did things in Norway was the only way for Mama." Her mother believed that her Norwegian cultural practices were the superior and correct approach and so expressed a kind of self-righteousness.[51]

The cycles of farm life, particularly those required in forging a farm on new land, made pressing demands on women. Carrie Young writes about her mother:

> No matter how busy the pioneer women were with their own tasks, when their husbands came to them and said they were needed, they dropped everything and went. From the time she was married my mother always helped my father outside. The first year she helped him clear the rocks from his homestead quarter and both of her own—a bone-crushing job. My father dug out the largest rocks from the soil with a pickax, and my mother helped him carry or roll them onto a flat stone boat pulled by a team of horses.

Even though the land was much richer and less rocky than in Norway, breaking new fields required picking rocks, as reported in many accounts of homesteading. For Bertine Sem Sannes, "although household tasks increased with the birth of each child, Bertine never completely removed herself from work in the fields. One of her babies was born in a field, far from the house, where she was picking rocks with [her husband] Erick."[52]

In recognizing the value of their labor, women could assert limits. Lester Skjerven's mother exercised her right to draw boundaries on the basis of the sacrifices she had made in the past. Amanda Skjerven reported on the bargain her mother-in-law made in agreeing to move from Minnesota: "His mother had told him that if she moved to North Dakota, she didn't want to leave Rochester 'cause that's where her people were; that's where they came. And she said, 'If I move out to North Dakota, I'm not going into the fields to work or anything. I'm through with that.' And she stayed by that. She never did go. Although she sure did her share of work. Plenty of it, but not in the fields like she had done there." Amanda admired the many talents of her mother-in-law and also implied that she found her negotiation fair and reasonable.[53]

That Norwegian women worked in the fields did not mean Norwegians abandoned a gendered division of labor. Most jobs had a gender label and a preferred hierarchy. In field work, men were preferred, then big boys second, hired men third, women next, and smaller children last. However, the necessity of flexibility was understood. Young reports, "Even in later years if my brother wasn't home and my father couldn't get a hired man my mother would often go out into the fields and help my father rake hay or operate the binder that tied the wheat into sheaves."[54]

The account of an interview with Johanna Tvedt, which compared her life in Norway with that in the United States, revealed that she was able to adapt to field work despite her distaste for it:

> Life in Norway had been constant work, but she found that it had been nothing compared to what was expected of her in America. Obligated to her sister and brother-in-law for the price of the passage, they put her to work. The hired man was released so that Johanna would not suffer from idleness and beside her house work she cultivated corn and did other farm work generally required of a hired man. In only a matter of days Johanna found that America was not going to be such a paradise.[55]

Perhaps Norwegian women were exploitable because they were new to the country. They often worked as domestic and farm servants. Lester Skjerven of Nelson County explained how Norwegian women contributed to the family economy: "They had to be along stacking hay, and work out in the field. Mother was telling about women [that] had little babies. They'd have the baby in the cradle at the end of the field and they'd make a round and come back and look after the baby. And go again." His wife, Amanda, elaborated that the workday was not yet over after working the fields: "And then come in and do your . . . housework and the cooking. And the men could rest." The lack of equitable leisure time was not lost on her. She carefully chronicled the skills and cumulative labor of her mother-in-law.[56]

While farm-making called on women of all ethnic groups to adapt, it seemed that Norwegian women were disproportionately likely to continue to work outdoors, which triggered scorn by the dominant culture. Handy-Marchello finds an "anti-rural sentiment" voiced in a larger cultural context that celebrated bourgeois womanhood and exercised suspicion toward those who were foreign born, did not speak English, and worked at physical labor. Levorsen recalls the tensions between farm women and town women, which corresponded to an ethnic divide: "It seemed that the 'Yankees' could take the settlers good butter, fresh eggs and hard-earned cash, but to take their hand in friendship was another matter." Handy-Marchello explains that "women's labor helped stigmatize their groups as un-American or hard on women." According to Levorsen, women worked with animals back in Norway and felt no disgrace in it. But in the United States, doing animal chores connoted poverty and foreignness. Ingrid Semmingsen writes that Yankees "took it for granted that immigrants would do the hardest work and get the least pay."[57]

In this, Norwegian and Dakota women shared a stigma. In the nineteenth century and through the early twentieth, dominant bourgeois Euro-American society constructed dichotomies as a way of defining and preserving middle-class white womanhood, distinguishing the ideal woman, who was dependent and decorative, from useful, hard-working immigrant, Indian, and black women. Indian women historically had been viewed by white society as unequal drudges because Indian women worked hard and, from the dominant perspective, Indian men did not work hard enough. Ironically, the strenuous and skilled labor that made Indian women integral to the economic endeavors of their families and communities prompted the dominant culture to cast aspersions on them. The values of respect and honor within Dakota and Norwegian cultures are different matters and ripe for future investigation.[58]

For our purposes, however, on the reservation, both Dakota and Norwegian women seemed relatively oblivious to the outside valuations as they went about their lives and raised their children as best they could. Occasionally, they had to confront prejudice, on and off the reservation. My grandmother, Helene Haugen Kanten, recalled being a student in a local day school just south of the reservation in Eddy Township. Because she did not come to North Dakota until the age of eleven, what little English she spoke was laced with a strong Norwegian accent. Tired of being ridiculed by a teacher for her inadequate English and by students who called her a "squaw" because she lived on the reservation, one day she exploded with frustration. She wrestled the teacher down on a bench, sat on her, and with a shaking finger scolded, "You be good. You be good." Like Dakotas, Norwegians were forbidden to speak their language in schools and were disparaged as foreigners in Yankee communities. In contrast, when they went to a store or attended a Lutheran church on the reservation, they could be greeted in their mother tongue.[59]

Operating Farms and Cultivating Community. If women worked on farms and if they owned land, did that make them farmers? Some women who worked in the field considered themselves farmers, not just partner farmers or farm wives. Some were even given the occupational designation of "farmer" in the census, which defined the job category as "a person in charge of a farm." A report based on the 1900 census found that foreign-born women in North Dakota were more likely to be farmers than any other occupation except domestic servant. Among the foreign-born women, Norwegians were more likely than any other group to be farmers. The few adequate options for making a living as a single woman made agricultural labor appealing, particularly if a woman had children to support. Trina Dahl was widowed when her children were small. Trina "ran the farm alone. She lived a most laborious life and still she lived to be one of the very oldest members of the community. The *Wells County Free Press* had an article about her when she was 95 years old and was out in the field attempting to shock grain." In another example, Sigrid Tufte Myhre Ostrom, whose husband died after failing to prove up his preemption and before he proved up his homestead, took over the homestead in 1896, at the age of twenty-six. She had four little children, the youngest of whom was eight months old. In 1900, she took title to the land; the census listed her as the head of the household and a farmer. She stayed on her homestead until 1907, when she remarried and moved to her new husband's farm with her children.[60]

Bjorne Knudson described the importance of his mother's labor in the fields while his father earned income for the family through carpentry: "Mother would try and farm and I can remember when she would have three horses on a walking plow. We called it a walking plow, because you had to walk behind it and hold it as you plowed the ground. So we farmed, as the kids got a little older, us kids, we helped her all we could." In the 1920 U.S. manuscript census, Charlotte Knudson's occupation was listed as "none;" her husband was listed as a farmer.[61]

Most of the few women I have found identified in the manuscript census as farmers on the Spirit Lake Dakota Reservation were widowed heads of households. Working in the fields and selling farm products did not earn a woman the title of *farmer,* clearly a valued and contested term. Lois Olson Jones declared that her aunt, Ida Olson, was not a "real farmer." Ida *owned* the land, but her father and her brother *farmed* her land. Owning land could mean working the land, leasing it, or managing a farm. For Jones, the hallowed title of *farmer* required that the person work the land.[62]

Women sought a voice in major decisions about the farming enterprise. Marriage led some women to assert their status as co-owners of their husbands' farms, even if their names were not on the deed. North Dakota law entitled married women "to hold as her separate property all real or personal estate owned by her at the time of her marriage and all that she may acquire afterwards." Laws insured that a widow received at least one-third of her husband's property after he died and that a homestead estate went to the surviving spouse. Sigri, who immigrated from Norway as an adult, found a good marital prospect in Hans, an affable man with two quarters of land. Sigri "was a smart woman and probably a much better manager than Hans," according to Levorsen. When Hans traveled to Norway, she stayed behind to run the farm and supervise the tenant: "It was her land now wasn't it?"[63]

The authority women assumed in ownership is evidenced in their use of the word "we," a perspective that assumes a common purpose, if not commonly owned land. In her letters home to Norway, Sigrid Lillehaugen speaks in the "we" voice. For example, she wrote, "We have put up well over 100 tons of hay and we have rented out just as much from the other quarter that we have taken as Homestead Land." While Lillehaugen more subtly suggested her ownership of the land than did Sigri, her phrasing nonetheless indicates that she believed homesteading to be a communal enterprise, not just her husband's responsibility.[64]

A dispute about farm management arose between a couple who owned land and were each used to running their own farms. Levorsen tells the story of Tostein and Tella:

> I no longer remember whether Tostein came to Tella's homestead as a hired man or whether she came to his as a hired girl. However as the years passed everyone, Tostein and Tella most of all, chose to ignore that the two were not married. It was said that when Tella first came into the community she chewed and spit tobacco just like a man. She smoked as well. Gradually she gave up the chewing and tried to smoke only in private.
>
> The two lived peacefully together most of the time, but occasionally they got into furious disputes about farm management. At such times Tella might snatch the pipe out of Tostein's mouth and puff furiously until the smoke billowed around her. Thus refreshed, she was ready to enter into the argument again.

The example illustrates Norwegian homesteaders' continued cultural isolation from hegemonic norms of femininity. At the same time, this dispute suggests that land ownership, independence, and a sense of entitlement prompted women to voice their opinions and exercise their decision-making power.[65]

Women also brought valuable resources to their household economies by cultivating community networks. Their social relationships affected resources available in the community as a whole as well. When an unnamed Indian visitor came to Ella Halvorson Dolbak's house off of the reservation one day when she had no fresh bread to offer, her mother gave the gift of wool socks she had knit. Her mother expressed concern that on this brisk day in late autumn the visitor was "cold on his feet." The socks were received with a smile and mutual appreciation. E. R. Manning, whose mother was Norwegian and whose Yankee father was the publisher of the *Sheyenne Star,* had multiple pairs of moccasins. He recalled that Annie Grey Wind, a Dakota woman who lived nearby, would occasionally bring her children and join the Mannings for a midday meal. His mother would give her their castoff clothing. In return, "she'd always give us moccasins. So I had moccasins; I'd wear moccasins all the time."[66]

Those relationships potentially translated into good will and a basis for doing business. In a land-scarce environment, having land to lease or rent meant a landowner could use discretion about with whom to make an agreement. Consistent with Sonya Salamon's research, landowners made decisions based on their ongoing relationships with other farmers, whether kin or neighbors. Ingemund Peterson appreciated not having to go all the way to Fort Totten to pay his rent, so when his Dakota landlord showed up annually to collect, Ingemund was relieved.[67]

Negotiating business relationships could be complicated, as Patrick Langstaff discovered, when a piece of land had multiple owners and a farmer assumed the person with whom he or she was dealing was the sole owner. Solomon Fox was a central Dakota landowner on the reservation, and many white farmers went directly to him to make an agreement, confident of his honor and ownership status.[68]

Presumably because it was a landowner's market, those who wanted to rent had to cultivate relationships with landlords. The Knudsons rented land from Mike Gord (as well as Mary Blackshield, as mentioned previously), on whose land they lived. One particularly desperate year, the Gord family began showing up for the midday meal unannounced but hungry. Thereafter Mrs. Knudson would, in anticipation, set places for them at the table. Hospitality not only strengthened the community safety net; it also ensured her family's good relationships with their landlords.[69]

Converging Logics in the Meanings of Land

In the early twentieth century, a confluence of global forces and local conditions brought two peoples together. Dakotas, through territorial dispossession and war, migrated to Spirit Lake and negotiated a treaty with the U.S. government to establish a reservation. Through a coincidence of timing, Norwegians migrated internationally and across North America in search of land, arrived in North Dakota, and found themselves poised to take advantage of the Indian land newly available at Spirit Lake. As a result, the Norwegians were major beneficiaries of government policies that further diminished Dakota lands. Thus the two groups lived together on the reservation, both adapting to a culture not their own but attached to the land, rooted in kin networks, and committed to a rural way of life.

In this context, Dakota and Norwegian women owned land, largely with different legal statuses. Most Dakota women owned their allotments with the land in trust, although some owned their land as citizen Indians. Norwegian women homesteaded, improved the land, made claims, and filed for patents to take title. Both occasionally bid on land for purchase. Dakota and Norwegian women frequently leased their land and sometimes cultivated part of it themselves. They farmed; they managed; they negotiated. In addition, most women grew their own gardens, providing produce for their families.

By 1929 Norwegians owned more land on the Spirit Lake Reservation than did Dakotas. Even when women did not own land themselves, they worked the fields and were actively involved in the land-taking process. They acted as partner farmers in the context of their kin networks. Like Dakota women, Norwegian women valued their land, sought to hold onto it, and were centrally involved in providing resources for their families through their labors. More detailed comparative studies of women's landowning in subsequent generations will uncover what was distinctive to some racial-ethnic groups and what was universal, what endured and what was characteristic only of a temporary moment of converging historical forces.

On average, Spirit Lake Reservation landowners' holdings were half the size of landholdings in North Dakota as a whole, and women's average acreage was smaller than men's. The Dakotas' average landholdings were less than half the size of those owned by Scandinavians. Because most Dakotas owned land in trust and multiple heirs subdivided entitlement, subsequent generations faced restrictions on land use. If owning land was a potential indicator of well-being, then the Dakotas continued to struggle. Landlessness in the wake of dispossession was a tribal issue as well as a personal and familial one.

Demographic concentration on the reservation gave both groups a visible cultural presence. A majority of tribal members continued to live on the reservation, even with the dearth of economic opportunity outside of farming or leasing land. They considered Spirit Lake their reservation, which even in destitute times was of symbolic importance (both positive and negative). Dakotas continued to live in family groups when possible, as the plat maps attest. It is evident that Norwegians also understood the power of demographic density; they exercised similar efforts to live near people with a shared ancestry. The critical mass enabled them to continue to speak their language and establish their own places of worship.

In the long run, women aspired to attain greater security for themselves and their families. In a country where land equals wealth, land ownership, even of relatively small parcels, confers some power. Larger landholdings translated into more resources, a greater political voice, and increased economic well-being. Conversely, owning less land or none at all led to impoverishment and further displacement. In an era during which the safety net was local, social, and noninstitutional, people without land were more vulnerable to hunger and dire poverty. Still, bountiful harvests or profitable commodity prices could never be guaranteed, and owning land did not ensure adequate nutrition, access to cash resources, or freedom from poverty.

My own great-grandmother stayed on the reservation into her old age, leaving the cultivation of land to her grandsons. The homestead was sold out of the family after she died in 1936. My grandmother married and moved to Saskatchewan in 1910 with her husband's family, only to homestead again. My family history aside, people of Norwegian descent can still be found on the reservation today, as landowners and as tenant farmers, alongside Dakotas. The tensions of the competing cultural logics have shifted over the past one hundred years of shared history and intertwined kinship networks, though they continue to shape the relationship between the two groups.

Notes

1. I extend my appreciation to those who patiently and astutely read earlier drafts of this essay: Andrew Bundy, Mignon Duffy, Anita Ilta Garey, Clare Hammonds, and Debra Osnowitz. Grey Osterud lent her expert eye and generous insights multiple times, and my argument is stronger for it. My understanding of Indians' perspectives on the past has been immeasurably aided by Louis Garcia, honorary tribal historian of the Spirit Lake Dakota, who has been conducting interviews and keeping research journals for forty-five years. David Deis designed the regional map, and Robert Rose provided invaluable skill in generating the GIS map. I also thank Betty Bergland and Lori Lahlum for having the foresight to undertake this project and for their generosity in sharing sources.

Helene Haugen Kanten, interview by author, 1977. The data for this article comes primarily from two sources: oral history interviews and plat maps (see note 3). The 106 oral histories that constitute the heart of the project convey the distinctive perspectives of the people who lived this history and of their immediate descendants who remain at Spirit Lake today. The limitations of the written records have made oral histories especially valuable in interpreting the dynamic between the Norwegians and the Dakotas during the process of reservation land taking. Few letters and diaries from the immigrant homesteaders remain. The Dakotas' perspective has been especially elusive. A people with an oral rather than written tradition who were reeling from dislocation and population decline, the Dakotas left few documents about themselves. I have analyzed seventy-two of the 1,214 oral histories collected by the State Historical Society of North Dakota in 1975–76, including all the interviews done with Scandinavian residents of the three counties on and adjacent to the reservation. Since only two SHSND interviews were with Native Americans who lived at Fort Totten, I purposely sought out Dakota narrators. Between 1999 and 2008, I personally conducted twenty-seven interviews with people who grew up on and near the reservation, six of those with Dakota narrators. Over the past three decades, I have conducted an additional seven interviews with members of my extended family.

2. At its founding, it was called the Devils Lake Sioux Indian Reservation. Throughout the essay I refer to the reservation as Spirit Lake, as it was originally called by the Dakota people. However, the lake itself is still called Devils Lake. To make matters more confusing, the town north of the lake is called Devils Lake as well.

3. If the landowner was born in Norway, Sweden, or Denmark, or at least one of his or her parents was born there, I consider that person Scandinavian. With common ancestral background came language, culture, and often, in those first several generations, values about land. For the purposes of this essay and to streamline language, I refer to the first and second generation as simply *Scandinavian* or *Norwegian,* acknowledging their ethnic and cultural identification but not their immigration status. The same guidelines apply to those I classify as *German,* although most of those living on the reservation are second-generation Germans who emigrated from Germany (not Russia, like so many in the state). *Yankee* is a catch-all term to describe those born in the United States whose parents were also born in the United States, so they are at least second-generation U.S. born.

Finally, *Canadian and Other Foreign-born* combines those of differing nationalities who were born outside of the United States. These categories encompass many fewer people, so for analytic purposes I have grouped them together.

The Native Americans who lived on the reservation also had diverse origins. Although Dakotas of several different bands constituted the vast majority, some of the Turtle Mountain Band of Chippewa were allotted land at Spirit Lake and lived on the reservation. Despite historic rivalries, intermarriage over the years has blurred boundaries between tribes, nations, and ethnicities. I use the term *Indian* to refer to all of the Native American landowners on the reservation. Originally, it was land designated for the Dakota people, and because they were the majority of the Native American population, I often use *Dakota* interchangeably with *Indian*. My terminology notes specific (albeit socially constructed) ethnic identities at particular moments in time.

My analysis of land ownership begins with plat maps in 1910 and 1929 where individual landowners were recorded on the one-mile-square sections within a surveyed grid of thirty-six square-mile townships. I used the maps to build a database of property owners in the eighteen townships on which the reservation falls. Over the course of a decade, I searched the U.S. manuscript census and town histories and queried locals about the gender and ethnicity of the landowners. Through this labor-intensive process, I have been able to identify the ethnicity of all but 10 percent of the 1,349 landowners on the reservation in 1929 and the sex for all but 5 percent. Next I used SPSS to generate descriptive statistics of landowners and Geographic Information Systems (GIS) to array the information spatially. For a more in-depth discussion of my strategies for gathering information about the landowners, see Karen V. Hansen and Mignon Duffy, "Mapping the Dispossession: Scandinavian Homesteading at Fort Totten, 1900–1930," *Great Plains Research* 18.1 (2008): 67–80.

4. To what degree this convergence of issues—costs and gains—for other immigrant groups operated on reservations elsewhere is unclear. This is an important area for future research. For a discussion of what some of those payments to the tribe looked like, see Louis Garcia, "Where Is Aspen Island?" in *A Message from Garcia: The History and Culture of the Spirit Lake Dakota* (Tokio, ND: The author, 2000).

5. Louis Garcia, "Who Are the Cut-Heads?" in *A Message from Garcia*. According to Garcia, the Cut-Heads subdivision of the Yanktonai, or Ihanktonwanna, a northern branch of the Nakota, did not sell any of their land to the U.S. government and never received a reservation of their own. They had claimed as their territory all the land from the Red River to the Missouri River in North Dakota. That said, they participated in the treaty that created the Spirit Lake Reservation in 1867. See also Gary Clayton Anderson, *Kinsmen of Another Kind: Dakota-White Relations in the Upper Mississippi Valley, 1650–1862* (St. Paul: Minnesota Historical Society Press, 1997); Garcia, "Where Is Aspen Island?"; Gary Clayton Anderson and Alan R. Woolworth, eds., *Through Dakota Eyes: Narrative Accounts of the Minnesota Indian War of 1862* (St. Paul: Minnesota Historical Society Press, 1988).

6. The fort buildings were transferred to the Bureau of Indian Affairs in January 1891 and became part of the Fort Totten Indian Boarding School. Merlan E. Paaverud, Jr., "Swimming with the Current: Education at the Fort Totten Indian School," in *Fort*

Totten: Military Post and Indian School, 1867–1959, ed. Larry Remele (Bismarck: State Historical Society of North Dakota [hereafter, SHSND], 1986), 46–56.

7. Frederick E. Hoxie, *A Final Promise: The Campaign to Assimilate the Indians, 1880–1920* (Lincoln: University of Nebraska Press, 1984); Francis Paul Prucha, *The Great Father: The United States Government and the American Indians* (Lincoln: University of Nebraska Press, 1984). Francis Paul Prucha, ed., *Americanizing the American Indians: Writings by "Friends of the Indian" 1880–1900* (Cambridge, MA: Harvard University Press, 1973). F. O. Getchell, Annual Report, RG 75/A003/B038/C002//E035, Kansas City Regional Archives, National Archives and Records Administration, Fort Totten, ND, 1902.

8. The Dawes Act specified eighty acres and forty acres for women and children respectively, but new legislation amended the law in 1891.

9. Mari Sandoz, *These Were the Sioux* (New York: Hastings House, 1961), 105. Phillip John Young, interview by author, 2005. On the tension between nomadic and sedentary economies and use of land, see Hugh Brody, *The Other Side of Eden: Hunter-Gatherers, Farmers and the Shaping of the World* (London: Faber and Faber, 2001).

10. Prucha, *The Great Father.* Janet A. McDonnell, *The Dispossession of the American Indian, 1887–1934* (Bloomington: Indiana University Press, 1991).

11. *Land Allotment Act,* 179, 58th Cong., 2d sess. (27 Apr. 1904).

12. Katherine Harris, "Homesteading in Northeastern Colorado, 1873–1920: Sex Roles and Women's Experience," in *The Women's West,* ed. Susan Armitage and Elizabeth Jameson (Norman: University of Oklahoma Press, 1987), 174. Barbara Handy-Marchello, "Women and the Homestead Law: Standing Equal before the Law of the Land," paper, The Lincoln Legacy: The Homestead Act, Bismarck, ND, 2008.

13. Cherry Wood Monson, Betty Loe Westby, Cherrie Lane Anderson, and Stella Rasmusson Payachek, *Warwick Memories* (Warwick, ND: privately published, 2002), 256. "Winners in Ft. Totten Land Lottery," *Sheyenne Star,* 1 Sept. 1904. Eunice Davidson and David C. Davidson, interview by author, 2008.

14. Leasing was not a panacea for the Dakotas or for others who rented their land. However, I do not have space to develop a critical discussion of the practice in this essay. See, for example, McDonnell, *The Dispossession of the American Indian.*

15. Odd S. Lovell, *The Promise of America: A History of the Norwegian-American People* (Minneapolis: University of Minnesota Press, 1984). Elwyn B. Robinson, *History of North Dakota* (Lincoln: University of Nebraska Press, 1966).

16. John C. Hudson, "Migration to an American Frontier," *Annals of the Association of American Geographers* 66.2 (1976): 242–65. Jon Gjerde documents extensively how this worked in a community in Wisconsin: Jon Gjerde, *From Peasants to Farmers: The Migration from Balestrand, Norway to the Upper Middle West* (New York: Cambridge University Press, 1985).

17. Theresse Nelson Lundby, Kristie Nelson-Neuhaus, and Ann Nordland Wallace, eds., *Live Well: The Letters of Sigrid Gjeldaker Lillehaugen* (Minneapolis, MN: Western Home Books, 2004), 74. Hudson, "Migration to an American Frontier."

18. Robinson, *History of North Dakota;* William C. Sherman and Playford V. Thorson, eds., *Plains Folk: North Dakota's Ethnic History* (Fargo: North Dakota Institute for Regional Studies [hereafter, NDIRS], 1988).

19. Getchell, Annual Report, 1902. The Bureau of Indian Affairs enumerated American Indians, but not European Americans, within reservation boundaries. The U.S. Census Bureau collected data and distilled it by county, not by other administrative districts.

20. William C. Sherman, *Prairie Mosaic: An Ethnic Atlas of Rural North Dakota* (Fargo: NDIRS, 1983); Carlton C. Qualey, *Norwegian Settlement in the United States* (New York: Arno Press and the New York Times, 1970).

21. John C. Hudson, *Plains Country Towns* (Minneapolis: University of Minnesota Press, 1985). Monson, et al., *Warwick Memories.*

22. Glen Allen Mumey, "The Parity Ratio and Agricultural Out-Migration," *Southern Economic Journal* 26.1 (1959): 63–65. The U.S. Department of Agriculture assessed the farm out-migration rates in the 1920s as between 1.4 and 2.9 percent. These are well below the figures for the 1940s and 1950s, which reach as high as 7.8 percent in 1952. Mumey clarifies that the measure of farm out-migration "excludes persons who continue to live on farms while working elsewhere" (64). As I have noted, farming does not preclude work for wages: Karen V. Hansen, *Encounter on the Great Plains: Nordic Newcomers and Dakota Survival, 1900–1930* (Oxford University Press, forthcoming 2012). See also Hudson, "Migration to an American Frontier." Karel Denis Bicha, "The Plains Farmer and the Prairie Province Frontier, 1897–1914," *Journal of Economic History* 25.2 (1965): 263–70. Lundby, Nelson-Neuhaus, and Wallace, eds., *Live Well*, 74–75. *Land Allotment Act.*

23. Barbara Handy-Marchello, *Women of the Northern Plains: Gender and Settlement on the Homestead Frontier, 1870–1930* (St. Paul: Minnesota Historical Society Press, 2005), 26. Sherman, *Prairie Mosaic;* Stanley Lieberson and Mary C. Waters, "Ethnic Groups in the Flux: The Changing Ethnic Responses of American Whites," *Annals of the American Academy of Political and Social Science* 487: Immigration and American Public Policy (1986): 79–91. John C. Hudson's study of the Historical Data Project found high rates of local residence by "pioneer offspring." He finds that 50.4 percent of Norwegians' adult children lived in the same county as their parents, and another 10.1 percent lived in another North Dakota County (58). Only Germans from Russia had a higher rate of intergenerational geographic stability. John C. Hudson, "The Study of Western Frontier Populations," in *The American West: New Perspectives, New Dimensions,* ed. Jerome O. Steffen (Norman: University of Oklahoma Press, 1979), 35–60.

24. Handy-Marchello, *Women of the Northern Plains,* 26.

25. Hansen, *Encounter on the Great Plains.*

26. Two important studies occasionally refer to the land women own but do not analyze the gendered variation on land ownership among Native women. Emily Greenwald, *Reconfiguring the Reservation: The Nez Perces, Jicarilla Apaches, and the Dawes Act* (Albuquerque: University of New Mexico Press, 2002); Melissa L. Meyer, *The White Earth Tragedy: Ethnicity and Dispossession at a Minnesota Anishinaabe Reservation* (Lincoln: University of Nebraska Press, 1994).

H. Elaine Lindgren, "Ethnic Women Homesteading on the Plains of North Dakota," *Great Plains Quarterly* 9.3 (1989): 157–73. In her study of nine counties, Elaine Lindgren found that women claimed an average of 12 percent of homesteads. H. Elaine Lindgren, *Land in Her Own Name: Women as Homesteaders in North Dakota* (Fargo: NDIRS, 1991), 53. The percentages ranged between 6 and 20 percent. In five of the townships in those counties she studied, women filed claims for 30 to 32 percent of the homesteads. Only two townships out of the three hundred she studied lacked women filing. Lindgren argues that homesteading varied little by ethnicity but rather by chronology. There were more women homesteading later, especially after 1900. None of the counties she studied included reservation land, so none included Native Americans. Although women of all ethnic groups homesteaded, Lindgren found that Anglo-Americans claimed the most homesteads in the settlement period following 1900; Norwegians did so only "moderately." Howard A. Turner, "The Ownership of Tenant Farms in the North Central States," ed. U.S. Department of Agriculture (Washington, DC: Government Printing Office, 1926), 26.

27. Turner, "The Ownership of Tenant Farms," 26. In comparing regions, the study surveyed ten counties in southeastern North Dakota and one adjacent county in South Dakota. The 1920 study of rented farms revealed that on average men owned more land than women: 374.6 acres compared to 232 acres. In their general study of land ownership in the United States, Anne B. W. Effland, Denise M. Rogers, and Valerie Grim found that in 1946 men owned about one-third more acreage than women; women's parcels were consistently smaller: "Women as Agricultural Landowners: What Do We Know About Them?" *Agricultural History* 67.2 (1993): 235–61. F. O. Getchell, Annual Report, RG 75/A003/B038/C002//E035, Kansas City Regional Archives, National Archives and Records Administration, Fort Totten, ND, 1903.

28. Davidson and Davidson, Interview.

29. Bureau of Indian Affairs, Land Sale Card, Records of the Fort Totten Indian Agency, RG 75/A003/B038/C002//E035, National Archives and Record Administration, Regional Archives, Kansas City, MO, 1913–25. Bjorne Knudson, interview by author, 1999.

30. Berthe Haugen, "Homestead Entry, Final Proof," Department of Interior, Devils Lake, ND, 1912. Gust Berg and Annie Berg, interview (Bismarck: SHSND, 1976), 55A. The 1929 plat map shows that Ida Olson, aunt to Lois Olson Jones, owned land near the Bergs. A 1946 national study documented that "the vast majority (85%) of female landowners lease out their land": Effland, Rogers, and Grim, "Women as Agricultural Landowners." Women were more likely than men to own the land but not operate the farm. Furthermore, women were "more dependent on income from agriculture, specifically land rentals, than men landowners" (250).

31. Erling N. Sannes, "'Free Land for All': A Young Norwegian Woman Homesteads in North Dakota," *North Dakota History* 60.2 (1993): 24–28.

32. Sannes, "'Free Land for All.'"

33. Lori Ann Lahlum, "'Everything Was Changed and Looked Strange': Norwegian Women in South Dakota," *South Dakota History* 35.3 (2005): 189–216. Lois Olson Jones, interview by author, 2005.

34. Elizabeth Hampsten, *Read This Only to Yourself: The Private Writings of Midwestern Women, 1880–1910* (Bloomington: Indiana University Press, 1982), 34.

35. Julius Fjeld, interview (Bismarck: SHSND, 1975), 1029A&B. Sannes, "'Free Land for All.'"

36. Mark R. G. Goodale and Per Kåre Sky, "A Comparative Study of Land Tenure,

Property Boundaries, and Dispute Resolution: Case Studies from Bolivia and Norway," *Journal of Rural Studies* 17 (2001): 183–200. Handy-Marchello, *Women of the Northern Plains*, 28. Effland, Rogers, and Grim, "Women as Agricultural Landowners."

37. Mary Neth, *Preserving the Family Farm: Women, Community and the Foundations of Agribusiness in the Midwest, 1900–1940* (Baltimore, MD: Johns Hopkins University Press, 1995). Hudson notes the importance of "well-used information networks specific to ethnic groups which formed a bond between the widely scattered enclaves, and the usefulness of these informal networks in spreading information about economic opportunities when and where they arose": "Migration to an American Frontier." Also see Sonya Salamon, "Sibling Solidarity as an Operating Strategy in Illinois Agriculture," *Rural Sociology* 47.2 (1982): 349–68.

38. Stanley B. Eliason, interview by author, 2005. Jon Gjerde, "Chain Migrations from the West Coast of Norway," in *A Century of European Migrations, 1830–1930,* ed. Rudolph J. Vecoli and Suzanne M. Sinke (Urbana: University of Illinois Press, 1991), 158–81. Barbara Handy-Marchello, "Land, Liquor and the Women of Hatton, North Dakota," in *The Centennial Anthology of North Dakota History,* ed. Janet Daley Lysengen and Ann M. Rathke (Bismarck, ND: SHSND, 1996), 228.

39. Barbara Levorsen, *The Quiet Conquest: A History of the Lives and Times of the First Settlers of Central North Dakota* (Hawley, MN: Hawley Herald, 1974). Lahlum, "'Everything Was Changed.'"

40. Lundby, Nelson-Neuhaus, and Wallace, eds., *Live Well.* Handy-Marchello, *Women of the Northern Plains*, 28. Norman Forde, interview by author, 2006.

41. Grace Lambert, interview (Bismarck: SHSND, 1976), 1101A&B.

42. Jones interview. Davidson and Davidson interview.

43. Handy-Marchello, *Women of the Northern Plains;* Joan M. Jensen, ed., *With These Hands: Women Working on the Land* (Old Westbury, NY: Feminist Press, 1981); Joan M. Jensen, *Calling This Place Home: Women on the Wisconsin Frontier, 1850–1925* (St. Paul: Minnesota Historical Society Press, 2006); Paula M. Nelson, *After the West Was Won: Homesteaders and Town-Builders in Western South Dakota, 1900–1917* (Iowa City: University of Iowa Press, 1986); Neth, *Preserving the Family Farm.*

44. Handy-Marchello, *Women of the Northern Plains*, 4, 5. Also see Deborah Fink, *Agrarian Women: Wives and Mothers in Rural Nebraska, 1880–1940* (Chapel Hill: University of North Carolina Press, 1992); Joan M. Jensen, *Promise to the Land: Essays on Rural Women* (Albuquerque: University of New Mexico Press, 1991); Nancy Grey Osterud, *Bonds of Community: The Lives of Farm Women in Nineteenth-Century New York* (Ithaca, NY: Cornell University Press, 1991).

45. Carrie Young, *Nothing to Do but Stay: My Pioneer Mother* (Iowa City: University of Iowa Press, 1991), 50.

46. Thomas Pearson and Grace Pearson, interview (Bismarck: SHSND, 1976), 685B, 686A&B. Levorsen, *The Quiet Conquest,* 45.

47. Handy-Marchello, *Women of the Northern Plains*, 9, 53. Hampsten, *Read This Only to Yourself.* Glenda Riley, *The Female Frontier: A Comparative View of Women on the Prairie and the Plains* (Lawrence: University of Kansas Press, 1988). Neth, *Preserving the Family Farm.*

48. Patricia C. Albers and Beatrice Medicine, "The Role of Sioux Women in the Production of Ceremonial Objects: The Case of the Star Quilt," in *Hidden Half: Studies of Plains Indian Women,* ed. Patricia C. Albers and Beatrice Medicine (New York: University Press of America, 1983), 123–40. Patricia C. Albers, "Autonomy and Dependency in the Lives of Dakota Women: A Study in Historical Change," *Review of Radical Political Economics* 17.3 (1985): 109–34. Hilde Bjorkhaug and Arild Blekesaune, "Masculinisation or Professionalisation of Norwegian Farm Work: A Gender Neutral Division of Work on Norwegian Family Farms?" *Journal of Comparative Family Studies* 38.3 (2007): 423–34.

49. Bjorkhaug and Blekesaune, "Masculinisation or Professionalisation." Handy-Marchello, "Land, Liquor and the Women of Hatton, North Dakota"; L. DeAne Lagerquist, *In America the Men Milk the Cows: Factors of Gender, Ethnicity, and Religion in the Americanization of Norwegian-American Women* (Brooklyn, NY: Carlson Publishing, 1991).

50. Levorsen, *The Quiet Conquest,* 52, 75.

51. Levorsen, *The Quiet Conquest,* 54.

52. Young, *Nothing to Do but Stay,* 66. Sannes, " 'Free Land for All.' "

53. Lester Skjerven and Amanda Skjerven, interview (Bismarck: SHSND, 1976), 680A&B.

54. Young, *Nothing to Do but Stay,* 66.

55. Johanna Tvedt, interview by Mark Olson, typed summary, NDIRS, Fargo, 1971.

56. Skjerven and Skjerven interview.

57. Handy-Marchello, *Women of the Northern Plains,* 97, 158. Levorsen, *The Quiet Conquest,* 105. Ingrid Semmingsen, *Norway to America: A History of the Migration,* trans. Einar Haugen (Minneapolis: University of Minnesota Press, 1978), 133.

58. For a discussion of these issues, see Albers and Medicine, eds., *The Hidden Half;* Bonnie Thornton Dill, *Across the Boundaries of Race and Class: An Exploration of Work and Family among Black Female Domestic Servants* (New York: Garland, 1994); Jacqueline Jones, *Labor of Love, Labor of Sorrow: Black Women, Work, and the Family from Slavery to the Present* (New York: Basic Books, 1985). Katherine M. Weist, "Beasts of Burden and Menial Slaves: Nineteenth Century Observations of Northern Plains Indian Women," in *The Hidden Half,* ed. Albers and Medicine, 29–52.

59. Esther Kanten Hansen, interview by author, 1995. According to Helene's daughter, Esther Kanten Hansen, the teacher ceased to pick on her after this incident.

60. 1910 Census, "Instructions to Enumerators." Stephen Ruggles, et al., "Integrated Public Use Microdata Series: Version 4.0 [Machine-Readable Database]" (Minneapolis Population Center, 2008). Handy-Marchello, *Women of the Northern Plains,* 49. Levorsen, *The Quiet Conquest,* 89. Carol Russell, *Sigrid: Sigrid Tufte Myhre Ostrom and Her Ancestors and Descendants: The History of an American Pioneer Woman with Roots in Hallingdal and Aurland, Norway* (Annandale, VA: The author, [1995]).

61. Knudson interview.

62. Jones interview.

63. Carole Shammas, Marylynn Salmon, and Michel Dahlin find that in Bucks County, Pennsylvania, in 1890, "couples rarely bought houses together; not even 1 percent did so. Almost all property was in the name of an individual; four out of five times it was a man."

This figure changed dramatically over the twentieth century; in 1980 it was 63.3 percent: *Inheritance in America from Colonial Times to the Present* (New Brunswick, NJ: Rutgers University Press, 1987), 172. Lemuel H. Foster, *The Legal Rights of Women: Adapted for Use in Every State by Means of a Brief Synopsis of the Laws Relating to Property Rights, Dower, Divorce, the Rights of a Widow in the Estate of Her Husband, Etc. Containing Much Other Helpful Advice, Information, and Direction for Women in Every Walk of Life* (Detroit, MI: Women's Publishing Co., 1913), 62, 101. Levorsen, *The Quiet Conquest,* 84.

64. Lundby, Nelson-Neuhaus, and Wallace, eds., *Live Well,* 14–15.

65. Levorsen, *The Quiet Conquest,* 98.

66. Ella M. Halvorson Dolbak, interview (Bismarck: SHSND, 1976), 50A&B. Erland Reed Manning, interview (Bismarck: SHSND, 1975), 317A&B.

67. Sonya Salamon and Ann Mackey Keim, "Land Ownership and Women's Power in a Midwestern Farming Community," *Journal of Marriage and the Family* 41.1 (1979): 109–19; Sonya Salamon and Vicki Lockhart, "Land Ownership and the Position of Elderly in Farm Families," *Human Organization* 39.4 (1980): 324–31. Ingemund Peterson, interview by author, 1999.

68. Patrick Langstaff, interview by author, 1999.

69. Knudson interview.

❖
❖❖

PART III

Constructing Gendered Identities and Meanings

The final section of the book examines the expressive legacies of the Norwegian immigrant women found in their fiction and nonfiction writings. These writings provide a vast body of primary source material for exploring the thoughts, experiences, and imaginative worlds of Norwegian immigrant women. Examining these writings not merely as historical documents of immigration but as cultural artifacts that construct gendered frameworks gives readers a deeper and broader view into this past. Furthermore, they enhance our understanding of the gendered dimensions of migration and settlement as their neglected works posit new and fresh perspectives. Focus on Norwegian American women's novels and on women's life writings bring new dimensions to Norwegian American cultural expression. An examination of these expressive artifacts enables readers to enter the imaginative worlds they created and appreciate the sense of identity they constructed.

Professor of Norwegian language and literature Ingrid K. Urberg discusses the fictional creations of four Norwegian American female novelists. Drawing on folkloric modes central to Norwegian literature and the literary theories of Blanche Gelfant on urban immigrant literature, specifically the concept of the hungry heroine, Urberg illuminates the desire and visions of Norwegian immigrant women represented in the central characters of novels. Starved for knowledge, experience, dignity, and opportunity, these protagonists signify the longings of young Norwegian women immigrating to America in search of their dreams. Urberg suggests that these fictional characters may reflect their creators' lives; they certainly evoke the hopes of many Norwegian women, as seen in Lønnå's study and found in letters of ordinary Norwegian immigrant women. Immigration and cultural historian Betty A. Bergland draws on feminist and cultural theory, along with scholarship on autobiography, to examine the life writings of Norwegian immigrant women. Used mostly by historians as documentary evidence, women's life writings (diaries, letters, memoirs, and collective autobiographies) have been overlooked as cultural artifacts that convey the values, ideas, and self-conceptions of the writers. While the immigrant women avoided full-length autobiography, they recorded their lives extensively in shorter and more fragmentary forms that convey cultural patterns. Bergland argues that the prevailing sense of self in these immigrant women's writings emphasizes a collective identity, a "we" rather than the "I" more commonly found in American autobiographies, and so conveys ethnic retention of collective values.

CHAPTER 8

The "Hungry Heroine" in Norwegian American Fiction

Ingrid K. Urberg

"Jeg maa ud og faa Luft . . ."
"I must leave and get some air . . ."

"Hun længtede ud, ud . . ."
"She longed to get away, away . . ."

Introduction: The Unsung Hungry Heroines

The dissatisfaction and longing revealed in these brief passages are representative of the female protagonists of late nineteenth- and early twentieth-century novels written by Norwegian immigrant women in the United States. These characters—girls and women who are eager to move to America from Norway to pursue educational and career opportunities as well as gender equality—are, using the language of American literary critic Blanche H. Gelfant, hungry heroines.[1]

Gelfant coined the phrase "hungry heroine" to describe a character type frequently found in American urban fiction. These young female protagonists, hungry for knowledge, are often immigrants or children of immigrants who actively seek out knowledge in schools, at work, and in libraries in American cities. Gelfant argues that these urban heroines, who transcend their fears by taking control of their lives and whose own experiences closely mirror those of real women, are often overlooked, while their counterparts, namely those women who are unable to escape their fears and whose passivity results in their succumbing to madness, suicide, or self-starvation, have traditionally received more critical attention. Similarly, in Norwegian American fiction, the young female protagonists who actively seek knowledge, education, and a better life have been neglected. These characters, overlooked in Norwegian American literary scholarship, are worthy of attention, not least to counter literary stereotypes such as the reluctant female immigrant, reinforced by traditional models of literary criticism. An examination of these figures is also important in that it facilitates the development of a methodology to examine a group of women writers who have been largely ignored. This methodology—combining Gelfant's observations about hungry heroines with structural elements found in fairy tales such as lacks, quests, tests, helpers, opponents, and rewards—may be used to analyze other texts. These fictional heroines reveal much about both real and perceived differences in educational and vocational opportunities for girls and women in Norway and the United States around the turn of the century. Much information about Norwegian American history, cultural attitudes, and gender roles can be gleaned from this literature.[2]

Significantly, hungry heroines, all rebels in various ways, are the rule rather than the exception in novels written by Norwegian immigrant women at the end of the nineteenth century, before the appearance of Gelfant's heroines at the beginning of the twentieth century, and they continued to appear in Norwegian American women's fiction after the turn of the twentieth century. In addition to providing a link between Norwegian-language fiction and English-language fiction produced in America, the hungry heroines reflect the experiences and attitudes of the female immigrants who authored these works. These protagonists and their creators actively search for ways to appease their longings through migration and are successful in their quests.

The Hungry Heroines' Creators

Though the creators of the hungry heroines came from different generations, socio-economic groups, and geographical regions in Norway, all lived for extended periods in the American Midwest in urban settings and found the opportunities and inspiration to write there. Like the protagonists in their novels, the writers Ulrikka Feldtman Bruun, Aileen Berger Evanson, Drude Krog Janson, and Palma Pederson were initially positive about the migration process and viewed America as a place of opportunity. For them, the migration and American experiences created outlets for literary and other passions such as social activism. These four Norwegian American authors wrote novels which start in Norway and in which the female protagonists move from Norway to America, equating America with their freedom. Parallels to the movements and experiences of the protagonists can be found in the lives of the authors: Norway being associated with a lack of educational and career paths for girls and women, and America providing the promise, dream, and, to some extent, realization of greater opportunities. The lives and works of Bruun, Evanson, Janson, and Pederson demonstrate how they drew on personal experiences and observations in describing social realities, including differences in educational opportunities and gender roles for girls and young women in Norway and America. Gelfant writes about "the hungry heroines of real life." In her context, these women are Willa Cather and Edith Wharton, but they are also found in the Norwegian American tradition.[3]

Norwegian American Literature: Origins and Overview

The novels written by Bruun, Evanson, Janson, and Pederson are part of a rich Norwegian American literary tradition. A brief introduction to this literature is needed to meaningfully frame a closer analysis of these authors and their works. This overview notes how traditional Norwegian American literary history and criticism has "privileged the image" of Ole E. Rølvaag's Beret Holm, a reluctant female immigrant. It also notes why this type of literary scholarship silences many women authors, highlighting the value of developing a new model to examine certain Norwegian American novels. The use of this model makes more authors available for serious consideration and gives them a collective voice. Previously overlooked fictional characters, including the hungry heroine, are then available to the reader.[4]

From the earliest days of Norwegian migration to the United States, immigrants produced literature that described their perceptions of social realities both in the old and new countries, providing a bridge between the two. Today these written sources continue to provide valuable insights into the Norwegian, Norwegian American, and American cultures of the nineteenth and early twentieth centuries. The most frequently employed genres in the early years of immigration were letters, guidebooks, and poetry. Immigrant letters, or America letters as they were called, were often widely circulated in the immigrants' home communities, and these fueled the America fever which spread across Norway in the mid- to late-nineteenth century. Social conditions, including differences in gender roles in the old country and the new, were noted in these letters. Guidebooks also outlined conditions in the United States. Though the factual reliability of these sources varies greatly, valuable information about political, religious, and social realities on both sides of the Atlantic can be gleaned from their pages.

While nonfiction and poetry dominated Norwegian immigrant literature through the 1860s, fiction gradually emerged as a vehicle in which immigrants recorded their perceptions of the old and the new. This appearance and eventual flourishing of fiction was due more to social and economic developments within the Norwegian American and broader Scandinavian American communities than to mainstream American literary currents. The establishment of numerous Scandinavian-language newspapers and publishing houses provided a forum where immigrants could read fiction, often serialized, from their home countries, receive inspiration to write, and publish their own works. Influential publishing and literary figures included University of Wisconsin professor Rasmus B. Anderson, editor and publisher of the Norwegian American newspaper *Amerika*. Anderson encouraged members of the Norwegian diaspora to write in order to create an immigrant literary tradition. The presence of such individuals and the success of the press and publishing houses are reflections that Norwegian as well as Danish and Swedish immigrants moved beyond a daily struggle for survival and had the time and resources to consciously cultivate and create immigrant literary cultures. Through plays, short stories, and novels, immigrant writers related their feelings about the country they had left and their hopes and dreams for themselves, their children, and their compatriots in their adopted country. Social realities and differences in both Norway and the United States are highlighted in many of the Norwegian works of fiction, and, indeed, many scholars, including historians and sociologists, argue that one of the most valuable aspects of this body of literature is the picture it provides of the immigrant experience and of life among Norwegian and other Scandinavian Americans: their daily existence, values, perceptions of the new country, and connections to the old. Perhaps the best-known and most extensive study conducted on this premise is Dorothy Skårdal's *The Divided Heart* (1974), and the use of fiction in history continues to gain acceptance. In her essay "The Literature on Women Immigrants to the United States," Dorothea Schneider, a scholar of German immigration and literature, argues that the study of fictional immigrant accounts is vital to obtain a complete and balanced view of the history of women immigrants in the United States.[5]

Norwegian American literature has been studied extensively, and much has been written about its origins, development, and decline, as well as about the lives and works of individual authors who contributed to this tradition. The most recent and comprehensive study of this body of literature is Orm Øverland's *The Western Home: A Literary History of Norwegian America* (1996). While Øverland's book and selected other studies have partially addressed the marginalization of women authors within this tradition by taking a relatively integrated and balanced gender approach to Norwegian American fiction, and while other studies have addressed marginalization head on, there is still work to be done before the voices of many Norwegian American women authors are rediscovered or, in some cases, uncovered for the first time. Norwegian American women writers, along with other female immigrant and ethnic writers who wrote and published in languages other than English (often gaining audiences in these languages) had to deal with a triple marginalization. They were marginalized not only due to their immigrant status but also due to their literary language and their gender. Norwegian immigrant women wrote letters, diaries, memoirs, poetry, short stories, and novels. Though a number of nonfiction works and a few short stories have been translated into English, making them accessible to a wider audience, this is not the case for novels. The first and only Norwegian language novel penned by a woman in the United States to be translated into English was *A Saloonkeeper's Daughter (En saloonkeepers datter)*, by Drude Krog Janson, originally published in 1887 in Copenhagen and reprinted in 1889 in the

United States. The English translation did not appear until 2002 as part of the Longfellow Series of American Languages and Literatures. Critics and scholars frequently dismissed these novels; some continue to dismiss them due to aesthetic concerns. However, if one excludes works with marked aesthetic weaknesses or flaws while looking at Norwegian American literature, focusing on "quality" at the expense of "vision," much of the social and cultural value of these novels is lost. In the case of novels by Norwegian American women, this social and cultural value includes illuminating and exposing the patriarchal structure of Norwegian and Norwegian American society at the end of the nineteenth and early twentieth centuries. This dismissal for aesthetic reasons along with the dearth of novels by Norwegian American women novelists in English account for some of the marginalization that continues to this day. An examination of Norwegian American literary history reveals the extent of this silencing: the literary voices of these women have, in the language of Tillie Olsen, been silenced, in some cases by exclusion, in other cases by segregation, and in other cases by being seen but not heard.[6]

A look at the best-known female protagonist in Norwegian American fiction, Rølvaag's Beret Holm, is a case in point. Rølvaag's trilogy about Per Hansa, Beret Holm, and their family, originally published in Norwegian between 1924 and 1931, is regarded as the artistic high point of Norwegian American literature, and these works have received a great deal of critical attention since their publication. Beret, a reluctant yet strong female immigrant who is unhappy and never feels at home in America, has become the prototypical nineteenth-century Norwegian immigrant woman in both the Norwegian American popular and literary imagination; indeed, other works of Norwegian American fiction and nonfiction contain Beret-like figures. However, it is important to recognize that Beret represents only one type of immigrant experience and attitude, and this is strikingly evident upon an examination of Norwegian-language novels written by Norwegian American women. The majority of these works contain female protagonists who provide a striking contrast to Beret, namely girls and young women who are active and willing participants in the migration process. These characters—eager to immigrate to America to pursue educational and career opportunities as well as gender equality—are hungry heroines.[7]

The Hungry Heroine and the Fictional Folktale Model

Gelfant incorporates the language, and to some extent the structure, of the fairy tale in her examination of the hungry heroines and their quests with references to "happy endings" and "fairy tale transformations." Building on Gelfant's work, this study applies the language of the folktale to the hungry heroines found within Norwegian American women's novels, examining gender issues and

tivity. Among his writings were: "Salmer og Sange for Kirke og Hjem," 1883; "Jesus-Sangene," 1893; "Lys og Frihed: Prædikener," 1892; "Har Ortodoxien Ret?" He published a Unitarian paper, "Saamanden," and several novels dealing with Norwegian-American life. Unitarianism did not make very strong appeals to the Norwegians. Janson himself drifted over to Spiritualism, and the Unitarian congregations he founded have faded away with the exception of one, on Mt. Pisgah, at Hanska, Minnesota, served by Amandus Norman. Janson returned to Norway in 1894. The Norwegian Congregationalists published a hymnal that has been quite extensively used in some of the Norwegian Lutheran churches of Chicago.

b. *Poetry and Fiction*

The oldest piece of poetry written by a Norwegian-American was composed for a Fourth of July celebration on the good ship Ægir in 1837. The poet was Ole Rynning. The poem struck the keynote for two or more generations of sweet singers of Norwegian birth and descent —a love of two countries. It was entitled "Til Norge" (To Norway). The second stanza has been rendered, in free translation, by Theodore C. Blegen as follows:

Wm. Ager

Hans A. Foss

Kr. Prestgard

Wm. M. Pettersen

Jon Norstog

Peer O. Strømme

Poets and Novelists

Image of authors (all men), from Norlie, History of the Norwegian People in America

positioning the hungry heroines as protagonists in the Vladimir Propp–inspired fictional folktale model:

(lack(s) / at childhood home → quest / out into the world → magical opponent + helper → test(s) → reward / establishment of new home).

Though the female protagonists of Norwegian American fiction are both active and urban after their move to the United States, these factors do not lead to undue tension with the fictional folktale model. Not only are active female protagonists part of the folk literature tradition but folk literature has always been a part of urban life. Placing the Norwegian American hungry heroines into the universal and timeless fictional folktale model demonstrates how the authors use their protagonists to examine and challenge social and gender attitudes and structures in Norway and America. Folk literature often contains social criticism, so the use of the folktale model to examine gender attitudes and social criticism in these novels does not lead to undue tension, either.[8]

Using the language of the folktale in this literary analysis is also appropriate when the works are placed within a wider Norwegian American literary context. Many early Norwegian American works of fiction, including Hjalmar H. Boyesen's *Gunnar* (1874) and H. A. Foss's *Husmands-gutten* (*The Cotter's Son*) (1885), are success stories patterned after Bjørnstjerne Bjørnson's peasant tales, in which Bjørnson relies heavily on the structure of fictional folk or fairy tales. The novels in which the hungry heroines are found are not exceptions. As a result, the fictional folktale model, which traces the physical and spiritual journey of the protagonist of a tale and which is helpful when analyzing Bjørnson's tales, is also useful in a study of these works. The typical protagonist is a young woman or man in a threshold situation, experiencing the transition from youth to adulthood, and the following elements are generally present in such tales:

lack(s) → quest → magical opponent + helper → test (s) → reward
(at childhood home) (out into the wider world) (at new home)

While on their journeys, the protagonists, both female and male, are often assertive and highly active. However, this type of female protagonist has often been overlooked in traditional folk literature scholarship. Torborg Lundell, in her study of gender biases in the folklore indexes of Finnish folklorist Antti Aarne and American folklorist Stith Thompson, has pointed out the disparity between the direct and indirect characterization of heroines as being mainly passive and the unmistakably active heroines found in many fictional folktales. Though these indexes register thematic events and character types that reoccur in folk literature, Lundell has noted their misrepresentation and lack of representation of certain characters and themes involving active girls and women. The focus of the indexes is, instead, on female passivity. The fate of being overlooked and neglected has also befallen the active heroines of Norwegian American fiction, who have, until this point, gone largely unrecognized, though not so much due to misrepresentation as to lack of representation.[9]

This study provides an introduction to the hungry heroine in Norwegian American fiction by examining five novels written in Norwegian between 1884 and 1925 and applying the fictional folktale model to the protagonists' journeys to America, with emphasis on Janson's *A Saloonkeeper's Daughter*. It will become clear that a number of these stories contain elements of social criticism, and the journeys of several of these young women, from oppression to rebellion to freedom, serve to indict patriarchal aspects of nineteenth-century Norwegian society and, in some cases, Norwegian American society as well. This type of social criticism was typical of writers of the Modern Breakthrough (1870–90) in Scandinavia, and Janson consciously and openly participated in this movement. The Modern Breakthrough followed Romanticism, and its writers wrote realistic and naturalistic works about societal problems (the position of women, prostitution, poverty, etc.) with the intent of instigating critical dialogue about these issues. Henrik Ibsen (1828–1906), Bjørnstjerne Bjørnson (1832–1910), and Amalie Skram (1846–1905) are three of the best-known Norwegian authors from this period who wrote, among other things, about women's lack of agency. Their realistic and naturalistic works garnered attention and criticism, often negative, upon publication and performance. Though Skram was harshly criticized during her lifetime for her open and frank descriptions of sexuality, prostitution, and marital discord, literary histories chose to focus on her works about poverty in the decades following her death—temporarily silencing those works critical of the position of women in society and marriages—while Ibsen's works about these topics have received continuous attention. Bjørnson's literary influence among Norwegian Americans has already been mentioned, but it is interesting to note how he was moved and influenced by his 1880 visit to the United States, during the height of the Modern Breakthrough. Though aware of the disparity between educational opportunities for women in Norway and the United States before his trip, Bjørnson experienced the positive impact of the extensive educational system firsthand when he attended the "Congress of Women" in Boston, writing in the Norwegian press, "The first two hours I was there, were, I believe, the finest I have experienced; for I sat as if in the future, and had difficulty controlling my emotion. The finest women of America, with a cultural background equal to that of the best men, well-traveled and well-read, several of them with university degrees, as doctors, etc., arose, one after the other, to express their views on the matter at hand with ability, sincerity, and moving conviction."[10]

Author Profiles

Of the four authors highlighted in this chapter, Ulrikka Feldtman Bruun (1854–1941)—novelist, poet, essayist, and temperance worker—appears to have the most in common with hungry heroine characters. A voracious reader and a writer of verse from a young age, she excelled in school growing up in Kristiansund as the youngest of nine children. Frustrated by the lack of educational opportunities for girls and women in Norway, she emigrated to America, apparently by herself, at the age of twenty-one. She spent a year at Kalamazoo College in Michigan before moving to Chicago, where she devoted the rest of her life to combating social ills and improving the quality of life among Scandinavians in America. In addition to opening a small Scandinavian reading room which served as a base for her temperance activities, Bruun established a number of aid organizations in Chicago, edited a Norwegian Danish temperance paper, wrote

Ulrikka Bruun, from Norlie, History of the Norwegian People in America

temperance themed fiction and nonfiction, and traveled extensively throughout the Midwest, lecturing about temperance issues. Bruun married shortly after moving to Chicago. Her novels, pietistic and didactic in tone, have never received more than passing critical attention.[11]

Palma Pederson (b. Anderson) (1879–1950) was the most prolific Norwegian American female novelist to publish in Norwegian and the only one to consider herself a full-time author. Pederson published a collection of poetry as well as three melodramatic novels: *Ragna* (1923), *Under the Lash of Responsibility (Under ansvarets svøbe)* (1924) and *Geniuses (Genier)* (1925). She also left behind a detailed account of her authorship in hundreds of letters written to Rasmus B. Anderson over the span of two decades. Pederson's works led to a polarized debate in the press, drawing in such figures as Rølvaag, and she received "Det Norske Selskab af Amerika's" prize for her first novel. Øverland points out the disparity between her "effusively pretentious poetic persona" and her poor Norwegian writing skills, while acknowledging the contributions she made to

Norwegian American literature by creating strong female characters in a literary culture dominated by men.[12]

A look at Pederson's childhood in Porsgrund, Norway, reveals a strong autobiographical link between Pederson and the character of Gudrun *(Under the Lash of Responsibility, Geniuses)*, one of the hungry heroines to be discussed in this study. Pederson's parents, as Gudrun's, were unable to care for her due to financial and substance abuse problems, so she was sent to a children's home. Like her fictitious character Gudrun, Pederson caught "America fever" while listening to her teacher's stories. This led to her emigrating to Coon Prairie, Wisconsin, to live with her grandmother shortly after she was confirmed. Pederson's dominant interest appeared to be escaping the confines of her class and social situation in Norway rather than pursuing a higher education, but she showed an interest in writing from a young age. Pederson eventually moved to La Crosse, Wisconsin, to work as a maid and then married her employer after his wife died. Despite caring for three children, Pederson managed to write poetry, but after the death of her husband in 1920, she chose to remain single and devote more time to writing.[13]

Drude Krog Janson (1846–1934) was, and remains, the best known of this group of authors. Though she was at a different life stage than Bruun, Evanson, and Pederson when she immigrated to Minnesota, she was still keenly interested in the opportunities women were afforded in the United States. She was in her thirties and brought her six children with her when she moved to Minneapolis in 1882. She joined her husband Kristofer Janson, who had emigrated the year before, with his wife's encouragement, to serve as a Unitarian minister among Norwegians. Her correspondence, essays in the Norwegian feminist journal *Nylænde* and in the Norwegian American journal *Saamanden,* and her first novel, *A Saloonkeeper's Daughter,* reveal her awareness of the American women's rights movement; she was involved in this movement as well as other social causes while in the United States. Janson remigrated to Norway in 1893. She was the only Norwegian American women novelist who published in Norway and who appears to have kept in close touch with Norwegian literary and cultural figures and trends, including her close friend Bjørnstjerne Bjørnson, during her years in the United States. This reflects both her privileged background (Janson was the daughter of a minister and member of parliament and she was privately tutored at home, as was common for the upper class) and the contacts she made in her life with her husband, who was poet and writer with a theological degree. Janson was often dismayed by what she viewed as the cultural backwardness and closed-mindedness of the Norwegian Americans, including their views on gender, and she and Kristofer blamed the Norwegian Lutheran clergy for encouraging such attitudes. This view is reflected at the end of Janson's *A Saloonkeeper's Daughter* when Astrid, the protagonist, finds her place not among the Norwegian American Lutherans but among American Unitarians.[14]

Drude Krog Janson and family, ca. 1890

In contrast to Bruun, Evanson, and Pederson, Janson does not appear to have been particularly concerned with her relationship with the Norwegian American literary establishment, finding publishers for her works in Scandinavia where she had contacts and connections. Unlike Evanson and Pederson, Janson did not write about creating or being part of an immigrant writing tradition. In addition, she was the only writer in this group to remigrate, moving back to Europe in 1893 after her marriage ended. Truthfully depicting social attitudes and circumstances among the Norwegian Americans, rather than creating or contributing to a literary tradition among this group, was clearly foremost in Janson's mind. This was probably due to the relatively early date of her first novel and her inability and unwillingness to identify with most Norwegian Americans and their culture. Though Janson's *A Saloonkeeper's Daughter* received mixed reviews (one Norwegian reviewer reacted negatively to her feminist message), the work was quite popular with the Norwegian American public as evidenced by the four editions by 1894.[15]

The correspondence of Janson, Pederson, and other Norwegian American writers not covered in this chapter reveals that societal gender roles and attitudes had an effect on their productivity as writers. Pederson, however, was the only one to state that she was blatantly discriminated against due to gender role expectations of the time. Not only did she believe being a woman made it difficult to get her work acknowledged and published, she felt that at times it colored the criticism she received. Pederson also alluded to widespread discrimination against Norwegian American female writers, stating that the Norwegian press used "the language issue" as an excuse not to print the works of Norwegian American authors, particularly those of women. It is important to note that Pederson was prone to making statements which she was unable to back up and often had conspiracy theories. However, the forms of discrimination which she described can be subtle and may be difficult or impossible to substantiate, and it is important to register her perceptions. Other female writers, including Helen Egilsrud, had similar experiences with and distrust of the male-controlled Norwegian American literary establishment, recognizing the potential for abuse of power and silencing by this body.[16]

Aileen Berger Evanson, who was named Aaslaug Berger when she emigrated from Norway to attend the University of Minnesota in 1921, is yet another author whose motivation to travel to America links her to the hungry heroine she created. Evanson was active in a Chicago theatrical company called "The Norwegian Players" in the 1930s, and a series of letters she wrote to the historian Theodore C. Blegen concerning her plays and productions, as well as his responses, have been preserved in the Norwegian-American Historical Association Archives in Northfield, Minnesota. These letters reveal that Evanson found the Norwegian American audience to be unsupportive, and she was most frustrated by Norwegian Americans' lack of a sense of humor and their unwillingness to accept a portrayal of Norwegians as being less than heroic. Though she contemplated giving in to this pressure, Blegen advised her not to compromise her artistic sensibilities. In this same letter, Evanson commented on another obstacle facing twentieth-century Norwegian American authors, namely the difficulties associated with the linguistic transition that was taking place among Americans of Norwegian descent. The fact that her novel *Family in America: A Chicago Story* (*Slekt i Amerika: Chicago fortælling*) does not appear to have been reviewed in the Norwegian American press is apparently linked, at least in part, to its being published in the mid- to late 1930s, at a time when Norwegian was being used less and less by Norwegian Americans.[17]

This brief look at the lives and literary careers of Bruun, Evanson, Janson, and Pederson reveals that, though they represented several generations and came from different socioeconomic and educational backgrounds, they all saw America as a place where girls and women had economic, educational, and social opportunities not available in Norway. However, most of these authors expressed frustration with the slow progress and narrow-mindedness of various elements of the Norwegian American population, not least the clergy and literary establishment, which made it difficult for these possibilities to be realized. Though these Norwegian American women authors produced novels which vary dramatically in aesthetic and literary quality and tone—some characterized by pietism, others by melodrama and social realism—all contain a vision of America as a land of gender opportunity. The possibility of realizing these opportunities is embodied in the hungry heroine, a character type also found in other works of American fiction. During the analysis of the novels it is important to keep in mind that the authors who construct these characters challenge patriarchy as they draw on their own experiences.

Hunger for Knowledge and Resistant Father Figures

As the name implies, one striking similarity of the hungry heroines is their hunger or, in the language of the model, lack. Hunger is used both literally and metaphorically to denote a void that is generally recognized by the person experiencing it. In other words, hunger implies discontent and desire, and these girls and young women are, without fail, discontented with the limited educational, vocational, and social possibilities in Norway that exist for individuals of their gender and/or class, and they long for greater opportunity. Most pervasive is their hunger for knowledge and education—from a young age they enjoy school, devour the books and reading materials to which they have access, and hope to continue their studies or establish careers. However, due to gender expectations and familial pressures and considerations, most are forced to stop their formal education or give up their career plans in Norway, but not before their appetites have been whetted and dreams of accomplishing great things have been awakened. This leads to increasing discontent and feelings of frustration and longing, for now they have a sense of the wider world and suspect what they are missing by remaining at home. The sense of potential loss is reinforced by what their mothers tell them of their own lives, of missed opportunities and waylaid careers.

Astrid Holm, the protagonist of Janson's *A Saloonkeeper's Daughter*, the best-known Norwegian-language novel written by a woman in the United States and the only one to be published in both Norway and the United States in its day, is an avid reader with big dreams for the future. Early in life, Astrid displays and gives free rein to a vivid imagination and creativity while exploring the contents of an old attic chest belonging to her mother. She wants to become an actress and devours the plays she chances upon. However, her mother, who gave up an acting career when she married, forbids Astrid to follow this path unless her merchant father gives his consent. This does not diminish Astrid's career aspirations. Her reaction when hearing her father's plans to emigrate to America from their home in Kristiania (Oslo) is to tell him of her goals. Though her father makes it clear that acting is forbidden, Astrid believes she will have greater freedom to choose in America. The protagonist's father serves as an obstacle to his daughter's intellectual and personal development. He is both unable and unwilling to provide either money or support for his daughter's further education, so Astrid's discontent at home creates a longing for the possibility of something better, a longing for a more complete life.

Perhaps this hunger is felt most strongly and expressed most demonstratively by Ragna Aastad, the assertive protagonist of Ulrikka Feldtman Bruun's *The Enemy's Pitfalls (Fjendens faldgruber)* (1884). Ragna's goal is to become an independent woman, and she dreams of making something great of herself. From a young age, Ragna is caught up in the world of books and has a burning desire to attend school beyond the compulsory level, but her father, a respected farmer, is adamantly opposed to this plan. Both Ragna's hunger and her recognition of the need to get away from her father and Norway to appease this hunger are clear in numerous passages. For example, as a girl in Norway, "She [Ragna] felt so dejected, that she was discontent with herself and the entire world. Thoughts of leaving and making something of herself constantly occupied her—so much so that she could not rest." Later, "If I could just go to school, then I could make something of myself, she often complained, and she was right. Think of being able to read as much as one desires." Finally, shortly after her move to America, Ragna reflects, "My father can give me bread—but that is all he can give me. He has never attempted to satisfy my intellectual hunger, or my thirst for knowledge." Ragna's dominant interest is clearly education, and she is aware of its transformative possibilities. Like Gelfant's heroines, she yearns to be transformed.[18]

Though Ragna's father is adamantly opposed to her plans and desire for change, her mother Sigrid lends an empathetic and understanding ear. Sigrid Aastad tries to console her daughter by telling her she was also hungry and longed for knowledge in her youth, but with time this longing disappeared. Though she admits it is unfortunate to suppress one's good qualities, Sigrid points out that people would starve to death if everyone became educated and no one was left to work. This argument does not convince Ragna, who refuses to resign herself to a similar fate. The restrictions imposed on her by family and society do not stifle Ragna's dreams but rather instill in her a longing to leave, and she is caught up in the America fever sweeping her rural home district.

Both Kate Crosby, in Aileen Berger Evanson's *Family in America* (undated), and Gudrun Skjoldhammer, in Pederson's *Under the Lash of Responsibility* (1923) and *Geniuses* (1925), are from the twentieth century. Kate's longing to study is just as intense as that of her older "sisters," and though she theoretically has greater educational opportunities in Norway than they had, she is unable to muster the courage to ask her stepfather, a lawyer, to let her study at the university in her hometown of Oslo. The father figure, once again, stands in the way of opportunity. Kate confides in a friend that her burning desire to travel to the United States is motivated by two factors. In addition to her wish to visit the country of her birth and reconnect with her American grandmother, Kate also hopes that this grandmother will allow her to study.

In *Under the Lash of Responsibility*, Gudrun first becomes aware of her *læse-tørst* and *kundskabstørst* (her thirst for reading and knowledge) when, as a girl of eleven, she is removed from the custody of her alcoholic parents and placed in a children's home in Telemark. Gudrun reads an illustrated edition of *Pilgrim's Progress* and then devours every book she can find: "When the grown ups took her lamp away at night, she read by the light of matches until her eyes watered. Sometimes she read by the light of the moon until she fell asleep with the book in her hand." Gudrun's longing to leave Norway is tied not merely to her thirst for knowledge but to other societal restrictions and attitudes as well. Gudrun has been branded as the daughter of alcoholics, and she realizes no matter what she accomplishes in the future, she will never be judged on her own merits. Gudrun does not resent her father as much as she does the patriarchal society, not least the church and the ministers who foster these restrictive and judgmental attitudes.[19]

Gelfant points out how physical movement, to the city from a town or countryside or even a few blocks within a city, is part of the hungry heroine's development and eventual transformation. In the works under consideration here, the protagonists' intense feelings of longing are awakened not only by education and the exercise of the mind but at times by geographical movement within Norway and later by relocation to America. A striking example is found in Janson's *A Saloonkeeper's Daughter*. When Astrid is seventeen, she accompanies her father on a business trip from Kristiania to Bergen. As they travel through the countryside and the fjord district, her senses are awakened and she sees herself as a princess in a magical forest. The trip becomes a revelatory experience when she realizes how different she is from her father. Astrid begins to understand who she is, and, while sitting in the theater in Bergen, she recognizes a call to become an actress: "now she understood what the minister had meant, when he spoke about the job of following one's inner calling." In her contribution to *Women's Writing in Exile,* Susan Standford Friedman notes that "the voyage over geographic space is an extended metaphor for the process of one person's coming to know who she is." For Astrid and other hungry heroines, the process of self-realization begins in Norway with travel or relocation, and the process accelerates in America.[20]

Alienation and Lack of Acceptance

The protagonists, without fail, are also discontented in Norway because they feel out of place. Their feelings of alienation are rooted in a variety of circumstances, ranging from societal and economic pressures to familial situations. The patriarchal system in place in nineteenth-century Norway, a system often embodied in the father figure, instills in these young women deeply ingrained feelings of marginalization because they act, feel, and think in ways that do not fit into society's narrow definition of acceptable female behavior and strictly defined roles. They are made to feel, or are explicitly told, that they are outsiders and abnormal, and these feelings are directly or indirectly responsible for their leaving home. While the oppressive patriarchal system leads to rebellion, this effect is unintended by the father figure. Once again the parallel to Gelfant's heroines is clear: "While critics may have overlooked the hungry heroine, other characters find her subversive . . . All see her potential for subversiveness. She refuses to stay where she 'belongs,' and by leaving home and abandoning men, she destabilizes the family." Heroes in folk tales often leave home and destabilize family as well.[21]

In *A Saloonkeeper's Daughter* Astrid Holm is made to feel different and alienated by society and her familial situation. Astrid, who had a lonely childhood due to her mother's ill health, feels increasingly lonely and helpless after her mother's death, and she is shunned by her girlfriends after her father declares bankruptcy. Astrid is not interested in domestic duties and, while her aunt's friends spend their time talking about household chores, not only is bored but realizes how unlike these women she is. Astrid's aunt patiently lectures her, telling her she will never amount to anything if she does not apply herself to learning, but she fails to acknowledge the fact that Astrid is teaching herself English. The strictly defined gender roles cause Astrid to feel that she is destined to be a failure in this system: "Astrid was so tired of these talks. They made her feel hopeless and incompetent, and she felt as if her life was like that of a slave." Astrid's father tells her to be content and sensible when he sees in his daughter too much of his independent wife, whose spirit he broke, and Astrid cannot help but wonder if her father would have treated a son in the same way: "Did he have any idea how cruelly he was treating her?—How he callously trampled on all her dreams and hopes. And wasn't it because she was a woman that he dared to treat her in such a way? Would he have dared to treat her in such a way if she had been a man? What right did they have to bind her and destroy her because she wasn't a man?" Though Astrid is filled with questions, it appears her father and the society he represents will not provide her with the answers and opportunities she craves.[22]

These feelings of being different are strong for Ragna Aastad in *The Enemy's Pitfalls*. Much to the dismay of her parents, she is uninterested in traditional women's roles and duties such as washing, cooking, sewing, and marriage, and she spends, in their opinion, an inordinate amount of time reading. However, while Ragna's mother is concerned that her eighteen-year-old daughter, who can neither weave nor spin properly, is unsuited for anything but reading and writing, she is sympathetic to Ragna's plight. Ragna's father, on the other hand, is more callous. He reprimands her for not being content, like other people, and he tells her she is crazy and will never amount to anything: "You

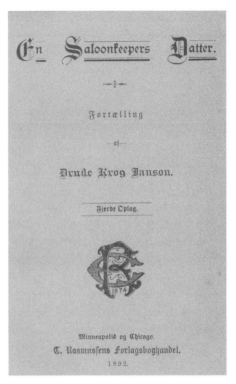

A Saloonkeeper's Daughter *title page*

have read far too much. If you didn't have all of these damned books, you would work and be satisfied like everyone else, but now you are disturbed and you are not good for anything." Such sentiments, representative of society as a whole, certainly play a role in Ragna's realization that she doesn't have much in common with others, and she often gives voice to her status as an outsider. For example, on the way to America, she tells a traveling companion that she is far different from other people, restless and strange, which is not surprising since this is what she has been told throughout her young life. Though Ragna feels innately different from others, one must ask to what extent a patriarchal society has instilled these feelings in her.[23]

Bruun's discussion of Ragna and her desire for freedom is similar to that of Janson's discussion of Astrid Holm in *A Saloonkeeper's Daughter* a few years later. This use of freedom is earlier than in the works cited by Gelfant, and it appears that Bruun and Janson were cutting-edge voices of their day. Indeed, the outlooks and choices of a number of protagonists in the novels being considered here would have been viewed as highly controversial or even subversive.

Gudrun's status as outsider is related to her parents' alcoholism and the failure of society, particularly the civil servants, to deal with this problem in a com-
passionate, non-hypocritical fashion. In *Under the Lash of Responsibility,* Gudrun
becomes increasingly angry and distraught over the destructive gossip spread
about her family as she reaches adolescence, and when her friends abandon her
after a particularly ugly rumor circulates, Gudrun decides to emigrate.

Mothers as Helpers and Transformative Travel

At times the lack of opportunities and lack of acceptance in Norway are so
oppressive that a heroine feels as if she is being imprisoned or suffocated. Astrid
Holm *(A Saloonkeeper's Daughter)* likens her condition in Norway to that of a
bird in a cage, while Ragna Aastad *(The Enemy's Pitfalls)* feels as if she is being
strangled and says she must leave to get some air. The lack in these cases is more
than mere discontent: it is a life-threatening force. Both Astrid and Ragna have
mothers who were forced to give up their dreams and careers and smother their
own longings, which may account for the strong reactions of their daughters.
These young women realize if they submit to authority rather than rebel, they will
end up broken and repressed like their mothers. While the mother figures function as helpers without being aware of their role, the father figures, who initially
appear to function as opponents, also inadvertently aid their daughters in the
process of liberation. Three of the protagonists are motherless by the end of the
novels, but the memories of their mothers inspire them to achieve their goals.
The mothers resemble those described by Gelfant—helpers who are "lurking in
the background" and who want their daughters to have a better life.[24]

These examples demonstrate that rather than succumbing to familial and
societal limitations, the heroines challenge these forces and attempt to escape
them. Their longing is not passive but accompanied by action. As mentioned
earlier, the young women are voracious readers who take advantage of the limited educational opportunities available to them in Norway. On discovering
that this only increases their appetite and longing, they either initiate a move to
America or agree to a move initiated by a family member. They are not reluctant
immigrants.

A striking example is found in Janson's *A Saloonkeeper's Daughter.* During the
year in which her father is in America preparing to send for his family, Astrid
becomes increasingly positive about the move, equating America with a fulfillment of dreams. She is hopeful her father will be more understanding of her in
this new setting, and her bitterness toward him is temporarily forgotten: "She
could no longer stand it in Norway. Gradually, all her dreams were focused on
America, for she was so young and vibrant with hope and zest for life that she
had to dream. In America she would begin to live again, and she dreamed of

endless sun-lit plains where people were happy, where all could follow a call, and where no one treated others harshly because of prejudice." Astrid's reaction to being on the ship on her journey to America is one of relief, for here she is free from the stifling restrictions at home: "How refreshing it was out at sea, and how wonderful it was to breathe here!"[25]

In *Under the Lash of Responsibility,* Gudrun writes to an aunt who lives in the Midwest and asks her to send a ticket. The following description of Gudrun as her ship leaves port in Telemark reveals her eagerness to leave Norway and her optimism for the future: "The desire to travel was in her blood, her courage swelled up and she looked at the future with increased optimism. Somewhere out there, something was waiting for her, something that was for her alone to carry out in the world. She would build a city on burned ruins." Gudrun's hopes for the future are unmistakable.[26]

Ragna from *The Enemy's Pitfalls* begs her parents to allow her to travel to America because America fever burns in her veins. At one point, she tells her mother, "Let me travel to America where there is freedom and equality, and where a poor, dejected woman has the opportunity to show the world that she is suited for more than washing and cooking." Kate from *Family in America* also experiences this unrelenting yearning, and when her stepfather proposes that she spend more time in Chicago with her American grandmother, she realizes this could be a potential turning point in her life: "And suddenly a burning desire to travel overwhelmed Kate. It was inevitable—something for which she had unknowingly been waiting. Wanderlust welled up inside her and the fairy tale out there enticed and beckoned her." Clearly Astrid, Kate, and their like-minded sisters hope to find not only the opportunities denied them in Norway but also adventure and a break from their everyday routines. America calls, beckons, and entices them, and their sense of adventure, as reflected in use of fairy tale images, is strong.[27]

America: A Land of Opportunity, Challenges, and Rewards

Though their expectations differ, the hungry heroines share the hope that displacement will bring with it opportunity, and in the end they give America a chance. This hope is realized, for the American experience satiates their cravings and rebellion leads to freedom. Though, in the beginning, the protagonists experience disappointment and difficulties, America ultimately provides education, opportunities, jobs of which they had only dreamed in Norway, a sense of place, and, most importantly, a relief from alienation and isolation. All of them find a person or community offering acceptance, and with these persons or communities they establish connections.[28]

Astrid Holm, for example, after two unhappy relationships with Norwegian

American men in *A Saloonkeeper's Daughter,* forms a pact for life with a woman doctor who has been shunned by the Minneapolis Norwegian American community, which finds her to be too radical, and Astrid chooses to become a Unitarian minister. Astrid's creator, Janson, was herself a Unitarian and married to a Unitarian minister, and Janson appears to have drawn on their own tension-filled relationship with the mainstream Norwegian American community in Minneapolis in painting Astrid's situation. Ragna Aastad in *The Enemy's Pitfalls* ends up marrying, which she had vowed never to do, and decides not to continue her medical studies. She finds great fulfillment in motherhood, referring to it as her highest calling, but as the novel draws to a close she tells her recently immigrated mother with satisfaction that she has a marriage in which she does not cook or sew and one in which she and her husband solve problems together. Kate Crosby divorces her first husband, a self-satisfied, working-class Norwegian American from Chicago who expects her to be content with the role of a traditional wife. She decides to remarry at the end of *Family in America* with the intention of living in a free and independent relationship. Social reform is to be the center of her life, not traditional familial responsibilities. Gudrun continues to pursue her writing career in La Crosse, Wisconsin, after her marriage, and her call as a writer is the most important thing in her life. Her artistic breakthrough comes shortly after the death of her husband, and the reader of *Under the Lash of Responsibility* is led to believe that despite numerous marriage proposals, Gudrun chooses to remain single and devote herself to her writing. None of the heroines end up in a marriage which leads to the loss of self or identity.

These rewards do not come easily, however. The protagonists experience increased feelings of isolation and alienation upon arrival in America. They struggle to adjust to their new homes, and some become so discouraged that they are tempted to give up their quest for a better life or even life itself. In *A Saloonkeeper's Daughter* Astrid, upon arriving in Minneapolis, is shocked to discover that her father runs a saloon. Her hopes for increased opportunities and a chance to follow her calling are dashed, and, "unable to fulfill her dream and become an actor, which would allow her to govern both the space and the gaze of others, Astrid turns into an observer, subjugated by the new space." Astrid's sense of alienation becomes so intense that she deteriorates physically and emotionally, worries about her mental health, and contemplates suicide. During the day she sits in her room, avoiding the sun and people, but at night she walks the streets: "She crept around abandoned and lonely. There was not one person in the entire teeming city who knew her or who could help her in her distress." Astrid's loneliness is palpable.[29]

Likewise, Kate, who is ostracized from her American relatives after marrying a poor working-class man in *Family in America,* becomes apathetic upon realizing she is pregnant. She experiences physical and mental turmoil, becomes deathly ill, and loses her unborn child. Even Ragna, sitting in her lonely attic room in the months after immigrating to America, awakens to the cold, grey reality in *The Enemy's Pitfalls* that one must work or starve in America, and she compares herself to a lonely bird in the forest.

Total alienation, a result of leaving the childhood home and a failure to establish new ties, leads to temporary passivity and despair in these cases, while a lesser degree of alienation proves to be positive and leads to constructive activity. Total alienation is akin to severe starvation, with its lack of both the desire and ability to eat. Neither Kate nor Astrid displays her characteristic penchant for books, learning, and creativity during these low periods. Astrid sits in a rocking chair with a book, but it remains unopened, for she

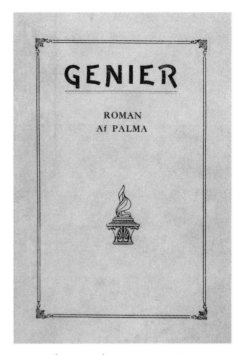

Genier (Geniuses) by Palma Pederson

cannot collect her thoughts. It is as if her hunger has disappeared. While a certain amount of alienation is motivating, too much is paralyzing.

It is useful to note that the sense of alienation is most vivid in the works of Janson and Bruun, both intensely interested in women's rights and social issues. Though Janson and her husband Kristofer participated in social, cultural, and literary activities while in Minneapolis, they were looked at with distrust by many mainstream Lutherans due to their liberal religious and social views, and they were often treated as outsiders. It appears that just as hunger and isolation were necessary for their literary protagonists to realize their full potential, so a certain degree of alienation aided these writers in their creative processes.[30]

Astrid, Kate, and their counterparts regain their appetites for learning and life and emerge from these crises as stronger individuals because they are able to muster the strength and will to cut ties to persons and things that are detrimental to their development and establish new, constructive bonds. Indeed, the key to their success and survival is their ability to take control of their own lives. The result is an awakening—a new direction in life and a tremendous sense of empowerment, though this only comes after tests and dangerous enticements have been overcome.

The most interesting example of this enticement and awakening theme is found in *A Saloonkeeper's Daughter*. Astrid, who is disgusted by the superficiality, pretentiousness, and drunkenness that characterize the Norwegian American community in Minneapolis, is drawn into this society after being engaged to Mr. Smith. Fancy dinners, champagne, and boat trips on Lake Minnetonka become routine, but Astrid feels as if she has sold herself, like thousands of other women, and the idea of marrying for money and appearances rather than for love repulses her. She recalls a line from Ibsen's play *The Feast at Solhaug (Gildet på Solhaug)* (1856), spoken by Margit, a despairing young woman in an unhappy marriage. Margit has just sung a ballad-like verse about a woman taken into the mountain by a troll that, she realizes, reflects her own situation of being enticed and bought: "Red-gold ring, surrounding my life, With gold did the Mountain King secure his wife." Janson's insertion of this literary reference reveals how intimately familiar her audience was not only with Ibsen, but also with the oral-formulaic tradition. This underscores the ability of readers to view Astrid and the other female protagonists as heroines in the fictional folktale framework.[31]

Only after meeting and getting advice from her hero Bjørnson, then on a speaking tour of the Midwest, is Astrid able to break her engagement to Smith as well as ties to her father and the Norwegian American community. The scene in which she takes leave of her father and younger brother is reminiscent of Nora's leaving in Ibsen's *A Doll House (Et dukkehjem)* (1879). Astrid accuses her father of killing her mother, who, unable to follow her calling, died from spiritual hunger and thirst, and Astrid tells him defiantly that he will not succeed in doing the same to her, for she will fight for her life. In her parting words to her father she remembers her suffering mother: "I am no longer your daughter—all the evil in me comes from you—I have at times believed that you were my evil angel." Astrid breaks free and leaves to start a new life with Helene. Her talk with Bjørnson has helped her gain the strength to choose her own destiny. Though Bjørnson functions as an important helper and catalyst, and Astrid's encounter with him is a revelatory and transformative experience, Astrid is "the agent of her own salvation."[32]

Kate *(Family in America)* is representative of those heroines who are enticed by a darker aspect of American society, namely materialism. Money rules the Crosby family, and Kate, who initially despises the role money and possessions play in the life of her American relatives, begins to wonder if they might have their priorities straight. Eventually Kate, like Astrid, is able to break free, both from her unsatisfactory marriage with her first husband and from the philosophy that enslaves her family, to lead a life of freedom in learning, study, and social reform.

The protagonists also encounter dangers and enticements of a more tangible nature, but by using their own powers, mental and physical, they escape from these situations. Three of the young women are targets of unwanted sexual advances, and all of them use their wits and fists to escape unharmed. However, while the heroines frequently call on their inner strengths and abilities for assistance, other helpers are abundant. They include maids, housekeepers, kindly couples, doctors, and ministers, who provide financial and moral support as well as good advice. Remembrances of things past also function as helpers. Three of the four protagonists are motherless by the ends of the novels, but the memories of their mothers, of their sacrifices and, in some cases, tragic fates, inspire the heroines to achieve their goals.

Displacement as Opportunity and Transformation

It is only after Astrid and Ragna have moved to America that they are able to articulate and acknowledge the extent to which they have been oppressed by their Norwegian fathers and society. The passage in *A Saloonkeeper's Daughter* in which Astrid, recently arrived in Minneapolis, laments being a girl is revealing. At the beginning of this passage Astrid speculates that her father would have given her more freedom had she been a boy. She uses the pronoun "he," but by the end of the passage she is using the pronoun "they." She asks, "What right did they have to bind and destroy her because she wasn't a man?" Astrid realizes her father represents a larger system. In *The Enemy's Pitfalls,* an entry from Ragna's diary articulates her recognition of oppression and the reasons she cannot return to Norway, despite occasional pangs of homesickness. Clearly the process of displacement both plays a literal role in and is a metaphor for the maturation of the hungry heroines. It is a reflection of the process of self-discovery and growth. Intrinsic to this self-discovery and liberation is the recognition of oppression; displacement functions as a catalyst in this process.[33]

One may ask if any travel would have had the same result. The American writer H. D., in exile in England, saw the break from home—rather than the destination—as key to self-development. In 1918, H. D. advised her fellow writer Bryher to travel to the United States: "Don't go with the false idea that America will give you *anything* you don't already possess. But the break from England may give you a spiritual impulse that will carry you on . . . Go to America!"[34]

Does America give Kate, Astrid, Else, Ragna, and the other hungry heroines of Norwegian American fiction something they don't already possess? It appears that while the mere process of travel, the breaking of old ties and establishment of new ones, does indeed lead to maturation and self-realization, America, as has been outlined, offered most of these women and their creators specific opportunities as well as communities that were unavailable in Norway and other more homogeneous societies with rigid social, gender, or class systems. In America, the hungry heroines are not only able to find themselves and recognize their true calling, but they are also given the opportunity to realize this calling. Ragna and Astrid meet, and are inspired by, other women who have studied and have careers, role models they were unable to find in Norway. For example, Astrid benefits from her association with Helene, a woman physician who, though she has often been treated as an outsider due to her sex, has been allowed to pursue her calling in America. Her example inspires Astrid to take up the ministry. Since the heroines have the freedom to pursue their callings, their initial feelings of alienation are drastically diminished or disappear. In their cases, the hope that "displacement equals opportunity" is realized. Oppression has been replaced by opportunity and freedom. Just as the father figure is transformed from a negative to a positive force, so displacement—a negative force in Norway—becomes a positive force in America.[35]

Optimism and sense of place and empowerment are mirrored in the thoughts, words, and actions of several of the hungry heroines at the close of their journeys. At the end of *A Saloonkeeper's Daughter,* Astrid stands in the pulpit of a Unitarian church in Chicago, preparing to preach at her ordination service. Though still an idealist, as reflected in her desire to help other women realize their callings, Astrid's naiveté has been replaced by realism. She no longer believes, as she did when she played Laura in Bjørnson's *The Newlyweds* (*De Nygifte*) (1865) shortly after coming to Minneapolis, that she can change the Norwegian Americans overnight. She has realized her true calling is not to be an actress but, rather, a minister, and she accepts that she will have to start with an American congregation, though she hopes one day to have a mixed American and Norwegian American congregation. As she looks out over the gathering of Americans, she recalls the last time she spoke publicly to so many people, a group of hostile Norwegians in Minneapolis who shouted her down. The congregation, by contrast, looks at her with mild, friendly faces, eager to listen. Not only does Astrid feel at home, but she is sure of her calling and, as she preaches on a text from the Gospel of Matthew on hunger and thirst, she finally realizes that her hunger and thirst have been satisfied and that she has arrived at her destination: "She had as her text 'blessed are they who hunger and thirst for righteousness sake.' *She had herself almost died of hunger and thirst—but now she was satisfied.* She lifted her head and looked out over the gathering. She felt that her words had power. She belonged here. She had not mistaken her calling. Finally she had arrived."[36]

Idealism and a sense of place and empowerment are also found in the closing paragraph of *Family in America.* Kate originally planned to study language and history and was later encouraged by her materialistic grandmother to study business, but she has now decided, on her own, to study sociology and social economics, since she wants to learn to understand how society can be changed to make the world a better place. The man she loves decides to follow her, the transformed Kate, so that she has a companion on this new journey: "Slowly a feeling of completeness came over Kate. And as she looked at him, she suddenly knew how the rest of her life would be; it would be with Olai as her spouse by her side, but in an independent existence with work to occupy her, with her achievements to strengthen her sense of self. She would be in control of her own destiny. A modern life!" Clearly Kate is in a position where she can pursue her plans.[37]

The sense of calling and empowerment is also present at the end of each of these novels; the protagonists are saved and delivered from their hunger. Only after finding themselves are they able to enter into fulfilling partnerships with others. According to Gelfant, before the end of the novels, few of the hungry heroines in American urban fiction find men who love "the self-created" people these women have become. Often, the novels conclude in an open-ended fashion, with the heroines declaring their independence rather than having demonstrated "tangible accomplishments." Notably, Kate and Ragna find such men, while Gudrun makes a conscious choice to remain single. Astrid enters into a pact with a woman, a choice surely viewed as subversive by mainstream society. The quests of these young women have led them from oppression at home, to rebellion, to a new home where they are free to choose their paths and partners in life. They are ready to embark on other journeys with renewed desire and optimism, reflected in their declarations of independence, driving them on.[38]

The spiritual nature of the protagonists' reward is striking and provides yet another link to Gelfant's work. Though material betterment is at times part of this reward, it is clearly not the most important. In fact, materialism is vehemently criticized in all of these novels, and the novels of the hungry heroines are closer to the spirit of Bjørnson's peasant tales than to H. A. Foss's popular Norwegian American imitation *The Cotter's Son*, in which the material reward is stressed.[39]

Unlike the characters in Bjørnson's peasant tales, as well as in the novels of early Norwegian American male writers who were heavily influenced by Bjørnson, the majority of the hungry heroines are city dwellers once they arrive in America. Why do these women, unlike their male counterparts, gravitate toward the cities? Circumstance, in the form of familial and other connections, initially brings Kate, Ragna, and Astrid to the cities of Chicago and Minneapolis, and they choose to remain in cities. If their quests are to be successful, they must be near the schools and the jobs that are available there. The urban setting is necessary because the dominant interest of the early hungry heroines was education rather than land. Their male counterparts, who are hungry for land and the material benefits it provides, gravitate toward the countryside. Gelfant points out that "the heroines of immigrant background evoke the perennial legend of America as a Golden Land. They see a new Canaan where 'learning flows free like milk and honey.'" Notably, this Canaan is located in urban America. Urban America, and the educational opportunities it affords, functions as both reward and new home when the folklore model is applied to the journeys of the Norwegian American hungry heroines.[40]

Of course, since Bruun, Janson, and Evanson lived in Chicago and Minneapolis, it was also logical for them to describe, relate, and react to urban situations. Janson provides a detailed picture of late nineteenth-century Minneapolis, including its Norwegian American community, which is particularly well done. Evanson related in her correspondence that her novel, set in Chicago in the depression years, was based on the lives and experiences of actual people in Chicago. In addition, Janson, Bruun, and Evanson were educated women who had families, jobs, and responsibilities but who also had the means to write, unlike their sisters in the countryside whose lives were more labor intensive and who, if they felt a calling to write fiction, were perhaps unable to do so.[41]

Finally, it should be noted that these novels contain a considerable amount of social criticism with vivid descriptions of urban ills. *A Saloonkeeper's Daughter* is a well-developed *tendensroman,* or novel which focuses on and aims to facilitate debate about specific societal problems and issues. Though the hungry heroines find and make responsible use of educational opportunities and social freedoms in America, a number of women and men in the works of Bruun, Evanson, Janson, and Pederson fall victim to poverty, materialism, domestic violence, prostitution, and drunkenness. These characters serve as reminders that displacement does not necessarily lead to self-discovery or growth but may, in some cases, lead to a loss of self.[42]

Though the hungry heroine plays a prominent, even dominant, role in Norwegian-language novels by Norwegian immigrant woman, Dorthea Dahl's only novel, *The City on the Hill (Byen paa berget),* provides a contrast. Dahl first gained attention for her short stories about everyday life, and when her novel came out in 1925 it was received favorably by the Norwegian American literary establishment. The reviewer, C. A. Mellbye, placed her writing on the level of Rølvaag and Bojer, and the critic and author Waldemar Ager said *The City on the Hill* was a genuine Norwegian American novel, one of the most significant written up to that point. Dahl's female protagonist, Frederikke, is American born, unlike the hungry heroines, and though she displays independent thinking at times, disagreeing in religious and other matters with her parents and her husband Otto, she finds meaning in raising her children in a fairly conventional marriage. Throughout her writing career, Dahl, who emigrated with her family to the United States when she was a toddler, placed emphasis on the experiences of second- and third-generation Norwegian Americans, providing another contrast to the works of Bruun, Evanson, Janson, and Pederson.[43]

How do women within other immigrant literary traditions position their female protagonists in the American social, cultural, and gender landscape? A critical look at social, gender, and class issues is found in some of the better-known German American novels and short stories published by urban German immigrant women in the second half of the nineteenth-century. While some of these works highlight the privileged position of women in the United States, the women in these novels tend to make more conventional choices in terms of relationships than the hungry heroines in Norwegian American fiction. Hunger for educational opportunities in the United States does not appear to be a focus of these works. In Therese Robinson's *The Exiles (Die Auswanderer)* (1852), the main female character Clothilde is a daughter of a professor. She leaves Germany with her fiancé Franz as a political exile. In the United States, she becomes the German tutor of two young southern women, but her relationship to Franz is highly traditional, and she dies from grief shortly after he is killed. In Fernande Richter's *"Ein Farm Idyll in Süd Missouri"* ("A Farm Paradise in Southern Missouri"), the young female protagonist and her family have actually left Germany to escape academia for life on a farm in America. In addition, the protagonists in these works live in rural rather than urban settings.[44]

Conclusion

The correspondence of Bruun, Evanson, Janson, and Pederson reveals that they, like the heroines they created, actively grasped hold of the American experience, both its positive and negative aspects, using it as a springboard to create. Sometimes they were frustrated with the challenges of being in a new environment, while at other times they found them refreshing. A number of the narratives which they produced contain striking tensions, some attributable to social tensions and differences in the Norwegian, Norwegian American, and American societies. In Janson's *A Saloonkeeper's Daughter* this tension is found in the life of the protagonist Astrid, who must leave the Norwegian American environment in order to realize herself. In Bruun's *The Enemy's Pitfalls* this tension is found in the mixture of feminism and pietism, which Øverland points out was present in the Woman's Christian Temperance Union, in which Bruun was highly active. Øverland also mentions how Evanson infuses modern, urban elements into older literary structures, providing yet another type of tension. Clearly, the way in which Bruun, Janson, Evanson, and Pederson integrate their hungry heroines into traditional folktale structure reflects another melding of and tension between older literary structures and new ways of thinking, such as in feminism.[45]

The segregation and focus on the novels of Bruun, Evanson, Janson, and Pederson in this study has been carried out for purposes, in the words of Tillie Olsen, of discovery and illumination. It is hoped that by listening to the voices of the hungry heroines and their creators, the picture that has already been drawn of the Norwegian American experience by literary scholars will become more multifaceted and gender balanced. Perhaps others will be encouraged to look for hungry heroine figures in other multilingual American works with similar results. By listening to the stories of these young women, we are provided with a more rounded view of motivations for emigration as portrayed in fiction, and light is cast on the gender perceptions of America held by a number of female Norwegian immigrant authors. The works and lives of these authors serve as a reminder that while North Americans hold the Nordic region up as a progressive model in terms of gender equality today, America was often viewed as the land of opportunity and promise for women at the turn of the twentieth century.[46]

Notes

1. First quotation from Ulrikka Feldtman Bruun, *Fjendens faldgruber: fortælling for ungdommen* (Chicago: Rasmussen, 1884), 20. Second from Marie Bang, *Livets Alvor* (Warren, MN: The author, 1901), 115. Translations are mine unless otherwise indicated.

2. Blanche H. Gelfant, "Sister to Faust: The City's 'Hungry' Woman as Heroine," in *Women Writing in America: Voices in Collage* (Hanover, NH, & London: University Press of New England, 1984), 206–7.

3. Gelfant, "Sister to Faust," 222.

4. "Privileged the image" is a phrase used by an anonymous peer reviewer. I thank the two anonymous reviewers of this essay for their useful comments and suggestions.

5. The novel was a major form of recreational reading in English-speaking America by the beginning of the nineteenth century. German-language novels were being written and published in the United States before mass emigration from Norway started in the mid-1860s. Dorothy Skårdal, *The Divided Heart: Scandinavian Immigrant Experience through Literary Sources* (Lincoln: University of Nebraska Press, 1974). Studies of other ethnic literatures have used this premise as well. For an example, see Patricia Herminghouse, "Radicalism and the 'Great Cause': The German-American Serial Novel in the Antebellum Era," *America and the Germans: An Assessment of a Three-Hundred-Year History*, ed. Frank Trommler and Joseph McVeigh (Philadelphia: University of Pennsylvania Press, 1985), 1:306–19. Dorothea Schneider, "The Literature on Women Immigrants to the United States," *Actes de l'historie de l'immigration* 3 (2003): 12, available: http://barthes.ens.fr/clio/revues/AHI/articles/index.html, accessed 29 Oct. 2010.

6. The Norwegians, Swedes, and Danes were but a few of the immigrant groups which produced flourishing literatures between about 1870 and 1930. At this time, numerous other non–English language literatures including Arabic, German, and Yiddish emerged to portray the experiences of both ethnic groups and individuals. See Ingeborg Kongslien, "New Narratives in Norwegian and Nordic Multicultural Literature, or 'Rewriting What it Means to be Norwegian,'" *Scandinavica* 44.1 (2005): 154. In recent years there has been a movement to make American literary scholars and the general public more aware of these works originally written in languages other than English and to encourage their categorization as American multilingual or ethnic literature. The Longfellow Institute,

established in 1994 in Cambridge, Massachusetts, to promote the study of non-English literatures written in the area which is now the United States, has made some of the most significant contributions to this effort. These include the publication of the Longfellow Institute Series in American Language and Literatures, edited by Marc Shell and Werner Sollors and published by the Johns Hopkins University Press. *The Multilingual Anthology of American Literature* (New York and London: New York University Press, 2000) is one work in this series that provides a broad assortment of fiction originally written in other languages. This anthology contains the texts in the original along with English translations. A number of texts in Norwegian, Danish, and Swedish are included, among them "The Copper Kettle," a short story by the Norwegian American writer Dorthea Dahl, translated into English by Orm Øverland.

Orm Øverland, *The Western Home: A Literary History of Norwegian America* (Northfield, MN: Norwegian-American Historical Association, 1996). In his 2007 article about Drude Krog Janson's *A Saloonkeeper's Daughter,* Øverland outlines how American literary and historical scholarship has privileged texts written in English, despite the multilingual nature of the United States since its inception. Øverland convincingly argues for its inclusion, stating, "American thoughts are no less American for not being expressed in English . . . American literature may be different from what we have assumed—and larger" (191). He points out the continued marginalization by writers like Janson today when he writes, "the minorities of the 1880s may not be considered minorities today—and therefore remain invisible . . . Thus, some writers may not have been considered interesting a hundred years ago because they wrote about minorities while they today may be excluded because they are not considered minority writers" (193). See Orm Øverland, "Recovering an Unrecognized Novel—Discovering American Literature," *Intercultural America,* ed. Alfred Hornung (Heiberg: Universitätsverlag Winter, 2007), 187–207.

Drude Krog Janson, *En saloonkeepers datter* (Minneapolis and Chicago: Rasmussen, 1889) was first published in Copenhagen in 1887 as *En ung Pige (A Young Girl).* This novel is the only one under consideration here that has been translated into English. Gerald Thorson's translation came out in 2002. Edited and with an introduction by Orm Øverland, *A Saloonkeeper's Daughter* is part of the Longfellow Series of American Languages and Literatures published by the Johns Hopkins University Press. See also Asbjørn Grønstad and Lene Johannesen, eds., *To Become the Self One Is: A Critical Companion to Drude Krog Janson's* A Saloonkeeper's Daughter (Oslo: Novus, 2005).

For a detailed discussion of types of silencing and marginalization, refer to Tillie Olsen, *Silences* (New York: Delacorter Press, 1965). My dissertation—"A Sense of Place: America Through the Eyes of Norwegian-American Women Novelists" (University of Wisconsin–Madison, 1996)—contains information about silencing in the Norwegian American context. This dissertation is the first and only work that collectively studies Norwegian American women writers who published fiction in Norwegian while focusing on issues of gender and marginalization. This essay relies heavily on sections of my unpublished dissertation.

7. Beret is a complex and multifaceted character who undergoes development throughout the trilogy. In the early years she is a reluctant immigrant who suffers from

anxiety and struggles with her mental and emotional health in the harsh prairie environment. After her husband's death in a snowstorm, Beret displays strength and stubbornness. Firmly clinging to the religion and language of her homeland, she raises her children and becomes a successful farmer in her own right. Though she commits herself to life in the new world, she is unwilling to build bridges outside of her ethnic community, and this stance affects her relationship with her children, particularly her eldest son.

8. Gelfant, "Sister to Faust," 221. I was first introduced to this model while studying at the University of Wisconsin–Madison under Niels Ingwersen. It is based on the work of the Russian folklorist Vladimir Propp, whose *Morphology of the Folktale* was originally published in 1928 and appeared in English in 1958. Fictional folktales are also referred to as fairy tales and magic tales. The melding of older literary models with seemingly new character types and ways of thinking leads to interesting tensions in these works, some of which have been noted in previous studies. Orm Øverland has pointed out that Aileen Berger Evanson's *Slekt i Amerika. Chicago fortælling* (*Family in America: A Chicago Story*)—an author and a work that will be discussed in this study—"is interesting for the way in which it integrates old structures with modern urban elements" (Øverland, *The Western Home*, 261). The old structures he refers to, however, are not folk literature models but the "on-both-sides-of-the-ocean" structure so typical of Norwegian American literature (261–62).

9. Bjørnstjerne Bjørnson (1832–1910) was one of the most influential Norwegian political and literary figures of the nineteenth century. A prolific writer, he penned poetry, plays, and fiction, and he was awarded the Nobel Prize in Literature in 1903. Bjørnson's peasant tales—*Synnøve Solbakken* (1857), *Arne* (1859), and *En glad Gut* (*A Happy Boy*) (1860)—were extremely popular and led to his literary breakthrough. Known for his patriotism and oratory skills, Bjørnson was also a proponent of Scandinavian cooperation, especially around the time of the dissolution of the union between Norway and Sweden in 1905. He is also remembered for writing the words to the Norwegian national anthem and for his role in incorporating children into the celebration of Norway's national day.

Torborg Lundell, "Gender-Related Biases in the Type and Motif Indexes of Aarne and Thompson," in *Fairy Tales and Society: Illusion, Allusion, and Paradigm,* ed. Ruth B. Bottigheimer (Philadelphia: University of Pennsylvania Press, 1986), 149–61.

10. For a discussion of Drude Krog Janson's engagement in the women's cause, see Anne Holden Rønning, "*A Saloonkeeper's Daughter* and the Woman Question," in *To Become the Self One Is,* 31–42. Bjørnson quotation, *Dagbladet,* 16 Nov. 1880, translated by Einar Haugen in *Land of the Free* (Northfield, MN: Norwegian-American Historical Association, 1978), 68. Girls' schools existed in Norway throughout the nineteenth century, but the pupils were denied entrance to higher education at the university level. The Norwegian writer Mauritz Hansen, who with his wife established a girls' high school in Kristiania in 1817, tried to prepare his gifted daughter for the university entrance exam but died (1842) before his plans could be realized. A good friend—the poet C. N. Schwach—told Hansen's widow that the idea of women students at the university was utter nonsense, and it took another forty years before the University of Kristiania admitted its first female student (see Francis Bull in *Norsk biografisk leksikon*). In the late 1880s,

only fifteen women students would enter the university every year, and by the end of the century, no more than twenty-five to thirty. In America, on the other hand, women's colleges existed since the late 1830s (Mount Holyoke), and even during the first half of the century some women attended general colleges (Oberlin, 1837). The idea of coeducation came with the establishment of the state universities after 1870.

11. See Urberg, "A Sense of Place," 190, for a listing of specific biographical sources.

12. For those works that have not been translated into English, I have used the title translations suggested by Orm Øverland in *The Western Home.* The letters are in some respects more valuable and interesting than Pederson's frequently dismissed novels, and they paint a detailed and intriguing portrait of the only Norwegian American female novelist who considered herself to be a full-time writer. Pederson's letters to Rasmus B. Anderson are found in the Rasmus B. Anderson Papers at the Wisconsin State Historical Society in Madison, WI. Additional detail on Pederson's correspondence is found in Urberg, "A Sense of Place," 125–84, as well as in Kristin Risley, "Palma Pederson," in *Kindred Hands: Letters on Writing by British and American Women Authors, 1865–1935,* ed. Jennifer Cognard-Black and Elizabeth MacLeod Walls (Iowa City: University of Iowa Press, 2006), 193–216. Øverland, *The Western Home,* 247.

13. See Urberg, "A Sense of Place," 199–200, for a listing of specific biographical sources. Pederson's pen name was Palma.

14. See Urberg, "A Sense of Place," 197, for a listing of specific biographical sources.

15. Henrik Jæger, review of *En ung Pige* by Drude Krog Janson, *Dagen,* 18 Nov. 1887, 1–2; Øverland, "Recovering an Unrecognized Novel," 188. In this article (187–206), Øverland discusses the myriad ways in which Janson's multifaceted novel can be read: as an American novel, as an immigrant novel, as a realistic novel—which includes "local color"—as a feminist novel, as a *Bildungsroman,* as a historical novel, and as a queer novel. In my analysis of *A Saloonkeeper's Daughter,* I have focused on reading the text as an immigrant novel, as a feminist novel, and as a *Bildungsroman.*

16. Drude Krog Janson's correspondence is housed in the manuscript collection (*Håndskriftsamlingen*) at the University of Oslo and in the Buslett Papers and Rølvaag Correspondence in the Norwegian-American Historical Association Archives in Northfield, MN (hereafter, NAHA). An example of a writer not covered in this study is Dorthea Dahl (1881–1958). Dahl was the only first-generation Norwegian American woman novelist to publish her work in both Norwegian and English, and she is best known as a short story writer, publishing over a hundred stories during her literary career. Dahl's correspondence to Ole Rølvaag reveals that traditional female responsibilities slowed and even threatened to put an end to her writing at times, though she did not appear to resent this fact or regret the time she spent with her family. Dahl's letters to Rølvaag are also found in the NAHA archives.

Palma Pederson, letter to Rasmus B. Anderson, 31 Dec. 1933, Rasmus B. Anderson Papers, Wisconsin State Historical Society, Madison. Pederson, as well as many other Norwegian American authors, struggled with Norwegian orthography and felt the press and publishers were quick to use poor orthography as a convenient excuse to unjustly dismiss works by Norwegian American authors. A more detailed discussion of Rølvaag's review of Pederson's novel *Ragna* and her reaction is found in Øverland, *The Western*

Home, 247–48, as well as in Urberg, "A Sense of Place," 140. Male writers such as Simon Johnson (1874–1970) were also hurt by negative reviews by critics such as Rølvaag. See Øverland, *The Western Home,* 275–76.

Egilsrud's concerns are outlined in a letter she wrote to Carl Hansen in 1937, now held in the Hansen Papers in the NAHA archives. The Norwegian American literary establishment included the heads of the publishing houses, newspaper and magazine editors, literary critics, and Norwegian professors—such as Rasmus B. Anderson and Ole E. Rølvaag. Most of those who held power were male, a number were clergy, and many knew each other well. The exclusionary nature of this establishment is reflected in the existence of all-male literary societies, including Ygdrasil (Madison, WI) and Symra (Decorah, IA). Information about the Norwegian American press can be found in Øverland's *The Western Home.*

17. Øverland, *The Western Home,* 261. Aileen Berger Evanson, letter to Theodore C. Blegen, 13 Apr. 1937, NAHA Publication Papers, NAHA archives.

18. Bruun, *Fjendens faldgruber,* 17–18, 48, 90. The latter passage is an excerpt from Ragna's diary. Gelfant, "Sister to Faust," 210.

19. Palma Pederson, *Under ansvarets svøbe* (Eau Claire, WI: Fremad, 1923), 44.

20. Gelfant, "Sister to Faust," 219. Janson, *En saloonkeepers datter,* 8–9. Susan Standford Friedman, "From Exile in the American Grain: H.D.'s Diaspora," in *Women's Writing in Exile,* ed. Mary Lynn Broe and Angela Ingram (Chapel Hill and London: University of North Carolina Press, 1989), 101.

21. Gelfant, "Sister to Faust," 210.

22. Janson, *En saloonkeepers datter,* 34–35, 57–58. Though Astrid expresses these thoughts while in America, they also apply to the way she was treated in Norway.

23. Bruun, *Fjendens faldgruber,* 48.

24. Ragna uses the verb *kvæler* to describe her feeling of strangulation. Ragna's mother uses the passive form of this verb, *kvaltes,* when she describes what happened to her years before. Gelfant, "Sister to Faust," 215–16.

25. Janson, *A Saloonkeeper's Daughter,* 23, Gerald Thorson's translation.

26. Pederson, *Under ansvarets svøbe,* 20.

27. Bruun, *Fjendens faldgruber,* 20. Aileen Berger Evanson, *Slekt i Amerika: Chicago fortælling* (Duluth, MN: Fuhr, n.d.), 6, 8.

28. Gelfant, "Sister to Faust," 219. Gelfant points out that the hungry woman in American urban fiction, like the immigrant, hopes that "displacement means opportunity."

29. Astrid's father emigrated before his children, and in the letter in which he sent for them, he lied about his work and financial situation, writing that he was doing well in the wine business. His feelings of shame over being a saloonkeeper were not tied to ethics but rather to class. He felt it beneath a man of his breeding and background to be a common saloonkeeper but decided that he had no choice due to his lack of English language skills. He knew this news would be upsetting to his daughter, while at the same time he hoped that her presence would draw respectable men to his saloon. Kristina Aurylaite, "Spaces of Access and Prohibition in Drude Krog Janson's *A Saloonkeeper's Daughter,*" in *To Become the Self One Is,* 171. Janson, *En saloonkeepers datter,* 61.

30. For an in-depth look at the Jansons' years in America, see Nina Draxten, *Kristofer Janson in America* (Boston: Twayne, 1976).

31. Janson, *A Saloonkeeper's Daughter*, 99, Thorson's translation. Refer to 155n99 for further contextual information.

32. Janson, *En saloonkeepers datter*, 231. Ken Luebbering, "Redefining 'American': The Creation of Identity in *A Saloonkeeper's Daughter*," in *To Become the Self One Is*, 63.

33. Janson, *En saloonkeepers datter*, 58.

34. Friedman, "From Exile in the American Grain," 94.

35. Powerful female characters who serve as negative role models are also found: for example, Kate's materialistic grandmother, the family matriarch in *Family in America*. This theme of displacement leading to opportunity and transformation, but at the cost of loneliness, albeit sometimes temporary, associated with cutting ties to one's previous patriarchal community, provides an interesting parallel to contemporary migration narratives by non-Western women who now live in Western countries. Fateme Behros's Swedish novel *Fångarnas kör (The Prisoners' Choir)*, published in 2001, provides an example. Ingeborg Kongslien points out how the protagonist, who immigrates as a young woman to Sweden from Iran, gradually gains freedom and self-reliance in her new, more liberal surroundings. This personal growth comes at a price, for at the end of the novel she is free but a bit lonely, though it is clear she—like Gelfant's heroines and the hungry heroines of Norwegian American fiction—has strength and a purpose, with plans to write a book about her experiences. Kongslien, "New Narratives in Norwegian and Nordic Multicultural Literature," 155.

36. Janson, *En saloonkeepers datter*, 263, italics added.

37. Evanson, *Slekt i Amerika*, 87.

38. Gelfant, "Sister to Faust," 215, 220.

39. A scene which calls to mind Bjørnson's peasant tales, and Foss's imitation as well, is found at the end of Ulrikka Feldtman Bruun's first novel, *Lykkens nøgle (The Keys to Happiness)* (Chicago: The author, 1880), when Bruun's protagonist Thyra Viking returns from America with her fiancé to be married in her home village. As in Bjørnson's stories, the poor, underprivileged farmer's child has made good. She has received an education and marries a person she loves, though this outcome had seemed impossible due to poverty, class, and other differences. Thyra's return, like that of Ole Haugen to his home village in *The Cotter's Son*, may seem like a mixture of triumph and revenge, but it also leads to a religious revival in the area, so the spiritual reward is shared by the community.

40. Gelfant, "Sister to Faust," 217.

41. The only nineteenth-century novels I have been able to locate by Norwegian American women that have clear rural settings in America are Drude Krog Janson, *Tore: fortælling fra prærien* (Kristiania: Verdens Gang, 1894), a naturalistic work that I treat in depth in my dissertation, "A Sense of Place," and Ingerid Bergum, *Familien paa Stjerneklip* (Chicago: The author, 1893). Though Bergum's frame story is set in rural Wisconsin, the heroine in this imitation of a Bjørnson peasant tale remains on Stjerneklip, a Norwegian farm. It is noteworthy, however, that Bergum's Antonia plans to move to America with her fiancé in order to escape her abusive father. Antonia is the initiator, though she

doesn't carry through with her plans due to her father's change in attitude. Bergum paints America in a positive light, as a haven for the poor. Aileen Berger Evanson, letter to T. C. Blegen, 13 Apr. 1937, Theodore C. Blegen Papers, NAHA archives.

42. These novels contain the two themes that dominate nineteenth-century Norwegian American fiction: success stories and temperance. It is also noteworthy that while Gelfant demonstrates the deep entrenchment of young immigrant women yearning for knowledge in American urban fiction, she has also written about those women who do not succeed in an urban setting (Gelfant, "Sister to Faust," 204).

43. Dorthea Dahl, *Byen paa berget* (Minneapolis, MN: Augsburg, 1925). C. A. Mellbye, review of *Byen paa berget* by Dorthea Dahl, *Lutheraneren* (9 Sept. 1925): 1141. Waldemar Ager, review of *Byen paa berget* by Dorthea Dahl, *Reform.* 8 Oct. 1925, 4.

44. Martha Kaarsberg Wallach, "Women of German-American Fiction: Therese Robinson, Mathilde Anneke, and Fernande Richter," in *America and the Germans: An Assessment of a Three-Hundred-Year History,* ed. Frank Trommler and Joseph McVeigh (Philadelphia: University of Pennsylvania Press, 1985), 1:331–42.

45. Øverland, *The Western Home,* 112, 261.

46. Tillie Olsen uses these terms—discovery and illumination—in her discussion of "legitimate reasons for grouping" women writers together: see page 187 in *Silences.*

CHAPTER 9

Collective Identities in Life Writings of Norwegian Immigrant Women

Betty A. Bergland

> "One may regret that she did not write a full-length autobiography recording her experiences and observations and revealing the mature growth of her personality."
>
> Theodore C. Blegen in 1955
> Preface to *The Diary of Elisabeth Koren, 1853–1855*

Theodore C. Blegen's regret that Elisabeth Koren did not write a "full-length autobiography" might extend to other Norwegian immigrant women. In some ways, Koren is atypical of nineteenth-century female immigrants: the wife of a minister called to serve a congregation in Iowa, the daughter of an educator and political figure in Norway, and the recipient of a private education. Else Elisabeth Hysing Koren (1832–1918) represented a privileged social class, unlike most Norwegian women immigrating to the United States. At the same time, however, Koren personified typical patterns of mid-nineteenth-century immigrant women: she migrated as a married woman, traveled with a larger group, settled in the Midwest, and, significantly, documented her life. In writing about their lives, Norwegian immigrants shared common ground—whether part of mid-nineteenth-century family migrations or single, youthful migrations of the late nineteenth and early twentieth centuries, and whether rural or urban, single or married, laborers or professionals. Norwegian female immigrants recorded their experiences in diaries, letters, reminiscences, and oral histories—considered fragments—though not in the "full-length autobiography."[1]

Before exploring what these women did and did not write, it is meaningful to consider Blegen's observation. As a historian of immigration, he no doubt imagined the full accounting of Koren's life might have offered a richer, fuller delineation of the immigrant experience—the interior life as well as more nuanced reflections of an educated woman in the midst of a vital immigrant community. Blegen also may have embraced the prevailing view of autobiography as the most mature, transparent, and superior explication of a life. Traditionally, historians and literary scholars have accorded autobiography a privileged place, especially in contexts of American culture and its emphasis on the individual. This tension between American cultural values and Norwegian immigrant women's avoidance of autobiography might be understood, in part, by a comment Rasmus B. Anderson (1846–1936) made on the writing of his own autobiography. A second-generation immigrant, scholar, and influential figure in Norwegian American life, Anderson wrote in the preface to his autobiography that he refused constant appeals from friends to write his life story because "the constant use of the 'I' is distasteful to me."[2]

The single, first-person pronoun that Anderson found distasteful is the centerpiece of autobiography. Furthermore, in the American context of westward expansion and rugged individualism, especially pervasive in American writings surrounding migration, the "distasteful I" may be even more elevated. Eventually, in the context of World War I and the era of growing Americanization, Anderson consented to write his autobiography. The professor of Scandinavian languages at the University of Wisconsin–Madison titled his life story simply *An Autobiography*. He thus joined many, mostly male, first- and second-generation immigrants of this era writing life stories. While a few Norwegian immigrant men wrote full-length autobiographies, Norwegian immigrant women avoided them. Many Norwegian immigrant women left written records, but they did so in fragmentary pieces: diaries and letters that might be shared with family and communities; fragments of life writing in reminiscences and memoirs that captured significant moments or events; as-told-to "autobiographies" that signified continuity across generations; and collective narratives that told stories of families or communities. In effect, these women generated life writings while avoiding Anderson's "distasteful" first-person pronoun central to autobiography.[3]

Why, one might wonder with Blegen, did Norwegian immigrant women avoid the "full-length autobiography"? This chapter examines that question as it explores the patterns of life writings by Norwegian immigrant women. Central to the discussion is the distinction between the singular "I" of a full-length autobiography and the plural "we" found more often in fragmentary life writings of women. These writings reflect a patriarchal worldview that excluded women from much of public life and posit a countervailing and alternative perspective that signifies a more inclusive and collective identity. At the same time, these writings recognize the "self" as more fragmented, divided, changing, and relational. I argue that the collective and fragmentary narratives of Norwegian immigrant women (as opposed to the individualized reconstructions of a perceived coherent "self" found in most traditional autobiographical forms) represent the cultural retention of a community-oriented sensibility in the immigrant generation and provide evidence of a collective sense of identity (as opposed to the more Americanized individualized identity). What inferences might we draw from the relative absence of the distasteful "I" and the affirmation of "we"? An examination of these overlooked texts and women's self-constructions reveals enduring values and suggests neglected dimensions of the transmission of culture and legacies.[4]

Immigrant Narratives in Contexts of Life Writing

Scholars have diverse theories on the beginnings of autobiography. Some trace its origin to St. Augustine's fifth-century *Confessions;* others associate the form with the emergence of modernity and its greater individuation, especially evident in Jean-Jacques Rousseau's secularized "confession," *Les Confessions,* which appeared in the late eighteenth century, 1782–89; and others emphasize the proliferation of the form in the twentieth century, especially in testimonials linked to global transformations through migration, wars, decolonization, and globalization. Scholarship today demonstrates the temporal and geographic reach of autobiography and its pervasiveness around the globe. Though the autobiography appears nearly universal, the genre resonates especially in American history and culture because of the ethos surrounding the individual. In addition, the notion that the individual may represent the group has led to inferences about individual autobiographies, so that Andrew Carnegie came to represent Americans and Frederick Douglass came to represent slaves in the antebellum South.[5]

This representative dimension becomes problematic in gendered contexts of history and culture, especially with migration. Empirical evidence demonstrates overwhelmingly that men (not women) wrote autobiographies: early compilations of American autobiography incorporate virtually only men, and any cursory examination of the genre demonstrates the preponderance of male narratives. Numbers, however, convey only part of an analysis of the male-dominated genre—scholars demonstrate how the "distasteful I" of autobiography signifies patriarchal male identity and has done so for the last five hundred years. Sidonie Smith argues persuasively: "The poetics of autobiography, as the history of autobiography, thus remains by and large an androcentric [male-centered] enterprise." In short, she claims that autobiographies of men dominate the field, and that the male experience has come to represent normative human experience. In other words, the male signifies the universal subject.[6]

The tension between claims of the universality of the male subject in autobiography and the presumed representative nature of autobiography means not only that women, and women's experiences, have been unrepresented or under-represented but also that women have often remained unimagined, or unreadable. This is also evident in immigrant autobiographies. The question then becomes, if the universal subject tends to be male and the autobiographical form remains androcentric, how have women conceptualized and written their lives—and what is the significance of this difference? Feminist scholars often assert that women have demonstrated a different conception of the self from that of men: their identity is more often intertwined with others' lives. Such a self-conception subsequently leads to a more collective rather than individualistic worldview. Such is the case, I argue, with Norwegian immigrant women's self-conceptions and is evident in the life writings.[7]

Norwegian Immigrant Women's Life Writing

Norwegian immigrant women wrote about their lives—in diaries, letters, reminiscences, oral histories, and collective autobiographies—like other women. In examining Norwegian immigrant women's life writings, we first might ask which key analytical categories are most determinative in shaping their life writings— gender, ethnicity, or class. Norwegian scholar Marie Wells identifies strong nationalist, heroic, and masculine patterns in both biographical and autobiographical writings in Norway in the period of migration, yet radical and feminist voices also appear in autobiographical writings in the late nineteenth and early twentieth centuries in Norway. One might then argue that the form itself is not inherently androcentric, but given patriarchal cultural formations at this time, both in Norway and the United States, it is likely that the form would emphasize the lives of men. As tension exists within both countries between democratic and patriarchal tendencies, they are found also in autobiographical expressions. Examinations of Norwegian life writings, in fact, reveal both individuated and collective examples; however, in Norwegian immigrant women's life writings a collective sensibility prevails.[8]

Norwegian immigrant women avoided individuated life histories because nineteenth- and early twentieth-century gendered ideologies, in both Norway and the United States, limited public roles for women. Because autobiographies were generally equated with public lives, women's life writings tended to be circumscribed to relationships surrounding women—families and communities—and found in diaries, letters, reminiscences, and collected narratives. The paradigm of the classic immigrant autobiography, of the lone figure traveling to America and becoming a successful American, is difficult to find among Norwegian immigrant women's writings. Rather, in fragmentary life writings, women tend to portray themselves in the context of relationships (often transatlantic), within a family, within a larger institution such as a church or hospital, or within the greater Norwegian American community. While writers may assure families at home of their well-being and describe overcoming hardships, the emphasis is on "we" and continuity with the past.

This analysis is organized around genres of life writing that correspond with historical patterns of migration—from rural to urban and from predominately family migration to single migration. The analysis also exposes relational patterns that convey a more collective and communal sense of self than has been generally acknowledged or documented. To develop this analysis, the chapter examines five categories of life writings of Norwegian immigrant women: 1) diaries and journals; 2) letters; 3) reminiscences and memoirs; 4) as-told-to autobiographies; and 5) collective autobiography.[9]

Each of these forms of life writing conveys relational patterns within a larger community and illuminates the writer's conceptual understanding of the self by how she situates herself (temporally and spatially) and in relationship to others. What dominates in all these genres is a collective sense of identity—alliances with family, institutions of religion or service (churches, parsonages, schools, and hospitals), or broader communal interests—rather than the individualized representation of paradigmatic immigrant autobiographies. Feminist scholars generally find a more collective sense of identity in women's life writings than in men's life writings. Those findings, coupled with those of this study, suggest that gender is *as* significant a determining factor in shaping life writings as is national origin or ethnicity.[10]

Diaries: Wives and Mothers in the Home

Blegen may have shared Virginia Woolf's view when she wrote the diary "does not count as writing." Nonetheless, the diary has a long history and proliferates today. In other words, in writing her diary, Koren had much company. Rachel Cottam argues that the form is characterized by hybridity (implying multiple selves, or parts of oneself) and diversity (meaning various forms). The reader's expectation, however, is that a diary or journal represents an immediate experience and uses everyday language. Perhaps most distinctive about the diary is its paradox, as Cottam argues: it is "communication that is not to be communicated." She explains that "as a text the diary comes to stand as an embodiment of the paradoxical and elusive self, revealed yet always remaining hidden, simultaneously public and private." Perhaps for these reasons, the diary is also often seen as a feminine genre, reflecting oppositional modes: "the subversion of traditional linguistic structures and conventions of representation—in particular, through nonlinearity, interruption, and lack of closure—allow meanings to emerge that have been repressed by [phallocentric] realistic discourses, and call into question the patriarchal order those discourses sustain." Consequently, diaries may be valuable not only for exposing historical conditions but also for providing an understanding of women's sense of self and its dynamic shift over time.[11]

Although diaries in the late twentieth century may be more associated with privacy and secrecy, the earlier century posited a different logic for the diary form. Lillian Schlissel wrote in the introduction to her now classic work, *Women's Diaries on the Western Journey,* that over eight hundred diaries recorded the Yankee westward journey. She wrote, "As a general category, the nineteenth-century diary is something like a family history, a souvenir meant to be shared like a Bible, handed down through generations, to be viewed not as an individual's story but as the history of a family's growth and course through time." A similar argument can be made about immigrant diaries of the nineteenth century. The public function, of course, may exist alongside the oppositional modes (noted above), making the diary a meaningful text for examining not only historical conditions but also immigrant women's self-conceptions and cultural contradictions.[12]

Lillian Schlissel and Elizabeth Hampsten, along with other women's historians of the West, have found hundreds of diaries of Yankee women written during their westward journeys. Few diaries of Norwegian immigrant women have emerged, though many more may be hidden from view; those known to us reveal rich detail and insight into migration from a gendered perspective. Several diaries of Norwegian immigrant women have been translated and published; in addition to Koren, the diaries of Linka Keyser Preus and Elizabeth Fedde may be most well known. Mostly studied to gain historical knowledge about early immigrants, these diaries are also scrutinized for the self-conceptions they provide. Koren and Preus, both wives of ministers, migrated in the mid-nineteenth century and lived in immigrant communities in Iowa. Fedde, a deaconess who assisted in the establishment of hospitals in Norwegian communities in New York and Minneapolis in the 1880s, describes the daily life of professional women in medical service on both sides of the Atlantic at the turn of the twentieth century. All three women convey a collective sense of self. This analysis focuses on Koren.[13]

Perhaps the most well-known diary among Norwegian immigrant women is *The Diary of Elisabeth Koren, 1853–1855*. While Koren may not be wholly typical, the self-conception in her writings is. She migrated from Larvik, Norway, to Winneshiek County, Iowa, as the new bride of Ulrik Vilhelm Koren (1826–1910), a theological student, recently ordained in Norway. After accepting a ministerial calling to a new congregation in northeastern Iowa in 1853, Ulrik and his new bride departed their homeland on September 5, 1853. Twenty-one years old and from a "sheltered home," as David Nelson notes, Koren possessed the advantages of an educated family—her father Ahlert Hysing taught at the cathedral school in Bergen, became headmaster of the modern school in Larvik, represented the region at the *Storting* (the Norwegian Parliament), and served for a decade as mayor of Larvik. Koren received a private education in Copenhagen and benefitted from the upbringing of the privileged class—aboard ship she read Charles Dickens, Frederick Schiller, and Washington Irving, not the typical reading of emigrants. Although in this period most migrating adult women were married and traveled with husbands and children, few came from her social

Else Elisabeth (Hysing) Koren,
Herbjorn Gausta, 1883

class or shared her education; furthermore, as the wife of a minister she would have been accorded a special position in the immigrant community, occupying a distinctive place in the new-world settlements. Though atypical in these respects, Koren produced a diary that describes the conditions and daily life of typical immigrant women. Furthermore, if examined through a gendered lens, her diary represents patterns evident in other life writings of Norwegian immigrant women: she foregrounds the "we" in her narrative and situates the self relationally within the community she shared.[14]

The Diary covers the period from September 15, 1853, when she and her husband sailed from Hamburg, Germany, and continues until December 3, 1854, nine days before the birth of her first child; several letters to her father in 1855 constitute the final chapter of the published version. While the narrative is clearly a diary, there are hints that the diary would be shared. At one point early in the journey she wrote: "I sit here now waiting for coffee, and reflect how odd it is that you are now having your morning coffee at home." The "you" here is not clarified, but presumably it would be her father (and/or siblings) to whom she wrote once they were settled. The direct address ("you") implies a conversation (or letter) and suggests a more public than private document. She also reported on several occasions that her husband read *The Diary* nearly daily, indicating her intentions to share it. When her children published fragments of *The Diary* during her life, the public function was also exposed. *The Diary* covers about fifteen months; with the letters to her father, it covers two years in over three hundred pages. Viewed generally, one-third of *The Diary* addresses their travels to northeastern Iowa; nearly two-thirds is devoted to their sojourn with others and in a temporary home; and the last two chapters (only forty pages) conclude the narrative with their move into the just-built parsonage and their new life. As they settled in, Koren wrote on October 20, 1854, "this is really a new existence for me. I have more to look after . . . it is as if I had just been married." Indeed, the responsibilities of marriage and motherhood eclipse a continuation of the life writing, as is the case with many women.[15]

Readers do not see a whole life here, and in some ways it is problematic to draw inferences from this relatively brief and transitional period—she is a young bride throughout the narrative, traveling, a sojourner in others' homes, and in transition. When she arrived in their just-built home (the parsonage), and took up the role of housewife, she seemed to do so with gladness, the fulfillment of her travels. As they moved in, she wrote, "now for the first time I began to under-stand rightly what 'home' means, our own house." But this is no ordinary home; the responsibilities placed on the minister's wife were great, something to which she alluded: "I hope I may be somewhat as I ought to be . . . [and] not become cross or upset . . . I hope I can manage everything for Vilhelm as I desire." The year was 1854, and for middle-class women clear guidelines existed for managing a proper home—in Norway and the United States.[16]

The self-portrayal of the young Koren as she departs for America on Sep-tember 15, 1853, is a thoughtful and observant woman eager for adventure as she records the events of the journey—the weather, sunsets, land sightings, the food, the dullness of the days, other passengers, the sick, and the dead. She described passing the time with reading, sewing, and writing in her diary while she also did crocheting, tatting, and lace making. Traveling in a first-class cabin, she had little contact with other passengers, but she described them. Of the second-class passengers, she wrote that they "come with their rugs which [they] spread out and sit on, and play chess or cards and infect the air with their vile tobacco." Of the steerage passengers, she wrote, "Early in the morning there is a throng of steerage people on the deck below; the women usually make their toilet there and eat breakfast . . . [and later] running about with their tin pails to fetch their midday meal, grouping themselves as but they can about the deck to eat it." One might argue that this is more descriptive than critical, and her central distinction is between the cultivated and not cultivated, but a critical view is apparent. Given her commentary about fellow passengers in first class, it is easier to see that her critique may be associated with a moral compass rather than class superiority, although these may be linked. Throughout *The Diary,* she remains critical of the vain and arrogant, the talkative and boastful, the silly and lazy—regardless of their class.[17]

The largest section of *The Diary,* when she and her husband stayed tempo-rarily with other settler families (until the parsonage was built), conveys a rich sense of the frontier Norwegian American settlements in northeastern Iowa and illuminates a sense of herself, others, and relational patterns in the community. From December 21, 1853, to March 7, 1854, she and Vilhelm resided with Erik and Helen Egge and their children—and the following months with the Sørlands. The immigrants lived in close proximity and Koren observed the people she occasionally referred to as "farm folk." She alternately found these farm folk "good people" that she admired and "uncultivated," dull companions. When her husband began traveling to settlements to develop congregations, Koren remained in the homes of others, sometimes described as "strangers." During this time she assisted with household chores, watched the children, knit and sewed, took walks, visited neighbors, and received visitors. When alone and sitting quietly, her thoughts tended to cross the Atlantic; moods of melancholy and loneliness surfaced, despite efforts to fight them. After several months of sharing a fifteen-by-sixteen-foot room of the cabin, the Korens' presence became "too burdensome" for Helen Egge, so they moved to the loft of another young family and subsequently to an empty cabin of Erik and Guri Skaarlias. During these months of living in close proximity to fellow Norwegian Americans, Koren conveyed a strong sense of their interdependence in the community: they shared labor, food, stories, letters, newspapers, information, skills, and comfort. Koren portrayed herself as of them, not above them.[18]

In the last six chapters, *The Diary* begins to capture what it meant to be the kind of wife Koren would become—first in her temporary home and then in their own parsonage. While a sojourner with others she wrote, a "young wife" needs "a home of her own to look after." Later, she wrote to her father that she would have a girl to help her, "so I begin to feel my dignity as a housewife." Many domestic tasks were shared by all women on the frontier—cooking, washing, starching, ironing, filling mattresses with straw, quilting, crocheting, sewing, and mending. Even Koren made pork sausage, headcheese, and pickled onions. As the minister's wife, other responsibilities were expected of her. Throughout *The Diary,* others come to her for medicine or advice on injuries, inflammations, or illnesses. With their significant library, including medical books, the Korens were sought out for medical advice. Furthermore, the minister's wife was expected to provide a welcoming social environment for the larger community. As they moved into their new home, she wrote, "May it be a truly peaceful and loving home! May I do all I can to make it so." In one of the last entries in *The Diary,* she noted preparations for a bridal party and a baptism, where she served four workers and six church trustees at the same table for dinner—nine days before she gave birth to her first child. She recognized that as part of her role—not only a *housewife* but also a *minister's wife*—she must be prepared to be healer and host for the whole community. Her life was defined in relationships.[19]

Koren was foremost a *wife.* In passages that convey a tender affection between husband and wife, Koren wrote of their marriage, "My consort and I are good friends today," "He is very naughty and has been teasing me all forenoon," and "There are not many who have so excellent a husband as I." She often wrote of their cozy evenings together, reading by the fire, glancing at one another, not speaking but content. Still, left alone while her husband traveled, she confessed to loneliness, melancholy, and a longing for him to return. Toward the end of *The Diary,* in the new parsonage, she reflects on his absence with a rare candor for a nineteenth-century diarist: "I thought it was very sad to sit here alone, and that it would be a terribly long time before Vilhelm would return, and more such fancies. But then I was ashamed of myself and chased such ideas out of doors; but just the same I could not help longing for Vilhelm, and I must be allowed to do that, no matter how pleasant things are." Socialized to be obedient, Koren was also taught to be thankful and not complain; yet she felt and expressed her loneliness and longing—and claimed the right to express these feelings. Koren conceived of herself as a *housewife* and as *a minister's wife*—with all the demands, expectations, and social constructions involved at the time—but she was also Vilhelm's wife, a woman, expressing feelings and desire.[20]

Koren was a young woman (only twenty-one years old) as she immigrated to the United States and began her new life. *The Diary* narrates the transition period as she prepares for this "new existence." At this stage, her central relationship was with her husband; her self-conception centered on that alliance. The central spatial or temporal reality of *The Diary* is the home—and eventually the parsonage. Of course, that site signifies not only Koren's world but also a pivotal place in Norwegian American communities. Significantly, *The Diary* concludes just before she gave birth—before the demanding complexities of domesticity, motherhood, and parsonage life. The so-called others (Americans and Indians) receive only brief mention. In this fragment of a life, readers acquire only a glimpse of a self in the process of becoming the parson's wife and a central figure in the community. Those she sometimes called strangers (her new neighbors and the farm folk) emerge as *her* community—the Norwegian immigrants of northeastern Iowa she and her husband served.

Koren did not write a full-length autobiography, but her detailed diary, encompassing several years of her life, conveys a sense of self deeply linked in relationships within family and community. Diaries of other immigrant women (published and unpublished manuscripts of women in urban and rural areas) may be less developed and detailed but nevertheless share commonalities with Koren—the emphasis on relationships within families and communities and the sense of self as "we."

Letters: Daughters, Sisters, Wives, and Mothers on the Homestead

The epistolary form is the oldest of all life writings and is seen to originate with the beginning of writing itself. The first forms are found in the third and second millennium BCE in cuneiform. Taught in classical Greece, letter writing emerged with the Romans, who gave the first examples to the Western world through the rules of Ciceronian rhetoric. Thus, from the beginning, there were rules about letter writing, though there are fewer today. French scholar of the letter Bernard Bray notes that today "letters are expected to be artless expressions of the writer's personality." Yet, even now, when many see in letters the authentic voice of the writer—unmediated and transparent—scholars recognize the rules or construction of letters. Nonetheless, what is at the core of all letter writing (including in the modern period) is the relationship between writer and recipient. Thus, Bray asserts, in the examination of letters the "essential requirement is that the addressee, and the relationship that the writer has with him and her, should be the main consideration." That relationship affects not only tone and subject of the letter, Bray writes, but also the medium, the arrangement of text, forms of address, degree of care, salutation, and closing, as well as the method of sending. Thus, any discussion of letters must consider the writer, the recipient(s), and their relationships.[21]

The letters immigrants sent home—often identified as America letters— were sent by all groups throughout the nineteenth and early twentieth centuries. Many scholars have collected, translated, preserved, and published examples that provide a rich source for both researchers and general readers alike. Some letters were intended for publication in newspapers, but most were intended for families. They provided the most reliable information about the new world, suggests Blegen in his introduction to *Land of Their Choice,* and so, he writes, they "constitute a composite diary of everyday people at the grass roots of American life." Consequently, they are often seen as the documents of immigration. Because of their immediacy and specificity, they informed the audience not only of the well-being of the writer but of the details of the new world—the journey, conditions of settlement, the American social and political life, the development of the expanded community, and prospects for migration. Orm Øverland argues that the letters were central to the chain migration (serial migration of family or neighbors following each other as links in a chain), a central feature of mass migration. Solveig Zempel in the introduction to her collection, *In Their Own Words,* emphasizes that the letters provided and helped sustain contacts with the family. Thus, they served two critical functions during what Roger Daniels calls the "century of migration" (1820–1924)—stimulating migration and connecting families.[22]

In the twentieth century, they have served as a critical and historical source on migration studies, as scholars testify—from Blegen to Odd S. Lovoll, Øverland, Øyvind Gulliksen, and, more recently, Zempel and Lori Ann Lahlum. Øverland also suggests they constitute a "folk literature," a collection of diverse writings of the people. Whether treated as folk literature, historical source, or curiosity, the letters have received much scholarly attention. This focus emphasizes letters as a form of life writing that can inform us about self-constructions. Bray argues, "Indeed, letters undeniably reveal the whole personality," from the shape of the letters on the page to its contents.[23]

Of course, both men and women wrote letters, yet it is noteworthy that the earliest collections of immigrant letters from the mid-nineteenth century are those of women, including those of Gro Svendsen, Elise Wærenskjold, and Caja Munch.

These earliest letters, from the 1840s, 1850s, and 1860s, came from women in a higher social class than most immigrants, yet as mass migration developed after the Civil War, laboring women also sent letters home. The literacy in Norway played a role, but perhaps equally significant was the reduction of postal rates after 1870, as noted by Øverland. This made it economically more feasible for agricultural and domestic workers to write and send letters. Like the diary, letters contain much immediate detail and a focus on a limited period of time. While letters generally do not signal a self-conscious reconstruction of a life as an autobiography might, inferences about the self, the other, and the community might be drawn from them—through the scope and content, linguistic structures, organization, form, and the unsaid. Also, relational patterns in the letters can lead to inferences about "self," "other," and community. Since the letters helped maintain contacts with families, they provide evidence for the nature of these relationships, as they also contributed to the maintenance of family networks—what anthropologist Micaela di Leonardo called "kinwork." Thus, like diaries, the letters served larger social and public functions.[24]

Beret Holm, the fictional character in *Giants in the Earth,* may be the most well-known Norwegian immigrant among non-Norwegians, but Svendsen may be the best-known female immigrant among historians—essentially because of her letters. In 1950, Blegen and Pauline Farseth translated and edited the collection entitled *Frontier Mother: The Letters of Gro Svendsen,* which included letters written from 1861 to 1877, the last just before her death. At the time of publication, as Blegen wrote, Svendsen's letters represented a "new and essentially unknown story." For a variety of reasons these letters are much used by historians: the collection is accessible to English readers, the letters engage, and they represent a coherent collection. Consequently, Svendsen is often viewed as a representative Scandinavian immigrant. Historians from Blegen to David Gerber have studied Svendsen's letters primarily for the social history of migration. Blegen sees her as representative of the "frontier mother," possibly meaning that her articulation of complex responses to frontier conditions is typical: she faced adversity on the frontier "resolutely" and "energetically" and she occasionally "hints of protest and nostalgic backward glances at the comfort and security she had left." What is unusual in her extended collection of letters is the unity of time and place, in contrast to the isolated or fragmented nature of many America letters; all her correspondence is written from Estherville, Iowa, to her family in Hallingdal, Norway, giving readers a sense of temporal and spatial continuity—as well as continuity of subjectivity. For these reasons, focusing on her letters is meaningful for exploring self-constructions.[25]

All the letters (with the exception of the first) are sent to her immediate family that she designates invariably as "Precious [or Beloved] Parents, Sisters, and Brothers"; she signs them "devoted daughter [or sister]" and, in the last ones,

"Devoted children, Ole and Gro N. Svendsen." Thus, the relationship between writer and recipient is made explicit. The correspondence, for all its rich social history and evocation of frontier life, also signifies the deep bond of the parent-child relationship. Svendsen married and left home at the age of twenty-one. Much of the correspondence represents the anguish and guilt she felt in leaving her parents and siblings behind, a grief shared by many—especially those sensitive to filial loyalty and the duty of a nineteenth-century, rural child to parents. Repeatedly, she writes of worry for them, despite her love for her husband. The relational contexts and patterns of the letters reveal much about the self.[26]

Gro Svendsen, n.d.

The sense of self in the letters is one in relationship— with parents, siblings, husband, children, in-laws, cousins, and neighbors—both in Norway and in Iowa. These relational patterns are evident not only in her salutations and closings (often with lists of named individuals) but also in the content of her letters. She reports news of the immediate family (husband, children, in-laws, and brothers) as well as news of the community (cousins, neighbors, the congregation, the civic community, and the larger Norwegian midwestern population) as it moves to Rock County, Minnesota, or to the Red River Valley. Svendsen reveals what can be found in other Norwegian immigrant women's writings in the Midwest—preoccupation with the larger community.[27]

Most striking and revealing, however, are the self-revelations conveyed in linguistic constructions—her use of "I" and "we." Throughout the letters she uses the first person plural ("we") to convey their life and conditions. In reference to daily life, she may refer to the immediate family and their labors, as in "we cut barley," "we cut oats," "we cut 184 bushels of wheat," or "we set up our household." These constructions convey shared endeavor and egalitarian relationships rather than individualized or gender-specific labor. Also, in writing about their well-being, she writes in the plural form, whether about the immediate or extended family: "we are well," "we are now well-housed," "we were compelled to buy our land for $480," "we had to borrow," and "we had to buy another house." In the midst of economic depressions and ravages by locusts for several years in a row in the 1870s, she seeks to assure her parents of their well-being: "we have not too much wealth . . . we have not much material wealth . . . [but] we have not suffered any want." What is striking throughout the collection is Svendsen's sense of self as a partner on the prairie with her husband and a member of a broad community. As a letter writer, she is a mediator, a voice of the migrants to her family, a daughter and sister—not simply an individuated self. Essentially, the letters represent relational patterns of an emigrant daughter, relational patterns that are inclusive, defining her new-world life in the form of "we."[28]

Blegen writes of Svendsen that she was "skillfully articulate, a woman who had mastered the art of revealing herself freely, effectively, and with imitable gusto in the letters." She does use the "I" in the letters, but it is not the "I" of a self-absorbed autobiographer Anderson found distasteful; rather, it is the "I" of individual acts for which she might be held accountable—such as "I have filled the paper with much nonsense" or "I wanted to write" but failed to. Also significantly, she uses the "I" to express sincere and deep emotion to parents and siblings. She uses the "I" apologetically to her parents when much time has lapsed between letters: "I am deeply grieved . . ." (for not writing sooner) and "I pray your forgiveness for not writing more." She expresses guilt for leaving her parents: "I know I cause you much worry and sorrow" or "now and then I reproach myself for leaving you alone . . . on the other hand, you mustn't think for a moment that I regret my choice." She admits to hiding fears when her husband fought in the Civil War: "I tried desperately to conceal from you the thoughts closest to my heart." At the same time she expresses joy in reading, in exploring the region, and especially in the context of relationships: "My grief was turned to joy when I have received so many letters at one time," "I can never be too thankful for having such a kind husband," and "I was overjoyed to get a daughter." She imagines her parents' pleasure in seeing their American lives: "I know it would give you great joy [to be here]" and "You would be happy because we are happy." She writes much and often of her children: "they are my greatest joy," "unspeakably dear," and "precious gifts."[29]

Svendsen clearly represents herself in relationship—as a daughter, sister, wife, and mother. Although the "we" of the letters generally refers to the immediate and extended family, she also encompasses the larger community. She writes of the neighbors, "now that we have our own land and a wagon and oxen, we are self-sufficient and can even help others. It's wonderful to be able to do so." She also serves the larger community as its letter writer. Furthermore, they join the church, she writes, because they "could not continue to be outsiders." The close links between the various farms and communities in northern Iowa is clearly demonstrated as she instructs would-be emigrants when and where to arrive to meet others already settled and how to find lodging and transportation. The familial relationships represent the primary ones in the letters, but larger community relationships remain vital. As the home represents the central temporal/spatial reality for both Koren and Svendsen, the links between the homestead and the larger community become more evident in Svendsen's letters.[30]

Similar patterns of familial and extended relationships can be found in the letters of other immigrant women, both in the pre– and post–Civil War migrations.

Three women whose letters are reproduced in the volume *In Their Own Words: Letters from Norwegian Immigrants,* edited by Solveig Zempel, arrived after the peak year of Norwegian migration (1882) and represent that mass migration from a broader sector of society. Each of the three women in this post–Civil War collection represent different stages or patterns of migration for women: Berta Serina Kingestad (emigrated in 1883) represents single migration; Barbro Ramseth (1888) represents a later family migration; and Bergljot Anker Nilssen (1923) represents twentieth-century, urban migration. All maintained correspondence for many years with their families in Norway. The letters reveal many details of living and working conditions as well as meaningful patterns of self-conceptions, not unlike their predecessors—an emphasis on "we," on family and community, and on relationships.[31]

Kingestad migrated from the area of Stavanger at the age of twenty-three as a single woman. Like many others similar in age and status, she took a position as a domestic; however, Kingestad was pregnant at the time of migration and gave birth seven months later. Subsequently, she married and bore another child; however, her short life ended at age thirty after contracting tuberculosis. Most of the letters (fifteen of twenty-three) are addressed to her sister Anna and the remainder are addressed to her parents and brother. In her letters, Kingestad gives much attention to her working life and what she describes as "her situation." For example, she seeks melioration and peace for her "terrible sin" and acknowledges that she "wounded and offended the hearts of [her] dear parents." She writes of finding solace with an aunt that came over in the same circumstance. Even while attempting to repair wounded hearts, Kingestad—like her predecessors—also aims in the letters to preserve relationships at home.[32]

Barbro Ramseth (1838–1913), migrating with her husband and five children in 1888, represents both typical and atypical patterns of migrant women. Typically, she came from a rural area of Tynset in Hedmark (north of Oslo), worked first in a country inn in Norway, married, migrated with her husband and children, and settled in rural Wisconsin near an uncle. Atypically, she was fifty years old when migrating at a time when most emigrants were much younger and often single. Like her earlier counterparts, she wrote to her "often remembered dear old Father," to her sister, and to her extended family—"My dear ones, often remembered all at *Gammeludstumoen."* In these letters, from 1888 to 1904, she updates her family on their living conditions—health, economic circumstances, schooling, labor, and marriages of the children—often in some detail. She also reports on the neighbors from Tynset, and for a period they exchange local newspapers in letters. While she offers little introspection, she includes expressions of piety, as well as judgment of individuals in the community (for leaving the church, excessive drink, and not working). She does, however, offer intermittent and contradictory comments about their migration: "I regret we came here," and later, "I am glad we came here." Like Koren and Svendsen, she alludes to melancholy. In a letter dated December 4, 1889 (about a year after migrating), she writes, "I often feel rather melancholy" at the thought of not seeing the family again. What is most striking in this collection of letters is the sense of a family and community that she would preserve through information and correspondence, like a mediator engaged in kinwork. Her sense of self—like that of Svendsen and others—is clearly identified with family and community both in Tynset and in north and central Wisconsin.[33]

Bergljot Anker Nilssen (1891–1930) represents urban migration, but also return and remigration as well as professional migration—in short, changing migration patterns in the 1920s. Born into a professional family (her father was a schoolteacher and principal), Nilssen attended a teacher's college, married, and immigrated with her husband in 1915 to Superior, Wisconsin; they returned to Norway in 1917 and, years later, remigrated with their son to Chicago, where her husband took a position as an engineer. Nilssen's letters (totaling twenty-eight) from Chicago cover the years from 1923 to 1929 and are addressed to family—mostly parents-in-law, mother-in-law, or all. She writes of their family life, health and sickness, the progress of their son (and later birth of their daughter), her husband Karl's work life, domestic chores, social gatherings with other Norwegians, and the economic conditions in Chicago. Her letters also serve as a catalyst for the migration of her brother Skjala and brother-in-law Egil. Since most of the letters are addressed to her parents-in-law, and several times she notes her husband's neglect of correspondence, Nilssen illustrates the concept of kinwork: she maintains the contact with her husband's family and so preserves and maintains filial bonds across the Atlantic.[34]

The America letters constitute a rich body of primary source material, or folk literature, most often used by social historians as evidence of migration patterns. By examining these letters through a gendered lens and exploring the ways in which they convey a sense of self among women, we gain greater understanding about relationships between recipient and sender as well as about gendered dimensions of migration. The America letters, despite their fragmentary nature, illuminate these relationships and reveal permutations of the "we" in its various formulations.

Memoir/Reminiscence: Fragmented Selves in Communities

Mrs. Gunhild Andrine Jakobsdaughter Larsen (1835–19??) began her life story not with her birth but with her baptism in Knut Langeland's church in Larvik, Norway, when she received her "baptismal name, Gunhild Andrine." She concluded the life narrative with her own confirmation in Muskego, Wisconsin, but then added a two-page description of her wedding day, including many contextual details, such as rescheduling the event because of the American election of 1856 and identifying candidates, parties, and wagers on the election. She notes that the "feelings of the citizens were divided and quite agitated," while "there was a sharp difference of opinion among our people," implying they wished to avoid acrimony on the wedding day. The first half of her five-page, single-spaced typescript is devoted to three stages common in immigrant narratives: 1) early life in Norway (including descriptions of visits from "religious people of the haugian [Haugean] movement [a pietistic movement in Norway named after the lay preacher Hans Nielsen Hauge (1771–1824)], to which our family belonged"); 2) the transatlantic journey in 1844 aboard the ship *Washington* (including reports of Norwegian Lutheran pastor J. W. C. Dietrichsen and his sermons at sea); and 3) early days around Muskego (emphasizing the arrival of ministers and building that community). While the religious sensibility frames her narrative and life, the truncated and somewhat formulaic, chronological pattern can be found also in nonreligious reminiscences and short memoirs. Nonetheless, her brief details convey conceptions of the "self" and the "other" consistent with the life writings of other immigrant women, with an emphasis on the "we" and the community. Especially noteworthy are the added notes on her wedding day, offering context that is public, political, and patriarchal but also giving greater meaning and legitimacy to that personal occasion and her life.[35]

The memoir is distinguished from autobiography, writes Helen M. Buss, in that the autobiography makes "the individual life central," while memoir tends to focus on the times in which the life is lived and the significant others of the memoirist's world." Buss also observes that the form has been essentially ignored, both by historians, who see it as "inaccurate and overly personal," and by literary critics, who view it as "superficial" and "incomplete." More recently, scholars see "the subversive and revisionary possibilities" in the genre for what many call the subaltern (the oppressed, exploited, and invisible) or those "excluded from the mainstream culture and its generic expressions." One could argue that Larsen illustrates this potential. Reminiscence, on the other hand, refers to the "everyday activity of recalling and recounting past experience." In the words of Rena Feld, it is a "personal, spontaneous response to particular moments in life." More often reminiscence is spoken than written; however, it is common and occurs at all ages, especially at turning points in a life, such as at a birth, a marriage, or a death. Sometimes it is associated with a life review. Although a reminiscence is often linked to a single event, a number of "life reviews" by immigrant women (two to twenty pages of a life history) are labeled "reminiscence." Many fragments of life writing by immigrant women can be characterized as reminiscence: brief, unpublished, written for progeny, and often an accounting of the writer's

Carl Gilbertson–Anna Hoegh wedding gathering, showing the importance of extended family and communities, Spring Grove, 1895

life. Both memoir and reminiscence signify a fragmented narrative. Yet those fragments can illuminate self-conceptions in the same way slips of the tongue, dreams, or snapshots can reveal an individual's inner life. Whether or not these fragmentary narratives have "subversive" possibilities, they are rich sources. As in Larsen's reminiscence, brief details illuminate.[36]

Larsen's father was a wagon maker in Norway, and he had a "workshop in a large courtyard with a roof over" and a gate to the street. She wrote, "peasants drove into this court yard with their produce which was then in safe-keeping until sold. Sleeping quarters were also provided for such strangers." Although religious rites of baptism, confirmation, and marriage constituted the central events of Larsen's life narrative, she described a community of visitors and strangers with whom she seemed to identify. In her brief but detailed and graphic descriptions, she links her own life to significant persons or developments of the times. During the ship's crossing, she describes the stormy weather and the state church representative, J. W. C. Dietrichson, getting "doused with water" while he gave sermons; the seamen, she recalled, claimed that the "helmsman steered the ship for that purpose." The detail democratizes the small group and humanizes the church leader while exposing challenges to the state church. In Wisconsin, they first lived in a house "dug into a mound" that had been the print shop for

Nordlyset; later her father and uncle purchased land from Reverend Clausen and built a "large, long house of hewn logs, according to the Norwegian style of building." She identifies major male figures in the community by noting schooling by Landsverk and Stangeland, confirmation by Tobias Larsen Roisland, and marriage by Rev. H. L. Thalberg. Linking her life with major (male) figures within Norwegian history seemed to validate her narrative and give it meaning; in the process she also includes the larger community. The description of her wedding (added after her confirmation) emphasizes not so much the marriage but the context of a political election and the divisions it generated. In so doing, Larsen shows herself as a witness to a broader history and society and so gives structure and meaning to her life by focusing on public events and figures while foregrounding the community in which she lives.[37]

Although more common from the second generation, reminiscences and memoirs can be found in the immigrant generation. Frequently, these were written by pastor's wives, such as Thalette Galby Brandt, Lulla Preus, and Ragnhild Thinn Thvedt, or those with an education, such as the deaconess, Elizabeth Fedde, who left behind a memoir and a diary. Of course, women of more ordinary circumstances also left behind fragments of life stories. One might speculate about why we do not find more memoirs in the immigrant generation, for as participants and witnesses to a mass migration, they had much to write about during their time. Øverland's study of Norwegian American literature, *The Western Home,* identifies only three published memoirs by women: Christie Monson, Preus, and Thvedt. Several reasons may account for this: a significant factor would be the rigors of survival that gave little time for such pursuits, especially in the first generation; the attitudes toward female writings, especially in the publishing world, may have discouraged writing, along with women's limited presence in the public sector. The unpublished reminiscence of Larsen represents many other short, unpublished narratives in archives or awaiting discovery.[38]

As-Told-To Autobiographies: Diachronic Relationships with Immigrant Past

Erna Oleson Xan's *Wisconsin, My Home: The Story of Thurine Oleson as Told to Her Daughter* represents a body of Norwegian immigrant life writings in which one generation (usually the second or third generation) resurrects the stories heard in the family and writes the narrative of the immigrant, invariably told in the voice of the subject (the mother or grandmother). Often written as a way to preserve stories and traditions or recapture the past for the third generation, the genre may be another way to avoid the "distasteful I." Within categories of life writing, the form is seen as a variation of collaborative autobiography. Scholar of autobiography C. Thomas Couser refers to collaborative autobiography as "inherently ventriloquistic" and potentially problematic: "Naïve readers may assume that the writer serves as the subject's dummy, but the text often owes more to the writer than the subject. The danger of reading collaborative auto-biography is of attributing solely to the subject a narrative not originating with him or her and not edited by him or her." Although the genre may be viewed as problematic (representing the writer's voice for the teller's voice and realign-ing events or contexts), the form also attempts to achieve what we might call a diachronic relationship with the past. Specifically, one might argue that the very fact of preserving the stories, memories, and traditions of the earlier immi-grant generation—that is, the very act of re-creating these stories—represents an effort to expand a sense of community in time and create a diachronic rela-tionship with the past.[39]

While there are many of these narratives among immigrant life writings, Xan's is certainly representative and possibly the most well known. Because of the complexities of interpreting the sense of self within the multiple voices in the collaborative autobiography genre, I only touch on Xan's narrative. Published in 1950 by the University of Wisconsin Press, the narrative (dedicated to "the Oleson children") is divided into twelve chapters, only the first of which is set in Norway. The teller of the tales, Thurine Oleson, is born in Wisconsin, a second-generation immigrant; she tells the tales to her daughter, Erna Oleson Xan, a third-generation immigrant. Xan, the author, writes in the first person but uses her mother's voice: "One of my earliest memories is of Mother rocking by the window in the old log house, smoking her clay pipe and crying about Norway." She explains the immigrants from Telemark migrated to the town of Winchester in Wisconsin. Oleson continues: "I was the first child born of my parents in the New World. What I shall tell you of the Old Country are the stories I heard when these old friends got together, and when, after supper night after night, Father and Mother talked of Norway and nothing else." The chapter describes daily life in mid-nineteenth-century rural Norway, foodways, weddings, Christmas rituals, family relations, the decision to emigrate, and the journey. At the end of the chapter, Xan writes that Oleson states, "And so it began, the lifelong talk about Norway that has never ended to this day." In subsequent chapters, Oleson/Xan conjure up the past through ever-widening circles of family and community. While Oleson/Xan use a first person singular form, the narrative encompasses siblings, neighbors, church, children, and kinfolk as well as larger local and national communities. Despite the complex nature of the "I" in this as-told-to autobiography, the self-construction must also be interpreted as a col-lective "we," one that includes an expansive temporal and spatial reach. The best example of a collective autobiography, however, is the book often referred to simply as *Souvenir*.[40]

Collective Autobiography: Citizens "Shoulder to Shoulder with Men"

On July 13, 1925, eighty-five Norwegian American women gathered in St. Paul, Minnesota, calling themselves the Norse American Centennial Daughters. Their first act was the unanimous approval of Mrs. Alma A. Guttersen's offer "to complete a history of the Centennial reports, historic facts about our women, and newspaper articles about their work." Consequently, the lives, labors, and contributions of Norwegian American women emerge in a souvenir book published in 1926—*Souvenir, Norse-American Women, 1825–1925: A Symposium of Prose and Poetry, Newspaper Articles, and Biographies, Contributed by One Hundred Prominent Women*. Five years after women's suffrage was achieved in the United States, and in the wake of nearly three quarters of a century of the women's movement, the book emphasized the contributions of Norwegian American women to the building of America. Rather than foregrounding the "distasteful I," the lengthy book foregrounds a multiplicity of voices—a community of women in a collective autobiography. The book is dedicated to the women who have "unselfishly and gladly *worked shoulder to shoulder with the men,* contributing their full share to the accomplishment and prosperity that has resulted, in America." The dedication asserts the values these women affirm: citizenship, collective labor and identity, equality with men, and a democratic and inclusive America. The preface (written by Alma A. Guttersen) restates this affirmation of gender equality articulated in the dedication. Describing a shared labor associated with pioneer life, Guttersen repeats the vision of gender equality: "Just as the fathers among those early pioneers shared in the intimate phases of home life, the mothers worked shoulder to shoulder with their men-folk in the fields contributing their full share to the accomplishments and prosperity that resulted."[41]

The 1925 centennial and the women's *Souvenir* emerged in the wake of World War I and the concurrent Americanization movement that sought the assimilation of immigrants into American culture and society. The discourses of the centennial and *Souvenir* reflect that assimilation model. If the centennial organizers sought to demonstrate that Norwegian immigrants had become Americans, then the women's *Souvenir* sought to demonstrate that the women remained intimately involved in that process: they, too, contributed to the communities, the prosperity, the achievements. Ignored by scholars as neither literature nor history, the collection still represents a significant document of women's collective sense of self in the early twentieth century. Furthermore, it signifies an alternative identity to the "distasteful I"; the collective identity is based on a sense of community over time and space.[42]

Most of the ninety-five entries are brief (less than five pages), written by diverse women, including speeches, newspaper articles, biographies, new essays, poetry, photographs, lists of women's associations, clubs, and short biographies of prominent women. The book's organization begins with a chronological orientation, starting in 1825 and positing a gendered history. The first entries focus on the ship *Restauration* that brought the first Norwegian immigrants in 1825; these entries including photographs (of an early Bible, a copy of the sloop, and female descendants of the "sloopers") and a narrative of "The First Lady of *Restaurationen*," Martha Larsen, the wife of Lars Larsen, who led the expedition. The entry on Martha Larsen sets the tone for the whole volume, which is focused on women. Originally a speech presented at the Minnesota State Fair grounds on June 7, 1925, this short essay by Hanna Astrup Larsen (editor of the *American Scandinavian Review* and descendant of the Larsens) describes Martha Larsen but also evokes "the Norwegian women in America" by alluding to gendered traditions brought there. She writes, "The respect and comradeship which Norwegian men give their women have old traditions. As far back as 'Ejaal's Saga' we read of Bergthora's saying, 'I am Ejaal's wife and I have as much to say in our household as he has.'" Larsen goes on to assess these cultural—and gendered—traditions over time: "The Norwegian-American man has held to these traditions of this race. Within the home, he has given his wife and sister an honored place. Outside of the Home he has been—shall I say less generous? He has been very slow to accord her opportunities for higher education. In the church he has accepted her drudgery, but listened little to her counsels. He has had little use for her intelligence and none for her qualities of leadership. Nevertheless, all this is changing and has already changed." In Larsen's view, Norwegian traditions of gender equity appear alongside a gendered critique, a duality that reflects the post-suffrage historical moment (in Norway and in the United States) in which women voiced gratitude for achievements, yet discontent for continuing inequity with cries for full equality.[43]

The subsequent organization of the volume is unspecified; the ninety-five entries follow neither a clear chronology nor a topical structure. Some essays are in Norwegian, but most are in English. The editors contributed numerous entries, but many come from other women, some anonymous. Subjects include women's roles as mothers, wives, and pioneers; emerging professions and the labor of women, especially teaching, nursing, midwifery, missions, and domestic service; the continuation of women's traditional crafts in the new world, such as quilting and weaving; women's contributions in fields such as music, literature, art, and social welfare—especially for orphans and the elderly; and the deaconess movement. Essays also discuss organizations of Norwegian American women: secular ones, such as the Dotres of Norge (Daughters of Norway) and the Progressive Literary Club; and religious ones, such as the Women's Missionary Federation and Daughters of the Reformation. Also found are essays by Norwegian American women on contemporary problems, including peace and national defense.

Fifty short biographies included toward the end of the collection provide a more detailed portrait of Norwegian American women. Although the biographies vary in length and detail, some generalizations emerge. Most of the women deemed prominent enough to receive a biography are married (thirty-nine out of fifty); nearly half indicated some postsecondary education (twenty-three out of fifty), although many entries did not note education, so the number may be higher; most were second-generation immigrants (eighteen out of the thirty-two who identified an immigration generation); most reside in Minnesota (eighteen out of fifty); several reside in North Dakota (nine) and a few in Iowa and Hawaii (four each); the remaining women are scattered throughout the other states (one or two in each, slightly higher concentration in the West). Virtually all women worked

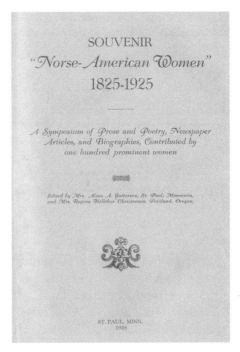

Title page for Souvenir, Norse-American Women, 1835–1925, *edited by Alma A. Guttersen and Regina Hilleboe Christensen*

outside the home, usually before marriage and mostly in teaching, but other professional areas include mission work, child and social welfare, music, accounting, banking, and cooking. This seems to demonstrate that, in the second generation, Norwegian American women were likely to pursue some postsecondary education, seek employment in areas linked to women's professions, marry, and remain in regions of their forebears or in areas of other Norwegian settlements.[44]

Entries represent the diversity of women's experiences and interests, including matters social, political, cultural, religious, and of international peace, demonstrating the complexity of the collection and the collective autobiography. The range of the topics, the scope encompassing all regions of the country, and the varied aspects of women's lives speak to the diversity and complexity of Norwegian American women. Placed in its historical context, the entries reflect the progressive reforms and thinking of the era. Though some historians argue that World War I ended the progressive reforms, these essays address those reforms and reflect the active engagement of Norwegian American women in the continuation of those efforts. Three essay entries illustrate not only this engagement with progressive reforms but also signify a diversity of women's concerns and activities—as well as their collective and community-oriented sense of "self."[45]

One entry, simply titled "Sketches," draws attention to the social and economic issues of young, immigrating women from Norway and to an effort to raise consciousness of their conditions. The six brief sketches describe risks of single, migrating girls traveling alone across the country, as the opening of the first sketch reveals: "How many of the girls reared in the United States have studied the problems of the new comers? Many of them leave home at an early age and while still in their teens are transplanted and expected to grow and develop without growth being retarded." The tragic story of Anna Brevig follows. Losing her mother as a young girl, Anna felt alienated when her father remarried and she was encouraged to join her sister in America. With a ticket from her father, she traveled to Seattle, where she learned her sister had moved to Los Angeles. Anna worked as a domestic for a Norwegian family in Seattle (who exploited her) until her sister (having contracted tuberculosis) sent for her. Nursing her sister back to health, Anna contracted the disease, received a return ticket to Norway, but died crossing the Atlantic. Less tragic but also disturbing stories portray related struggles of vulnerable women in a foreign land. One sketch describes a young girl who lost her purse containing money and the address of her destination. In another sketch, a young, immigrant girl worked for her aunt as a domestic but was wrongly accused of theft and set off on her own. Another describes a young girl tricked and deceived while traveling by train. Another conveys the pay discrimination young girls faced: Sarah explained that both she and her brother worked binding grain in the fields near Dawson, Minnesota, but he received $1.50 a day for field work while she received $1.00 for field work *and* domestic chores. These sketches expose perils facing young girls from Norway but also convey the social conscience of the editors (married, middle class) and their alliance with and advocacy for these young women.[46]

A second, striking entry evokes cultural awareness and continuity with transnational connections. "The Baldishol Committee" describes a gift to President and Mrs. Coolidge of a tapestry from Norwegian American women on the occasion of their visit to the Twin Cities for the 1925 centennial. Representative of medieval art and dated from 1180 CE, the original Baldishol tapestry depicts the months of April and May and is believed to be a fragment of a larger panel. Kristi Sexe, "an accomplished [Norwegian] artist," wove a copy of the tapestry, spinning and dyeing her own wool. The Baldishol Committee decided to present the tapestry to the White House as "a suitable present" and a "token of gratitude" for Coolidge's participation in the centennial. The labor of the women in securing and carrying out this gift of gratitude is not described, but in many ways it signifies complex transnational exchanges and foregrounds a gendered perspective: the gift presents a traditional Norwegian craft (weaving) associated with

Baldishol tapestry fragment, presented as a gift to the White House from Norse-American Women

women; a female artist (Sexe) re-created the original work; and the collaboration of women extended a gesture of gratitude on a national scale.[47]

A third exemplary entry illustrates the political and transnational dimension of the volume and the women's broader sense of self in a global context pursuing world peace. Written in Norwegian, the essay "Norwegian American Women's Commitment to World Peace" by Helen Egilsrud must be seen in the context of the international women's and peace movements surrounding World War I. In this entry, Norwegian American women affirm their commitment to and offer proposals for achieving world peace—proposals to be submitted to all U.S. senators, congressmen, and leading advisors: 1) Codification of International Law; 2) Progressive World Organization for Peace, International Co-operation; 3) Referendum—Vote of the People—on War; 4) Worldwide Reduction of Armaments to Police Status; and 5) Worldwide Education for Peace. While the women's vision is idealistic, elements of these strategies can be found in Woodrow Wilson's writings, in the formulations of most peace groups at the time, and in the Kellogg-Briand Pact of 1928 (ratified by sixty-two countries) that renounced war. This advocacy for international peace clearly situates Norwegian American women within the international women's progressive and peace movements of the time. Furthermore, that the Norwegian American women include this entry demonstrates their conception of themselves as linked across national borders.

Indeed, this essay suggests a self-construction embracing not only the recent, young, immigrant women, their sisters in Norway, and ancestral mothers but also those united in a vision of shared humanity and peace.[48]

The final, one-page entry, labeled "A 'Thank You,' an Apology, and a Request," reveals a tension at the core of the collective autobiography. The "Thank You" is directed at all contributors and advisors for the volume—evoking a contribution model of history. The "Apology" reaches out to those excluded, to the absent voices: "In gathering material, we find the half has not been told: only a fraction of the accomplishments . . . is recorded in this book. Thousands of autobiographies and biographies should have been on the honor roll, completing the history of women's work." The "Request" seeks additional material for a second volume and "a more complete history." These closing comments reflect both the tension and the vision of the women as they seek to negotiate and balance their place in the new world. A desire to demonstrate women's contributions—how they stood "shoulder to shoulder with men"—risks exclusion and the egoism of a "distasteful I" in patriarchal narratives; on the other hand, the apology aims to recognize the lost voices and lives while offering an alternative and inclusive narrative of "we." The concluding paragraph affirms the vision of an inclusive, diverse, and collective "we" as signifying Norwegian American women: "The Norse-American women have carved their names on the slabs of fame as homemakers. They are also to be found as students and graduates of our colleges and universities, teachers, doctors, nurses, missionaries, artists, musicians, authors, in clubs, churches, business etc." Notably absent, however, in this closing statement are the laborers most visible in the immigrant generation—domestics, seamstresses, cooks, laundry workers, farmers and homesteaders, clerks and office workers. One can only assume the editors also included them in the pantheon of worthy citizens.[49]

Conclusion

Norwegian immigrant women avoided full-length autobiographies. While they wrote what today is described as life writing, their contributions fall into categories often devalued, dismissed, or ignored—diaries, letters, reminiscences and memoirs, oral history, as-told-to autobiographies, and collective autobiographies. While social historians have drawn on many of these writings for historical evidence, they may also be read for understanding self-conceptions of immigrant women and gendered perspectives of migration. Consistently, these women's narratives convey the sense of a fragmented self but also emphasize the "we" of extended families, communities, and transatlantic alliances. These women's self-constructions, avoiding the "distasteful I" and emphasizing the "we" of the community, represent a deeper continuity with the past—and old-world democratic and egalitarian values—than the representation of the individual-ized "I" in the autobiography elevated in the American context. Furthermore, the self-constructions of the immigrant women convey cultural traditions and values as enduring as the more visible elements of culture often associated with ethnic retention—language, food, dress, objects, and rituals. Identifying, acknowledging, and understanding these neglected life writings that posit an alternative self-construction help us rethink the legacies of migration, especially in their gendered dimensions.

Notes

1. Theodore C. Blegen, "Preface," *The Diary of Elizabeth Koren, 1853–1855,* trans. and edited by David T. Nelson (Northfield, MN, Norwegian-American Historical Association [hereafter, NAHA], 1955), v. Blegen describes the memories as "rich and deep"; scenes and events as "vivid," fresh, and "significant in themselves."

2. Rasmus B. Anderson, *Life Story of Rasmus B. Anderson Written By Himself,* 2nd ed. rev. (Madison, WI: N.p., 1917), xvii . The lengthy volume, nearly seven hundred pages in its final form, ironically conveys little reticence about using the "I" form, yet in his dedi-cation (to "those of Norwegian birth or descent who have helped to make America") he also acknowledges the larger community. Anderson's candid reluctance about writ-ing autobiography reflects a cultural value conceivably shared by immigrant men and women but more prevalent among women.

3. The term *autobiography* traditionally has had a specific meaning referring to an individual writing his or her life story, embedded in the meanings of the elements *auto* (self), *bio* (life), and *graph* (writing). More recent scholarship has placed autobiography in a broader context of "life writing," a category that encompasses shorter autobiograph-ical texts such as memoirs and reminiscences, journals and diaries, and the epistolary form as well as biography, autobiographical fiction, and auto-ethnography.

On immigrant men writing life stories, see, for example, Edward Bok, *The Ameri-canization of Edward Bok* (New York: C. Scribner's Sons, 1922); Andrew Carnegie, *Auto-biography of Andrew Carnegie* (Boston and New York: Houghton Mifflin Company, 1920); Jacob Riis, *The Making of an American* (New York: Macmillan, 1902); and Andreas Ueland, *Recollections of an Immigrant* (New York: Minton, Balch and Co, 1929). The classic American autobiographies that provided models include two major works: Ben-jamin Franklin, *The Autobiography of Benjamin Franklin,* in numerous versions but first published by his grandson, William Temple Franklin, in 1818; and a work published a century later, Henry Adams, *The Education of Henry Adams* (Boston: Houghton Mifflin, 1918). Of course, these successful immigrants represent an impossible model for immi-grants not male and not white and a difficult model for white male immigrants who were unskilled wage workers. During this time Hamilton Holt, editor of the progressive (and previously abolitionist) periodical *The Independent,* made an effort to be more inclusive as he published eighty so-called "life-lets" in a volume entitled *The Life Stores of Undis-tinguished Americans As Told By Themselves* (New York: The Independent, 1906). Holt writes they would also represent the "five great races of mankind, the white, yellow, red, brown and black" ("Note," 1906 edition).

Regarding women writing life stories, researchers always allow the possibility of new discoveries. To date, my searches for Norwegian immigrant women's autobiographies have been unsuccessful, though they sometimes led to ambiguous narratives. Some works that may be listed as autobiographies often prove to be second-generation, "as told to" autobiographies, biographies, or adaptations. Some second-generation women have written their mother's stories in the "I" form, for example, "Alma" (Alma A. Gutterson, co-editor of *Souvenir),* which *was* written by a daughter but is identified in archival records as an autobiography. Also important is that extant studies of Norwegian American autobiographies focus only on men. For example, in his chapter on autobiographies in *Twofold Identities: Norwegian-American Contributions to Midwestern Literature* (New York: Peter Lang, 2004), Øyvind Gulliksen argues that there is a "large corpus of Norwegian-American autobiographies," 67n2. His examples represent prominent men: Laurence M. Larsen, *The Logbook of a Young Immigrant* (Northfield: NAHA, 1939); John Widtsoe, *In a Sunlit Land* (1952); and recently published works in Norway: Knut Lundeberg, *Glimt fra mit liv* (1992); and Kristian Prestegard, *Fra Heidal til Decorah* (1996). The two representative examples analyzed are the autobiographies of Andreas Ueland, *Recollections of an Immigrant* (New York: Minton, Balch and Co., 1929); and Ø. Ø. Rønning, *Fifty Years in America* (Minneapolis, MN: Friend Publishing Company, 1939). Laurence Larsen became a scholar of the European Middle Ages and president of the American Historical Association (though he emigrated as an infant and might be considered second generation); Andreas Ueland was a successful attorney in Minneapolis; Kristian Prestegard edited the *Decorah Posten* for fifty years, although he told his life story to his daughter and this manuscript was published posthumously.

It should be noted that immigrant women's autobiographies representing other ethnic groups do exist; however, immigrant women are less represented in the genre than may be assumed. Among immigrant women who wrote autobiographies, Eastern European Jewish immigrant women figure prominently. Included among autobiographers for this immigrant group, one finds Mary Antin, Emma Goldman, Anzia Yezierska, Rose Schndiderman, and Hilda Polacheck, the latter less prominent than the other women. Polacheck grew up in the neighborhood of Hull House and tried throughout her life to publish her autobiography. Not until the ethnic revival and the second wave of feminism did her daughter, Dena J. Polacheck Epstein, assist in publishing the work two decades after her death, as *I Came a Stranger: The Story of a Hull-House Girl* (Urbana and Chicago: University of Illinois Press, 1989).

4. In this essay I have focused on the immigrant generation and exclude second-generation immigrant narratives. Migration historians usually use the term *second-generation immigrant* to refer to those born in the United States or who migrated as infants but whose lives were steeped in both the immigrant and American cultures. This generation often experienced significant tensions between the two cultures. Autobiographies by second-generation Norwegian immigrants can be more readily found and reflect a more assimilated sensibility.

5. For example, see selected works by Philippe LeJeune, *L'Autobiographie en France*

(Paris: A. Colin, 1971), *Je est un autre, l'autobiographie de la literature aux medias* (Paris: Editions du Seuil, 1980), *Moi aussi* (Paris: Editions du Seuil, 1986), and *On Autobiography*, trans. Katherine Leary, in Theory and History of Literature Series, Vol. 52 (Minneapolis: University of Minnesota Press, 1989); Françoise Lionnet, *Autobiographical Voices: Race, Gender, Self-Portraiture* (Ithaca, NY, and London: Cornell University Press, 1989); Mary Jo Maynes, *Taking the Hard Road: Life Course in French and German Workers' Autobiographies in the Era of Industrialization* (Chapel Hill: University of North Carolina Press, 1995); and Katherine Goodman, *Dis/closures: Women's Autobiography in Germany Between 1790 and 1914* (New York: P. Lang, 1986). See also Margaretta Jolly, ed., *The Encyclopedia of Life Writing: Autobiographical and Biographical Forms*, 2 vols. (London and Chicago: Fitzroy Dearborn Publishers, 2001), which encompasses all periods and regions of the globe.

6. See, for example, *De/Colonizing the Subject: The Politics of Gender in Women's Autobiography*, eds. Sidonie Smith and Julia Watson (Minneapolis: University of Minnesota Press, 1992), and *Women, "Race," and Writing in the Early Modern Period*, eds. Margo Hendricks and Patricia Parker (London and New York: Routledge, 1994). Quotation from Sidonie Smith, *The Poetics of Women's Autobiography: Marginality and the Fictions of Self-Representation* (Bloomington and Indianapolis: Indiana University Press, 1987), 15.

7. This tension can be illustrated in Mary Antin's autobiography, *The Promised Land* (1912). Though the work is often seen as the paradigmatic immigrant autobiography, it is the work of a woman. She stands for the universal (male) subject, as I have argued elsewhere, essentially by erasing gender. Antin, who wrote her autobiography at the age of thirty when she was a wife and mother, concluded her "life" story when she completed high school, thoroughly Americanized, still a teenager, before the messy matters of adulthood, marriage, sexuality, children, and gendered struggles. Indeed, she wrote her narrative, the classic immigrant autobiography, by denying femaleness and adulthood, thus signifying the universal subject. Still, this work has been viewed as "the classic immigrant autobiography."

8. Marie Wells, "Norway," in *Encyclopedia of Life Writing*, 1:664–65. Wells discusses what she sees as manifestation of the more democratic spirit of the country found in family history *(slektshistorie)* and local history *(bygdehistorie)*—forms in which identity is linked historically (in the ancestral family, often the farm) and spatially (in the community). Such forms can also be linked with more collective concepts of subjectivity. See also Marianne Gullstad, *Everyday Life Philosophers: Modernity, Morality and Autobiography in Norway* (Oslo, Stockholm, Copenhagen, and Boston: Scandinavian University Press, 1996).

Gulliksen's chapter on autobiographies in *Twofold Identities* examines two autobiographers: Andreas Ueland and Ø.Ø. Rønning. The former represents an individualized and heroic American success story, while the latter demonstrates more of a collective narrative, although dimensions of Rønning's work evoke the universal male subject. The first half of the work (1–111) is devoted to a chronological narrative of his life, while the second half considers "People Worth Knowing," suggesting a more collective sensibility and identification with others. Nevertheless, of these twenty-eight "people worth knowing," twenty-seven are men, while the sole female is a minister's wife. Rønning, an active writer, publisher, and editor, emigrated at the age of seventeen to study in the United States. Although he uses Anderson's distasteful "I," he wrote the autobiography, he asserts, because it would be "fun" and "to throw light on life and work" of Norwegian Americans in the new world.

9. This essay is organized around representative samples of life writing in the five categories and does not aim to provide a comprehensive study of all life writings by Norwegian immigrant women. I argue, however, that these representative examples illuminate other writings.

10. M. M. Bakhtin argues that our image of the human being is always situated in time and place, what he refers to as a chronotope, quite literally the time/place of human beings. He argues in *The Dialogic Imagination,* ed. Michael Holquist, trans. Caryl Emerson and M. Holquist (Austin: University of Texas Press, 1981), "the image of man [*sic*] is always intrinsically chronotopic" (271). For further discussion of the chronotopic reading of immigrant autobiography, see Betty Ann Bergland, "Reconstructing the Self in America: Patterns in Immigrant Women's Autobiography" (diss, University of Minnesota, 1990). For other studies using a spatial analysis, see, for example, *Mapping the Self: Space, Identity, Discourse in British Auto/Biography,* ed. Frederic Regards (Saint-Etienne, France: Publications de l'Universite de Saint-Etienne, 2003).

11. Virginia Woolf, cited in her "Diaries and Journals: General Survey," in *Encyclopedia of Life Writing,* 1:267. The diary and journal discussed together here may convey different meanings: in English, the term *diary* is also used for "formal planning"; whereas, the French use the word *agenda* for formal planning and *journal intime* for diary. In Norwegian, the term *dagbok* translates as both diary and journal, literally as "day book." Cottam, *Encyclopedia of Life Writing,* 1:268. That a journal may not always be intended for secrecy is suggested by Gro Svendsen, who copies entries from her journal in letters to her brother to convey details of the journey to America and her first impressions.

12. Lillian Schlissel, *Women's Diaries of the Westward Journey* (New York: Schocken Books, 1982, 1992), 10. See also Elizabeth Hampsten, *Read This Only to Yourself: The Private Writings of Midwestern Women, 1880–1910* (Bloomington: Indiana University Press, 1982), which emphasizes the private and oppositional dimensions of women's life writings.

13. Elizabeth Fedde, "Diary, 1883–88," trans. and ed. Beulah Folkedahl, *Norwegian American Studies and Records* 20 (1959); Caroline Dorothea Margrethe Keyser, *Linka's Diary on Land and Sea, 1845–1864,* trans. and eds. Johan Carl Keyser Preus and Diderikke Margarethe Brant Preus (Minneapolis, MN: Augsburg Publishing House, 1952), and in a new translation, *Linka's Diary: A Norwegian Immigrant Story in Words and Sketches,* eds. Marvin G. Slind and Gracia Grindal (Minneapolis, MN: Lutheran University Press, 2008); and *The Diary of Elisabeth Koren.*

14. *The Diary of Elisabeth Koren.* Extracts from this diary were published in 1914 by her children, titled *Fra Pioneer Tiden: Uddrag af Fru Elisabeth Korens dagbog og breve fra femtiaarene.* E. Clifford Nelson and Eugene Fevold noted in *The Lutheran Church Among Norwegian-Americans: A History of the Evangelical Lutheran Church* (Minneapolis, MN: Augsburg Publishing House, 1960) that Koren, along with a few other new theological students, were "reinforcements" because of the lack of "clerical manpower to meet the spiritual needs of the frontier" (1:162). David T. Nelson writes that with a "tendency

toward deafness," a young Elisabeth was sent to Copenhagen "to address the issue." The schools there provided nothing for girls, however, so she received private lessons from some of the teachers. For more discussion of Koren and *The Diary*, see L. DeAne Lagerquist, *In America the Men Milk the Cows: Factors of Gender, Ethnicity, and Religion in the Americanization of Norwegian-American Women* (Brooklyn, NY: Carlson Publishing, Inc. 1991), note index references, 248.

15. Koren, *The Diary*, 23, 324. She addresses "you" on Monday, 24 October 1853, aboard the sailing ship *Rhein*. The link between letters and diaries is also found in Caja Munch's letters to her family: see *The Strange American Way: Letters of Caja Munch from Wiota, Wisconsin, 1855–1859*, trans. Helene Munch and Peter A. Munch (Carbondale and Edwardsville: Southern Illinois University Press, 1970). Koren's "Conclusion to the Norwegian edition" published in 1914 confesses that when her children wished to print the diary and letters, she initially opposed them and could not believe that "these simple and unadorned notes are worth it" (369). *The Diary* might be imagined with six divisions: the transatlantic journey (chs. 1–4); the land journey via train, steamer, and canoe across the Mississippi River (5–6); their residence sharing settlers' cabins (7–13); residence in a temporary house on their own (14–17); arrival in their new parsonage (18–19); and the letters to Elisabeth's father in 1855 (20).

16. Koren, *The Diary*, 314, 324. American readers familiar with U.S. women's history may recognize here the nineteenth-century model of the ideal woman, outlined in Barbara Welter, "The Cult of True Womanhood, 1820–1860," *American Quarterly* 18.2 (Summer 1966): 151–74. Welter argues that middle-class American women were guided in their domestic roles through the day's popular literature and clergymen's advice on the cardinal virtues of the "ideal woman": domesticity, submissiveness, purity, and piety. Catharine Beecher, *Treatise on Domestic Economy, For the Use of Young Ladies at Home and at School*, first published in 1841 with numerous editions, provided guidelines for managing a household. The Norwegian counterpart was to be found in Koren's library, *Lærebog I de forskjellige grene av husholdning* (*Textbook on the Various Branches of Housekeeping*) by Hanna Olava Winsnes (Kristiania, 1845).

17. Koren, *The Diary*, 3–4. When they disembarked in New York, she wrote of the steerage passengers: "the steerage folk were taken ashore on a tug . . . a throng of people so clear and well dressed that we did not recognize them" (60). In her descriptive passages narrating the journey inland she also comments on the masses: in the steamer from Chicago to Milwaukee in the "elegant saloon" of mixed classes, she is critical of the pride and arrogance, high and low, of the woman in silk "from top to toe" and much taken with herself and her finery, as well as of the man with heavy, dirty shoes sullying the "lovely carpets" (74). She also complained of the coaches filled with an "unpleasant mixed company, which one must put up with here where there is only one class" (73).

18. She often remarks on the "rustic manners" of the farm folk and refers to them as "nature's children" (121).

19. Koren, *The Diary*, 212, 226, 324. It was common in Norway for large farmsteads, and especially the parsonage, to hire young girls for household chores. On medical practices, see Kathleen Stokker, *Remedies and Rituals: Folk Medicine in Norway and the New Land* (St. Paul: Minnesota Historical Society Press, 2007), esp. ch. 3, "The Pastor as

Doctor." Stokker writes, "Ministers and ministers' wives did much of the doctoring and dispensing of medicine in rural nineteenth-century Norway and Norwegian America" (61). Koren recalls unpacking her books was her greatest pleasure. In addition to the medical books, she refers to works on natural history, folk ballads, fairy tales, household management, and fiction by Norwegian, German, and British writers.

20. Koren, *The Diary*, 238, 237, 249, 331. The entry expressing longing is dated 30 Oct. 1854, when she was pregnant with her first child. She gave birth on 12 Dec. 1854.

21. Bernard Bray, "Letters: General Survey," trans. Monique Lamontagne, *Encyclopedia of Life Writing*, 2:551, 553. See also Bernard Bray with Christoph Strosetzki, *Art de la lettre, art de la conversation a la epoque classique en France: actes due colloque de Wolfenbuttel* (Paris: Klincksieck, 1995).

22. Theodore C. Blegen, ed., *Land of Their Choice: The Immigrants Write Home* (Minneapolis: University of Minnesota Press, 1955), v. Orm Øverland, "Letters as Links in the Chain of Migration from Hedalen, Norway, to Dane County, Wisconsin, 1857–1890," in *Interpreting the Promise of America: Essays in Honor of Odd Sverre Lovoll*, ed. Todd W. Nichol (Northfield, MN: NAHA, 2002), 79–103. Roger Daniels, *Coming to America: A History of Immigration and Ethnicity in American Life*, 2nd ed. (New York: Perennial, 2002).

23. Orm Øverland, "Learning to Read Immigrant Letters: Reflections towards a Textual Theory," in *Norwegian-American Essays*, ed. Øyvind T. Gulliksen, et al. (Oslo: NAHA-Norway and the Norwegian Emigrant Museum, 1996), 210. Like literature, there are conventions of letter writing and guidebooks that circulated in the nineteenth century and that may raise questions about the degree of authenticity in this folk literature. Also, it is often impossible to determine contexts that contribute to the letters, the subtexts, and the unsaid. Bray, "Letters," in *Encyclopedia*, 2:552. The present essay is more concerned with self-conceptions, especially the gendered constructions, and not "personalities." However, the element of self-revelation is fundamental to both views.

24. Øverland, "Learning to Read Immigrant Letters," 224. See Micaela di Leonardo, *The Varieties of Ethnic Experience: Kinship, Class, and Gender Among California Italian Americans* (Ithaca, NY: Cornell University Press, 1984). Examining the important work women did in maintaining the kinship networks of these dispersed first-, second-, and third-generation immigrants through writing letters, sending cards notifying of births, death, and marriages, and so on, di Leonardo describes this labor as "*kinwork.*" Significantly, when women left an area (through moves or divorces), kinwork also declined along with connections to extended families.

25. Pauline Farseth and Theodore C. Blegen, eds. and trans., *Frontier Mother: Letters of Gro Svendsen* (Northfield, MN: NAHA, 1950), v. Blegen's thoughtful introduction provides a biography of Svendsen, a descriptive analysis of the letters, and commentary on the conditions of frontier life they describe. See Øyvind T. Gulliksen, "Interdisciplinary Approaches in American Immigration Studies," in *Interpreting the Promise of America*, 31–51, especially 43–45. Gulliksen points out that Svendsen's letters appear in *Immigrant Voices: Twenty-four Narratives of Becoming an American*, ed. Gorden Hunter (New York: Signet Classics, 1999), as the sole representation of Scandinavian immigrants. David A. Gerber also discusses Svendsen in "The Immigrant Letter between Positivism and Populism: The Uses of Immigrant Personal Correspondence in Twentieth-Century American

Scholarship," *Journal of American Ethnic History* 16.4 (Summer 1997): 3–34, esp. 20–22. For a more general discussion of immigrant letters, see David A. Gerber, "Epistolary Ethics: Personal Correspondence and the Culture of Emigration in the Nineteenth Century," *Journal of American Ethnic History* 19:4 (Summer 2000): 3–23.

26. The first letter fragment, addressed to "my beloved friend" in 1861, presumably is written to Ole, her future husband, on the matter of securing permission to marry; she requests that he come to her parents and speak to them. The longing and guilt communicated in later letters is also the anguish Ole Rølvaag gives to the character of Beret Holm.

27. See, for example, Betty Bergland, "Cultural Memory and Migration in Orabel Thortvedt's Narrative: 'Buffalo River: A Tale of the Emigrant and the Pioneer,'" in *Norwegian American Essays 2008: Migration and Memory*, ed. Oyvind Gullicksen and Harry T. Cleven (Oslo: NAHA-Norway, 2002), 15–40.

28. Farseth and Blegen, *Frontier Mother*, 72, 123, 136, 138.

29. Farseth and Blegen, *Frontier Mother*, v, 27, 119, 120, 126, 128, 134.

30. Farseth and Blegen, *Frontier Mother*, 53, 128–29. Blegen notes her writing for the newspaper *Emigranten* but not her unpaid labor as a community letter writer. Svendsen commented that many can write but "few can compose"; she tells them she has no time, but there is no one else, so "I usually yield," and "my earnings are a thank-you" (125). She includes these details in a letter to her parents to explain her not writing.

31. Solveig Zempel, ed. and trans., *In Their Own Words: Letters from Norwegian Immigrants* (Minneapolis and Oxford: University of Minnesota Press in cooperation with NAHA, 1991) provides the reader with rich historical documents in English of extended correspondence for eight emigrants (three women) from Norway during the post–Civil War era. The multiple letters over time from one individual provide more context and understanding for each example. Zempel also provides biographical material on each letter writer.

32. Zempel, *In Their Own Words*, 33.

33. Zempel, *In Their Own Words*, 102–28.

34. Zempel, *In Their Own Words*, 157–84.

35. Gunhild Andrine Jacobsdatter Larsen, unpublished manuscript, P210, 1923 and 1925, Norwegian-American Historical Association, Northfield, MN (hereafter, NAHA). Larson's narrative might be representative of other short typescripts that provide a life review and may be found in family papers, especially those of fathers, husbands, and brothers. In the last page of her manuscript she takes issue with some claims in O. M. Norlie's *History of the Norwegian People*, questioning whether Søren Bache's accident with a loaded gun led to a woman's death and his departure from Muskego in despair.

36. Helen M. Buss, "Memoirs," *Encyclopedia of Life Writing*, 2:595. Memoir is also an older term, appearing in the *Oxford English Dictionary* in the early sixteenth century, whereas the term *autobiography* appears first in the late eighteenth century, Buss explains, when individualist narratives were growing out of the revolutionary and romantic periods. Often the word *memoir* is used as a generic term for autobiography; however, most scholars of life writings distinguish between the two forms. Memoirs may also be briefer. Because memoirs focus more on the times, they may be especially useful to

social historians. Buss notes that *autobiography* is the more elevated term, since literary historians have chosen these as the culture's "central originating life stories," contrasted with the scandalous narratives of "fallen women" who wrote their memoirs in the eighteenth century. For more on the topic of the oppressed or invisible, see subaltern studies as a critical field. Scholars often point to the importance of memoirs in the twentieth century that testify to horrific events we might seek to deny; for example, the works of Elie Wiesel on the Holocaust that use the term *memoir.*

One might see subversive potential in other unpublished reminiscences of immigrant women. One example: the three-page typescript (labeled "Olson?") found in the Knut Gjerset Papers, P683, box 5e, folder 7, NAHA. Born in Norway in 1879, Olson migrated from the family farm to Kristiania (Oslo) and worked as an apprentice in a tailor's shop for eight years before migrating to Chicago, following typical patterns of single, female migration. With a trade she quickly found work with a "Scandinavian clientele," fell in love, became pregnant, and raised her son alone "in a little flat in Chicago" as she continued working. When her son was three, she married a Norwegian widower and farmer in Wisconsin and so found a home to provide "a normal childhood" for her son. Still, she wrote at the end of her short memoir, "working and taking care of my baby [in Chicago] as being the happiest time of my life." (Gjerset, who was involved with the centennial in 1925 and the formation of NAHA, was planning an encyclopedia of Norwegians in America; presumably this manuscript was to be part of that project.)

Rena Feld, "Reminiscence," *Encyclopedia of Life Writing,* 2:742–43. Because the form is usually associated with the spoken word, it is more recently linked with psychotherapy, experiential learning, and ethnography.

37. Larsen, *Logbook of a Young Immigrant,* 1–5.

38. The memoir of Elizabeth Fedde is certainly interesting for its depiction of the life of a professional nurse and deaconess who helped establish hospitals in the United States. Still, we must consider her a sojourner, not an emigrant, since she remained in the country only from 1883 to 1896. Nevertheless, she challenges some of the patterns in immigrant women's writing as she conveys confidence working with American physicians, consular officials, and clergy to serve the poor and sick. At the same time, she avoids the "I" by emphasizing the work and not the self. She is discussed elsewhere and, most recently, in Kristin Kavli Adriansen, "Sister Elizabeth Fedde: A Light of Hope to Sick and Needy Immigrants in New York City," in *Norwegian American Essays 2008,* 59–84.

For some examples of Norwegian immigrant and Norwegian American women's reminiscences and memoirs, see Astrid Ihme Bacon, "Bridges of Brotherhood," unpublished manuscript, P832, NAHA; Mrs. R. O. Brandt, "Social Aspects of Prairie Pioneering: The Reminiscences of a Pioneer Pastor's Wife," *Norwegian American Studies and Records* 7 (1933): 1–46; Elizabeth Fedde, "The Memoirs of Sister Elizabeth," trans. P. J. Hertsgaard, unpublished manuscript, P801, NAHA; Eleanor Merriken, *Looking for Country: A Norwegian Immigrant's Alberta Memoir* (Calgary: University of Calgary Press, 1999); Christie Monson, "Hvorledes en sognebydg i midtre Iowa ble til," *Jul I Vesterheimen* (1947), "En Bolig har du vaert oss," *Jul I Vesterheimen* (1952): 37–40, and "Den gamle Emigrantkisten," *Jul I Vesterheimen* (1956): 33–45; Lulla Preus, "Minder fra den gamle Paint Creek Prestegaard," *Symra* 7 (1911): 1–15; Grace Rollag, "Erindring fra Gamle dage,"

1927, unpublished manuscript, P329, NAHA; Ragnhild Thinn Thvedt, *Nogle Minder Fra en Norsk-Amerikansk Prestegaard* (Eau Claire, WI: Fremad Publishing Company Press, 1940). Orm Øverland, *The Western Home: A Literary History of Norwegian America* (Northfield, MN: NAHA, 1996), see references, 381–426.

39. Erna Oleson Xan, *Wisconsin My Home: The Story of Thurine Oleson As Told To Her Daughter* (Madison: University of Wisconsin Press, 1950). C. Thomas Couser, "Collaborative Autobiography," in *Encyclopedia of Life Writing*, 1:223. See also by Couser, *Altered Egos: Authority in American Autobiography* (New York: Oxford University Press, 1989) and *Vulnerable Subjects: Ethics and Life Writing* (Ithaca, NY: Cornell University Press, 2004). For other examples of as-told-to autobiographies, see also Ann Guttormsen Hought with Florence Ekstrand, *Anna: Norse Roots in Homestead Soil* (Seattle, WA: Welcome Press, 1986). Ekstrand asserts that the stories were taken "verbatim" from Anna's letters, journals, and calendar pages, while other stories "were written as she told them." Even if these claims are accurate, Ekstrand organizes and structures the material, weaving the pieces into a coherent narrative that Anna may not have imagined. In another example by Martha Reishus, *The Rag Rug* (New York: Vantage Press, Inc., 1955), Reishus recalls stories of her grandmother, using the rag rug as a metaphor and telling the stories with drama, dialogue, and the omniscient voice of a novelist.

40. Xan, *Wisconsin My Home*, 3, 30.

41. Mrs. Alma A. Guttersen and Mrs. Regina Hilleboe Christensen, eds., *Souvenir "Norse-American Women" 1825–1925: A Symposium of Prose and Poetry, Newspaper Articles, and Biographies, Contributed by One Hundred Prominent Women* (Minneapolis, MN: Lutheran Free Church, 1926), 276. The work, copyrighted in 1926 by Mrs. Gilbert Guttersen, St. Paul, Minnesota, is 455 pages in length, including the index but no table of contents.

Dedication, *Souvenir*, iii, italics added. Orm Øverland refers to the work as an anthology in his study *The Western Home*, 397. This assessment is reasonable and accurate. When attempting to characterize women's life writings, the concept of a "collective autobiography" provides an interpretive framework and suggests a theoretical perspective. Guttersen identifies herself in the work variously as Mrs. Alma A. Guttersen, Mrs. Gilbert Guttersen, Alma A. Guttersen, and A. A. G. The multiple formulations of her name reflects, I would argue, the shifting position of women in the 1920s in the wake of the first wave of the women's movement and suffrage victories; it may also suggest the fragmenting of women's lives. I use the form Guttersen employs in each usage. Alma A. Peterson, preface, *Souvenir*, 7.

42. For a discussion of the centennial and its assimilation ethos, see April R. Schultz, *Ethnicity on Parade: Inventing the Norwegian American Through Celebration* (Amherst: University of Massachusetts Press, 1994). (Schultz does not discuss the *Souvenir* book.) For a discussion of the effects of World War I and the Minnesota Public Safety Commission on Norwegians in the Upper Midwest, see Carl H. Chrislock, *Ethnicity Challenged: The Upper Midwest Norwegian-American Experience in World War I* (Northfield, MN: NAHA, 1981).

43. Hanna Astrup Larsen, "The First Lady," in *Souvenir*, 17. Larsen noted, especially, educational opportunities for women, particularly in Norwegian American colleges that

graduate as many women as men. The allusion to *Egil's Saga* probably resonated with her audience in 1925. Sometimes described as the greatest of Icelandic sagas and written about 1230 by Snorri Stuluson, *Egil's Saga* centers on the complex character of Egil Skallagrimsson and gives a broad view of the Viking era.

44. Following the fifty short biographies, the editors include several short lists of women with minimal information (usually name, residence, and vocation or avocation) with intriguing categories: "Women Who Have Made Good in Their Chosen Life Work" (247 entries); "A Few of Our Musical Women" (45 entries); "Women Prominent in Community Work in Minnesota" (149 entries); "Honor Roll of Deceased" (ca. 65 entries); "Honor Roll of WMF" (recognizing Sister Caroline Thompson, who died in a shipwreck returning from the mission field in Madagascar); "Women Memorialized by Organizations, Relatives and Friends" (eight and a half pages of names); and *Ledende Kvinder (Leading Women)*, discussing five individuals.

45. The richness and range of the material warrants a more complete analysis and interpretation of this fascinating document.

46. "Sketches," in *Souvenir*, 198–207, is an anonymous submission. It is not clear whether these sketches were submitted or culled from newspapers or other sources.

47. "The Baldishol Committee," in *Souvenir*, 272–75. The committee consisted of six officers, twenty-six women from Minneapolis, and twenty-three from St. Paul; the gift stipulated that the tapestry always hang in the White House. The original Baldishol tapestry resides in the Museum of Applied Art in Oslo. For more on the Baldishol tapestry, see Aase Bay Sjvold, *Norsk billedvev* (Oslo: C Huitfeldts Forlag, 1975), and Helen Engelstad, *Refil, bunad, tjeld: Middelalderens billedtepper i Norge* (Oslo: Gyldendal Norsk Forlag, 1952).

48. Helen Egilsrud, "Norsk-Amerikanske kvinders indsater for verdensfred," in *Souvenir*, 129–31. The formation of the Women's International League for Peace and Freedom (dating to 1915, the oldest continuous peace group in the world) is a central example of this effort. Also indicative of the international women's movement is the International Council of Women (ICW), established in 1888 with nine charter members, including Norway and the United States. Meeting every five years, the ICW gathered in Washington, DC, in 1925 and the Norwegian delegation was invited to the Norse Centennial in St. Paul, Minnesota, where they met with Norwegian American women. Several entries address the exchanges of Norwegian and Norwegian American women. *Souvenir*, 129. See, for example, Thomas J. Knock, *To End All Wars: Woodrow Wilson and the Quest for a New World Order* (Princeton, NJ: Princeton University Press, 1992), who argues that women in the progressive and peace movement were influential in shaping Wilson's vision of peace in the World War I era.

49. Guttersen and Hilleboe, *Souvenir*, 450.

Epilogue

In many ways this book serves as an introduction to gendered perspectives in Norwegian American history. It clearly demonstrates that from the ancestral villages and communities in Norway to the farms, small towns, and urban communities of the United States, gendered dimensions shaped the migration and settlement process. In addition, the book offers strong evidence that gendered conditions and perceptions shaped experiences and possibilities for the immigrant generation and their progeny in the new land. At the same time, the heretofore neglected dimensions of women in Norwegian American communities illustrate their critical role in the economic survival of families and communities, their centrality in maintaining kinship networks, their contributions to the social welfare of the larger society, and their participation in the racial hierarchies of the nation that provided them benefit. Furthermore, this book demonstrates how women's writings, their literary expressions in fiction and nonfiction, provide rich documentary material for examining not only their imaginative and subjective lives but also considering the cultural and social values of the Norwegian American descendants intimated in these writings. This collection provides a foundation for rethinking Norwegian American history from a gendered perspective while it also points in directions for further research and study. Much remains to be explored.

First among topics for more exploration would be issues of class. How did Norwegian immigrants and Norwegian Americans negotiate tensions surrounding gender and class, both within their ethnic enclaves and with the American society? To what degree did ethnic identity mute class differences? Norwegian immigrants left a more rigid class structure in Norway for the promise of a more egalitarian society with diverse opportunities. How significant were (and are) class differences for the immigrant generation and its progeny? How were men and women affected differently? In farming communities, class stratification may have been more blurred as many homesteaders and small landowners aspired to larger holdings. How did these economic and social differences develop in small rural communities? While class distinctions may have been more fluid in rural areas, how did these differences emerge in large urban areas—for example, in ethnic institutions, churches, and neighborhoods and within marriages? Class tensions also lead to exploitation. Preliminary research has revealed exploitation of young immigrant girls in urban areas, and in large cities, such as Chicago, Minneapolis, and Seattle, evidence found in police records (that include nationalities of perpetrators) documents sexual exploitation in prostitution. More work is needed in all of these areas.

These questions lead to a second topic requiring more research—Norwegian immigrant labor and labor organizing from a gendered perspective. Some work has been done on labor activism among Norwegian immigrants, but focused work on women remains unexplored, especially in the significant area of domestic service. A large body of historical literature has emerged on domestic service in the United States during the last few decades, but a sustained analysis of Norwegian women's domestic service remains absent, although a majority of the single Norwegian immigrant women arrived as domestic servants. Many questions remain: for example, how did their experiences differ in urban and rural areas? In Norwegian and American households? How were women's lives shaped by this position, a position common in Norway both for laboring and middle classes but often scorned in American communities? How did their experiences compare with those of other domestic servants, for example, Scandinavian and Irish immigrant women, or African American and, more recently, Asian and Latino immigrant women?

Norwegian immigrants did not represent the large numbers found in other European migrations during the Industrial Era—for example, over four million Italians migrated to the United States, contrasted with fewer than a million Norwegians in this era—but Norwegians did contribute to labor organizing. Much scholarly work has addressed Norwegian labor and labor organizing, but what contributions did Norwegian immigrant women make? Norwegian immigrants counted among the founders of the Nonpartisan League formed in North Dakota in 1915 to challenge corporate control of pricing, storage, and sale of agricultural commodities, but what involvement did the women have and how might we understand that engagement? Also, since Norwegians represented the most rural of all European migrations, a large percentage lived in farming communities and small towns, where the laboring conditions differed from that of the industrial regions; nevertheless, Norwegians were part of populist, progressive, and socialist movements in the Midwest, yet little is known about the involvement of women in these efforts. Furthermore, radical newspapers can be found in these communities until after World War I, when radical groups and publications (throughout the country) came under assault in the first Red Scare. Did women contribute to the radical newspapers? Certainly, it is important to note that the emphasis on class and labor has tended to mute the category of gender (see Alice Kessler-Harris's 2007 book, *Gendering Labor History* for evidence of this); however, the place of women and the gendered dimensions of labor organizing, especially in the progressive, populist, and radical movements at the turn of the twentieth century, provide a meaningful avenue for research.

A third area is suggested by the Norwegian American women's involvement in the transnational women's movement of the late nineteenth and early twentieth centuries. What positions did Norwegian immigrant women and their daughters take on women's rights and the women's suffrage movement? Did Norwegian American women gain representation in the International Council of Women, the National Women's Suffrage Association, the Women's Peace Party, and other organizations of the turn-of-the-century reform movements? How did Norwegian immigrant and Norwegian American women contribute to Progressive Era movements? Evidence suggests that Norwegian American women were involved in health, education, and social reforms, including temperance, in the United States. What were their contributions? Were there gendered differences among Norwegian men and women on these issues? In a related area, the gendered dimensions of the mission field offer rich possibilities, especially since a substantial group of Norwegian American women left from the Midwest for the mission fields in China and Africa, particularly, starting in the late nineteenth century and continuing into the mid-twentieth century.

A fourth area of study that is rich with potential is family and domestic life. Social historians of migration have considered this a critical sphere because families tended to migrate together, so topics surrounding family life—courtship, marriage, sexual practices, birthing, family rituals, kinship networks, and extended families—have all been addressed in immigration history. Still, more work remains to be done. How did immigrants manage domestic life, especially in the wake of shifting gender roles in the early twentieth century as well as differences between the American and Norwegian cultural attitudes toward domestic practices? How did women and men negotiate sexuality and childbirth? How did they adapt or challenge prevailing mores in the American contexts when conflicting values were formulated by ethnic churches and secular American cultural ideas? In the emerging field of the construction of masculinity, how did Norwegian cultural values compete with or challenge images of manhood in the dominant culture?

A fifth under-examined area for research is the relationships with other ethnic and racial groups in the United States. Although not known for its cultural diversity, the Upper Midwest is home to numerous Indian tribes and one of the major urban reservations in the country (in Minneapolis). Also, Mexican migrant labor on farms in the Midwest has been an important presence since the immigration restriction laws of the 1920s; generations of Mexican farm laborers worked and lived in Norwegian communities. Furthermore, the region has one of the highest concentrations of recent African immigrants (from Somalia, Ethiopia, Liberia, and other areas), as well as one of the highest concentrations of Hmong and Vietnamese in the United States. What have been the historical relationships between Norwegian immigrants and non-European residents? How have intersections of race, class, and gender shaped interactions, attitudes, and interethnic relations over time in the area? Has the Lutheran church and Lutheran Social Service(s) (formed in 1865 by Swedish Lutheran minister Eric Norelius) affected intercultural and interethnic relationships in the region? What racial attitudes emerge in the historical literature? What tensions develop over racial and ethnic hierarchies, and how have these changed over time? In his book *The Promised Fulfilled,* Odd S. Lovoll touches on the absorption of Viking-era myths and symbols in racist, neo-Nazi groups in the United States, yet much might be explored here surrounding contributions of Norwegian Americans to these movements. What have been the gendered dimensions among Norwegian immigrants in these borderlands where diverse ethnic and racial groups converge? What have been the gendered dimensions in constructions of whiteness, in the maintenance and resistance to racial hierarchies, and how have Norwegian immigrants and Norwegian Americans understood these categories and their place in such hierarchies?

Sixth, more work needs to be done incorporating migration to the entire continent of North America. Significant numbers of Norwegians also migrated into Canada; some started there and migrated south into the United States, but others remained in Canada. Most studies of Norwegian immigration neglect the migration to Canada and to other parts of the globe during this period. This can be explained in part by geographic distances but also by institutional divisions—universities, academic associations, journals, and scholarly networks—that tend to use the nation-state as a framework for analysis, although this propensity is shifting. In the twenty-first century, with global connections and our advanced technologies, we should be able to expand the scope of migration studies more easily to include comparative studies, especially those that encompass all of North America.

Finally, one might explore more fully the progeny of the immigrants and the long-term effects of immigrant and ethnic cultural patterns—within individuals, families, communities, and regions—from a gendered perspective. What influences, if any, have the political and cultural patterns and practices of this immigrant group had on the regions where they settled? How have second, third, and fourth generations (and beyond) understood their relationship to the past, to immigrant cultures, and how have women, especially, affected these cultural retentions and patterns? In geographic regions where Norwegians represent a significant percentage of the population—the Upper Midwest and the Pacific Northwest—these areas are also often described as progressive. What correlations, if any, can be made with the immigrant generation and the progressive cultures in these areas, especially using a gendered perspective?

Unquestionably, other topics of research might also be posited. The point remains, in the words of prolific scholar and historian Lovoll, that work on immigration from Norway and Norwegian American history has "just begun."

Selected Bibliography

Based on the holdings of the Norwegian-American Collection,
National Library of Norway

Compiled by Dina Tolfsby

Dina Tolfsby created the core of this bibliography from the extensive holdings of the Norwegian-American Collection at the National Library in Oslo, which may be the largest single collection of published materials on all aspects of life in Norwegian America. A bibliography that included all published materials either about Norwegian American women or by Norwegian American women would be too unwieldy. Therefore, this bibliography is not comprehensive. Instead, it focuses on published primary sources and scholarly works, with the goal of making these materials accessible to researchers on both sides of the Atlantic.

Norwegians and Norwegian Americans began collecting primary materials, especially letters sent to Norway, in the 1920s and 1930s. Some of these letters and collections were then translated and published. As such, there is a rich body of primary source materials, largely letters, that is available to an English-reading public. This bibliography includes published and, for the most part, translated documents of the first generation and important accounts from the second generation. Works of fiction, with the exception of the authors noted in the chapters, are not addressed here. Women also wrote for Norwegian American periodicals and stories about women appeared in such publications. These are not included in this bibliography. Scholar Orm Øverland provides coverage in his comprehensive treatment of literary production in *Norwegian America, The Western Home*. Odd S. Lovoll's *Norwegian Newspapers in America: Connecting Norway and the New Land* is also useful to readers interested in newspapers. In addition to the published sources, a list of major repositories for manuscript collections is included, as are two key websites that contain primary sources.

The secondary source material is broader in scope and includes many works that address life for the second and even third generation of Norwegian American women. Academic treatments of topics that include a significant Norwegian American women's history component are found here, too. These secondary works are scholarly in nature. As such, local histories, short pieces published in periodicals, pamphlets, and so on, which are valuable sources for historians, are excluded from the scope of this bibliography. Of note, some of the most interesting work on Norwegian American women is being done by graduate students in Norway, and many of these theses are written in English.

Some can be found in the United States at the Norwegian-American Historical Association Archives.

Published Primary Sources

Books

Blegen, Theodore, C., ed. *Land of Their Choice: The Immigrants Write Home.* Minneapolis: The University of Minnesota Press, 1955.

Bonhus, Emma Quie. *From Lantern to Yardlight.* Minneapolis, MN: Lund Press, 1948.

Deen, Tilla Regina Dahl. *Chronicles of a Minnesota Pioneer.* Minneapolis, MN: Burgess Pub. Co., 1949.

Drewsen, Gudrun Løchen. *Man Minnes Mangt.* Oslo: Aschehoug, 1937.

Gulliksen, Øyvind T. *"Saa Nær hverande": Ei samling Amerikabrev fra Midtvesten til Nissedal 1850–1875."* Vol. 9 NAHA—Norway and Nissedal Historielag. Bø, Norway: Bø Trykk A/S, 1999.

Guttersen, Alma Amalia Petersen, and Regina Hilleboe Christensen, eds. *Souvenir "Norse-American Women," 1825–1925: A Symposium of Prose and Poetry, Newspaper Articles, and Biographies, Contributed by One Hundred Prominent Women.* St. Paul, MN: Lutheran Free Church Publishing Co., 1926.

Hought, Anna Guttormsen, and Florence Ekstrand. *Anna.* Seattle, WA: Welcome Press, 1986.

Koren, Elisabeth. *The Diary of Elisabeth Koren, 1853–1855.* Translated and edited by David T. Nelson. Northfield, MN: Norwegian-American Historical Association, 1955.

Koren, Elisabeth, and V. Koren. *Fra Pioneertiden.* Decorah, IA: Udgivernes forlag, 1914.

Levorsen, Barbara. *Quiet Conquest: A History of the Lives and Times of the First Settlers of Central North Dakota.* Hawley, MN: The Hawley Herald, 1974.

Lien, Linda Frances, ed. *Hannah Kempfer: An Immigrant Girl.* Fergus Falls, MN: Annika Publications, 2002.

Lillehaugen, Sigrid Gjeldaker. *Live Well: The Letters of Sigrid Gjeldaker Lillehaugen.* Edited by Theresse Lundby, Kristie Nelson-Neuhaus, and Ann Nordland Wallace. St. Paul, MN: Western Home Books, 2004.

Merriken, Ellenor R. *Looking for Country: A Norwegian Immigrant's Alberta Memoir.* Calgary: University of Calgary Press, 1999.

Munch, Caja, and Johan Munch. *The Strange American Way: Letters of Caja Munch from Wiota, Wis., 1855–1859, with an American Adventure; Excerpts from Vita Mea, an Autobiography Written in 1903 for His Children.* Translated by Peter Andreas Munch and Helene Munch. Carbondale: Southern Illinois University Press, 1970.

Nilsen, Frida Rebekkah. *Growing Up in the Old Parsonage.* Lake Mills, IA: Graphic Publishing Co., 1975.

Nilsen, Ole, and Birgitte Evensen Nilsen. *Letters of Longing.* Minneapolis, MN: Augsburg Publishing House, 1970.

Østgård, Bjørn Gunnar, ed. *America-America Letters: A Norwegian-American Family Correspondence.* Northfield, MN: Norwegian-American Historical Association, 2001.

Øverland, Orm, ed. *Fra Amerika til Norge IV: Norske Utvandrerbrev 1875–1884*. Oslo: Solum forlag, 2002.

Øverland, Orm, and Steinar Kjærheim, ed. *Fra Amerika til Norge I: Norske Utvandrerbrev 1838–1857*. Oslo: Solum forlag, 1992.

———. *Fra Amerika til Norge II: Norske Utvandrerbrev 1858–1868 (Med et tillegg av brev 1836–1857)*. Oslo: Solum forlag, 1992.

———. *Fra Amerika til Norge III: Norske Utvandrerbrev 1869–1874 (Med et tillegg av brev 1845–1867)*. Oslo: Solum forlag, 1993.

Pettersen, Anna. *Langt Ud*. Minneapolis, MN: O. W. Lunds trykkeri, 1903.

Preus, Caroline Dorothea Margrethe Keyser. *Linka's Diary, on Land and Sea, 1845–1864*. Translated and edited by Johan Carl Keyser Preus and Diderikke Margrethe Brandt Preus. Minneapolis, MN: Augsburg Pub. House, 1952.

———. *Linka's Diary: A Norwegian Immigrant Story in Word and Sketches*. Edited by Marvin J. Slind and Gracia Grindahl. Minneapolis, MN: Lutheran University Press, 2008.

Raaen, Aagot. *Grass of the Earth: Immigrant Life in the Dakota Country*. St. Paul: Minnesota Historical Society Press, 1994.

———. *Grass of the Earth: Immigrant Life in the Dakota Country*. Northfield, MN: Norwegian-American Historical Association, 1950.

Rasmussen, Janet Elaine. *New Land, New Lives: Scandinavian Immigrants to the Pacific Northwest*. Foreword by Odd S. Lovoll. Northfield, MN: Norwegian-American Historical Association and Seattle and London: University of Washington Press, 1993.

Solberg, Elizabeth Ronning. *The Long and Happy Life of Mrs. Peeleyant: An Autobiography*. Published by author, 1967.

Sponland, Ingeborg, and Mabel Louise Thorstensen. *My Reasonable Service*. Minneapolis, MN: Augsburg Pub. House, 1938.

Svendsen, Gro. *Frontier Mother: The Letters of Gro Svendsen*. Translated and edited by Pauline Farseth and Theodore C. Blegen. Northfield, MN: Norwegian-American Historical Association, 1950.

Wagner, Sally Roesch, ed. *Daughters of Dakota: Schooled in Privation*. Vol. 4, *German, German-Russian and Scandinavian Immigrants in South Dakota*. Yankton, SD: General Federation of Women's Clubs of SD/DOD, 1991.

Wærenskjold, Elise Amalie Tvede. *The Lady with the Pen: Elise Wærenskjold in Texas*. Edited by C. A. Clausen. Northfield, MN: Norwegian-American Historical Association, 1961.

Wærenskjold, Elise Amalie Tvede, and Charles H. Russell. *Confession of Faith: A Strong Woman's Statement of Her Faith*. Philadelphia: Xlibris Corp., 2001.

Westerskow, Nellie Simonsen. *From Arctic Splendor to Sunset Mountain*. Kremmling, CO: J. M. Simmons, 1992.

Xan, Erna Oleson, and Thurine Oleson. *Wisconsin My Home by Erna Oleson Xan as Told by Her Mother Thurine Oleson*. Madison: University of Wisconsin Press, 1950.

Zempel, Solveig, ed. and trans. *In Their Own Words: Letters from Norwegian Immigrants*. Minneapolis: University of Minnesota Press in cooperation with the Norwegian-American Historical Association, 1991.

Book Chapters and Journal Articles

Abrahamson, Laura. "Herding Cows and Waiting Tables: The Diary of Laura Aleta Iversen Abrahamson." *South Dakota History* 20.1 (Winter 1990): 17–50.

Blegen, Theodore C. "Notes and Documents: Guri Endreson, Frontier Heroine." *Minnesota History: The Quarterly of the Minnesota Historical Society* 10.4 (1929): 425–30.

Blegen, Theodore C., ed. and trans. "Immigrant Women and the American Frontier: Three Early 'America Letters.'" *Norwegian-American Studies and Records* 5 (1930): 14–29.

Bonhus, Emma. "En Nittiårig Prestekone Forteller." *Jul i Vesterheim* (1953): 44–48.

Brandt, R. O., Mrs. "Social Aspects of Prairie Pioneering: The Reminiscences of a Pioneer Pastor's Wife." *Norwegian-American Studies and Records* 7 (1933): 1–52.

Drewsen, Gudrun Løchen. "Kvinderne i Amerika: De Indfødte og De Indførte." *Nordmands-Forbundet* 3.8 (1910): 430–38.

Fedde, Elizabeth. "Elizabeth Fedde's Diary, 1883–88. Translated and edited by Beulah Folkedahl." *Norwegian-American Studies and Records* 20 (1959): 170–96.

Halvorsen, Helen Olson, and Lorraine Fletcher. "19th Century Midwife: Some Recollections." *Oregon Historical Quarterly* 70.1 (1969): 39–49.

Herseth, Lorna B. "A Pioneer's Letter [Walborg Holth]." *South Dakota History* 6.3 (Summer 1976): 306–15.

Jacobsen, Clara. "En Amerika-Reise for 60 År Siden." In *Symra: En Aarbog for Norske Paa Begge Sider Af Havet,* edited by Kristian Prestgard and Johannes B. Wist, 120–37. Decorah, IA: Decorah-Postens trykkeri., 1913.

———. "A Journey to America in the Fifties." *Norwegian-American Studies and Records* 12 (1941): 60–78.

———. "Memories from Perry Parsonage." *Norwegian-American Studies and Records* 14 (1944): 139–58.

———. "Minder Fra Perry Prestegaard." In *Symra: En Aarbog for Norske Paa Begge Sider Af Havet,* edited by Kristian Prestgard and Johannes B. Wist, 92–110. Decorah, IA: Decorah-Postens trykkeri., 1912.

Johnson, Pål Espolin, and Øyvind T Gulliksen. "Lina Alsakers Dagbok Fra 1886." In *Migranten,* edited by Anne Birgit Larsen and Reidar Bakken, 6–30. Hamar: Norwegian Emigrant Museum, 1989.

Levorsen, Barbara. "Early Years in Dakota." *Norwegian-American Studies* 21 (1962): 158–97.

———. "Our Bread and Meat." *Norwegian-American Studies* 22 (1965): 178–97.

Naeseth, Caroline Mathilde Koren. "Memories from Little Iowa Parsonage." *Norwegian-American Studies and Records* 13 (1943): 66–74.

Nichol, Todd W., ed. and trans. "A Haugean Woman in America: The Memoirs of Sigrid Eielsen." *Norwegian-American Studies* 35 (2000): 265–300.

Preus, Lulla. "Minder Fra Den Gamle Paint Creek Præstegaard." In *Symra: En Aarbog for Norske Paa Begge Sider Af Havet,* edited by Kristian Prestgard and Johannes B. Wist, 1–15. Decorah, IA: Decorah-Postens trykkeri, 1911.

Slind, Marvin G. "From the Immigrant Diary of Linka Preus." *Vesterheim* 5.1 (2007): 18–31.

Major Repositories for Collections about Norwegian America

United States
 Center for Western Studies, Augustana College, Sioux Falls, SD
 Iowa State Historical Society, Des Moines
 Luther College Archives, Decorah, IA
 Minnesota Historical Society, St. Paul
 North Dakota Institute for Regional Studies, North Dakota State University, Fargo
 Norwegian-American Genealogical Center and Naeseth Library, Madison, WI
 Norwegian-American Historical Association, Northfield, MN
 Pacific Lutheran University Library and Archives, Tacoma, WA
 Special Collections, University of North Dakota, Grand Forks
 State Historical Society of North Dakota, Bismarck
 University of Washington Special Collections, Seattle
 Vesterheim Museum, Decorah, IA
 Wisconsin Historical Society, Madison
Norway
 Norsk-amerikansk samling, Nasjonalbibliotek [Norwegian-American Collection, National Library], Olso
 Norsk utvandrermuseum [Norwegian Emigration Museum], Ottestad
 Riksarkivet [National Archives], Oslo
 Statarkivet [State Regional Archives], especially those located in Hamar, Stavanger, and Trondheim
 Sogn og Fjordane Fylkearkivet [Sogn og Fjordane County Archives], Leikanger

Websites (Both sites have materials in English.)

Det løftrike landet [The Promised Land], Nasjonalbibliotek, http://www.nb.no/emigrasjon/
Digitalarkivet [Digital Archives], http://digitalarkivet.uib.no/

Secondary Sources

Books

Beito, Gretchen Urness. *Coya Come Home: A Congresswoman's Journey.* Beverly Hills, CA: Pomergrante Press, Ltd., 1993.

Cayleff, Susan E. *Babe: The Life and Legend of Babe Didrikson Zaharias.* Illini Books edition, Women in American History. Urbana: University of Illinois Press, 1996.

Cole, Catherine C. *Norwegian Immigrant Clothing and Textiles.* Edmonton: Prairie Costume Society, 1990.

Gjerde, Jon. *From Peasants to Farmers: The Migration from Balestrand, Norway, to the Upper Middle West.* Cambridge, NY: Cambridge University Press, 1985.

———. *The Minds of the West: Ethnocultural Evolution in the Rural Middle West, 1830–1917.* Chapel Hill and London: University of North Carolina Press, 1997.

Handy-Marchello, Barbara. *Women of the Northern Plains: Gender and Settlement on the Homestead Frontier, 1870–1930*. St. Paul: Minnesota Historical Society Press, 2005.

Hunt, Linda. *Bold Spirit: Helga Estby's Forgotten Walk across Victorian America*. Moscow: University of Idaho Press, 2003.

Lagerquist, L. DeAne. *In America the Men Milk the Cows: Factors of Gender, Ethnicity, and Religion in the Americanization of Norwegian-American Women*. Chicago Studies in the History of American Religion, ed. Jerald C. Brauer and Martin E. Marty. Brooklyn, NY: Carlson Publishing, Inc., 1991.

Langlois, Janet L. *Belle Gunnes: The Lady Bluebeard*. Bloomington: Indiana University Press, 1985.

Lindgren, H. Elaine. *Land in Her Own Name: Women as Homesteaders in North Dakota*. Fargo: North Dakota Institute for Regional Studies, 1991.

———. *Land in Her Own Name: Women as Homesteaders in North Dakota*. Norman: University of Oklahoma Press, 1996.

Ljone, Oddmund. *"Mine Tårer Fløt Rikelig" Fortellingen Om Utvandrerkvinnen Gro Nilsdatter Fra Hallingdal*. Oslo: Gyldendal, 1975.

Lovoll, Odd S. *Norwegians on the Prairie: Ethnicity and the Development of the Country Town*. St. Paul: Minnesota Historical Society Press in cooperation with the Norwegian-American Historical Association, 2006.

Michelet, Maren. *Glimpses from Agnes Mathilde Wergeland's Life*. Memorial ed. Minneapolis, MN: [M. Michelet], 1916.

———. *Glimt Fra Agnes Mathilde Wergelands Liv*. Mindeutg. ed. Minneapolis, MN: [M. Michelet], 1916.

Nilsen, Frida Rebekkah. *Eyes of Understanding: A Biography*. Minneapolis, MN: Augsburg Publishing House, 1947.

Norwegian Lutheran Deaconess Society of Chicago. *Mission of Mercy . . . Women of Action: The Norwegian Lutheran Deaconess Society of Chicago*. [Chicago]: Lutheran General Hospital, 1985.

Øverland, Orm. *The Western Home: A Literary History of Norwegian America*. Northfield, MN: Norwegian-American Historical Association in cooperation with the University of Illinois Press, 1996.

Pederson, Jane Marie. *Between Memory and Reality: Family and Community in Rural Wisconsin, 1870–1970*. History of American Thought and Culture. Madison: University of Wisconsin Press, 1992.

Reishus, Martha. *Hearts and Hands Uplifted: A History of the Women's Missionary Federation of the Evangelical Lutheran Church*. Minneapolis, MN: Augsburg Publishing House, 1958.

Riley, Jocelyn. *Norwegian Pioneer Women: A Resource Guide*. Madison, WI: Her Own Words, 1995.

Rolfsrud, Erling Nicolai. *The Borrowed Sister: The Story of Elisabeth Fedde*. Minneapolis, MN: Augsburg Publishing House, 1953.

Russell, Charles H. *Undaunted: A Norwegian Woman in Frontier Texas*. Tarleton State University Southwestern Studies in the Humanities No. 20. College Station: Texas A&M University Press, 2006.

Stokker, Kathleen. *Remedies and Rituals: Folk Medicine in Norway and the New Land.* St. Paul: Minnesota Historical Society Press, 2007.

Young, Carrie. *Nothing to Do but Stay: My Pioneer Mother.* 1st ed., A Bur Oak Original. Iowa City: University of Iowa Press, 1991.

Book Chapters and Journal Articles

Adriansen, Kristin Kavli. "Sister Elisabeth Fedde: A Light of Hope to Sick and Needy Immigrants in New York City." In *Norwegian-American Essays 2008: "Migration and Memory,"* edited by Øyvind T. Gulliksen and Harry T. Cleven, 59–84. Oslo: NAHA-Norway, 2008.

Allen, Hans. "Lutheran Ladies' Seminary." In *Festskrift Til Den Norske Synodes Jubilaeum, 1853–1903/Synod for the Norwegian Evangelical Lutheran Church in America,* edited by H. Halvorsen, 176–80. Decorah, IA: Norske Synodes Forlag, 1903.

Alnæs, Barbara Ann. "Borghild M. Dahl, Second-Generation Norwegian-American Author." In *Essays on Norwegian-American Literature and History: Proceedings from a Seminar on Norwegian-American Literature and History,* edited by Ingeborg R. Kongslien and Dorothy Burton Skårdal, 187–97. Oslo: NAHA-Norway, 1986.

Barton, Arnold H. "Scandinavian Immigrant Women's Encounter with America." *The Swedish Pioneer Historical Quarterly* 25.1 (1974): 37–42.

Bergland, Betty. "Cultural Memory and Migration in Orabel Thortvedt's Narrative, 'Buffalo River: A Tale of the Emigrant and the Pioneer.'" In *Norwegian-American Essays 2008: "Migration and Memory,"* edited by Øyvind T. Gulliksen and Harry T. Cleven, 15–44. Oslo: NAHA-Norway, 2008.

Blegen, Theodore Christian. "Immigrant Marthas." In *Grass Roots History,* 65–80. Minneapolis: University of Minnesota Press, 1947.

Brungot, Hilde Petra. "Dorthea Dahl, Norwegian-American Author of Everyday Life." In *Essays on Norwegian-American Literature and History: Proceedings from a Seminar on Norwegian-American Literature and History,* edited by Ingeborg R. Kongslien and Dorothy Burton Skårdal, 175–85. Oslo: NAHA-Norway, 1986.

———. "To Keep and to Cultivate: Dorthea Dahl, a Norwegian-American Voice in Idaho." *Latah Legacy: The Annual Journal of the Latah County Historical Society* 30 (2001): 1–28.

Buckley, Joan. "Norwegian-American Immigrant Women as Role Models for Today." In *Norwegian Influence on the Upper Midwest: Proceedings of an International Conference, University of Minnesota, Duluth, May 22–24, 1975,* edited by Harald S. Næss, 98–105. Duluth: Continuing Education and Extension, University of Minnesota, Duluth, 1976.

Buckley, Joan N. "Martha Ostenso: A Norwegian-American Immigrant Novelist." In *Norwegian-American Studies* 28 (1979): 69–81.

Buraas, Anders. "Pioneren Agnes Mathilde Wergeland, Historiker, Dr.Philos. (1857–1914)." In *De Reiste Ut: Syv Fortellinger Om Agnes Mathilde Wergeland, Ole Evinrude, Anders Furuseth, Knute Rockne, Harry Irgens Larsen, Hans Christian Heg, Ole Bornemann Bull,* 13–41. Oslo: Aschehoug, 1982.

Ericson, Kathryn. "Triple Jeopardy: The Muus vs. Muus Case in Three Forums." *Minnesota History: The Quarterly of the Minnesota Historical Society* 50.8 (1987): 298–308.

Fink, Deborah. "Anna Oleson: Rural Family and Community in Iowa, 1880–1920." *Annals of Iowa* 48.5–6 (1986): 251–63.

Fletre, Helen. "Det Litterære Samfund (The Literary Society of Chicago)." In *Essays on Norwegian-American Literature and History: Proceedings from a Seminar on Norwegian-American Literature and History,* edited by Ingeborg R. Kongslien and Dorothy Burton Skårdal, 365–72. Oslo: NAHA-Norway, 1986.

Fløystad, Ingeborg. "Kvinnene i (Det Ville) Vesten: En Gren av Amerikanske Kvinners Historie og Norske Immigrantkvinners Plass i Den." *Historisk tidsskrift* 66.2 (1987): 209–22.

Flå, Vibeke. "Økt Kvinneutvandring Fra Nord-Norske Byer På Slutten Av 1800-Tallet Og Fram Til 1915." In *Norwegian-American Essays 1996,* edited by Øyvind Tveitereid Gulliksen, David Mauk, and Dina Tolfsby, 171–87. Oslo: NAHA-Norway: Norwegian Emigrant Museum, 1996.

Gilbertson, Laurann. "Careers of Service: The Norwegian Lutheran Deaconesses." *Vesterheim* 5.1 (2007): 42–48.

———. "Patterns of the New World: Quiltmaking among Norwegian Americans." *Uncoverings* 27 (2006): 157–96.

———. "Religion and Norwegian-American Quilts." In *Proceedings of the 4th Biennial Symposium of the International Quilt Study Center & Museum.* Digital Commons@ University of Nebraska—Lincoln. http://digitalcommons.unl.edu/iqsc4symp/3/.

Gjerde, Jon, and Anne McCants. "Fertility, Marriage, and Culture: Demographic Processes Among Norwegian Immigrants to the Rural Middle West." *Journal of Economic History* 55.4 (Dec. 1995): 860–88.

———. "Individual Life Chances, 1850–1910: A Norwegian-American Example." *Journal of Interdisciplinary History* 30.3 (Winter 1999): 377–405.

Gloppen, Jaspreet Kaur. "Ole E. Rølvaag's Beret and the Female Gothic." In *Norwegian-American Essays 2008: "Migration and Memory,"* edited by Øyvind T. Gulliksen and Harry T. Cleven, 227–42. Oslo: NAHA-Norway, 2008.

Grindahl, Gracia. "The Americanization of the Norwegian Pastor's Wives." In *Norwegian-American Studies* 32 (1989): 199–207.

———. "Linka's Sketchbook: A Personal View of the Norwegian Synod." In *Scandinavians in America: Literary Life,* edited by J. R. Christianson, 258–66. Decorah, IA: Symra Literary Society, 1985.

Gulliksen, Øyvind T. "The Trimming of Their Lamps: Norwegian-American Immigrant Women Writers in the Midwest." *Vesterheim* 5.1 (2007): 32–41.

Handy-Marchello, Barbara. "Land, Liquor and the Women of Hatton, North Dakota." In *The Centennial Anthology of North Dakota History,* edited by Janet Daley Lysengen and Ann M. Rathke, 223–231. Bismarck: State Historical Society of North Dakota, 1996.

Hansen, Karen V., and Mignon Duffy. "Mapping the Dispossession: Scandinavian Homesteading at Fort Totten, 1900–1930." *Great Plains Research* 18 (Spring 2008): 67–80.

Haugen, Einar. "Celia Thaxter and the Norwegians of the Isles of Shoals." In *Fin(s) De Siècle in Scandinavian Perspective: Studies in Honor of Harald S. Naess,* edited by Faith Ingwersen and Mary Kay Norseng, 171–78. Columbia, SC: Camden House, 1993.

Hinton, Paula. "'The Unspeakable Mrs. Gunness': The Deviant Woman in Early-Twentieth-Century America." In *Lethal Imagination: Violence and Brutality in American History,* edited by Michael Bellesiles, 327–52. New York: New York University Press, 1999.

Janson, Kristofer. "Kvinden Skal Være Manden Underdanig." In *Præriens Saga: Fortællinger Fra Amerika,* 5–60. Chicago: Skandinavens bogtrykkeri, 1885.

———. "Wives Submit Yourselves Unto Your Husbands." *Scandinavia* 2.1–4 (1885): 13–20, 49–56, 76–80, 101–3.

Jenson, Carol. "The Larson Sisters: Three Careers in Contrast." In *Women of Minnesota: Selected Biographical Essays,* edited by Barbara Stuhler and Gretchen V. Kreuter, 301–24. St. Paul: Minnesota Historical Society Press, 1977.

Lagerquist, DeAne. "As Sister Wife and Mother: Education for Young Norwegian-American Lutheran Women." In *Norwegian-American Studies* 33 (1992): 99–138.

Lahlum, Lori Ann. "'Everything Was Changed and Looked Strange': Norwegian Women in South Dakota." *South Dakota History* 35.3 (Fall 2005): 189–216.

———. "Growing Up in Norwegian-American Communities: A Preliminary Study of Childhood, Adolescence, and Young Adulthood." In *Norwegian-American Essays 2008: "Migration and Memory,"* edited by Øyvind T. Gulliksen and Harry T. Cleven, 105–36. Oslo: NAHA-Norway, 2008.

Langeland, Åse Elin. "Kvinden Og Hjemmet: Sixty Years of Success / Norskdommens Høydepunkt: 1880–1914, the Golden Age of the Norwegian Immigrant Community in Minneapolis–St. Paul." In *Norwegian-American Essays, 2004,* edited by Orm Øverland and Harry T. Cleven, 164–83. Oslo: NAHA-Norway and Norwegian Emigrant Museum, 2005.

Laut, Agnes C. "Guri Endreson: A Daughter of the Vikings." *The North Star* 3.1 (Dec. 1920): 37–51.

Legreid, Ann M. "'Over the Beds Hung Baskets Where the Children Slept': Case Studies in Frontier Population Dynamics." In *Norwegian-American Essays,* edited by Knut Djupedal, Øyvind T Gulliksen, Ingeborg R. Kongslien, David C. Mauk, Hans Storhaug, and Dina Tolfsby, 115–31. Stavanger: NAHA-Norway, Norwegian Emigrant Museum and Norwegian Emigration Center, 1993.

Lindgren, H. Elaine. "Ethnic Women Homesteading on the Plains of North Dakota." *Great Plains Quarterly* 9.3 (1989): 157–73.

Miller, Deborah L. "Reading Norwegian-American Cookbooks: A Case Study." In *Interpreting the Promise of America: Essays in Honor of Odd Sverre Lovoll,* edited by Todd W. Nichol, 175–91. Northfield, MN: Norwegian-American Historical Association, 2002.

Muthyala, John. "Gendering the Frontier in O. E. Rölvaag's *Giants in the Earth.*" *Great Plains Quarterly* 25.4 (Fall 2005): 229–44.

Nichol, Todd. "Wedding Customs among Norwegian-American Lutherans, 1850–1950 / Substantial or Relational Explanations? The Exclusion and Inclusion of Newcomers:

The Norwegian Case." In *Norwegian-American Essays, 2004,* edited by Orm Øverland and Harry T. Cleven, 25–45. Oslo: NAHA-Norway and Norwegian Emigrant Museum, 2005.

Rasmussen, Janet E. "Gender and Ethnicity." In *Essays on Norwegian-American Literature and History,* edited by Øyvind Tveitereid Gulliksen, Ingeborg R. Kongslien, and Dina Tolfsby, 41–48. Oslo, Norway: NAHA-Norway, 1990.

———. " 'I Met Him at Normanna Hall': Ethnic Cohesion and Marital Patterns among Scandinavian Immigrant Women." In *Norwegian-American Studies* 32 (1989): 71–92.

———. " 'I Was Scared to Death When I Came to Chicago': White Slavery and the Woman Immigrant." In *Fin(s) De Siècle in Scandinavian Perspective: Studies in Honor of Harald S. Naess,* edited by Faith Ingwersen and Mary Kay Norseng, 194–202. Columbia, SC: Camden House, 1993.

———. "*Nylænde* Presents America." In *Scandinavians in America: Literary Life,* edited by J. R. Christianson, 104–13. Decorah, IA: Symra Literary Society, 1985.

———. " 'We Were Brought Up to Work': Family Values and Scandinavian Immigrant Women." *Selecta: Journal of the Pacific Northwest Council on Foreign Languages* 7 (1986): 137–41.

———. "Women and Domestic Service: An Oral History Report from the Pacific Northwest." In *Norse Heritage . . . Yearbook,* 88–97. Stavanger: Norwegian Emigration Center, 1989.

Risley, Kristin A. "Palma Pederson (1879–1959)." In *Kindred Hands: Letters on Writing by British and American Women Authors, 1865–1935,* edited by Jennifer Cognard-Black and Elizabeth MacLeod Walls, 193–216. Iowa City: University of Iowa Press, 2006.

Rossbø, Sigrid. "Drude Krog Janson, Norwegian-American and Norwegian Writer." In *Essays on Norwegian-American Literature and History: Proceedings from a Seminar on Norwegian-American Literature and History,* edited by Ingeborg R. Kongslien and Dorothy Burton Skårdal, 49–60. Oslo: NAHA-Norway, 1986.

Russell, Charles H. "The Bigamous Marriage of Elise and Wilhelm Wærenskjold." In *Norwegian-American Essays, 2004,* edited by Orm Øverland and Harry T. Cleven, 245–54. Oslo: NAHA-Norway, 2005.

Ruud, Curtis D. "Beret and the Prairie in Giants in the Earth." In *Norwegian-American Studies* 28 (1979): 217–44.

Sannes, Erling N. " 'Free Land for All': A Young Norwegian Woman Homesteads in North Dakota." *North Dakota History: Journal of the Northern Plains* 60 (Spring 1993): 24–28.

Schwieder, Dorothy. "A Tale of Two Grandmothers: Immigration and Family on the Great Plains." *South Dakota History* 31.1 (Spring 2001): 38–47.

Scott, Larry Emil. "The Poetry of Agnes Mathilde Wergeland." In *Norwegian-American Studies* 30 (1985): 273–92.

Selkurt, Claire. "The Domestic Architecture and Cabinetry of Luther Valley." In *Norwegian-American Studies* 30 (1985): 247–72.

Semmingsen, Ingrid. "Kvinner i Norsk Utvandringshistorie." In *Migranten,* edited by Anne Birgit Larsen and Reidar Bakken, 7–23. Hamar: Norwegian Emigrant Museum, 1988.

_____. "A Pioneer: Agnes Mathilde Wergeland, 1857–1914." In *Makers of an American Immigrant Legacy: Essays in Honor of Kenneth O. Bjork*, edited by Odd Sverre Lovoll, 111–31. Northfield, MN: Norwegian-American Historical Association, 1980.

——— . "Women in Norwegian Emigration." In *Scandinavians in America: Literary Life*, edited by J. R. Christianson, 75–91. Decorah, IA: Symra Literary Society, 1985.

Setterdahl, Lilly. "Adjusting to America." *The Palimpsest: Iowa's Popular History Journal* 68.5 (Fall 1987): 136–44.

_____. "Women in Norwegian Emigration/Kvinnan Och Hemmet: A Women's Journal Written in Swedish, Edited by a Norwegian, Published by a Dane." In *Scandinavians in America: Literary Life*, edited by J. R. Christianson, 92–103. Decorah, IA: Symra Literary Society, 1985.

Simonson, Harold P. "Beret's Ineffable West." In *"Etter Rølvaag Har Problema Han Stridde Med, Vorte Til Verdsproblem–" Rapport Fra Rølvaag-Konferansen I Sandnessjøen 7.-8. August 1995. Skriftserie. Vitenskapelige Arbeider/Høgskolen I Nesna Nr 27*, edited by Ole Karlsen and Renee Hilda Waara, 105. Nesna: Høgskolen i Nesna, 1995.

Slind, Marvin G. "Building an Ideal Image: The Creative Translation of the Linka Preus Diary." In *Norwegian-American Essays, 2004*, edited by Orm Øverland and Harry T. Cleven, 255–81. Oslo: NAHA-Norway and Norwegian Emigrant Museum, 2005.

Spånem, Magnhild. "Med Gro Jonsdotter Einungbrekke Frå Tinn Til Amerika." *Årbok for Telemark* (1981): 14–26.

Steiner, Dale R. "Gro Svendsen." In *Of Thee We Sing: Immigrants and American History*, 118–32. San Diego, CA: Harcourt Brace Jovanovich, 1987.

Torvik, Judith. "*Me* by Brenda Ueland, Feminist, Journalist, and Norwegian American." In *Norwegian-American Essays 1999*, edited by Ingeborg Kongslien and Dina Tolfsby, 207–23. Oslo: NAHA-Norway and Norwegian Emigrant Museum, 1999.

Wangsness, Sigrid Brevik. "*Kvinden Og Hjemmet*: A Magazine for Scandinavian Immigrant Women, 1901–1910." In *Norse Heritage . . . Yearbook*, 105–16. Stavanger: Norwegian Emigration Center, 1989.

Williamson, Erik Luther. " 'Doing What Had to Be Done': Norwegian Lutheran Ladies Aid Societies of North Dakota." *North Dakota History: Journal of the Northern Plains* 57.2 (Spring 1990): 2–13.

Theses and Dissertations

Adriansen, Kristin Kavli. "Sterk, Fri og Kallet: En Studie av Kallet i Lys av Søster Elisabeth Feddes Diakonissegjerning 1873–1896." Master's thesis, University of Bergen, 2007.

Almhjell, Unni Ohrvik. "Returned Female Norwegian Immigrants and American Domestic Service 1910–1970." Master's, thesis, University of Trondheim, 1994.

Alnæs, Barbara Ann. "Borghild M. Dahl Second-Generation Norwegian-American Author." Master's thesis, University of Oslo, 1978.

Austgulen, Catherine. "The Female Experience of a Round Trip to America: A Case Study of Norwegian Female Repatriation, 1920–1990." Master's thesis, University of Oslo, 2000.

Bakken, Anja. " 'Our Country Gives Us the Vote—America Refuses It': Norwegian-

American Suffrage Workers in Brooklyn and Minneapolis, 1880–1920 and Their Gendered Sense of Ethnicity." Master's thesis, Norwegian University of Science and Technology, Trondheim, 1998.

Beito, Gretchen Urnes. "The Constituency of Coya Knutson, 1954." Master's thesis, University of North Dakota, 1982.

Berg, Ellen L. "From Maids to Mothers: Single Norwegian Immigrants at the Turn of the Century." Bachelor's thesis, Carleton College (MN), 1996.

Blomvik, Kirsti Alette. "Heritage, Sisterhood, and Self-Reliance: The Evolution and Significance of the Daughters of Norway, 1897–1950." Master's thesis, Norwegian University of Science and Technology, Trondheim, 2002.

Brungot, Hilde Petra. "Dorthea Dahl: Norwegian-American Author of Everyday Experience." Master's thesis, University of Oslo, 1977.

Devik, Vigdis. "Privileged Family—Privileged Ethnicity: Ethnic Parental Polarization and Historical Contexts That Shaped the Life of Norwegian-American Columnist Brenda Ueland." Master's thesis, Norwegian University of Science and Technology, Trondheim, 2005.

Hagen, Monys Ann. "Norwegian Pioneer Women: Ethnicity on the Wisconsin Agricultural Frontier." Master's thesis, University of Wisconsin–Madison, 1984.

Hinton, Paula K. " 'Come Prepared to Stay Forever': The Tale of a Murderess in Turn-of-the-Century America." PhD diss., Miami University, 2001.

Hunt, Linda Lawrence. "Stepping Out: Helga Estby's Walk across America in 1896." PhD diss., Gonzaga University, 1997.

Krogh, Hilde. " 'We meet only to part': Norwegian Immigrants in Transition." PhD diss., University of Colorado–Boulder, 1990.

Lagerquist, L. DeAne. "That It May Be Done Also Among Us: Norwegian-American Lutheran Women." PhD diss., University of Chicago, 1986.

Lahlum, Lori Ann. " 'There Are No Trees Here': Norwegian Women Encounter the Northern Prairies and Plains." PhD diss., University of Idaho, 2003.

Langeland, Åse Elin. "Adjusting to America: A Study in *Kvinden og Hjemmet,* a Monthly Journal for the Scandinavian Women in America, 1888–1947." Master's thesis, University of Bergen, 2001.

Langlois, Janet L. "Belle Gunness, the Lady Bluebeard: Community Legend as Metaphor." PhD diss., Indiana University, 1977.

Lægdene, Anne-Marie. "Laura Ringdal Bratager: Norwegian-American Author." Master's thesis, University of Oslo, 1981.

Løken, Lise B. "Dr. Agnes Mathilde Wergeland: Historian, Poet, and American University Professor." Master's thesis, University of Oslo, 1995.

Madland, Hans Andreas. "Norwegian-American Pioneer Pastors and Spouses in the Upper Midwest, 1840–1860: Conflict of Values and Search for Identity." Master's thesis, University of Wisconsin–Eau Claire, 1991.

Mauuarin, Anne-Renée. "Fra Nyheter til Livstegn Norske Utvandrerkvinner Skriver Hjem: Amerikabrev i et Tidsperspektiv." Master's thesis, University of Oslo, 1997.

Røed, Lise Merethe Pavely. "The Reaction of Four Norwegian Immigrant Women to

Pioneer Life in America: A Comparison of Attitudes." Master's thesis, University of Oslo, 1977.

Rokstad, Camilla. "Bringing Home to America: The Significance of Holiday Traditions in the Establishment of a Norwegian-American Ethnic Identity in Seattle, 1880–1930." Master's thesis, Norwegian University of Science and Technology (NTNU), 2006.

Røssbø, Sigrun. "Drude Krog Janson Norwegian-American and Norwegian Author." Master's thesis, University of Oslo, 1983.

Sjo, Laila. "Gender and the Immigrant Experience as Depicted in the Fiction of Waldemar Ager, Ole Edvart Rölvaag, Abraham Cahan, and Henry Roth." Master's thesis, University of Bergen, 2001.

Solheim, Britt Janne. "Her Letters Home: Expressions by Norwegian Immigrant Women." Master's thesis, University of Bergen, 2004.

Urberg, Ingrid K. "A Sense of Place: America through the Eyes of Norwegian-American Women Novelists." PhD diss., University of Wisconsin–Madison, 1996.

Wegner, Madeleine Jean. "Feminists and Church Leaders: Norwegian-American Women in Transition, 1850–1920." Bachelor's thesis, Mount Holyoke College, 1982.

Williamson, Erik Luther. "Norwegian-American Lutheran Churchwomen in North Dakota: The Ladies Aid Societies." Master's thesis, University of North Dakota, 1987.

Winslow, Katherine. "Acculturation as Reflected in Dress of Norwegian Immigrants to North Dakota, 1870–1900." Master's thesis, North Dakota State University, 1983.

Fiction

Bruun, Ulrikka Feldtman. *Lykkens Nøgle: Fortælling*. Chicago: Trykt i Den Christ. Talsmands Bogtrykkeri, 1880.

Dahl, Dorthea. *Byen Paa Berget*. Minneapolis, MN: Augsburg Publishing House, 1925.

———. *Fra Hverdagslivet*. Minneapolis, MN: Augsburg Publishing House, 1915.

———. *Returning Home*. Minneapolis, MN: Augsburg Publishing House, 1920.

Evanson, Aileen Berger. *Slekt i Amerika: Chicago Fortelling*. Duluth, MN: Fuhr Pub. and Print. Co., n.d.

Janson, Drude Krog. *En Saloonkeepers Datter Fortælling*. Minneapolis, MN: C. Rasmussens Forlagsboghandel, 1889.

———. *A Saloonkeeper's Daughter*. The Longfellow Series of American Languages and Literatures. Baltimore, MD: Johns Hopkins University Press, 2002.

———. *Tore Fortælling Fra Prærien*. Kristiania: [s.n.], 1894.

[Pedersen] Palma. *Genier Roman*. Eau Claire, WI: Fremad Publishing, 1925.

———. *Ragna Novelle*. Eau Claire, WI: Fremad Publishing, 1924.

———. *Syrener: Digte*. La Crosse, WI: Forfatterindens, 1911.

———. *Under Ansvarets Svøbe Fortælling*. Eau Claire, WI: Fremad Publishing, 1923.

Contributors

BETTY A. BERGLAND is professor of history at the University of Wisconsin–River Falls. Her dissertation, "Reconstructing the 'Self' in America: Patterns in Immigrant Women's Autobiographies" (1990), generated articles in journals and edited volumes, including *Autobiography and Postmodernism; Memory, Narrative, and Identity; Ethnicity and Representation in American Literature;* and *The Encyclopedia of Life Writing.* Her current book project, "Norwegian Migration and Indigenous Peoples in the Upper Midwest," has led to numerous conference papers and articles in *Norwegian-American Studies* (2000), *Norwegian-American Essays* (2005), and *Competing Kingdoms* (2010).

LAURANN GILBERTSON received a BA in anthropology and an MS in textiles and clothing from Iowa State University. She is chief curator at Vesterheim Norwegian-American Museum in Decorah, Iowa, and previously served as the textile curator for nineteen years. In addition to writing for popular magazines, including *Piecework,* she has published scholarly articles and essays on Norwegian American quilts, Norwegian jewelry, and the use of clothing styles to date photographs of women.

KAREN V. HANSEN is professor of sociology and women's and gender studies at Brandeis University. Her major publications include *Not-So-Nuclear Families: Class, Gender, and Networks of Care* (2005); *A Very Social Time: Crafting Community in Antebellum New England* (1994); *At the Heart of Work and Family: Engaging the Ideas of Arlie Hochschild* (edited with Anita Ilta Garey, 2011); *Families in the U.S.: Kinship and Domestic Politics* (edited with Anita Ilta Garey, 1998); and *Women, Class, and the Feminist Imagination* (edited with Ilene J. Philipson, 1990), in addition to numerous articles that have appeared in sociology and history journals. Her chapter in this volume is part of the book-length project *Encounter on the Great Plains: Nordic Newcomers and Dakota Survival, 1900–1930* (forthcoming from Oxford University Press, 2012).

LORI ANN LAHLUM is associate professor of history at Minnesota State University, Mankato. She is the author of "'Everything Was Changed and Looked Strange': Norwegian Women in South Dakota," which appeared in *South Dakota History* in 2005 and won the 2006 Herbert S. Schell Award (best article published in the journal in 2005) from the South Dakota Historical Society. She is currently working on a book, *Norwegian Women, Landscape, and Agriculture on the Northern Prairies and Plains, 1850–1920,* for Texas Tech University Press.

ANN M. LEGREID is professor of geography and dean of the School of Business and Social Sciences at Shepherd University in Shepherdstown, West Virginia. She is the author of articles on Norwegian immigration, Norwegians in America, and Swedes in America that have appeared in various editions of *Norwegian-American Essays, Out of Scandinavia: Essays on Transatlantic Crossings of Cultural Boundaries,* the Nordic Conference Papers (1983), and *Wisconsin Land and Life: A Portrait of a State* (1997).

ODD S. LOVOLL is professor emeritus of history at St. Olaf College and was the first King Olaf V Chair in Scandinavian-American Studies; until 2005 he held an adjunct appointment at the University of Oslo. Lovoll's major English-language publications include *A Folk Epic: The Bygdelag in America* (1975), *The Promise of America: A History of the Norwegian-American People* (1984), *A Century of Urban Life: The Norwegians in Chicago before 1930* (1988), *The Promise Fulfilled: A Portrait of Norwegian Americans Today* (1998), *Norwegians on the Prairie: Ethnicity and the Development of the Country Town* (2006), and *Norwegian Newspapers in America: Connecting Norway and the New Land* (2010). In 1986, Lovoll was decorated by H.M. King Olav V with the Knight's Cross of the Royal Norwegian Order of Merit, and in 1989, he was invited to occupy a seat in the history section of the Norwegian Academy of Science and Letters.

ELISABETH LØNNÅ is a historian and writer in Norway. She earned her doctorate from the University of Oslo in 2004 with a dissertation on Helga Eng, one of the early female pioneers within Norwegian academia. In 2010 Lønnå published the book *Sjøens kvinner: Ute og hjemme (Women of the Seas: On Board and at Home),* a pioneer work on women sailors and sailors' wives. Other major publications include *Helga Eng: Psykolog og pedagog i barnets århundre (Helga Eng: Psychologist and Educator in "The Children's Century"),* published 2002, and *Stolthet og kvinnekamp: Norsk Kvinnesaksforenings historie fra 1913 (Pride and Feminist Struggle: The History of the Norwegian Association for Women's Rights after 1913)* in 1996.

DAVID C. MAUK, associate professor of North America area studies at the University of Oslo, is the author of *The Colony that Rose from the Sea: Norwegian Maritime Migration and Community in Brooklyn, 1850–1910* (1997) and *American Civilization, An Introduction* (5th edition, 2009) with John Oakland. He is the author of numerous essays on immigration and Norwegian America that have appeared in edited volumes and journals. His current work in progress, "The Heart of the Heartland: Ethnic Identity in the Capital of Norwegian America, 1850–2000," is an interethnic social history of the Norwegian Americans of Minneapolis/St. Paul and vicinity.

DINA TOLFSBY is curator for the Norwegian-American Collection at the National Library in Oslo, Norway. She served as project manager for *The Promise of America,* a website devoted to Norwegian emigration to America at the National Library of Norway: www.nb.no/emigrasjon/emigration.

INGRID K. URBERG is associate professor of Scandinavian studies at the Augustana Campus, University of Alberta in Camrose, Canada, where she teaches a variety of Norwegian language, Scandinavian literature, and Scandinavian culture courses. Her dissertation, "A Sense of Place: America Through the Eyes of Norwegian-American Women Novelists," examines Norwegian American women writers. She is currently working on an oral history project, "The Norwegian Immigrant Experience in Alberta."

Index

Page numbers in *italic* refer to illustrations, photographs, and tables

Picture Credits

About the cover image: "Domestic Staff with Work Utensils," 1890, Black River Falls, Wisconsin. The studio portrait of domestic workers signifies the diverse responsibilities these servants claimed and represents the work patterns of the majority of Norwegian immigrant and second-generation women at the turn of the century. The unidentified women most likely were employed at the Merchants Hotel and represent different national origins. However, federal census records, demographic patterns, and local histories support the conclusion that several of the women were Norwegian immigrants or American-born women of Norwegian ancestry. (Those of Norwegian ancestry represented the majority of domestic servants in the area.) Wisconsin Historical Society, Charles Van Schaick Collection, Image ID 1919

Page 25	Oslo Museum
Page 27	Painting by Asta Nørregaard; Norwegian Association for Women's Rights
Page 35	Photo archives, Hedmark Fylkesmuseum
Page 37	The Schröder Archives—Trøndelag Folkemuseum
Page 43	The Picture Collection, University of Bergen Library
Page 46	Photo by Nanna Broch; owner: Oslo Museum
Page 56	Photo by Anders Wilse; Norsk Folkemuseum, Oslo
Page 57	Norwegian Emigrant Museum, Hamar
Page 61	Map by David Deis, Dreamline Cartography
Page 64	From Jon Thallaug and Rolf H. Erickson, *Our Norwegian Immigrants* (Oslo: Dreyer, 1978)
Page 68 (top)	Courtesy Lawrence M. Nelson, Chicago
Page 68 (bottom)	From Maren Michelet, *Glimt fra Agnes Mathilde Wergelands liv* (Minneapolis, 1916)
Page 85	Ole Matthiason Aarseth photo, negative number 10776-A, Minnesota Historical Society
Page 88	Negative number 33302, Minnesota Historical Society
Page 91	O. S. Olson photo, courtesy Norwegian-American Historical Association, Northfield, Minnesota
Page 95	Melvin M. Holte photo, author's collection
Page 99	Photo courtesy of Latah County Historical Society, Moscow, Idaho
Page 103	Andreas Dahl photo, image number WHi-2371, Wisconsin Historical Society
Page 123	Negative number 100103, Minnesota Historical Society
Page 129	Negative number 58797, Minnesota Historical Society
Page 137	Edward Straus photo, negative number 28729, Minnesota Historical Society

The text of *Norwegian American Women* has been set in Arno Pro. Inspired by fifteenth- and sixteenth-century early humanistic types of the Italian Renaissance and in the tradition of early book types such as Venetian and Aldine, this Adobe Original typeface was designed by Robert Slimbach.

Book design and composition by Wendy Holdman.
Manufactured by Sheridan Books, Ann Arbor, Michigan.